1800

Spirit and Soul

Spirit and Soul

Essays in Philosophical Psychology

EDWARD S. CASEY

Spring Publications, Inc.
Dallas, Texas

SPRING PUBLICATIONS, INC.; P.O. BOX 222069; DALLAS, TEXAS 75222

The drawing of the plan of Stonington, Connecticut (by William Hersey and John Kyrk) is reprinted from Kent C. Bloomer and Charles W. Moore, *Body, Memory, and Architecture* (New Haven: Yale University Press, 1977), by permission of the authors and publisher. "Tribal Memories" is reprinted from Robert Duncan, *Bending the Bow.* Copyright © 1968 by Robert Duncan Reprinted by permission of New Directions Publishing Corporation

Interior art from *Old-Fashioned Frames and Borders* (Dover Publications, Inc., 1987). Cover designed and produced by Margot McLean, featuring a recent acrylic painting by the author

Library of Congress Cataloging-in-Publication Data
Casey, Edward
Spirit and soul : essays in philosophical psychology / Edward S.
Casey.
p.   cm.
Collection of previously published articles.
Includes bibliographical references.
ISBN 0–88214–346–8 (pbk.)
1. Imagination.   2. Memory (Psychology)   3. Archetype (Psychology)
4. Phenomenology.   5. Psychology and philosophy.   I. Title.
BF408.C22   1991
128—dc20   91–13223
                                                CIP

Dedicated to Connie, My Sister
Who has taught me much about Spirit
and still more concerning Soul

CONTENTS

ACKNOWLEDGMENTS

This book has been a long time in the making. Most of its component pieces stem from conversations and encounters with figures from another world than that to which I had become accustomed in professional philosophy—the world of archetypal psychology. The first (and most enduringly inspiring) figure I met in this world was James Hillman, with whom I discussed the controversial content of his Terry Lectures at Yale in 1972 (since published as *Re-Visioning Psychology*) and to whom I am indebted for ongoing dialogue in diverse times and places in the intervening years. Entering further into this newfound world, I was welcomed by others who were far advanced in their understanding of archetypal matters: above all, Mary Watkins (to whom I owe a significant reorientation of my thought), David Miller, Robert Sardello, Rafael López-Pedraza, Angelyn Spignesi, Charles Winquist, Paul Kugler, Robert Romanyshyn, Pat Berry, Gail Thomas, Charles Scott, Joanne Stroud, and Charles Boer. For their collective wisdom and their individual forebearance, I wish to thank warmly each of these persons. To Jan Larson I owe the delight of intense discussions following our common discovery of archetypal psychology. Marcia Johnson remains a lively source of wisdom in the domain of philosophical psychology.

The essays which compose this collection were written for rather different purposes and on divergent occasions. In terms of explicit subject matter, they range from perception to hallucination, from epistemology to film, from architecture to cognitive psychology, and from human minds to gods. But each essay is marked—and often re-marked several times over—by the basic concerns which I have sketched out in the Foreword. The result is a set of experiments in writing philosophical psychology which are not only pertinent to each other but are co-implicative in the end.

Edward S. Casey
Stony Brook, New York

FOREWORD
Spirit and Soul in Perspective

All goes onward and outward . . . and nothing
collapses.

—WALT WHITMAN
"Song of Myself"

I

PHILOSOPHY AND PSYCHOLOGY—how will this strange twain meet?
Or have they not always already met—but in a way unknown to each
other? Either way, whether we focus on the future or on the past, the two
activities remain alien for the most part, or they connect only at their
peripheries. What holds apart the two "fields"? (The very term "field," with
its connotation of a spatial spread having strict boundaries that connote
possession and property, only serves to aggravate the problem.)

Otherwise put: how are we to join—or to rejoin, or to see as already
conjoined—spirit and soul? This is difficult only because the two enter-
prises have tended to stake out such exclusive and extravagant claims upon
spirit and soul respectively. Ever since the speculations of Milesian *physikoi*,
the aim of philosophy has been to identify "the logos that is common to
all" (Heraclitus). By the time of Plato, the mind had been stratified in such
a way as to privilege intellect and reason above all middle and lower level
faculties. *Epistēmē* or pure knowledge was the goal of philosophical inquiry, and it took precedence over all mediated or image-bound cognition.
The hierarchy of mental faculties and the logocentric commitment varied
little in the ensuing two millennia of philosophizing in the West. In particular, the notion of "mind minding itself" (Aristotle) has recurred with
remarkable regularity across this span of time in the various guises of active reason, pure reason, rationality, and "thought about thought" (Collingwood).

When mind minds itself, it not only withdraws from the circumambient world but creates a circumstance in which the primary action is one of *separation*. Philosophy begins—and very often ends—in *diakrisis*, the making of distinctions,[1] teasing (and sometimes tearing) apart. Philosophizing has been and remains mainly a matter of analysis. Whereas psychology became analytical only in 1896 (when Freud coined the term "psychoanalysis"), philosophy has always been so. Aristotle's *Prior* and *Posterior Analytics*—the very titles open and close the issue—inaugurate an era in which "synthesis" became a technical term only by the comparatively late date of 1781, the year in which the first edition of Kant's *Critique of Pure Reason* was published (the text remains controlled nonetheless by the "transcendental analytic," especially its "analytic of concepts"). It did not take the comparatively recent rise of "analytical philosophy" in Anglophone countries to tell us that all of philosophy is analytical, however differently it may be so. And in keeping with this basic *nisus*, one of its primary tasks has been to separate spirit from soul—and both from body. This happens whenever *nous* is set against appetite, active reason against passive sensation, Intellect against Soul, *res cogitans* against *res extensa*, idea against impression, understanding against sensibility.

In each of these paradigmatic cases, which litter the field of philosophy like so many corpses left over from a Gigantomachia of Minds, one entity or activity has been *analyzed out* from the other. What one possesses the other must lack: activity (versus passivity), conceptuality (versus sensibility), ideality (versus empirical reality), etc. The parenthetical analysands are, moreover, demoted in importance by their very analyzability or "reducibility" (to use a term that is revealingly common to mathematics and to twentieth-century philosophy alike). Indeed, the very distinction between "analytic" and "synthetic" has been since 1781 the subject of increasingly close scrutiny: the analytic spirit must also analyze itself in its own name. The spirit is the spirit of philosophy itself; or, more exactly, it is philosophy *as spirit*.[2] The analytical is the mode by which the spirited part of human beings proceeds; its dominant expression in Western civilization is called "philosophy."

What then is "psychology"? Although of later cultural vintage (the word itself dates from the sixteenth century), it has been an at least implicit antagonist of philosophy from the beginning. It has played this role of loyal opposition insofar as it has attempted to account for that part of human nature which may be called *syncretic*.[3] In psychology, the *logos* is no longer given an exalted (and isolated) position as a Form, a universal, a concept, a notion. The *logos* is centered in soul by a centripetal force which operates by fusing, by *synkrisis*, rather than by separating. And soul, by the same stroke, is not seen as tending to itself alone in the isolationist manner of mind qua intellect or reason. Soul suffuses itself throughout the entire human system—into mind as into body. It also finds itself—perhaps even is found primarily—in world, that is, in concrete places (a theme to which

I shall return). This is no doubt why psychology began as the study of "feeling," a term that (as Whitehead argued) connotes connection of many kinds and at many levels.[4] Feeling also refuses to submit to the dichotomies so obsessively pursued by reason: is it active or passive, sensible or cognitive, idealizing or receptive-of-the-real? *Both* in every case, or else situated at the very border between the dualistic alternatives themselves—and so calling their very separateness into question. On this point ancient and modern thinkers are in accord. Plato locates feelings in the *thymos* or midriff portion of our being which is continuous with appetites on the one side and with intellect on the other. Collingwood positions feelings at the middle-range "psychical level," while Langer has found in feeling the matrix of mind itself.[5]

Psychology concerns thus the syncretizing aspect of our existence, whether it bears on the synthesis of robust emotions and pallid intellect (Collingwood points, after Spinoza, to "emotions of intellect"[6]), sensations and reasons (e.g., by showing how the former come pre-structured in Kantian "forms of intuition"), body and soul (as in the *expression* of emotion), one soul with another soul (in empathic understanding), or even soul and world (as in the idea of *anima mundi* as revived by archetypal psychology). In all of these ways (especially the last), psychology shows itself to be far less confining—far less interiorizing—than it is often taken to be. In taking to the psyche, not only do we take ourselves into our interior selves: we take ourselves out of ourselves. As Whitman suggests, we feel *out* as well as in: "onward and outward."

Psychologizing *is* syncretizing. Its syncretistic capacities extend even to the merging of psyche and spirit themselves—hence of psychology and philosophy. Psychologizing puts together what philosophizing tears asunder. In this sense psychology is more comprehensive than philosophy; and this is true of "analytical psychology" itself, whether of a Freudian or Jungian or Hillmanian cast. All incorporate Logos and Eros as a composite paradigm of the Psyche.

II

But you may be asking yourself: Has not the foregoing contrast between philosophy and psychology been just another instance of the kind of dichotomizing to which philosophy itself is so prone? Have I myself not been analytic and divisive? How can I escape from, or at least suspend, the dualizing penchant of the human mind? Not easily—no more easily than I can avoid the mind/body split itself. Indeed, there is something deeply prototypical about the Cartesian dualism which finds itself played out at other levels of human existence. Collingwood finds the relation between thought and feeling to be profoundly parallel to that between mental and bodily substance. Feeling, for example, seems

> simply to discover what was there independently of it, almost as if we
> were thinking about the anatomical structure and functioning of our body,
> which would no doubt exist and go on whether we thought or not.[7]

Surely Collingwood is descriptively right in the matter. Feelings, like sensations, are notoriously opaque—dense like the body itself—in contrast with the lambent transparency of thought. The habitual-and-sedimented is set over against the spontaneous.

It is just because such descriptive contrasts are so convincing to us in our first-person experience that each of us is easily drawn into a regressive and vicious dichotomizing. So powerful is the draw that two traditional efforts to overcome dualisms between mind and body, thought and feeling—indeed, between philosophy and psychology themselves—have been unavailing. One of these efforts is to *unify from above* by recourse to reason regarded as the only human faculty capable of holding together such disjunctive terms. But Kant wisely warned that reason unifies in two ways, neither of which is adequate to the task at hand. It does so *formally* by constructing an external architectonic structure or set of tautologies—and thus fails to capture the distinctive content of human experience. But it also proceeds *dialectically* by positing ultimate synthetic unities such as "God" or "Freedom"; but these latter are at best regulative, not constitutive, of experience as we know it: they miss the mark by going beyond the mark itself.

Another effort *unifies from below* by appealing to perception as the origin of all unity of experience. The unity is supposedly found in sensations as the ultimate experiential units; in opposition to a purely rationalist ploy, this characteristically empiricist move locates the unity of experience in an internal and intimate space, one engendered by our own bodily sensations. The difficulty is no longer that of over-unification from without but that of under-unification from within. For what is to unify these minimal units themselves? The traditional answer has been laws of "association" such as similarity, contiguity, and causality. However, such laws—which ended by being more influential in psychology than in philosophy itself—are nothing but ad hoc creations designed to fill in the glaring gaps between sensations themselves; their source, as well as their unity, is left unexplained.

It is evident that we must turn elsewhere in order to find a way in which philosophy and psychology can overcome their deep diremption from each other, a diremption that expresses itself in seemingly irreconcilable differences between thought and feeling, and between spirit and soul.

III

A major thrust of the essays lying below is that the main means of unifying spirit and soul are to be found in the two activities which with seeming innocence we name "imagination" and "memory." Detailed descriptions of the workings of these activities are offered throughout this book. For the present I want only to indicate their role in the context of concern which I have been sketching in the last few pages. This role is remarkably "esemplastic" (in Coleridge's word); it serves to reconnect the *disjecta membra* which we have seen to be the result not only of philosophy's analytical spirit but also of the very juxtaposition of philosophy and psychology, which appear to diverge ineluctably even as they are drawn into comparison.

Take *imagination* to start with. It unifies by an extraordinary form of upward mobility. Its very celerity and creativity are expressive of a *Heiterkeit* that often glitters and is gay. Imagining is typically realized in an upward rush, a "verticalizing" propensity underlined by Bachelard in *L'air et les songes*. Carried to extremes, this propensity leads to the separatist tendency which we have seen to underlie philosophy; sometimes it leads to a self-containment that may mean isolation from other modes of human *praxis*. Nevertheless, as I have argued elsewhere,[8] the autonomy of an act of imagining is "thin"; it can never create a domain that is entirely independent and self-sustaining. It does soar—and does so characteristically and with flair—but it does not soar so far beyond the world as to lose relationship with it altogether. Even when imagination is deemed "productive"—as Kant termed it—it retains a richly constitutive role that links sensibility upward to categories via a highly differentiated schematism for which it is the responsible agent.

The annealing power of imagining may be observed in two of its most characteristic upward movements as these are deployed in philosophy and psychology.

(i) *Up from Body to Soul*. Here the general principle is that imagining guides bodily being toward soul. We see this quite dramatically in many forms which the employment of "active imagination" can take in psychotherapy: e.g., drawing, painting, or dancing out a dream or fantasy. It is also evident in the Feldenkreis technique whereby certain critical bodily movements are anticipated in imagination—enticed and enacted in imagining as an essential step to corporeal action itself. Indeed, behavior modification, so antithetical to other forms of psychotherapy, often employs the patient's imagination in much the same anticipatory way—i.e., as an essential guide toward the transformation of conduct. In all of the preceding cases, what would otherwise be merely bodily behavior—chartable motions in objective space—becomes behavior informed by imaginative leaps that buoy it up and allow it to become the natural vehicle of feeling. This is perhaps most dramatically the case in Gestalt therapy and in psychodrama, where explicit emotion is induced by imaginative role-taking. But even where feeling is not the focus of the therapy, it still becomes more accessible—and thus subject to the soul-making that is the aim of any lastingly significant psychotherapy.[9]

(ii) *Up from Soul to Spirit*. In this case imagining leads soul through the realm of mute feeling to its expression in categories, concepts, and words. It is a matter of progressive *articulation,* which is achieved by a conjoint ramification and specification of the forms of feeling. This is not merely a process of "verbalization," even if such is a frequent fate of the process. A truly *noetic* imagining can find expression in categorial thinking that has not yet found words adequate to its level of insight. This happens whenever we find ourselves in a reflective or meditative state of mind and are pondering a topic without yet crystallizing our thought in language—not even in inner speech. It is just such a state that is under description when Hegel speaks of "absolute spirit." The thoughts of such a spirit are set forth in ontological sequence in *The Science of Logic* and in a quasi-historical format in *The Phenomenology of Spirit.* In both cases the movement to such purely philosophical thinking is from "subjective spirit," which is Hegel's term for soul; and it would not be possible without the intervention of an imagination that inspired the soul to think abstractly. Thus philosophy itself is made possible by imagination. As Whitehead has said, "philosophy is the welding of imagination and common sense into a restraint upon specialists, and also into an enlargement of their imaginations."[10]

In this doubly directed fashion imagination shows itself to be a spontaneously unifying factor in human experience, first linking body with soul (this step being most evident in psychotherapy) and then connecting soul with spirit (this being best seen in the production of categorial schemes in philosophy). In each case imagination works by an infusion of one form or level of human being into another form or level, thereby overcoming the dichotomous condition of the presumed starting-point. I say "presumed," for the situation is such that in human experience imagination has always already been at work and tempers even the most divisive circumstance. Human beings are not composed of two, or several, distinctly separate parts but of an indefinite plurality of modes of existing between which imagining moves in its Mercurial manner.

Nevertheless, this is not the only way in which we enjoy a non-diremptive existence. Imagination is not the only "point at which the activity of thought makes contact with the merely psychic life of feeling"[11]—just as it is not the only way in which body and soul can be combined in a perduring way. Its upwardly adhesive movement is matched by a downwardly synthesizing force—*memory.* Once more the movement occurs in two phases.

(i) *Down from Spirit to Soul.* Memory serves to lend weight to upward-flying thoughts through the dense accretions of a personal or inter-personal history and tradition. In remembering, we think back and down. *Andenken,* "commemorative thinking," means literally a thinking-at that aims at the origin of an event.[12] This "back" need not be temporal only; it can refer to a constantly available fund or source of experience and meaning. Nor need remembering occur in an explicitly scenic format. There may be merely the sense that 'I've been here before'; such a sense, however dim it may be, provides continuity to human existence. More importantly, the fund or source with which I reconnect gives mass or substance to what might otherwise be a wholly insubstantial state of affairs. Without something that I can recall—call up from the depths—every experience would present itself as altogether *de novo*. It is in just this respect that soul lends weight, psychic substance, felt gravity to any given situation. We re-flect ourselves through the remembering soul, which offers to the rational reflection of spirit a refractive index. Spirit would soar indeed—and precisely as abetted by imagination—were it not to have this reflective resource at its disposal. It is not surprising, therefore, that psychoanalytic therapy began with Breuer and Freud by encouraging an intense, rememorative reflection. Nor is it surprising that the abreaction of affect in its "strangulated" form was held to be achieved through an active remembering of traumatic moments. Memory brings spirit down to feeling as to its own body, a subtle but troubled body that is re-membered in mind.

(ii) *Down from Soul to Body.* The memorial movement continues downward to the actual, corporeal body. For soul seeks its own substance, its own bodily basis. A disembodied soul feels itself to be as homeless as a soulless spirit. The embodiment of soul proceeds through memory as well—now in the specific form of habitual remembering. We know our own body primarily as a "customary body" (in Merleau-Ponty's apt term)— as a massive network of habitual movements and responses. Only through an extraordinary technique such as rolfing do we elicit expressly recollective memories from the body proper. Short of this, the connection to the body is via a tacit remembering, which occurs more by adumbration than by clear delineation. Just as remembered feeling so often refuses to be pinpointed at the level of psyche, so the lived body resists easy categorization when it presents itself in its habitual bearing. Nevertheless, this same bearing lends depth to remembering and remembered soul, giving to its feeling and its interiority a dimension they would otherwise altogether lack.

Even if it is not the case that in the spirit–soul–body matrix "the way up and the way down are one and the same," still the two connective modes just sketched out do complement each other closely. Imagining and remembering co-ordinate their movements with regard to upward and downward respectively. For one thing, the former typically tends *forward* (into the future; into the not-yet-explored), while the latter moves *backward* (into the past; into the already-constituted). For another, the de-sedimenting power of imagining—its frequent flights and frivolities—is matched by the sober sedimenting action of remembering. One breaks up and breaks out while the other consolidates. The pursuit of the possible on the one hand is paired with the attachment to the actual on the other. What is "productive" in imagining aligns itself with what is "reproductive" in remembering. (For Kant, memory is termed "reproductive imagination.") This list of complementarities could continue almost indefinitely.

It is also important to realize that the two activities are *necessary to each other* and not just contingent counterparts; being necessary to each other, they are essential to human being as well. To paraphrase Kant: imagining without remembering is empty; remembering without imagination is blind.[13] Or to put the point psychologically: imagination without memory is manic; memory without imagination is depressive. Elsewhere I have argued for the co-ingredience of imagining and remembering in such diverse sectors of experience as historical reconstruction, screen memories, dreams, and time-consciousness.[14] Here I only want to underline the fact that without the continual and conjoint operation of imagination and memory human existence would indeed fall apart into warring factions, divided against itself. The syncretic strength of soul would be unable to counteract the separative strain in spirit, nor would the body be able to mediate between soul and spirit. Nor could reason or sensation adequately bring together our disparate aspects. Only imagining and remembering, working as coeval partners, can effect the holding-together which is a minimal condition of coherent existence.

This coadjutant holding-together is further reinforced by the fact that, in the end, both activities *hold out* and not just *in*. When we imagine something—say, the great god Pan—we imagine out to that figure, ex-tending ourselves body and soul in its direction. (Is this not what intentionality should always have meant and not the ensnarement in transcendental subjectivity which it came to connote?) So too we hold ourselves out when we remember—out to what we re-member in its very temporal separation from the present moment. If it is true that something is always held in as well (e.g., the past in traces or holographic regions of the brain), this does not lessen the extero-centric directionality of the act of remembering itself. No less than in the act of imagining are we held wholly within ourselves when we remember. In both cases we get out of ourselves—out of our skin and into the places of the world—by the very experiences of imagining and remembering (and often the two together in complex, equally ec-centric commixtures).

If all of this is indeed the case, then philosophy and psychology are themselves made more continuous with each other by the complementary and co-necessary actions of imagining and remembering. Each of these latter, and each with the other, draws spirit and psyche into a common enterprise in which the body is implicated as well. For it is manifest that we cannot confine either of these modalities of active life to spirit or to soul exclusively. There is an imagination of spirit as well as its own memory; and there is a psychic imagining as well as soul's own remembering. The twain between spirit and soul not only *will* meet but has already met in continual collusions of imagining and remembering, which, tied to each other, tie soul and spirit together. This is not an external unification effected by formal factors or by an imposed architectonic, nor is it a matter of an internal unification via the contents of experience. It is instead a co-constitution of spirit and psyche as co-inherent members of an existence that is held together in a bodily mode—held together, above all, by the *images* which imagining and remembering share—despite the deeply divisive tendencies which also compose our own being. To imagine and to remember are to hold in one's hands the "intentional threads"[15] by which a life comes to composition and compresence with itself.

IV

Now that we have explored certain internal links between philosophy in general and psychology in general, we need to ask more specifically what is the relationship between the *particular* kind of philosophy and the *particular* kind of psychology which are at stake in the essays set forth in this book. Once more we shall find a surprising convergence between things which at first might seem quite disparate. For what could be more divergent than an *archetypal* psychology and a *phenomenological* philosophy? Doesn't the "arche-typal" connote the primordial and the universal—the first of types, the type of types—while the "phenomen-ological" points to what lies on the surface of things, i.e., the derivative and particular, in short the apparent, the merely phenomenal? This preliminary contrast will not, however, sustain scrutiny. For one thing, a type is very closely related to an essence, which is the ultimate object of phenomenological description. For another, however primordial it may be, the archetypal must manifest itself within the realm of appearances—and precisely as a "primordial image" in Jung's apposite term.

The deepest bond between an archetypal psychology and a phenomenological philosophy is found in *manifestation*. A "phenomenon" is, after all, that which manifests itself to us in some salient way, and the aim of phenomenology as a description of the essential features of phenomena has been formulated by Heidegger as "to let that which shows itself be seen from itself in the very way in which it shows itself from itself."[16] Or we can say in plainer prose that phenomenology describes *structures of presentation*, whether these structures be gross or subtle. It gives to such structures what Vico calls a "true narration" (*vero narratio*). And it does so by going to "the things themselves" (*den Sachen selbst*) rather than to introspected representations of things. It is a matter of bringing things to light, *not* to the "natural light" of mind, but into the very light of day—into the "clearing" (*Lichtung*) as Heidegger terms it. In this luminous place there is no room for the empirical ego, for pent-up emotions and cooped-up thoughts, for the anthropocentric person, or even for "human being." The true domain of phenomenological description is *being-in-the-world*, and this latter cannot be construed in terms of strictly self-enclosed features of human subjectivity.

Archetypal psychology also moves decisively beyond egological self and its fugitive feelings and into a transpersonal dimension where what matters is the manifest image and the world in which it is set. This is ultimately a syncretic movement into world construed as *anima mundi*.[17] What Jung calls "collective" and Husserl "transcendental" implies a movement outward from the entrapment of personalized consciousness. No more than being-in-the-world can be reduced to determinate forms of egological presence by a *Verweltlichung* (i.e., "mundanification") can the world as archetypally alive—as ensouled—be kept within the confines of sensations or feelings that are the focus of so much psychology. For *archetypes are everywhere if they are anywhere at all*; and the way in which they abound is through a continual manifestation and proliferation: in dreams, in fantasies, in actions, in things themselves.

Phenomenology and archetypology thereby join forces in a conjoint move to the manifest. They do so in two major respects. First, each refuses to subscribe to the interiorizing tendency which has been so dominant in Western thought since Descartes; the epoch of subjectivity is severely contested. Second, each endorses a movement out and onto the world. "All goes onward and outward" in a world as indefinite in its limits as it is capacious in its contents. Both step into the light of place—not Hemingway's "clean well-lit place" but a diffusely lighted, amorphously luminous place whose proper name is "landscape."

Place and landscape have emerged as central topics in my most recent writing.[18] The places of landscape—"placescapes"—provide a circumambience, a setting, for archetypes as well as for structures of presentation. While phenomenology has become (in Heidegger's final formulation) a "topology of Being," archetypology can be conceived henceforth as an arche-*topology*. Perhaps we can even begin to speak of a new three-sided discipline: "arche-pheno-topology." Existing only in barely emergent form at this time, it may become a region within which philosophy and psychology can commingle more fully and freely than they have allowed themselves to do thus far in the modern and post-modern era.

By the same token, in shifting the emphasis from time to space we shall find ourselves questioning the interiority which, from Augustine to Husserl, has been considered an indispensable element of subjective time-consciousness. *Time takes in*, comprehending all events in a totalization so complete that only an all-encompassing Mind can be its proper locus. No wonder that Kant conceived of time as a pure form of the most inward sensibility. But archetypal and phenomenological structures are not only or altogether temporal, nor are they timely or timelike; they are, if anything, omnitemporal, panchronic. For this reason, they require specification in terms of space, the form of "outer" sense for Kant. If time takes in, *space moves out*. Space qua place locates: it furnishes outward abode in world. Space specifies; it gives local habitation.

Images also serve to specify. They occupy places in psyche; they *are* places of psyche, its place-holders. It is with images, then, that the ultimate rapprochement is to be made between archetypal psychology and phenomenological philosophy. Husserl spoke of "phantoms" as the proper objects of perception when it is described with phenomenological precision. Such phantoms are close cousins (and not just etymologically) of *phantasmata*, those "appearings" which for Aristotle constituted the basis of sensory knowledge of the world. It is in phantasy that the world first becomes known; and what we call "images" are only further specifications of phantasmal if not phantasmatic presences.

It seems almost redundant to add that images exist in common between imagination and memory and thus help to account for the deeply rooted links between the two activities to which I pointed in section III above. Hobbes said that "Imagination and Memory are but one thing, which for divers considerations hath divers names."[19] We need not go *this* far; but we do need to underscore the fact that images play back and forth between imagining and remembering: they are the free play of their enactments. They also furnish the *Spielraum*, the very play-space, for a psychology conceived archetypally and a philosophy considered as phenomenology. Images allow these two "fields" to *take place together*, to find a common ground—a shared placescape—and even on occasion to take each other's place.

Depth psychology commenced with the technique of free association, for which images give place and punctuation; active imagination carried the technique to still more expressly imagistic extremes. Phenomenology for its part eventuated in a technique termed "free variation in imagination," in which the unfettered projection of images is restrained only by what we can retain (in memory) of what is common to these images in their fictive freedom. Images connect even as they differentiate; they unite even as they separate. Images provide the primary places in which imagining and remembering, archetypal psychology and phenomenological philosophy, and finally psychology and philosophy themselves, come together. For each of these disparate dyads they constitute the "common but unknown root."[20]

1. For a contemporary extension of the same movement, see Robert Sokolowski, "Making Distinctions," *Review of Metaphysics* (1980).

2. Josiah Royce's remarkable book *The Spirit of Modern Philosophy* (1892) is thus doubly ironic: first because modern philosophy (i.e., since Hegel) has been explicitly concerned with "Spirit" (*Geist*) and then because philosophy, *at all times*, has been a matter of spirit.

3. Alfred North Whitehead might say "prehensive," which he contrasts with "separative" in his *Science and the Modern World* (New York: Mentor, 1965), p. 80 f.

4. Cf. Alfred North Whitehead, *Process and Reality*, ed. D. R. Griffin and D. W. Sherburne (New York: MacMillan, 1978), pp. 40–42, 51–53, 277–78.

5. See R. G. Collingwood, *The Principles of Art* (Oxford: Oxford University Press, 1938), pp. 163–64, 171; and Susanne Langer, *Mind: An Essay on Human Feeling* (Baltimore: Johns Hopkins University Press, 1967, 1973, 1982), vols. I, II, III.

6. Cf. Collingwood, *The Principles of Art*, pp. 266 ff.

7. Ibid., p. 163. I have been reverting to this unappreciated text as a resource of special value for philosophy and psychology alike; it confronts many of the matters which are central to this book.

8. E. S. Casey, *Imagining: A Phenomenological Study* (Bloomington: Indiana University Press, 1976), chap. 7.

9. This is not to deny that the opposite movement, i.e., from image to body state, may also occur by means of some of the same techniques I have just named. Then imagining gives to an image a local habitation in a habit.

10. Whitehead, *Process and Reality*, p. 17.

11. Collingwood, *The Principles of Art*, p. 171.

12. See Martin Heidegger, *What Is Called Thinking?*, trans. J. Glenn Gray (New York: Harper & Row, 1968), pp. 10 ff., 138 ff.

13. See Immanuel Kant, *The Critique of Pure Reason*, trans. N. K. Smith (New York: Humanities Press, 1950), A 51, B 75.

14. E. S. Casey, "Imagining and Remembering" in this volume, and also *Remembering: A Phenomenological Study* (Bloomington: Indiana University Press, 1987), chap. 11–12, especially the idea of "thick autonomy."

15. This phrase is used (in a different sense) by Maurice Merleau-Ponty in his *Phenomenology of Perception*, trans. C. Smith (New York: Humanities Press, 1962), p. 72.

16. Martin Heidegger, *Being and Time*, trans. E. Robinson and J. Macquarrie (New York: Harper & Row, 1962), p. 58.

17. See James Hillman, "*Anima Mundi*: The Return of the Soul to the World," *Spring* 1982.

18. See my essays "Getting Placed: Soul in Space" (in this volume) and "Keeping the Past in Mind" (*Review of Metaphysics II* [1983]). A book on the subject entitled *Getting Back into Place* is forthcoming from Indiana University Press.

19. Thomas Hobbes, *Leviathan*, ed. C. B. Macpherson (Pelican, 1968), p. 89. I consider the same statement in a very different light in "Imagining and Remembering," sections I and II below.

20. This is, of course, Kant's phrase for the origin of sensibility and understanding in *The Critique of Pure Reason*, A 15, B 29.

IMAGINING

Toward an Archetypal Imagination

I

EARLY IN *Psychological Types* Jung is driven to posit fantasy, and more particularly "creative fantasy," as a way of resolving the philosophical antinomies present in the work of Abelard and Schiller. Rejecting Abelard's conceptualism and Schiller's rational will as the proper "mediating standpoint," Jung sees in fantasy a way to conjoin the antinomical notions in question—realism and nominalism in Abelard's case, sensation and thought in Schiller's. It is in this austerely philosophical context that Jung introduces fantasy as a *tertium quid* that is capable of mediating between contradictory concepts:

> This autonomous activity of the psyche, which can be explained neither as a reflex action to sensory stimuli nor as the executive organ of eternal ideas, is, like every vital process, a continually creative act.[1]

In this inaugural statement, Jung stresses two characteristics of fantasy: its autonomy and its creativity. Its autonomy stems from its being "the mother of all possibilities," and its creativity is linked with its role in the formation of symbols.[2] But fantasy is held to be much more even than this. Its activity, not being limited to creativity as such, pervades all psychic acts and is not merely one psychological operation among others. As "the direct expression of psychic life," fantasy draws together and mediates between every aspect of psyche.[3] It is the universal solvent of mind.

As discussed in *Psychological Types,* fantasy may take at least three different forms: voluntary, passive, and active. Fantasy that is produced voluntarily as a mere concoction of conscious elements is dismissed as "an artificial experiment of purely theoretical interest" (*CW* 6, ¶711). Jung is primarily concerned with the other two types of fantasy, in both of which there is "an irruption of unconscious contents into consciousness" (ibid.).

The way this irruption is treated by the human subject determines whether the fantasy will be passive or active. If we are supine before the inrushing material, then the fantasy is a passive one, and we are in the position of the dreamer or the psychotic. But there is a different way of confronting the upsurge of unconscious contents in fantasy. Instead of allowing ourselves to be overcome, we can attempt to alter the course of the ongoing experience by becoming the agents of fantasy rather than its victims. The use of such active fantasy as a means of containing and guiding material emanating from the unconscious forms a prototype for what came to be called "active imagination."[4]

For it became increasingly clear to Jung that he could no longer confine his attention to fantasy alone. Under the impact of the alchemists' distinction between *phantasia* and *imaginatio,* he began to restrict the term "fantasy" (*Phantasie*) to what is merely "a subjective figment of the mind" (*CW* 13, ¶207n17). Imagination (*Einbildungskraft, Imagination*), in contrast, is said to be "an image-making, form-giving, creative activity" (ibid., ¶207n18). A genuinely active imagination epitomizes this creative activity and thus usurps the role that had formerly been given to fantasy alone:

> . . . fantasy is mere nonsense, a phantasm, a fleeting impression; but imagination is active, purposeful creation. . . . A fantasy is more or less your own invention, and remains on the surface of personal things and conscious expectations. But active imagination, as the term denotes, means that the images have a life of their own and that the symbolic events develop according to their own logic.[5]

As a way of "coming to terms with the unconscious," of "having it out with the unconscious," active imagination involves a two-part process which Jung describes as "synthetic":[6] (i) a general movement from the unconscious to consciousness—a progressive move which, in Freud's terminology, would be from primary to secondary processes. Synthesis here implies a change in psychic level or, more exactly, a change in the kind of awareness with which psychic contents are apprehended. In Jung's words, it is a matter of "releasing unconscious [contents] and letting them come into the conscious mind" (*CW* 7, ¶342). (ii) Subsequent elaboration and unfolding—in this case, the synthesis proceeds primarily at the conscious level as the contents delivered in the first synthesis are expanded and unfolded to reveal aspects which had not been apparent initially. These aspects are now focused upon and developed as the imaginative act proceeds. To be sure, the unconscious is still present as a motivating factor and as a source of new images. But it is kept in the background as one focuses on what is brought within the range of consciousness. Jung's instructions are to "give [the emerging content] your special attention, concentrate on it, and observe its alterations objectively. . . . Follow the subsequent transformations . . . attentively and carefully" (*CW* 14, ¶749).[7]

The activity proper of active imagination occurs during the elaborational phase: here "the passive process becomes an action" (*CW* 14, ¶706). Instead of merely contemplating the display of flowing images, the subject enters into dramatization or, more precisely, *self*-dramatization. The imaginer, from having been a mere spectator of his or her own unconsciously projected images taken as a form of "interior entertainment," becomes the dramaturge of his or her own psychic creations. In describing this culminating stage of active imagining, Jung revealingly adopts theatrical terminology:

> The piece that is being played does not want merely to be watched impartially, it wants to compel [the imaginer's] *participation*. If [the imaginer] understands that his own drama is being performed on this inner stage, he cannot remain indifferent to the plot and its denouement. (Ibid.; my italics)

By "participation" Jung does not mean acting out or concretizing the imagined drama: "we must not concretize our fantasies" (*CW* 7, ¶352). Nor does he call for psychodrama or guided daydreams under the tutelage of a mentor or a group. His recommendation is more subtle than this. As his choice of descriptive terms hints, the sense of participation involved in active imagination is akin to that of the playgoer in watching a moving stage drama. There is an imaginative merging of the spectator's self with one or more of the figures on the stage. At the same time, and as a precondition, there is what Coleridge called a "willing suspension of disbelief," that is, a bracketing of belief in the empirical reality of what is taking place: in short, the drama is a "drama of the psyche."[8]

Even though Jung is suspicious of what he denigrates as the "merely aesthetic" dimensions of active imagination, repeatedly warning that an overriding aesthetic concern undermines the experience itself, his description of the quasi-histrionic aspect of active imagining exhibits a shrewd insight into the cathartic and transformative effects of theatrical performances. Still more significantly, he draws on the same analogy with regard to the reality-sense which is involved in active imagination:

> If you recognize your own involvement, you yourself must enter into the process with your personal reactions, just as if you were one of the fantasy figures, or rather, *as if the drama being enacted before your eyes were real*. It is a psychic fact that this fantasy is happening, and it is *as real as you—as a psychic entity—are real*. (*CW* 14, ¶753; my italics)

As distinguished from voluntary fantasy or non-hallucinatory passive fantasy, the sense of reality is no longer that of mere possibility, of what might be. Yet, as distinguished from passive fantasy that is hallucinatory or from sensory perception, the reality-character is not of an overflowing plenitude or external presence. Rather, in active imagination we have to do with a distinctively psychical reality. But what kind of reality is this?

"The real," says Jung, "is what works" (CW 7, ¶353), and this efficacy of the real obtains no less in the psychological than in the perceptual or practical realm. Psychologically speaking, to "work" means to have an effect on one's psyche—to change it in some essential way. Something that is posited as merely possible will have no such transforming effect; it will not "work" psychologically and hence lacks genuine psychical reality. In Jung's view, it requires active imagination to convert the purely possible—the merely fantasied, the aesthetically contemplated—into the psychically real: active imagining "invests the bare fantasy with an element of reality, which lends it greater weight and greater driving power" (CW 16, ¶106). Accordingly, the specific function of dramatization in active imagining is to give to apprehended content the effective force which it lacks as the object of voluntary or passive fantasy. As dramatized, this content comes alive and comes to influence, by a kind of counterforce, the imaginer himself or herself: "if this crucial operation is not carried out, all the changes are left to the flow of images, and you yourself remain unchanged" (CW 14, ¶753).

Yet the ultimate source of psychical reality is found not in anything the imaginer himself or herself can do but in the primordial images or archetypes which inform and preform his or her imaginative activity. Archetypes, proclaims Jung, are "psychical realities, real because they work" (CW 7, ¶151). And they work, or have effect, precisely by structuring and subtending the specific imagistic contents which the active imaginer puts into dramatic form. For we do not experience archetypes themselves—that is, archetypes as *Dingen an sich*—but only their expressions in concrete images. In other words, active imagination is "a kind of spontaneous amplification of archetypes"[9]—a means for unleashing their prolific potentialities. To imagine actively is to make archetypal patterns psychically real: actual and effectual in the psychic life of the imaginer.

II

The above account of Jung's evolving theories of fantasy and imagination, far from pretending to be definitive, is meant only to serve as the prelude to a problem which confronts any form of archetypal psychology. Let us grant for the moment that imagination in its active form is capable of initiating experiences of archetypal significance,[10] leaving aside the question (to be treated in section III below) as to whether such imagination is to be regarded as the ultimate form of imagining. The more pressing problem takes the following form. What is to introduce and maintain *order* within the experiences induced by active imagining? What is the organizing principle for such experiences? Jung's own response is well-known:

"There are certain collective unconscious conditions which act as regulators and stimulators of creative [i.e., imaginative] activity and which call forth corresponding formations by availing themselves of the existing conscious material" (*CW* 8, ¶403). These conditions are, of course, the archetypes themselves, which act as regulative conditions for a specific imagined content by providing this content with a typological framework. Jung's own writings are a testament to this regulative function of archetypes, illustrating how dreams and fantasies lose their initially diffuse character when subsumed under various archetypal dominants. Yet, convincing as this demonstration is, what regulates the regulators? How do archetypes, which impart patterns to particular imagined contents, themselves form an ordered pattern? If there is a danger of endless and shapeless promiscuity at the level of images—a level which always tends to revert to the chaos of passive fantasy—is there not a comparable danger at the archetypal level itself?

One might be tempted at this point to respond by simply asking, so what? Why *not* infinite proliferation at every level? But if such proliferation were in fact the case, then we could neither refer to nor experience anything at all. A minimum of order is essential for any experience to be intelligible—that is, for it to cohere as *an* experience—no matter how seemingly formless it may appear at first. This principle of minimal ordering applies no less to the archetypal level than it does to everyday empirical experience: a complete absence of order at any level would eliminate the very possibility of experience at that level.

If the necessity of an at least minimal ordering of all experience is admitted, then we are in a position to discuss the specific problem of patterning among archetypes. How are archetypes ordered among themselves? This question, which arises from reflection on Jung's account of active imagination, concerns what we may call *archetypal topography*. By "topography" is meant a mapping of *topoi*, of places or sites. In archetypal topography, it is a matter of determining where archetypes are to be located in relation to each other and thus of what groupings they form. The importance of this task is affirmed by James Hillman in a statement which stands as a prolegomenon to the whole problematic with which we are here concerned:

> The discipline of imagination asks "where" [not "how" or "why"]; and by asking "where" and fantasying in terms of place, the psyche enlarges its interiority, the space by which it carries meaning.[11]

In pursuit of an adequate conception of archetypal topography, I shall divide this part of the essay into two subsections. In the first, I shall take up the position of those persons for whom the ultimate topography is to be conceived in terms of the specific structure of fourness. The second attends to alternative schemes which involve the positing of more complex configurations with more than four members. In both instances, however, we shall be dealing with ways of mapping the placescape of an imagination which is active and alive with archetypes. Thus we are seeking to discover how the general domain of archetypal space has been delineated and thereby to furnish a preliminary answer to the question of how archetypes are arranged among themselves.[12]

(i) *Fourness.* A four-figured pattern represents what is no doubt the most persistent and stable of archetypal arrangements, as the squat and stolid immobility of a regular four-sided polygon graphically suggests. The co-presence of four factors—especially when these factors are equivalent or at least countervailing—brings with it actual or potential characteristics of balance, solidity, and regularity as well as connotations of lastingness and totality. This is the case whether we are speaking of the four seasons, the four directions, or the four quarters of the heavens—or even of what Schopenhauer called "the four-fold root of the principle of sufficient reason." Hence it is not surprising that a number of those who have investigated archetypal groupings come up with a four-part configuration as their preferred pattern. We shall consider three cases in point: Jung himself, Bachelard, and Heidegger.

(a) *Jung.* Jung's special concern with fourness is too familiar to demand detailed discussion.[13] From his early isolation of four psychological functions to his later studies in mandala symbolism, *marriage quaternio* figures, and the psychology of transference, he found his conviction as to the archetypal ultimacy of a "quaternary system of orientation" (*CW* 13, ¶207) continually reinforced. Yet the most striking confirmation of the apparent universality of the four-part schema came through Jung's inquiries into alchemy. In medieval and Renaissance alchemy, he wrote, are "collected, as in a reservoir, the most enduring and most important mythologems of the ancient world" (*CW* 13, ¶353). These mythologems or archetypes cluster into groups of four at every important juncture in the alchemical imagination, whether it is a question of basic elements, of sensible qualities such as colors, or of the parts, limbs, and emanations of the mysterious Anthropos (*CW* 12, ¶¶333–35; *CW* 13, ¶215). In Jung's view, everything of significance that was attributed by alchemists to the cosmos is equally valid for the psyche, which unwittingly projects its own nature on external nature: "figures and laws were dimly perceived and attributed to matter although they really belonged to the psyche" (*CW* 12, ¶332). Therefore, if matter is apprehended as quaternary in character, this must mean that the psyche is similarly structured into four orientating faculties (each of which corresponds to a specific function type): *phantasia, imaginatio, speculatio,* and *agnata fides* (cf. *CW* 13, ¶¶206–12). Further, since for Jung the psyche comes to its highest realization in imaginative activity, imagination itself must be tetradic in nature. This follows from Jung's declaration that "the alchemical operation [which typically involves four stages] seems to us the equivalent of the psychological process of active imagination" (*CW* 14, ¶749; cf. ibid., ¶446). Yet it is a curious fact that Jung did not follow his own lead in this regard. Notably lacking in his writings is an explicit analysis of active imagination in terms of fourfoldness which his research into alchemy and other areas had shown to be fundamental. As we have seen, active imagination is instead described as a continuously unfolding procedure, with no hint of division into fourfold aspects, phases, or types.[14]

(b) *Bachelard*. It took the genius of Gaston Bachelard to suggest how this gap in Jung's theorizing might be filled. Bachelard, who was also a student of alchemy, noticed the striking analogy between the four ancient elements and the four medieval humors. Rejecting the theory of humors as an adequate basis for understanding poetic creativity, he opted for the notion of a material imagination which has precisely four types, each corresponding to one of the original four elements. Bachelard proceeded to spell out in evocative detail the character and primary modalities of each type of material imagining as it expresses itself in poetry. The result, which he considered to be at once psychoanalytical and phenomenological, provides us with a panoply of perspectives on the poetic imagination in action. He advances the thesis that the reader's material imagination—which is to be distinguished from the formal imagination that operates in understanding mathematics and natural science—contains *in nuce* four types of elemental imagining, but that in fact it will resonate most fully when confronted with literary images featuring just one or two preferred elements. Correspondingly, a poet's imagination will tend to express itself in terms of certain elements and not others: Poe's imagining is basically aqueous, E. T. A. Hoffmann's pyric, Shelley's aerial, and Rilke's telluric.

Suggestive and nuanced as Bachelard's analyses are, they are founded almost entirely on the experiences of reading and (to a lesser extent) of writing poetry. It is significant that when, following the publication of a series of books on material imagination,[15] Bachelard widened his horizons to a cosmic scale, he tended to replace imagination by revery as the central psychic experience, without showing the exact relationship between the two. Is revery a mode of imagining, or is it the other way around? On the basis of Bachelard's eloquent but elusive "poetics of revery," we cannot say which is the right relation. All that can be said for certain is that the earlier stress on material imagination as a fourfold psychic process has given way to an emphasis on revery and the cosmic.[16]

(c) *Heidegger*. Heidegger's horizons are cosmic too, but he manages to offer a more convincing system of archetypal classification. He does this without being influenced by Jung and within the context of ontology, not psychology. His aim in many of his later essays is to provide a "topology of Being," an explication (*Er-örterung*) of Being in terms of its primary loci or places of appearance, its "clearings." Being appears in, and through, "things," even the simplest physical things such as a jug of wine or a pair of shoes. In each case, the thing in question is interpretable in terms of four primary categories, which together form a permanent tetrad (*das*

Geviert). The categories or "members" of the tetrad are gods, men, earth, and sky. In this loose unity, each individual member expresses or reflects the three others in a perpetual mirror-game of mutual compresence.

The advantage of Heidegger's schema is that, though remaining fourfold in structure, it is more comprehensive than the specific tetralogy proposed by Bachelard. Thus the four ancient elements, which formed the exclusive basis for Bachelard's analysis, are subsumed under just two of Heidegger's *topoi:* air and fire under "sky," earth and water under "earth," as we can see in the following characteristic statement:

> The earth is that which bears and serves; it flourishes and fructifies, extended in the form of rock and water, opening itself as plant and animal. . . . the sky is the arched course of the sun, the march of the moon in its various phases, the brilliant movement of the stars, the seasons of the year and the decline of day, the obscurity and clarity of night, the amenity and severity of the atmosphere, the flight of clouds, and the blue depth of the aether.[17]

What is remarkable in this gnomic utterance is that not only are the four elements accounted for, but much else besides: animals, sun, moon, aether. Such themes fascinated the alchemists as well, and we can read Heidegger's musings on *das Geviert* as a modern correlate of an alchemical compendium. For Heidegger included, in addition to sky and earth, two other essential factors: man and gods. Just as the alchemists made Mercurius and other specific deities intrinsic to the alchemical process, so Heidegger does not fail to make gods (conceived precisely as messengers and thus as Mercurial figures) and men (understood as mortals, whose being is a being-toward-death) an integral part of the round-dance (*der Reigen*) performed by the foursome as an interpenetrating whole. The movement of this round-dance is isomorphic with alchemical distillation and sublimation, and in its uroboric circularity it recalls the cyclical movements of the alchemical *iteratio* that are so essential to the completion of the process.

Conspicuously lacking in the medieval alchemists' and in Heidegger's quaternary archetypology is an explicit acknowledgment of the role of the imaginal psyche as an independent factor. It is true that in alchemical treatises *imaginatio*, an act of meditation which is located in the heart (itself conceived as the seat of the soul), is invoked and is even "a key that opens the door to the secret of the *opus*" (*CW* 12, ¶400); and it is also true that Heidegger makes imaginative meditating, in the specific form of *Gelassenheit* or "letting be," crucial to the full realization of *das Geviert*. But Heidegger and the alchemists—albeit in extremely divergent ways—both fail to consider the imaginal psyche of fundamental importance in their cosmic concerns. Whatever the reasons for this omission—in the one case, it may be due to an attempt to eliminate all traces of humanism, in the other to an unwitting projection of the psychic factor—it remains a serious short-coming. If an archetypal topography is to be well-grounded, it must make explicit reference to a specifically psychical element and not allow this element to be a mere object of inference. Otherwise, the result is a one-sided affair, favoring cosmos over psyche. In their common stress on the cosmic, Heidegger and the alchemists—and Bachelard as well, especially in his last stage—exhibit their deafness to Jung's profound warning:

> The psychoid form underlying any archetypal image retains its character at all stages of development, though empirically it is capable of endless variations. (CW 13, ¶350)

It is not a matter of reducing archetypes to this psychoid form but of recognizing the strictly coeval status of psyche and cosmos. *Both* are essential: neither can be eliminated from an adequate archetypal analysis.[18] Archetypes, then, have a foundation equally in psyche—which is to say in imagination, for "image *is* psyche" (CW 13, ¶75)—and in the material world; and this is the case whatever their ultimate configuration may be.[19] So far, we have been treating theories in which this configuration is held to be tetradic. Are other patterns possible?

(ii) *Polyadic Patterns.* Not only are other patterns possible. They are *necessary.* Archetypes are simply too diverse and too manifold to be containable within any single kind of pattern, no matter how capacious or flexible it might be. The inadequacy of a given archetypal pattern does not stem from its lack of unifying power. We have just seen that Heidegger's tetrad of man, sky, earth, and gods is quite encompassing in character. It exhibits the truth of Jung's remark that a quaternity "always expresses a totality" (CW 13, ¶207). But it is neither unity nor totality that is at issue here. What is at issue is precisely the multiplicity of archetypes and, in particular, how this multiplicity resolves itself into ordered groupings in imaginal space. For this, we need a different kind of model. In Heidegger's schema, all the gods are lumped together under the one generic heading of "gods." But will the gods allow themselves to be classed together in such indiscriminate indifference? Are there not intrinsic differences between individual gods as well as between different groups of gods? And does such differentiation not tell us something essential about an archetypally alert imagination?

Even into this largely uncharted area of questioning, Jung once again leads the way. At one point in his "Septem Sermones ad Mortuos" he begins with a foreseeable adulation of the quadriform character of gods: "Four is the number of the principal gods, as four is the number of the world's measurements." But he continues in a quite unexpected manner:

> The multiplicity of the gods correspondeth to the multiplicity of man.
> Numberless gods await the human state. Numberless gods have been

men. Man shareth in the nature of the gods. . . . Measureless is the movement of both.[20]

Not only does this passage uphold the continuity between cosmos and psyche, but it does so precisely by recognizing the multiplicity of archetypal figures, a multiplicity which refuses to be reduced to—or even to be symbolized by—a fourfold arrangement. Thus Jung himself suggests how one might move beyond the numerolatry of which he has been accused by unsympathetic critics.[21]

Moreover, to make this move toward the multiple does not in any way diminish or undermine the role of imagination. For imagining, as inherently polymorphous in its appetites and actions, is the protean psychic faculty par excellence. As Henri Corbin writes, "to recognize the plurality that attaches to the Imagination is neither to devaluate it nor to negate it, but on the contrary to establish it."[22] The combined influence of Corbin and of Jung is evident in writings of Hillman, who is even more emphatic on this point:

> Archetypes would correspond to divine imaginal forms used as Aristotelian or Kantian conceptual categories. Rather than logical or scientific laws, mythical structures would provide the *a priori* structures within the caverns and the dens of the immeasurable imagination.[23]

The immeasurability of imagination at this level corresponds to the immeasurability of the gods, and vice-versa, for it is precisely through imagination that access to deities becomes possible.[24] Furthermore, Hillman, following Plotinus and Jung, holds that imagination is immeasurable in the specific sense that it is not numerable: it is "innumerably full of innumerable kinds of things . . . this third person, this imaginal region of the psyche does not submit to numbering."[25] This important statement calls for two comments. First, to say outright that archetypes or gods *cannot* be numbered is to prejudge the issue. There is no a priori reason why they cannot be given numerical attributes or, for that matter, still other quantitative characteristics. What should be stressed, however, is that any such numbering, though possible, will always be partial and provisional, for no single numerical schema can claim to be definitive. In other words, gods or archetypes may be numerable in particular groupings—e.g., in given mythical situations—while in the end being both numberless (i.e., inexhaustible by any finite set of numbers) and immeasurable (in the sense of not being finally determinable by means of quantitative determination).

Secondly, and more generally, we may say that the sheer multiplicity of phenomena of a given kind does not preclude their being arranged (or arranging themselves) into significant clusters, whether these clusters have a specifically numerical character or not. If so, this means that archetypal topography is a viable, and not a merely chimerical or desperate, undertaking. Despite the measureless multiplicity of archetypes, they (or, rather, various groups of them) may be found to occupy locations on an imaginary grid: locations which, though not fixed in the sense of being bound to a precise locus in an objective and public space and time, are nevertheless determinate and meaningful in relation to *other* imaginal positions. The gods, though assuredly not situated in relation to the sensible perceived world (between the two there is an absolute and unmeasurable difference), are still locatable intrasystemically, that is, in relation to each other. But to assert this is only to offer support for Hillman's own claim that archetypal psychology must "assume from the beginning that there is a place for everything, that everything can belong to one God or another."[26] There *is* a place for everything—for everything of archetypal significance.

Archetypal topography may be a risky pursuit, prone to errancy (though not, strictly speaking, to error), but it is a justifiable one if there are—indeed, *must* be—"transcendental topics" (in Kant's term) for all archetypal dominants. And this enterprise is to be carried out precisely by delineating and denominating mini-systems of archetypes. Each such system will contain a finite (but not necessarily specified) number of members, each of which derives its symbolic meaning from two factors: (1) its own intrinsic, auto-iconic (i.e., self-resembling, non-repeatable) nuclear signification; (2) its relationship with the other members of the mini-system in question (which is how its locus in imaginal space is determined). This is to grant to French structuralism that diacritical differences—that is, sheerly differential relations—between terms can be crucial. But it is at the same time to retain the terms themselves as indispensable nodes or terminal points with their own unique and inalienable significations. That such a conception of archetypal topography is not of merely theoretical interest can best be shown by a brief consideration of two exemplary cases.

(a) The first is to be found in Gilbert Durand's comprehensive treatise *Les structures anthropologiques de l'imaginaire*. Durand shows how groups of archetypes cluster around schemata determined ultimately by certain dominant reflexes and gestures. The resultant archetypal patterns are "well-defined and relatively stable,"[27] for every archetype can be classified in accordance with its precise position in one of two enormous collective units or "regimes," the nocturnal and the diurnal. These regimes are mutually exclusive of one another and yet jointly exhaustive of all archetypal structures. Any given structure—say, that of Promethean ascent—will have its *own* intrinsic signification ("ascent" remains a singular and directly describable *trajet*) while at the same time acquiring certain other properties from its relationship with *different* structures in the same sector of the same regime (e.g., from the association of Promethean ascent with images of height and of solar light). Thus both principles (1) and (2) as indicated above are at work in Durand's classificatory system: there is a core-meaning ("ascent") along with intrasystemic determinations by coordinate factors (height, the sun).[28] Moreover, although in Durand's overall project of "general archetypology" there are two, and only two, great regimes, the individual structures within each regime are numberless in the sense that there is no limit to the amount of particular structures that can be incorporated into a given group or subgroup inside a given regime. Yet the internal complexity of the system of classification ensures that this system is not merely accommodating and all-inclusive but also a means of locating archetypal structures in relation to each other. In other words, Durand's general archetypology is a genuine archetypal topography, a mapping of the primary *topoi* of the imaginal realm. The system is a system not only for classifying but for *finding* archetypal structures—for discovering and recognizing such structures within that "gigantic net" which is traced by archetypal topography.[29]

(b) In Frances Yates's *The Art of Memory* we find a quite different system proposed in a brilliant discussion of Guilio Camillo's "memory theater," which Yates regards as a quintessential expression of Renaissance psychology and cosmology.[30] In this instance, individual archetypal structures are arranged in two kinds of general regime: the regime of astral bodies and that of the successive stages of creation. Each regime is in turn divided into seven distinct subgroups, which correspond to the seven divine astral bodies and to the seven stages of creation. Thus specified, the two regimes are superimposed on each other, thereby forming a single cross-classificatory system with a powerful combinatory effect. Both of the primary types of classification, that of the astral gods and that of the stages of creation, serve to constellate a vast range of mythological material, which appears in the form of diverse epithetic images occupying determinate "seats" within each row of the memory theater.

This way of organizing pagan, Christian, and Cabalist lore was intended not just to improve one's powers of memory but to *provide places* for a mass of archetypal figures that would otherwise remain homeless and unrelated to each other. By becoming related to one another within the imaginal space of Camillo's theater, these figures gained a talismanic potency which stemmed, according to the Hermetic tradition that inspired the theater's design, from the magical influences of the astral bodies. Each of these celestial beings represents an archetypal dominant and is characterized, among other things, by a specific affective quality: Jupiter by tranquility, Mars by anger, Saturn by melancholy. Such an affective quality traverses and thus helps to collect together the whole series of diverse images that is arranged under each astral body. The quality is immediately intelligible—or, more exactly, psychologically recognizable—by itself, but it is made all the more meaningful through its differences from other astral-affective qualities: Saturnian melancholy becomes all the more efficaciously emblematic—hence valuable for the magical purposes to which the memory theater was to be put—by its contrast with Jovian tranquility. This contrast is heightened by use of the same image—say, Juno and the clouds—in different astral series and at different levels of the same series. Such intrasystemic complexity serves to specify archetypal dominants to a rare degree of precision and, above all, to provide for these dominants' appropriate places in the total scheme of things. Without the space to enter further into this fascinating blend of the classical art of memory with Hermetic and Cabalist currents in the Italian Renaissance, I want to stress only that Camillo's richly imaginative archetypal topography embodies the same two fundamental elements which would, I believe, be found to lie at the basis of any thorough charting of archetypal locations: a nuclear term (e.g., a name designating a given astral-affective quality) with its own semantic depth—a "shimmering symbol," as Jung called it (*CW* 13, ¶199)—together with a network of internal relations which gives this nuclear term a determinable locus in imaginal space.

III

Even if the case for the possibility of an archetypal topography can be made—and its actuality shown by reference to already existing models of archetypological classification—one might well wonder what all of this has to do with imagination, and especially with active imagination as described by Jung. Do the results of two such disparate inquiries as have been presented in sections I and II above have any significant relationship to each other? It is my conviction that active imagination and archetypal topography are in fact quite closely related, though not in the way that one might at first suppose. In order to show this, I shall sketch a somewhat more comprehensive picture of imagination than is found in Jung's writings on the subject. In particular, I shall distinguish among three types of imaginative experience, for each of which there is a different method of analysis. The types in question are conscious, everyday imagining; active imagination as depicted by Jung; and what we may call an archetypal or visionary imagination. The corresponding modes of analysis are phenomenology, depth psychology, and archetypal topography. In what follows, I shall say something about each type of imagining and the most appropriate approach to it.

(i) *Conscious Imagining*. This is the everyday phenomenon with which we are all familiar from its pervasive presence in the daytime world. It includes everything from flickering fancies to daydreams and reveries: all that Jung would range under voluntary and passive (but non-hallucinatory) fantasies. As distinguished from what happens in active imagination— which may nonetheless borrow its material content from diurnal fantasies—in ordinary conscious imagining we do not normally attempt to extend or deepen what flits before our bemused minds. Since fleetingness characterizes much of this garden-variety imagining, an analysis is called for which is at once cautious and objective. Phenomenology, using its primary procedure of "bracketing," provides in my view the most promising procedure for investigating this most elusive and ephemeral of psychic phenomena.[31]

The portrait which emerges from a phenomenology of imagination is that of a self-circumscribed and yet self-transparent act—one which is autonomous at its own level of experience, a level dominated by the imaginer's ego. This ego is capable of continuously controlling the course of imaginative experience. It is able to originate this experience by merely intending to do so—only rarely is such an intention thwarted—and may terminate the experience just as effortlessly. If an imagined object or event appears spontaneously, it is subject to immediate modification so as to accord with the imaginer's wishes. Moreover, there can be no mistaking of imagined content: whatever presents itself to the imagining ego *is* as it appears and cannot be other than it appears. Nothing corresponding to perceptual illusion (i.e., mistaking the identity or specific qualities of something actually given in perceptual experience) or to hallucination (i.e., mistakenly believing in the perceived presence of something that is not given in perceptual experience at all) takes place in conscious imagining. Instead, what appears appears with complete self-evidence, and this is true even if the character or structure of the imaginative appearance is radically indeterminate.

To the extent that conscious imagining is inherently controllable and its products unmistakable and self-evident, the imagining ego comes to savor an unobstructed, Apollonic freedom. Like Kierkegaard's "aesthetic man," the ego dwells in the realm of pure possibility where anything is or can become possible or, more exactly, where whatever is imaginable is possible and vice versa. In this realm, to be possible *is* to be; and since it is imagination that envisages what is possible, it becomes the arbiter of experience, determining and directing its course.

But this exhilarating freedom is as shallow as it is short-lived. As Kierkegaard saw with psychological acumen, a surfeit of imaginative possibilities may result in a peculiar form of breakdown, "the despair of infinitude."[32] Even more to the point, the freedom enjoyed by the self-controlling imaginal ego is psychologically illusory. As the very evanescence of everyday imagining attests, it is a freedom without foundation in the larger and less controllable life of psyche as a whole. The freefloating and rootless character of much conscious imagining indicates a need for reconnecting, like Antaeus, with stable sources of psychic strength. If this reconnection is not effected, the danger is that of sudden collapse—a collapse into the very opposite of what the conscious ego had come to expect. Instead of self-willed omnipotence, this ego finds itself overwhelmed by imaginal shapes and forces which it can no longer orchestrate. The ostensibly unlimited freedom of ego-dominated conscious imagining—its self-assured success—gives way to a state of unfreedom as the vengeful unconscious, heretofore neglected or suppressed, reclaims its rights. In other words, conscious control cedes to usurpation by the unconscious in a reversal that represents an *enantiodromia* of mind. In place of the fleeting fantasies of everyday egoic imagining, there is now the *fascinosum* of forms emanating from, and variously personifying, unconscious regions of mentation.

It is at this critical juncture that, as Corbin suggests, "it may be advisable to free . . . the Imagination from the parentheses within which a purely phenomenological interpretation encloses it."[33] For if a phenomenological account of conscious imagining shows the ego at an apogee of self-created autonomy, it would be a mistake to equate such an ego with mind *in toto*: egoic imagining is not equivalent to *all* imagining. In fact, such imagining itself leads, almost inexorably, to a different kind of imagining. And, just as we are now forced to acknowledge a new type of imaginative experience, so we must seek for a new way to describe this experience.

(ii) *Active Imagination.* The new world of imagination thus opened up— a world manifested in the personified figures of the unconscious, in nightmares, in toxic states, in psychopathology—is the province of depth psychology, the examination of psyche in its profundity. Present here is a second type of imaginative experience which is subject to at least two basic kinds of analysis in depth. On the one hand, a Freudian technique such as free association (which itself involves imagining) leads back to the remembered or reconstructed past of early childhood, with the distinct implication that all significant imagining represents the hallucinatory fulfillment of certain prototypical infantile wishes. In this perspective, depth psychology becomes a movement *à rebours*, traversing the recent past toward that primordial past (itself constituted partly or wholly by fantasy) which contains the secret of all present imagining. On the other hand, Jungian analysis leads out from one's stock of personal memories and fantasies into the *memoriae* belonging to a realm that is prepersonal in character. "Active imagination," as we have seen, names both the method for realizing this ec-centric movement and the experience of what the movement reveals. In imagining in this active way, an element of control remains present— not to confirm the ego in its self-appointed sovereignty, but to ensure that the unfolding of a given imaginative sequence is followed through as fully as possible. For in active imagining we are no longer marginally engaged in an evanescing activity of sheer ego-consciousness—or, for that matter, propelled backward by the magnet of repressed wishes—but taken up in a movement that is "dramatic" in the most pregnant sense of the term. No longer do we entertain or lull ourselves with what is merely possible and purely private. Nor do we allow ourselves to be overcome by the oppressive opposite of conscious imagining, that is, by passive fantasies of hallucinatory force. Instead, we enter into the drama of the psyche itself by participating in what is psychically real, in what is capable of changing us in some basic way.

Such imagining, though neither hallucinatory nor delusional, is *active* because we are ourselves the actors in the psychical play that is produced through the forceful elaboration of fantasies that might otherwise remain merely passive. In this process of self-dramatization, we come up against entities and events which derive, not from the fickle freedom of the conscious ego—not even from the constraint of a personal unconscious—but from the genuine autonomy of an objective, impersonal psyche. For we are experiencing neither the projections of an idle revery nor the personifications of petulant passions. Rather, in active imagining we confront the *dramatis personae* of a different proscenium of experience altogether. Or more exactly, such apparitional figures guide us, if we are willing to follow them, toward a different kind of imaginative experience through "a movement [born] out of the suspension between opposites, a living birth that leads to a new level of being, a new situation" (*CW* 8, ¶189). There is nothing self-contained about this new kind of imagining, which is disclosing and not enclosing in character.

Therefore, if active imagining begins with a procedure of concerted elaboration of fantasies, it ends with a breakthrough into the disclosure of a world which is not of our own making. And if this is the outcome, we cannot claim that active imagining is itself the ultimate kind of imagining. Crucial as it is, it remains, in Corbin's words, "an intermediary, a mediatrix."[34] In short, we must move beyond both ordinary and active imagining, and hence also beyond both phenomenology and depth psychology as methods for analyzing the imaginal component of human experience.

(iii) *Archetypal Imagination.* But where does such a move move us to? This is the appropriate question, for it is a matter of specifying the proper *place* of this last type of imaginative experience, the experience of an archetypal or visionary imagination. This place is "the place of . . . visions, the scene on which visionary events and symbolic histories *appear* in their true reality."[35] It is important to recognize that the "visions" in question need not be expressly theophanic in nature. The visionary imagination is potentially present at every level of human experience. It can be found in the imaginative transformation of even the most mundane object into a denizen of the *mundus imaginalis*, as in Kathleen Raine's description of the visionary transmutation of a simple vase of flowers before which she was seated or in her accounts of Blake's visions (for which a prototype is "to see a World in a Grain of Sand").[36]

Such en-visioning must not be confused with hallucinating, though certain hallucinatory states may prepare for or even induce imaginative visions. In full-blown hallucination, a demonstrably false claim is made concerning what is *perceived*—say, that I am now seeing a certain quasi-perceptual object, a 'knife,' when I am not in fact seeing any such object. In hallucinating, a would-be perception is substituted for an actual perception. From this point of view, having a genuine, non-hallucinatory vision is even comparable to conscious imagining: both are non-corrigible experiences which do not admit of verification *or* falsification by reference to the perceived world. But the analogy ceases here, for in visionary imagining I do not regard what I imagine as purely possible. Nor do I treat it as psychically real in the dramatic and dramatized form which is found in active imagination proper. Instead, I take the content of the experience to be psychically real in a sense that encompasses and yet transcends both perceptual and self-dramatized realities. Such imagining "posits real being"[37]—real *imaginal* being—but in such a way as to surpass the empirical existence characterizing the objects of natural science as well as the strictly subjective existence pertaining to those purely personal experiences that form the focus of so much psychological analysis.

The activity of archetypal imagining moves not only beyond ordinary conscious imagining by constellating contents from the personal and collective unconscious—as occurs in active imagining—but also beyond active imagination itself. As we have seen, it is the quasi-histrionic aspect of active imagining that allows the imaginer to become an active participant in his or her own imaginative projects—a participation which is noticeably absent from the spectatorial stance of revery or daydream. But self-dramatization, while a source of psychic strength and self-insight, is at the same time delimiting. It keeps the scene of imaginative action confined to the immediate vicinity of the imaginer's personal sphere of concern, with all that this implies of the particular and the peculiar, and may end up as an introverted method of ego-building. The story that is told through imaginative projections, personifications, and identifications is the story of the imaginer himself or herself—hence its potential value in therapy, but also its limitation and its danger.

Yet the stories spun out in active imagining are more than personal in signification, even if they owe their original attractive power to some profoundly personal *retentissement.* These stories are not only self-enactments: they dramatize and sensuously embody what is other than purely personal, what is extrapersonal. They are trying to tell us something not just about ourselves but about the archetypal dominants upon which they themselves are founded. The paradox is that active imagination, though permitting a first glance into this extrapersonal domain, is not adequate by itself as a means of exploring the entire domain. The core of active imagining remains, in Jung's words, "a method of introspection for observing the stream of interior images" (*CW* 9, i, ¶319). It is true that these images are latently rich in archetypal meaning, but to enter the archetypal region itself, an archetypal or visionary imagination is required which by its very nature transcends active imagining.

Because of this transcending movement—not to be confused with Jung's "transcendent function," which remains at the level of active imagination—it is tempting to speak with Corbin of visionary imagining as "magical." But if it is magical, it is not merely in Sartre's sense of escaping all causal explanation.[38] Rather, it is a magical act in the spirit of what Paracelsus called "true imagination" (*Imaginatio vera*), which transmutes gross matter into subtle, immaterial bodies; or in the sense of the hermetic psychology of imagination to be found in Pico della Mirandola, Ficino, and Bruno, for all of whom images were talismanic presences of the demonic.[39]

In any event, the aspect of visionary imagination which is of most concern to us is not its exact modus operandi—of this we know little—but its proper plane of experience. This plane is that of archetypal structures themselves, not in their separate imagistic fulgurations but in their joint con-figurations. If Jung is right in claiming that we do not know an archetype in itself, this is true only in the strict sense that we do not know *an* archetype by itself alone—that is, as a strictly singular entity. Instead, through visionary imagination we come to know *archetypes*—in the plural, always and only in the plural. For in the experience of visionary imagining we do not encounter individually isolated archetypes. Archetypal topography, the method which discloses the order inherent in the content of such imagining, reveals the presence of whole clusters of archetypes; and it is within these groupings alone that individual archetypes can be experienced and known. It is not accidental, then, that a visionary imagination is capable of disclosing a crowded canvas of angels or demons, planetary gods or supra-celestial beings. As Dürer put it, "he who wants to create dreamwork must make a mixture of all things."[40]

IV

A genuinely archetypal imagination, which is by no means easy to achieve, presents us with three paradoxes. An exploration of these will bring this chapter to its conclusion.

(i) The first paradox arises from two conflicting tendencies. (a) On the one hand, archetypal imagining represents the advent of a certain kind of consciousness, not the naive and shallow consciousness of an empirically determined and oriented awareness, but a more disciplined consciousness which may take at least two forms. First, the visionary state involves heightened awareness, a form of attention differing both from attention to the merely mundane and from the attention involved in dreaming. Second, to perform a topographical analysis of archetypes requires an act of intellection which is in itself an acute form of consciousness. If the first form of heightened consciousness—the peculiar attentiveness of the visionary state—is an activity of psyche, the second form (that required in archetypal topography as such) is an activity of intellect, hence of spirit. (b) On the other hand, although consciousness is thus enhanced in both of these respects—in soul and in spirit, its two basic modes of manifestation—*what* we come to experience in archetypal imagining is no longer of the character of, or based in, consciousness. The content that we come to experience is rooted outside of human consciousness, whether this consciousness presents itself in the form of the ego or in the more expansive format of the self. Therefore, just at the point when personal consciousness has reached its psychical zenith, psyche itself is surpassed. The impersonal, the nonhuman, is met with.[41]

There is no name for what is now imagined visionarily other than the names given to it—names that are themselves always plural in form—in folklore, in classical Greek mythology, in the symbols of dreams. If it is true, as Hillman suggests, that it is "through the imagination that man has access to the Gods,"[42] this access is attained only through a genuinely archetypal imagination, and, further, the deities reached in this way are named conjointly. To recognize this is not to revert to nominalism, for the names in question convey presences—they *are* presences. They are numinal, not nominal, names, each of which makes a sign to us from within the confraternity formed from all affiliated names. Through the numinosity of naming, we have to do with what Corbin calls the "archetypal essences, the eternal hexeities of Names."[43]

(ii) The second paradox follows closely upon the heels of the first. The latter, as we have just seen, combines the necessity of specific acts of consciousness with entry into a domain that is extraconscious and even extrahuman. Despite the ultimacy of this domain with regard to archetypal imagination—providing as it does the proper placescape of archetypal configurations—it is nonetheless not the most ultimate region of human experience. In particular, it is not ultimate from an ontological standpoint: it is not the culminating sphere of being. The further paradox, then, is that what is archetypally adequate is ontologically inadequate. (Which is not to deny that the converse may also be true: what is ontologically adequate is archetypally inadequate.) For the realm of archetypes, the "eighth clime" of the theosophers of Islam, is not to be mistaken for what the same theosophers call "the sphere of spheres," the sphere that encloses the cosmos as a whole.[44] This "supreme sphere" is the arena of Ideas, the eternal exemplars that give to the universe its formal character, a character at once original and final. These Ideas are not so much Names as Forms in the Platonic sense. Forms are ontologically ultimate, providing not only meaning but *being* to all that is.

It is true that archetypes also furnish meaning and being; but archetypal meaning is inseparable from the images in which it is embodied (hence this meaning is always expressed metaphorically), and being at the archetypal level takes the form of psychical reality. In contrast, the meaning of Forms cannot be exhausted by metaphorical expressions; as conceptual, such meaning cannot be condensed into images but remains the object of thought, the aim of what Aristotle called "active intellect." And the scope of Forms extends to the cosmos in its entirety and not only to that sector designated "Psyche." This is why the ultimate Form, the Form of Forms, must be the One. As Plotinus saw, only the One can bring together, within the compass of a single concept, the multiplicity of the many. Moreover, the inherent manyness of both the empirical and the archetypal worlds calls for the concept of a oneness which, while preserving this manyness, allows it to be thought under the aegis of unity. Instead of dominating from above in a topheavy manner, the Form of Forms is itself ingredient in and necessary to all multiplicities, serving as their essential conceptual correlate. In fact, multiplicities are found on all three levels: empirical, archetypal, and formal. But only at the last level does the specific multiplicity that is present—i.e., that of the Forms themselves—imply a unity that encompasses *every* kind of multiplicity. This unity remains, of course, formal and thus does not inhibit in any way the multifariousness present at any given level. Only when a unity is proposed *too soon* does it have an inhibiting effect, as occurs when a strictly Newtonian 'Nature' is posited as the unity of the empirical world or a monotheistic 'God' as the unity of the gods. Hence the most radical pluralism is not only compatible with oneness but even requires an open ontological One to ensure that unification does not occur precipitously or pointlessly. As Rafael López-Pedraza has observed, "the many *contains* the unity of the one *without losing* the possibilities of the many."[45] To put it differently: the many is related to the One in such a way as not to lose its inherent manyness.

Reflection on the above two paradoxes suggests this schematic structure:

Region of Being	Physis	Psyche	Spirit
Human Capacity	sensory perception; memory; ordinary imagining insofar as it merely replicates what is perceived	ordinary and active imagining insofar as they move us beyond the empirical realm; above all, archetypal imagining as the envisioning of clusters of archetypes	active intellect or the ability to grasp Forms as ultimate conceptual categories
Type of World	the empirical world of determinate loci in an objective space and time	the imaginal world: (a) as personified in the contents of the unconscious; (b) as dramatized in active imagination; (c) as a self-presenting domain of apparitional figures	the world of Ideas or Forms, including the Form of Forms or the One: all that is intelligible in a strictly conceptual sense

Despite its fastidious character, such a structure may help to make sense of the repeated claim of philosophers and theosophists alike that the imaginal exists midway between the sensible and the intelligible and that, as a consequence, imagination itself is irrevocably *intermediate* in status. Yet this very claim leads to still another paradox.

(iii) This paradox may be expressed in the form of a question: if imagination is intermediate in status, does it not become an act whose merely mediatory function is all too easily replaceable by other mediating acts? In order to answer this question, it needs to be pointed out, first of all, that the intermediacy of imagination has been an ongoing and largely unchallenged assumption within Western epistemology since the Greeks. Aristotle's cautious observations in his *De Anima,* Kant's sober speculations in *The Critique of Pure Reason,* and Collingwood's elegant account in *The Principles of Art* represent three remarkably continuous cases in point. Western philosophers would for the most part agree with the theosophers' judgment that imagination "has a mediating role *par excellence.*"[46] Yet it must be acknowledged that for most Western thinkers— though Collingwood, along with his Romantic precursors, is in this regard an exception—the assigning of an intermediate position to imagining has been a way, not of magnifying, but of denigrating and even of denying its powers. When Sartre speaks of imagining as "degraded knowing" (*savoir dégradé*),[47] he is articulating an inbred bias against imagination whose most virulent expression is found in the seventeenth-century Cartesian reaction to the Renaissance exaltation of the magical powers of imagining. Most post-Cartesian philosophers—and those psychologists who simply follow suit—would concur with Pascal's classic complaint that imagination is "the mistress of falsehood and error."[48]

The condemnation of imagination as cognitively dangerous arises in the context of theories of knowledge which restrict valid cognition to the survey of sensible particulars. Yet if such a stringent conception of cognition were to be enlarged, imagination's intermediate position would no longer count against it. For imagining would then be granted its *own* cognitive value, its own specific way of knowing—a way of knowing which might culminate in what I have termed archetypal topography. Further, imagination might become an essential point of access not only to archetypes but also to Ideas. Certain, if not all, Ideas might be best approached through imaginative activity, much as Plato considered myth to be the most accessible approach to Forms and Vico thought metaphor indispensable to the grasp of concepts.

If imagination is indeed intermediate in these crucial ways, it does not deserve the wholesale censure which it has received from so many Western philosophers. Though intermedi*ate*, it need not be only intermedi*ary*, a mere "mediating representation" in Kant's demeaning term.[49] If imagination mediates, it does so in a distinctive and irreplaceable manner. This is above all true of an archetypal imagination, which provides a necessary and unique *medium* within which archetypal realities come to be reflected in the form of vibrant images. Archetypal imagining as a *via media* is uneliminable insofar as it supplies structure to what is psychically real. As genuinely intermediate, it surpasses sensible particularity while foreshadowing strictly formal or ideational modes of being. It offers both a way *out* of the snares of sensationalism and a way *toward* a sphere of being that is ontologically ultimate. Paradoxically penultimate, the archetypal imagination upon which our entire analysis has been converging should not be taken as the concluding phase in the movement of mind as such. For mind knows no conclusion and is as unending as the application of an archetype or the scope of an Idea.

I shall not attempt on this occasion to resolve any of the above paradoxes. Unlike certain other paradoxes which the phenomenon of imagination presents—e.g., the conjunction of controllability and spontaneity—these paradoxes do not admit of easy explication, much less of direct dissolution. In other words, they are paradoxes which can, and perhaps *should*, be left standing just as they are. For as they are, they point to something profoundly characteristic of human imagining. This is that our very efforts to actualize, in the fullest possible way, what Jung called "the psyche's capacity for imaginative realization" (*CW* 13, ¶216) land us in a world which is neither perceptual nor conceptual in nature—nor, for that matter, merely imaginary in the derogatory sense of unreal. This intermediate world is an imaginal world, teeming with transmuted substances, subtilized sensuous forms, and legions of figures each with a proper place within the endlessly variegated topography of the *mundus imaginalis*. It is a world no longer human—or at least not exclusively or primarily human. It is *another* world, with *another* kind of reality, to which we have access through active imagination but which we explore by the exercise of an archetypal imagination. It is with reference to this world that Rimbaud said that "one must be, must make himself, a seer,"[50] for we come to know it only through the enactment of an authentically visionary imagination.

In its polymorphous and polyvalent profusion, imagination itself effects the dialectical movement that has been traced in this essay. Imagining changes character or type as it is embodied and realized in different regions of experience. We have witnessed a movement from a quotidian consciousness, in which the ego is pridefully capable of controlling its imagining and yet riding for a fall; to a state of being stunned by an avenging unconscious, though eventually coping with it by means of active imagining; and finally to an experience of an archetypally structured world, which is at once the fulfillment of a visionary imagination and an opening to a region of Forms. Though dialectical, this movement is not Hegelian in character, for the final stage is not simply the synthesis of the preceding stages. The dialectic is a sheerly qualitative dialectic of consciousness with no prearranged progress and no assured success. There is only a sense of radically shifting modes of awareness as the mind migrates from the nameless and nonfixed nature of conscious imagining, through the singularly named and potently personified contents of passive and active imagining, to the collectively named Names—to the archetypes, to the gods—of a luminously visionary imagination. This route is neither a mystical *via negativa* nor a philosophical royal road. Nor is it the only itinerary which the course of human imagining may take. But it does serve to mark off three critical way-stations by means of which imagination—that "link of links" as Bruno called it, stressing its ineluctable intermediate character— charts the soul's odyssey through the Medi-terranean multiplicity of the psychically real.

1.   C. G. Jung, *Collected Works*, vol. 6: *Psychological Types*, trans. H. G. Baynes and R. F. C. Hull (Princeton: Princeton University Press, 1971), p. 52, ¶78. Subsequent references to Jung's writings will be designated *CW*, followed by volume and paragraph numbers.

2.   Cf. ibid., ¶¶78, 187.

3.   Ibid., ¶722. Cf. also the statement at ¶433: "It is not a special faculty, since it can come into play in all the basic forms of psychic activity."

4.   For the history of this term in Jung's writings, see R. F. C. Hull, "Bibliographical Notes on Active Imagination in the Works of C. G. Jung," *Spring 1971*: 115–20.

5.   C. G. Jung, *Analytical Psychology* (New York: Vintage, 1970), p. 192.

6.   Concerning the synthetic character of active imagination, Jung says: "The images and symbols of the unconscious yield their distinctive values only when subjected to a synthetic mode of treatment" (*CW* 7, ¶122).

7.   There is a striking similarity between active imagination and the phenomenological technique of free variation in imagination. Jung's very terms—"alteration," "transformation"—point to a procedure in which "the material is continually varied and increased until a kind of condensation of motifs into more or less stereotyped symbols takes place" (*CW* 8, ¶173). Although free variation as described by Edmund Husserl is more systematic in character—since it involves varying each and every feature in an attempt to exhaust all possible variations—still the respective aims of the two methods are not so disparate as might be supposed. In free variation, an *eidos* or essence is sought. This *eidos* is the invariant factor in the variations which have been performed by means of imagination: it is what cannot be "imagined away," what keeps intruding itself. Similarly, Jung conceived archetypes—the ultimate, if not the immediate, objects of active imagination—as "constant, autonomous factors," as preformed patterns which keep emerging through all of the vicissitudes of active imaginings (cf. *CW* 9, ii, chap. 3). These "dominants" are given an explicitly a priori status by Jung, who mentions Kant in this connection: "the basic images and forms of imagination have in a way more resemblance to Kant's table of a priori categories . . . than to the scurrilities, circumstantialities, whims, and tricks of our personal minds" (*CW* 3, ¶527). Kant is also the philosophical patron of Husserl, and we might say that Jung and Husserl join forces precisely in their common concern for what is invariant or categorial. In the end, both provide a "transcendental" account of the conditions of possibility for certain kinds of experience. This is the case even though, as we shall see in section III below, the kinds of imaginative experience for which their respective methods are most appropriate differ decidedly in character. (There is also the difference that conditions of possibility are in Jung's view strictly unconscious; thus he speaks of "the unconscious a priori" which "precipitates itself into plastic form" (*CW* 8, ¶402). For Husserl, in contrast, the eidetic realm of the a priori is attainable by a conscious, albeit transcendental, ego. For Husserl's notions of free variation and the transcendental ego, see *Ideas*, trans. W. R. Boyce Gibson [London: Allen & Unwin, 1958], sec. 3–4, 23, and 49–50.)

8. *CW* 14, ¶753. We might say, in Husserlian language, that imputing existence within an objective space and time is "neutralized"—not so as to discredit the actively imagined performance or to make it unbelievable (as if it were merely fantastic or hallucinatory) but to make it all the more convincing at its own level. On neutralization, see *Ideas,* sec. 109–15.

9. Jung, *CW* 8, ¶403. Keeping in mind the distinction between archetypes and their imagistic amplifications may help us to understand one of Jung's more obscure utterances:

> Of the essence of things, of absolute being, we know nothing. But we experience various effects: from "outside" by way of the sense, from "inside" by way of imagination. We would never think of asserting that the color "green" had an independent existence; similarly, we ought never to suppose that an imaginative experience exists in and for itself, and is therefore to be taken literally. It is an expression, an appearance standing for something unknown but real. (*CW* 7, ¶355)

This very Kantian-sounding statement is in the end quite unKantian. Although Jung is granting with Kant that we can *know* appearances alone (in this case, imaginative appearances or presentations), he is asserting, in spite of a stated aversion to metaphysics, that the thing in itself can be characterized as real—that archetypes, as the ultimate psychical things in themselves, are metaphysically real because they are capable of producing certain "effects." Yet if Kant is right concerning the noumenal status of things in themselves, then we should not be able to say anything *at all* about them—not even that they are causally efficacious in some unknown way. In this dispute we must invoke Jung against himself: "whether we will or no, philosophy keeps breaking through" (*CW* 7, ¶201). It breaks through this time in the form of Jung's own thesis concerning the metaphysical status of archetypes. For even if the real is to be judged only by its effects, to assert the existence of these effects (as Jung explicitly does) is necessarily to presume the reality of their archetypal cause and thus to indulge in metaphysics despite Kant's and Jung's own warnings.

10. In at least one place, Jung even credits his discovery of archetypes to the procedure of active imagination: *CW* 8, ¶403.

11. James Hillman, *The Myth of Analysis* (Evanston: Northwestern University Press, 1972), p. 181.

12. I should indicate why I have not considered the triad to be in competition with other archetypal groupings. Jung's efforts to play down the significance of triadic arrangements and to seek for a fourth figure wherever possible are well known. These efforts were based on the sound intuition that a cluster of three elements often represents an essentially *intellectual* formation, in which the thinking function excels. One need only think of Plato's tripartite soul, Aristotle's three-step syllogisms, Spinoza's three-fold classification of cognitive faculties, Kant's triplistic judgment-forms, or Hegel's dialectic of thesis, antithesis, and synthesis in order to realize how spontaneously the human intellect adopts a triadic form in which to present its insights. Jung resorts to such a schema himself in his *theoretical* discussions of the transcendent function and of active imagination—both of which he terms "third things." As an instrument of analysis, the triad provides an economical means for bringing us efficiently, and yet comprehensively, to a conclusion. But if we are more interested in psychic *experience*—and especially in the archetypal origins of this experience—than in valid conclusions as such, we shall find ourselves driven to other models: first to the tetrad and then beyond.

13. For a discussion of the significance of the quaternity in Jungian theory and therapy, see A. Plaut, "The Ungappable Bridge," *Journal of Analytical Psychology* 18 (1973), esp. pp. 119–20.

14. It should be noticed, however, that dreams are analyzed in terms of four distinct phases in Jung, *CW* 8, ¶¶561–64.

15. This series is composed of the following books: *La psychanalyse du feu* (Gallimard, 1939); *L'eau et les rêves* (Corti, 1942); *L'air et les songes* (Corti, 1943); *La terre et les rêveries*

de la volonté and *La terre et les rêveries du repos* (Corti, 1948). Bachelard's concern with a psychoanalysis of the elements is indebted to Jung for the notion of the complex, as is acknowledged in the Conclusion of *La psychanalyse du feu:* "le feu est l'occasion, au sens très précis de C. G. Jung, 'd'un complexe archaïque fécond' " (p. 183).

16.   See especially Bachelard, *La poétique de l'espace* (Presses Universitaires de France, 1957) and *La poétique de la rêverie* (Presses Universitaires de France, 1960). The influence of Jung is marked in both of these works. Thus Bachelard says in the former that "en ce qui nous concerne, nous nous croyons obligé à établir l'actualité des archetypes" (p. 172).

17.   Martin Heidegger, "Bauen Wohnen Denken," in *Vorträge und Aufsätze* (Pfullingen: Neske, 1954), pp. 149–50. See also the essay "Das Ding" in ibid., pp. 163 ff.

18.   Perhaps this is what Jung meant to indicate by his choice of the otherwise baffling term "objective psyche." This term's deliberate ambiguity allows it to connote a mixture of cosmic and psychic factors.

19.   On the relation between psyche and matter, see Patricia Berry, "On Reduction," *Spring 1973,* esp. pp. 78–83.

20.   C. G. Jung, "Septem Sermones ad Mortuos," in *Memories, Dreams, Reflections* (New York: Random House, 1963), p. 386.

21.   Further evidence of this direction in Jung's thinking is provided by a statement which he made at Eranos in 1934: "The fact is that the single archetypes are not isolated . . . but are in a state of contamination, of the most complete mutual interpenetration and interfusion" (*CW* 9, i, ¶80; quoted by Hillman in *Myth of Analysis,* p. 264).

22.   Henri Corbin, *Creative Imagination in the Súfism of Ibn 'Arabí,* trans. R. Manheim (Princeton: Princeton University Press, 1969), p. 193.

23.   Hillman, *The Myth of Analysis,* p. 179. This statement should be compared with what has been said in note 7 above.

24.   See ibid., p. 180.

25.   Ibid., pp. 175–76.

26.   Ibid., p. 181.

27.   Gilbert Durand, *Les structures anthropologiques de l'imaginaire* (Presses Universitaires de France, 1963), p. 55.

28.   Durand's acute analysis has been simplified considerably in the above presentation. Promethean ascent is a specific archetype, while "ascent" as such is for Durand one of the two principal schemata corresponding to the "postural gesture" of verticality, which is itself the dominant gesture or reflex that functions as the corporeal analogue or basis of the diurnal regime. See *Les structures anthropologiques,* pp. 39–52 for a more complete analysis. "Archetype" is discussed at pp. 53–54 and "structure" at pp. 55–56.

29.   Gilbert Durand, "Exploration of the Imaginal," *Spring 1971:* 91.

30.   See Frances A. Yates, *The Art of Memory* (London: Routledge and Kegan Paul, 1966), esp. pp. 129–72.

31.   For a fuller statement of what is entailed in a phenomenology of imagination, see my "Toward a Phenomenology of Imagination" in this volume. It should be noted that the elusiveness of the image may be due as much to the imaginer's easily distractable attention as to the image's own ephemerality: *both* factors seem to be involved.

32.   See Sören Kierkegaard, *The Sickness Unto Death,* trans. W. Lowrie (New York: Doubleday Anchor, 1954), pp. 163 ff. On p. 165 Kierkegaard elucidates: "The self thus leads a fantastic existence in abstract endeavor after infinity, or in abstract isolation, constantly lacking itself, from which it merely gets further and further away." On "aesthetic" existence, see Kierkegaard's *Either/Or,* trans. D. F. Swenson et al. (New York: Doubleday Anchor, 1959), p. 40: "If I were to wish for anything, I should not wish for wealth and power, but for the passionate sense of the potential, for the eye which . . . sees the possible."

33.   Corbin, *Creative Imagination,* p. 3.

34.   Ibid., p. 189. The full statement is "An intermediary, a mediatrix: such is the essential function of the Active Imagination." It must be noted, however, that Corbin's use of "active imagination" differs from the above interpretation, which remains closer to Jung's original

conception. For Corbin, active imagination is fully archetypal in status. Hence it would be more nearly equivalent to what I describe below as "archetypal imagination." Its intermediate status derives from its position between sense perception and intellect. Cf. Corbin's article "Mundus Imaginalis" in Spring 1972, esp. pp. 9–12. For further discussion, see my "Imagination as Intermediate" in this volume.

35.   Corbin, Creative Imagination, p. 4. Corbin also speaks of "the place of apparition" (p. 189).

36.   See Kathleen Raine, The Divine Vision (New York: Haskell House, 1968) and Blake and Tradition (London: Routledge and Kegan Paul, 1969). Raine described her own "vision" in a recent BBC interview.

37.   Corbin, Creative Imagination, p. 180.

38.   See Jean-Paul Sartre, L'Imaginaire (Gallimard, 1940), pp. 161–62.

39.   See Frances A. Yates, Giordano Bruno and the Hermetic Tradition (London: Routledge and Kegan Paul, 1964) , passim.

40.   Albrecht Dürer, quoted by Ernst Kris, Psychoanalytic Explorations in Art (New York: Schocken, 1964), p. 199.

41.   In Corbin's description, it is a "waking state . . . the state characteristic of the gnostic when he departs from the consciousness of sensuous things" (Creative Imagination, p. 189). As a non-dreaming state which is focused upon the non-sensuous, visionary imagining should not be confused with hallucinating. For hallucinating, whether it occurs in dreaming or in waking life, is always concerned with sensuous content, even if this content is only pseudo-perceptual.

42.   Hillman, The Myth of Analysis, p. 180. It should be added that for Hillman access to the gods is also gained through psychopathology, as he has made clear in his 1972 Terry Lectures (Re-Visioning Psychology [New York: Harper & Row, 1975]).

43.   Corbin, Creative Imagination, p. 195.

44.   See Corbin, "Mundus Imaginalis," p. 4.

45.   The statement of López-Pedraza is in Spring 1971: 214.

46.   Corbin, "Mundus Imaginalis," p. 12.

47.   See Sartre, L'Imaginaire, pp. 81–82, 97, 118, 137–38.

48.   Blaise Pascal, Pensées, ed. L. Lafuma (Paris: Seuil, 1962), p. 54.

49.   Immanuel Kant, Critique of Pure Reason, trans. N. K. Smith (New York: Humanities Press, 1950), A 138 B 177, p. 181.

50.   Letter to Paul Demeny, 15 May 1871.

Toward a Phenomenology of Imagination

I

IN A BAFFLING but engaging prose piece, Samuel Beckett writes as follows:

> No trace anywhere of life, you say, pah, no difficulty there, imagination not dead yet, yes, dead, good, *imagination dead imagine.*[1]

In this puzzling but profound utterance, especially in its concluding three words, Beckett is pointing to the paradox of a mental activity which, conceived as a fixed faculty, is dead or dying but which, considered dynamically and in process, is very much alive. *The* imagination may indeed be dead, yet we keep on imagining—much as Beckett himself continued to write prose, while scorning the established forms of this literary medium. Indeed, imagining is so essential to human mental activity that its elimination would radically alter the character of the human mind. Disagreement may well arise as to how imagining should be described or explained, but it is difficult to deny its central place in much mentation. I say "central" and not, as one might have expected, "marginal." In dealing with imagination, we have to do, not with a peripheral phenomenon taking place in the wings of awareness, but with something that occurs on the center stage of consciousness. To imagine is not—or at least is not always—to indulge in an evasive maneuver carrying us away from the mind's principal preoccupations. It is not—or at least is not necessarily—to sidestep the real in order to enter or erect a separate mental domain which is unreal or surreal. The life of imagination is at one with the life of mind as a whole.

That imagining is crucial to a considerable portion of mental activity can be inferred not only from the frequent recourse which we make to concrete images and diagrams—to the devices of what Plato called *dianoia*—but also from the polymorphic use which human beings make of hypotheses and thought-experiments in everyday reasoning and in scientific theorizing. What John Dewey termed "dramatic rehearsal in imagination" occurs constantly when we dream, daydream, think, and even when we perceive. Indeed, it is rare to accomplish any of these quotidian activities without in some way making use of inherent imaginative powers. Perhaps only in the case of perceiving do we have the impression of participating, and then only on occasion, in a perfectly straightforward activity of Moorean simplicity. But it can also be argued that no act of perceiving is wholly unattenuated by nonperceptual elements, among which imaginative activity must be included. This can be seen, for example, in Wittgenstein's analysis of "seeing as." Referring to a scalene triangle whose bottom line is its longest side, he comments that "it takes *imagination* to see the triangle as fallen."[2] Not even this brief demonstration is needed to persuade us that imagining is ingredient in such diverse acts as daydreaming, dreaming, hallucinating, remembering, and anticipating. Although occurring differently in each case—so differently, in fact, that a separate investigation would be required just to establish these differences—imagining is genuinely immanent in these activities and is not an ad hoc addition to them.

The centrality of imagining extends to the social and political realm as well. To cite just one familiar example: when the slogan *"l'imagination au pouvoir"* appeared spontaneously during the May, 1968 uprisings in Paris, this was not a merely whimsical event. It was, at least in part, the expression of a profound distrust of the prevalent reality-oriented, rationalist-technocratic model of human action. The slogan called for a new emphasis on the *possible* in human affairs. It reflected and encapsulated the type of quasi-utopian political speculation that is found, among other places, in Marcuse's *Eros and Civilization.* Marcuse explicitly appeals to imagination as a means of realizing a freer, more playful sense of action and interaction. What is disappointing in Marcuse's program— as well as in the barricade mentality that failed, following the Paris rebellion, to think through the rhetoric of slogans—is that no convincing notion of imagination itself, supposedly the very organ of liberation, is offered. For a model for the act, Marcuse takes over the hierarchical, faculty-dominated theory of Schiller, who in turn owes much to Kant. The result is a warmed-over, twice-removed Kantian version of the phenomenon.[3] Needed here as elsewhere in contemporary appeals to imagination is a coherent and non-derivative account of precisely what imagining is—how it functions, what its primary traits are, how it relates to other mental acts.

It is a remarkable fact that such an account is lacking, not only on the contemporary scene, but, even more significantly, in the majority of Western theories of mind. The reason I call this conspicuous absence of an adequate account "remarkable" is that imagination stands out among human mental acts precisely in terms of its easy accessibility and its virtually assured success. On the one hand, perhaps no other mental act is so readily available to consciousness as is imagining. Undistracted and undisturbed by mundane concerns, the imaginer is fully present to what he or she imagines, and what he or she imagines in turn reveals itself totally and transparently. On the other hand, he or she can imagine just what he or she wants to imagine. No sooner does he or she desire to imagine something in particular than this something appears to him or her directly and without delay. What human experience could be less problematic? Or so it seems.

Or so it *seems*, for practically all extant descriptions and theories of imagination are beset with confusion and contradiction. The obfuscation takes two closely related forms. First, imagining is not decisively distinguished from other mental acts. Secondly, the intrinsic character of imagining is itself misdescribed or misunderstood. The combined result of these two forms of obfuscation is a denial, or at least a demotion, of the importance of imagination vis-à-vis the rest of mental activity. In particular, any autonomy which one might be tempted to ascribe to imagining on the basis of its ready availability and its self-incurring success is undermined by a tendency to consider it as second-rate in status.

This tendency to disparage imagination is as prevalent in commonsensical attitudes as it is in psychological or philosophical theories. When we say unthinkingly that "it was merely my imagination" or that "my imagination was playing tricks on me," we express, in the telling terms of ordinary language, the same dismissive frame of mind to which the mainstream of Western psychology and philosophy has given sophisticated elaborations and justifications. Within psychology, we find that associationism and, more recently, behaviorism consider the image to be a mere replica, trace, or combination of hypothetically simple, first-order sensations. Even the psychoanalysis of Freud, for all of its brilliant insight into fantasy, tends to equate imagining with daydreaming and to regard the latter as the mere result of a temporary remission of ego-control. Jung's analytical psychology underlines the therapeutic efficacy of what is called "active imagination" but never attempts to elucidate imagining itself in any detail. Moreover, active imagination is of interest not for its own sake but primarily as a vehicle for the unearthing of archetypal material. Piagetian psychology conceives imagining in the child as a form of "internalized imitation" which is displayed in symbolic play and is itself only a transitional stage in the development of full cognitive powers that will, ultimately, be free from reliance upon images. When Piaget ranges imagining under the general rubric of "egocentric representational activity," he might well be summing up a whole tradition of psychological theorizing on the topic.[4] In this tradition, imagining is viewed as a rear-guard picturing activity carried out internally to, and under the aegis of, the representing subject or ego. It is no wonder, then, that imagination has been assigned a distinctly minor role in many psychological portrayals of mind.

Imagination has fared little better in the hands of philosophers. In fact, in one basic respect it has fared worse. For philosophers have tended to confuse imagining not just with apparent allies such as daydreaming or symbolic play but also with such disparate acts as perceiving or thinking. This more radical confusion may be due to philosophers' being more theory-minded than their psychologist *confrères* and thus to their being even less attentive to descriptive detail. As a consequence, their accounts are typically truncated from below, lacking the firm foundation in exact description which should precede, or at least confirm, theory-building. Perhaps it has been assumed—wrongly—that such a foundation is not needed in view of the very accessibility and transparency of imagining. But on the contrary: imagination is a highly elusive phenomenon.

In any event, the sins of philosophical theorists in regard to accurate description have been especially grievous. They extend from the distant past into the most recent present, leaving us with a bewildering array of alternative conceptions. These conceptions range from Plato's and Hume's strict subordination of imagining to perceiving (for both philosophers, imagination is a weakened form of perception) through Aristotle's and Kant's attempts to make imagination an intermediary between sensation and thought ("the soul never thinks without an image," said Aristotle, and Kant echoes this by calling the image a "mediating representation") and down to the effort, on the part of the German and English Romantics and the French surrealists, to promote imagination into an extravagantly superordinate position.[5] The congenial but fatal error of Romantics and surrealists alike lay in overreacting to previous accounts and particularly in mistaking the importance of imagination in art for its supremacy in epistemology and metaphysics.

The most effective way in which to overcome former failures is not merely to reverse priorities. To claim that imagination is superior to all other mental acts is just as dogmatically unfounded as Plato's or Hume's efforts to impose on imagination a decidedly inferior role. In both instances, and in the case of the mediation theorists as well, a rigidly hierarchical view of mind is presupposed, and it is presumed that imagination must be given some standing, however precarious, within this hierarchy. But the enormous gamut of possible positions contained in such a stratified model—once one begins to differentiate levels of mind, there is no way to place an effective limit on the procedure—prevents us from concluding anything definite with regard to imagination's position in comparison with that of other mental acts. Not only is it not convincingly distinguished from such sibling acts as phantasy or memory—a weakness of psychological theories as well—but it is not securely situated in relation to such manifestly different acts as sensation or intellection, being affiliated with these latter in a variety of conflicting ways. The picture which thus emerges from a conspectus of former philosophical theories is one of disarray.

What also emerges from such an overview is a warning that, if the mind is considered to be a mere processor of sensations or as a series of successively higher functions, imagination will be denied a distinctive role of its own. In such a priori models of mental activity, imagining will almost always be consigned to a secondary or even tertiary status in which it merely modifies what is proffered to it by some supposedly superior cognitive power such as thought or by some putatively more original source such as sensation. In this way, the specificity of imagination as a unique mental act is overlooked. What is called for is an approach that respects essential, and not merely casual or contingent, differences between types of mental acts, accounting for each act in its own terms. In short, it is a matter of being open to what we may call *the multiplicity of the mental*. Only an acute sensitivity to the uniqueness of each kind of mental act will permit imagination to be viewed as a phenomenon in its own right. As Wittgenstein remarks:

> "But what is this queer experience?" Of course it is not queerer than any other; it simply differs in kind from those experiences which we regard as the most fundamental ones, our sense impressions for instance.[6]

If imagination truly differs in kind from other mental acts, then it merits a separate account that would allow its specific structure to be set free from the morass of misconception in which it has been so deeply mired in past theories of mind.

Now, it cannot be denied that imagination has been regarded by philosophers in the twentieth century in a manner significantly different from the way in which it was seen in the past. Formerly, one of the main motives for denigrating the role of imagination in human experience was that it represented a threat to reason; it stood for what was irrational or at least beyond rational control. Imagination was viewed, in Samuel Johnson's words, as a "licentious and vagrant faculty, unsusceptible of limitations, and impatient of restraint."[7] One of the primary tasks of philosophy, especially in movements such as Stoicism and eighteenth-century rationalism, was to help the individual defend against the incursions of imagination, incursions that upset the delicate balance between knowledge and passion. As a result, although imagination was continually taken to task for its vagaries, it was at least a matter of concern for such earlier philosophers, who waxed eloquent in denouncing (while often secretly admiring) its charms.

Twentieth-century philosophers, in contrast, do not regard imagination as threatening in the first place, since rational self-enlightenment and self-control are no longer predominant philosophical ideals. Yet for the most part these philosophers continue to play down the significance of imagining. This stems not from fear of imagination's beguiling and bewitching powers but from a conviction that imagination has become obsolete as a subject of serious philosophical reflection. Whatever its admitted use and relevance in everyday life, interest in it has dwindled considerably in professional philosophy, where it is either ignored altogether or treated with thinly veiled disdain. This near-eclipse of imagination as a topic of live discussion derives partly from a criticism and rejection of certain episte-mological notions (e.g., such as representation) which have formed the basis for many traditional conceptions of what imagining involves. But it also comes from an attempt to stress the primordiality of certain key concepts such as formal structure, ordinary language, or Being—which are thought to have been themselves unjustly neglected in the course of Western philosophy and which, by their very nature, leave little room for imagina-tion as a singular and significant human activity.

Exceptions to this twentieth-century trend of regarding imagination as obsolete are few in number: Croce, Collingwood, Bachelard, Ryle, and Sartre. The first three regard the use of imagination in artistic creation and enjoyment as paradigmatic. Like Breton or Schelling in this respect, they strive to exalt imagining on the basis of a somewhat delimited role. More-over, this very role has been questioned by a number of movements within modern art such as cubism, op art, and minimalism. In any case, recourse to aesthetic experience is not sufficient to shore up the seminal significance of imagination in its *non*-artistic avatars. Ryle, on the other hand, intro-duces a broader perspective by conceiving imagining as a form of pretend-ing or make-believe. But this conception overlooks the decisive objections of Collingwood, Ryle's immediate predecessor in the Waynflete Chair of Metaphysical Philosophy at Oxford University. For imagining is not merely pretending that something is the case: this is to take the part for the whole. Nor is it, as Ryle claims, "one among many ways of utilizing knowledge" (i.e., through its use of hypothetical thinking).[8] Turning imagination into a mere mode of knowing or thinking trivializes it as much as if it were considered a mode of perception.

Sartre shares something with all four of the figures just mentioned. He often seems to have art in mind as a model for what he terms "the im-aginary," especially insofar as the imaginary is identified with the unreal. And he ends by assimilating imagining to thinking: "the image is like an incarnation of non-reflective thought. Imaginative consciousness represents a certain type of thought: a thought which is constituted in and through its objects."[9] The consequence of this reductive move is that no provision is made for a specific activity which can be said to be unique to imagina-tion alone. Its nihilating character, by means of which it surpasses the real and constructs the imaginary, is found in greater or lesser degree in all other acts of consciousness. Thinking itself, with whose lower reaches imagin-ing is held to be continuous, is a separate mental act altogether. The paradox is that Sartre, a devastating critic of traditional views of imagina-tion, ends by committing both of the cardinal errors endemic in these same views. He confuses imagining with another kind of mental act, and he downgrades its importance vis-à-vis other mental acts. For imagining is understood not just as non-reflective thinking, but as "debased knowing"—knowing that is markedly inferior to pure knowing.[10] Hence if Sartre does represent a brilliant exception to the twentieth-century tendency to consider imagination as effete and obsolete, he nevertheless fails to avoid the pitfalls of the classical, logocentric conceptions of imagining which he had sought to undermine in *L'Imagination* (1936). As portrayed in *L'Imaginaire* (1940), imagination is just as ineptly distinguished from other acts and just as minor in its epistemological significance as it had been in the earlier proposals of Plato and Hume, Aristotle and Kant. The question thus becomes: is there some way of gaining a fresh view that does not end in such a stalemate, a view which neither overrates imagination nor supposes that it is moribund?

II

It is my contention that a renewed attempt at an adequate phenomenology of imagination offers one such way. This is so for at least two reasons. First, among available methods of philosophical analysis, perhaps only phenomenology is able to do full justice to a mental act as difficult to pinpoint as imagining. Despite its seemingly Byzantine complexity, phenomenology possesses the one sure virtue of affording a means for the patient probing of a phenomenon. Its very methodological apparatus—above all, its much-maligned and frequently misunderstood technique of "reduction"—induces the caution which is called for in investigating imagination. Secondly, included in this same apparatus is a procedure which itself makes an overt use of imagining—free variation in imagination. Husserl made this, along with reduction (which itself resembles imagination to the extent that both suspend the positing of existence), the cornerstone of phenomenological method. Free variation is the primary means for grasping essences. As Husserl affirmed, "Freedom in the investigation of essences necessarily requires that one operate on the plane of imagination."[11]

What matters here is not whether Husserl is finally correct in this last assertion. Rather, the crucial thing for our purposes is that phenomenology finds itself to be in a particularly advantageous position for describing imagination, since it is already intimately acquainted with this very act in one of its own ongoing procedures. No other philosophical method, with the possible exception of Descartes's method in the *Meditations*, makes so explicit or so extensive a use of imagining. And this is the case in spite of Husserl's abiding logocentrism, which prevented him from according to imagination a central place in his official philosophy of mind—where it is held to be the mere modification of memory.[12] Thus, even if we may agree with Wittgenstein when he says that "there is not a philosophical method, though there are indeed methods, like different therapies,"[13] a phenomenological approach holds out particular promise with regard to the task of describing the experience of conscious imagining. Let us now proceed to this task, whose pursuit will occupy the remainder of the present chapter.

For the sake of ordering the description of something which may at times appear to lack any intelligible order, the following account will be sub-divided into two sections. In the first, I shall take up imagination in its intentional character. In the second, certain essential traits of conscious imagining as a whole will be considered.

A. *Intentional Structure.* By the term "intentional structure" I mean that structure of imagination which emerges when it is regarded as analyzable into an *act* of imagining and an *object* (or content) imagined. That imagination can be analyzed in this fashion cannot be fully argued for here. I shall just assert that if all conscious mental acts are intentional in character—such was Brentano's original claim—then, a fortiori, conscious imagining must be intentional. Perhaps only Ryle among moderns seriously disputes the correlation of intentional objects with acts of imagining, assert-ing flatly that "there are no such objects."[14] This denial proceeds from the espousal of a constrictive ontology that refuses to accord an intrinsic ontic status to imagined entities. From a strictly descriptive standpoint, however, it is clear that imagined objects and states of affairs do present themselves to consciousness in experiences of imagining. The smile which, in Ryle's own example, a child imagines to be on a doll's face may not be objectively locatable on this face—admittedly it lacks the ontic status of the empirically real—but it is nonetheless experienced by the child as *present* there. This experience is sufficient to establish, if not the smile's existence, then at least its "intentional inexistence" (in the Scholastic term which Brentano took over for his own purposes). And this latter is all that is required to provide imaginative experience with an intentional structure—a structure which has a descriptive, if not an ontological, basis. In accordance with this struc-ture, imagining as intentional possesses two primary phases: an act-phase and an object-phase.

(a) *Act-Phase.* The act of conscious imagining can take place in at least three forms, each of which merits separate mention: imaging, imagining-that, and imagining-how.

(i) *imaging.* Most acts of imagining occur as imaging, that is, as the pro-jection and contemplation of imagined objects or events in a specifically sensory guise. By "specifically sensory" I mean as characterized by predicates that specify whether the imagined object is visualized, audialized, smelled in the mind's nose (in Ryle's expression), or felt in the mind's muscles. No act of imaging occurs in a sensory-neutral way. Every such act must be projective in a quasi visual, auditory, olfactory, kinesthetic, or tactile way—or in some combination of these sensory modalities. But while it is normal in perceiving to combine several modalities in a single experien-tial interfusion, in imaging we more typically entertain objects or events in just one privileged mode—and most frequently in visual terms. Yet by the same token we can, at will, supplement a given imaged sensory dimen-sion with other dimensions to form a fuller imaginative experience—by, say, imaging not only how a certain object looks but also how it might feel to the touch. No comparable "building up" of successive sensory dimensions is found in perception—which is, as Merleau-Ponty has so splendidly shown, a synesthetic, syncretistic experience from the very beginning.[15]

(ii) *imagining-that*. But in imagining we are not restricted to imaging disparate and unrelated objects or events. We can also entertain whole complexes of simultaneously apprehended entities—what we shall call "states of affairs." When we do so, we are imagining-*that*—imagining that such states of affairs obtain or take place. Imagining-that in this sense may occur in two forms, sensory and nonsensory. I can imagine in vivid sensory detail that a certain state of affairs is happening, as when I imagine that a speeding car is running me down: here imaging and imagining-that overlap. But I can also imagine that something is the case in a nonsensory way, as when I imagine that Oxford University admits only students from Reunion Island in the Indian Ocean. In this instance, I am projecting and contemplating a state of affairs that has no—or, more exactly, needs no—precise sensory form, for I can imagine that Oxford admits such students without visualizing these students in the setting of the University. This is not to deny that there is a tendency to fall back on imaging whenever possible, especially when we daydream or entertain conscious fantasies. In this respect, imaging seems to aid in imagining-that by depicting how a state of affairs would appear in concretely sensuous form. But imaging is not *necessary* to the enactment of imagining-that, and it is perfectly possible to imagine-that abstractly and without the support of imagistic detail. What is important is that we do not seek to reduce all imagining to imaging on the one hand (as Hume attempts to do) or to imagining-that on the other (as Ryle tries to do).[16] Each is a separate, live option for the imaginer.

(iii) *imagining-how*. The same point applies to imagining-how. This too can occur in a sensuous or in a nonsensuous manner. I may imagine how to tie a particular sailor's knot by projecting the various steps in an explicitly visual form. But I may also imagine how to solve a problem in mathematics without in any way concretely embodying my thought process or its objects: I just "run through" the projected steps in an abstract and sensuously unspecified way. It is true that imagining-how is closely related to imagining-that insofar as the former always involves the projection and contemplation of a certain state of affairs. But the state of affairs entertained in imagining-how includes a sense of personal agency: I imagine how I or someone else does something or gets somewhere, or how it is for myself or someone else to feel or perceive something in a certain situation. In sheer imagining-that, in contrast, I merely suppose that a given situation obtains, whether or not any human agent is involved in it. I can imagine, for instance, that the surface of the sun looks like a lunar landscape without injecting any sense of human presence. But I imagine *how* it would be to live on such a solar surface by projecting myself (or someone else) onto this surface as its inhabitant.

No doubt there are still other forms which acts of conscious imagining may assume. It seems, for example, that we can imagine something *as* in a sense that is slightly different from imagining-that: I can imagine myself as gregarious without necessarily imaging myself qua gregarious, imagining that I am gregarious, or imagining how it would be to be gregarious. But the three forms of imaging, imagining-that, and imagining-how do account for the vast majority of the acts of imagining which we enact or undergo.

(b) *Object-Phase.* In spite of Ryle's disclaimer, when we imagine we imagine something and not nothing. By the term "object-phase" I refer to *all* that we thus imagine—the entire intentional correlate or imaginative presentation. Constituting this correlate or presentation are three basic elements: imagined content, the imaginal margin, and the image.

(i) *imagined content.* By this is meant specifically *what* we imagine— that which is identifiable or recognizable as a certain thing or kind of thing. This content is equivalent to what we would report to others if asked about what we imagine. When I say that I imagined 'a five-legged lion,' I make reference to the specific content of what I have imagined. This specific content is composed of imagined objects and/or states of affairs. Thus I can specify, sometimes by name, both the object and the situation I imagine. Take Sartre's now-classic example: I imagine my friend Peter in Berlin.[17] Designated here is not only the person 'Peter,' but also a whole affair-complex 'Peter-in-Berlin.' 'Peter' names the partial specific content; 'Peter-in-Berlin' designates the total specific content.

But closer analysis reveals that the full imagined content includes not only particular objects and/or states of affairs but also their immediately surrounding context. We may call this contextual factor "the imagined world-frame of quasi-space-and-time," since it is a matter of the experiential field within which imagined objects and states of affairs appear. These latter do not emerge in a vacuum; they must appear as located somewhere, although not in the homogeneous, objective space and time of perception. *Where* they do appear is no neatly delimited region with set boundaries and measurable internal distances. Indeed, the site for the appearance of imagined objects and states of affairs is not so much a "place" or region as it is an amorphous field which, though difficult to specify itself, serves to frame and present specifiable imagined entities and events. This is done in ambiguous and non-determinate spatial and temporal parameters which are tailored to each case. In each successive instance, these parameters form a different mini-world of experience rather than contributing to, or being continuous with, the single, universal space and time of the perceived world (a world which is finally one world).

(ii) *imaginal margin.* The imaginal margin is that penumbral zone which surrounds imagined content, including even the world-frame. It is not only difficult to specify, but also strictly unspecifiable. In this regard, the nearest equivalent to the imaginal margin is Plato's Receptacle as it is found before the ingression of determinate sensible shapes. Like the Receptacle, the imaginal margin defies description. Yet it is felt to be an integral part of imaginative experience. This is easily confirmed by visualizing any given object or scene—say, the god Jupiter. It will be noticed that at the outer fringes of this imagined figure there is a nebulous area which cannot be said to be either strictly continuous or strictly discontinuous with the figure itself. The imaginative presentation just trails off indefinitely as it becomes progressively less distinct in identifiable content. (The same thing happens when we attempt to fill in the margin around 'Jupiter' with other figures: these latter are in turn surrounded by an undifferentiated qualitative halo.) Finally, when past a certain ill-defined point, we can no longer say what, if anything, is being presented to us. The imagined content seems to have run its course—evaporated, as it were—without, however, ceasing so abruptly as to leave us with an entirely empty abyss at its edge. Rather, there is a sense of *something*, not of sheer nothing, that continues to ring around the specifiable content and its world-frame. But, unlike the fringes of the perceptual field, it does not seem to surround the imaginer himself or herself on all sides. The marginal area remains projected in front of him or her, on the lateral edges of the plane of presentation. Thus the imaginal margin contributes to the irrevocably frontal, depthless character of the imaginative representation, which hovers before the imaginer at a certain indefinite and untrespassable remove. (This sense of remove is to be contrasted with the situation in perceiving, where we find ourselves always already enmeshed in the midst of a circumambient, three-dimensional world of palpable material things and persons.)

(iii) *the image.* I construe the term "image" not in its usual meaning—i.e., as a pictorial form of imaginative presentation—but rather as the mode of presentation with which imagined content is given to the imaginer's consciousness.[18] The image is not *what* is present to awareness—this is the content proper—but *how* this content is presented. Only rarely are we explicitly conscious of the image in this sense, but when we attend closely to imaginative experience we become increasingly aware of a multiplicity of modes of givenness, three of which may be mentioned here.

(1) *relative clarity.* Imagined content may be given with differing degrees and types of clarity. Contrast, for example, the comparative clarity by which the imaged face of an absent friend is given to me with the obscurity that infects a thirty-sided polygon which I am attempting to imagine. The imaged face springs vividly to consciousness, while the geometrical figure is present to mind—if it can be said to be present at all—only in an extremely diffuse way. Thus there is room for considerable variation in the clarity with which imagined content may be presented to us.

(2) *texture.* The texture or felt quality of imaginative presentations also varies considerably, depending on the specific imagined content. These presentations may give an impression of smoothness, as when we imagine a marble facade, or of coarseness, as in imaging a choppy sea. Although

imaginal texture is thus usually determined by the nature of what is imagined, it lacks the concretely tangible character of perceived texture. We are not tempted to reach out and touch imagined texture as we might be when perceiving or hallucinating. For there is an unbridgeable gulf between ourselves and the surface of the imaginative presentation; and we are convinced that this surface is impalpable.

(3) *directness*. Although imagined content always presents itself in the frontal way just described, it can be given more or less directly in any particular case. Thus I might first imagine a person whose face is turned directly toward me; but I might then go on to imagine the same person with his or her face averted or even turned completely away from me. The same is true of the person as a whole: s/he can be envisaged as standing directly before my imagining gaze or as given indirectly (for example, as reflected in a mirror).

What such "images" or modes of presentation point to is the highly variable character of imaginative experience. It is this variability which, combined with the inherent instability of imaginative attention, accounts for the strikingly evanescent quality of so much imagining. Only with the most disciplined mental exertion can I hold the same imaginative presentation constantly before my imagining mind; and even then it becomes questionable whether I can continue to say that it is "the same" presentation which is being contemplated throughout. Unanchored in an underlying and persistent spatio-temporal field, essentially unexplorable (nothing can be strictly speaking discovered there, for nothing pre-exists the very act of conscious projection by which imagined content is constituted), this presentation slides from the tenterhooks of concerted attention, quickly giving way to another presentation: "one glimpse and vanished," says Beckett.[19]

B. *Essential Traits.* Under this second main heading, I wish to consider six of the most prominent essential traits of imagination viewed as a total phenomenon. By "essential traits" I mean traits that are essentially necessary to imagining—indispensable to it in one way or another, as could be shown in each instance by the test of free variation. It should be forewarned that such essential traits, even when taken together, do not constitute a sufficient list. Their mere co-presence or collocation is not by itself enough to bring about an act of imagining. Still other traits would have to be cited if sufficiency were to be claimed and a complete description offered. In the meanwhile, adequacy of description must be the aim of the present limited endeavor. Accordingly, the following traits are selected for their representativeness and suggestiveness, not for their exhaustiveness. They will be grouped into three pairs so as to facilitate the analysis: spontaneity and controlledness, self-containedness and self-evidence, indeterminacy and pure possibility.

(a) *Spontaneity and Controlledness.* This first pair of essential traits is quite crucial, and I shall dwell on it longest. It possesses what we may call "option-necessity" in contrast with the "trait-necessity" of the other two pairs. Any given case of conscious imagining will be characterized by spontaneity or controlledness—*by one or the other, but not by both.* Thus these two traits are mutually exclusive—what is spontaneous cannot be simultaneously controlled and vice versa—and yet jointly exhaustive of that dimension of imaginative experience which has to do with the relative freedom with which the imaginer's consciousness operates. That they are mutually exclusive does not mean that one of them might not characterize the act-phase, and the other the object-phase, of a particular imaginative experience: I can be controlling an act of imagining when a certain imaginative presentation appears spontaneously. It only means that both traits cannot apply to precisely the *same* phase at the same time and in the same respect.

(i) *spontaneity.* There is a whole tradition which imputes spontaneity to imagining—extending from Kant and Schelling down to Collingwood and Sartre. But the existence of this tradition does not make it any easier to determine precisely what imaginative spontaneity consists in. Is this spontaneity simply a matter of acting without an efficient cause (as on Kant's original conception)? Is it an aspect of nihilation (as Sartre holds)? Approached phenomenologically, the spontaneity of imagination is not adequately characterized in either of these ways. Instead, the felt quality of imaginative spontaneity is to be described in such terms as "gliding," "floating," "sliding" into or before consciousness. There is something peculiarly automatic about spontaneous imagining—something that is strikingly self-generating, requiring no intervention by an outside agency (not even by the imaginer himself or herself). The imaginative act or presentation appears to arise sui generis and without having been willed into existence. If such self-generativity may be taken as the basic feature of spontaneous imagining, we can proceed to specify three ways in which it expresses itself.

(1) *effortlessness.* A spontaneously imagined entity or event arises without any conscious effort on the part of the imagining subject. This subject feels that he or she has contributed nothing of substance to the formation of the spontaneous appearance, and this is so even if he or she is convinced that his or her presence as the sole witness to this appearance is required. Nor does such an appearance emerge with any sense of belabored effort on *its* part. Rather, there is a sense of free facility in the phenomenon of appearing, a lack of inhibition or restraint. Nothing constrains the spontaneous imaginative act or presentation either to appear or not to appear; and if it does appear, it simply arises of its own accord.

(2) *surprise.* In encountering an apparently self-generated entity or event in the perceptual world, one's characteristic reaction is one of incredulity: "How did *that* happen?" One is simply astonished that such a thing as, say, spontaneous combustion could take place in an apparent absence or irrelevance of pre-existing conditions. All seemingly self-generated events,

perceived or imagined, carry with them an essential element of surprise. But where surprise may approach stupefaction in the case of perceived self-generation (where we "can't believe our own eyes"), in the case of conscious imagining our reaction is rarely this extreme: we are taken by surprise, but we are not swept away by it. Our mental composure is retained because it is not a matter of anything that undermines or threatens our habitual beliefs. For in imagining, committed beliefs—and disbeliefs, as Coleridge pointed out—are suspended from the start. By the same token, our basic stock of knowledge is not altered, since we do not, strictly speaking, learn anything from imagining, that is, anything that we do not in some sense already know.[20] Nevertheless, even though spontaneous imaginative experiences represent no threat either to knowledge or to belief, they are still capable of surprising us because of the way in which their self-generated character subverts our usual expectations as to causal agency and because they fulfill intentions of which we may not have been fully aware.

(3) *instantaneity*. Genuine self-generation, that is, generation ex nihilo, can only occur at a single stroke, since the transition from a state of non-being to one of being without the intervention of external agencies is an absolute one which does not brook intermediate, time-taking stages. Such a transition or "leap" between two wholly disparate states can occur only instantaneously, *totum simul:* in the timeless "moment" of which Kierkegaard speaks.[21] It is just such a sense of instantaneous explosion-into-being that is experienced in spontaneous imaginative acts and presentations. These leap to our mental eyes or ears in one fell swoop: they spring into being as if from nothing or, at least, from nothing that has been experienced immediately prior to their appearance. They can appear in this way to us only in the temporal format of the instant or moment.

It may be concluded that the spontaneity which characterizes many imaginative acts and presentations is clarified when it is viewed in terms of the general feature of *self-generativity*. For all three of the distinctive aspects of imaginative spontaneity—its effortlessness, surprising character, and instantaneous quality—can be seen as facets of the fundamentally self-generative nature of this spontaneity. In possessing such a sense of self-generativity, imagination is perhaps unique among mental acts. For no other mental act, with the possible exception of thinking, is spontaneous in such a thoroughly self-incurring manner.

(ii) *controlledness*. Tempting as it may be, it would be a mistake to regard *all* imaginative activity as spontaneous in character. A not inconsiderable amount of it is controlled by the imaginer in a way which complements, as well as contrasts with, the spontaneity of imagining. In fact, controlledness and spontaneity are complementary components of imagination's inherent autonomy. Spontaneity signifies that pole of imaginative experience at which acts and presentations appear in an autogenous, unexpected upsurge. Controlledness signifies the opposite pole, where the power of the imaginer over his or her own acts and presentations is most effectively expressed and experienced. In former accounts of imagination, controlledness has been much less discussed than spontaneity, but it remains a live option for imaginative experience—as Aristotle observed when he said that "imagining is up to us when we wish."[22]

Controlledness is exercised at three critical points in imaginative experience—i.e., its initiation, guidance, and termination.

(1) *initiation*. At any time I wish, so long as I am awake and undistracted, I can initiate almost any imaginative act or presentation which I desire. Let it be a scene in which an Abyssinian Abuna is officiating in a religious ceremony: even as I propose such a scene to myself as a possible imaginative project, it begins to unfold beneath my imaginative gaze. In this case, the initiation is comparatively easy. In other cases, my mental effort is somewhat more strenuous, as in imagining that an Abuna is taking a spacewalk. But no matter how complex or bizarre the specific subject-matter, I can, in normal circumstances of alert consciousness, initiate practically *any* imaginative act or presentation that I choose.

(2) *guidance*. Not only am I capable of initiating my own imaginative experiences in such autocratic fashion, I am also able to guide them afterward in whatever direction and manner I wish. Moreover, I can guide imaginative experiences which have not been initiated by me at all—including those which arise spontaneously and those which stem from strictly non-imaginative experiences such as perception or memory. Such non-self-initiated experiences can be brought under the imaginer's control: he or she "imaginifies" them and directs their subsequent course in whatever way is chosen. Because of these various possibilities—and still more, including even that of allowing the experience to slip momentarily out of one's control—it is in the moment of guidance that the imaginer's powers of control are displayed in their most impressive and extensive form. Here, above all, one is tempted to regard the imaginer as sovereign in his or her own sphere, for he or she seems able to direct imaginative acts and presentations with practically unlimited latitude. At whim, he or she can alter whatever is being presently imagined and move it in a different direction with respect to content, mode of presentation, time-sense, and spatial character; and he or she can also change at will the specific form which the act of imagining takes—from, say, sensuous imagining to non-sensuous imagining-that.

(3) *termination*. The imaginer can, finally, annihilate the very appearances which he or she has initiated and perhaps also guided: he or she can banish any given imaginative act or presentation from his or her mind merely by wishing to do so. No matter what its intrinsic fascination may be, and no matter what extraneous reasons he or she may have for continuing to imagine, he or she can always call a halt to it all. This can be done in either of two ways. On the one hand, he or she may choose to cease imagining altogether by attempting to empty one's mind of all particular conscious content (a difficult procedure which may require special

training) or by allowing himself or herself to become engrossed in a wholly different kind of activity, such as doing sums in one's head. On the other hand, a given imaginative experience can be deliberately supplanted by another, distinctly different imaginative experience: here, the initiation of the new experience is the termination of the old one.

The foregoing descriptions of controlledness have indicated that the imaginer's capacity of control is such that he or she can initiate, guide, and terminate imaginative acts and presentations at will. Implied by this finding is a still stronger claim which seems to follow directly from it: to wit, the imaginer cannot fail to imagine what, how, and when he or she wishes to. Insofar as this is the case, there would appear to be no effective limitations on one's imaginative powers. Yet is this really so? And if so, how are we to account for the common conviction (frequently reflected in philosophical theory as well) that imagination is, on the contrary, quite constricted in its scope? Let us digress for a moment in order to sketch an answer to these important questions.

It is evident that we cannot imagine absolutely anything we want to, and, in fact, two basic kinds of limitation upon one's imaginative capacity must be admitted. The first of these is conceptual or logical in character. There are some things which cannot be imagined because they are formed from contradictory concepts and thus are logically impossible—e.g., a square circle or a four-sided triangle. Of course, one can attempt to imagine such self-contradictory things and even (as in hallucinated states) come to believe that one has indeed imagined them. But, however far or wide one's imaginative capacity is stretched in this effort, what one does succeed in imagining will not qualify as a bona fide instance of the self-contradictory notion. Yet this essential restriction upon imaginative powers does not testify to their weakness or failure. For nothing, whether perceived *or* imagined, can possibly exemplify a conceptually contradictory notion. And where there is no possibility of success, we cannot talk, strictly speaking, of failure.

The second kind of limitation is empirical in character, namely, the contingent limits upon the individual imaginer's particular ability to imagine. It is undeniably the case that, from one person to another, there are discernible differences in the extent to which human imaginative powers are displayed. But these differences are neither so considerable nor so irresolvable as they may seem to be at a glance. In spite of differences of detail— for example, differences in the degree to which one can visualize or audialize—the general scope of imaginative capacity is remarkably similar from one imaginer to the next. This means that, if one cannot imagine something in one way (say, by visualizing it), one can usually succeed in imagining it in some other way (say, by touching it in imagination). Moreover, a given individual's imagination is capable of being trained, through disciplined exercises in imagining, to overcome marked deficiencies. Thus empirical limitations on a specific imaginer's ability to imagine, though significant, do not serve to curtail human imaginative capacity as such.

But the admission of these two kinds of limitation may still not fully allay the commonsense suspicion that our imaginative powers are inherently puny, revealing (in Sartre's phrase) an "essential poverty."[23] This suspicion is not wholly unfounded. Imagining—particularly in its humdrum, everyday embodiment—certainly does not manifest the cosmic dimensions which have been claimed for it by Bruno and Blake. What needs to be recognized is that the imaginer is for the most part able to bring forth the imaginative act or presentation which he or she desires or intends—at least this, but by the same token, *no more*. What is brought forth in controlled imagining is typically satisfactory, but only *just* satisfactory; it does not represent an embarrassment of riches.[24]

These brief remarks—which concern one of the most vexing problems to which the phenomenon of imagination gives rise—may be summed up with a statement that incorporates the qualifications just made: in principle the imaginer cannot fail to imagine what, how, and (for the most part) when he or she wishes to; but what one does succeed in imagining by virtue of one's capacity for imaginative control is *just* what one intends it to be and nothing more.

(b) *Self-Containedness and Self-Evidence.* In these two traits, we have to do with a straightforward "trait-necessity," that is, with the necessity that each of these traits characterizes all phases and aspects of a given imaginative experience and thus (as contrasted with traits exhibiting option-necessity) that *both* always hold good for the entirety of this experience. Further, instead of the two traits being complementary to each other, one is the necessary condition for the other: self-containedness is a precondition for self-evidence. But we shall see that both traits display a similar self-sufficiency.

(i) *self-containedness.* This essential trait will be discussed in terms of its appearance in the two primary intentional phases.

(1) *act-phase.* Each act of conscious imagining is self-contained insofar as it is experienced as complete and needing no supplementation by other acts. The act suffices for itself. This can be seen in two ways. First, the act sweeps out its own field of action, instead of entering a preconstituted field as in perceiving or remembering. It is not a matter of controlling what already lies within the imaginative field or of injecting new content into it (as in controlledness proper) but of determining this field's limits in terms of the imaginer's ongoing interests and concerns. Secondly, the act of imagining is self-contained by virtue of its strict discontinuity with other mental acts, both imaginative and non-imaginative. Not only is the act of imagining experienced as independent of efficient causation by other acts, it also presents itself as insulated from significant continuity of any kind with preceding or concurrent acts.

(2) *object-phase.* A quite similar analysis applies here. First, imagined content always appears within a field of awareness—what we earlier called the "world-frame"—which is delimited by the very activity of the imagin-

ing self. The content does not reach or refer beyond this field in any significant way, even if its component parts have been borrowed or derived from other experiences. Secondly, the imaginative presentation is felt to be self-contained in the sense of being experienced as strictly discontinuous with other presentations (whether imaginative in character or not). Reinforcing the self-containedness of the object-phase is the frontality of imaginative appearances. For each imaginative presentation is compressed into a single frontal appearance. Thus it is confined within a severely constrictive one-dimensionality which does not allow for the formation of meaningful connections with other presentations. Such connections require that phenomena be given in more than one dimension—or at least that they contain the promise of possessing other dimensions. Without these other dimensions, there is no sense of genuine discovery—of being able to uncover hidden aspects which will link up with what we already know of other phenomena. Contained within its own frontal surface, an imaginative presentation cannot refer meaningfully to anything other than itself. Therefore, if the self-containedness of the act of imagining can be said to be *self-enclosing*, that of the imaginative presentation can be said to be *self-enclosed*: ingathered in such a way as to preclude forming significant relationships with other experiential contents.[25]

(ii) *self-evidence*. From imagination's self-containedness we may infer something basic about the sort of evidence which is given in imaginative experience. This is precisely the strict irrelevance of evidence which is not indigenous to the phenomenon of imagination itself. Just insofar as an imaginative act or presentation is self-contained, no evidence from other sources can bear on a given case of imagining in any definitive way.[26] Each imaginative experience brings with it its own unique evidence and does not need to import evidence from alien acts. Consequently, imaginative evidence is to be judged by its own criteria. Let me mention three of these.

(1) *non-corrigibility*. Non-corrigibility is not to be confused with incorrigibility. Incorrigible evidence is evidence that is always and only true. Non-corrigible evidence is evidence which cannot be considered either true *or* false. If imaginative evidence is non-corrigible, then imagined content is neither falsifiable nor verifiable. There is no standard, internal or external, in whose terms this content could be judged true or false. As opposed to a case of perceptual illusion, there is nothing with respect to which the imaginer can be said to be mistaken. In spite of Pascal's warning that "imagination is the mistress of falsehood and error,"[27] we are not tricked or misled by what we imagine in the way that we can be fooled by a fake facade. For there is nothing other than, nothing beyond, what is immediately experienced in imagining—the imaginative presentation is, as it were, all facade—and thus there is no way that we could mistake a false appearance for a true one. In other words, there is no ultimate or standard-setting experience which could serve to correct the claims im-

plicit in imaginative experience as such. This experience is as ultimate as it can be (and as it needs to be) and sets its own standards. Thus imagining is strictly non-corrigible. Just as we cannot be proven wrong in our conviction *that* we are imagining on a given occasion, so we cannot stand corrected as to *what* we imagine on this occasion. There is, in short, an unimpeachable and unimprovable mutual compresence between the imaginative presentation, the act of imagining, and the conscious awareness of the imaginer.

(2) *apodicticity.* The apodicticity or strict indubitability of imaginative evidence follows from its non-corrigibility: there is simply no significant way in which to doubt that an imaginative act or presentation has exactly the form it appears to have. The imaginer's acquaintance with both phases of imaginative experience is total and is unshakably secure. As distinguished from the logically apodictic, however, it is not a question of grasping something as necessary, as *having* to be the way it is. Rather, it is a matter of being certain as to how imaginative phenomena appear once (and for whatever reasons) they *do* appear. For once they appear, they appear with indubitable evidence, hence as self-evident in a complete and unmediated manner which precludes the possibility of doubt.

(3) *all-at-onceness.* In perception, evidence is only more or less adequate. There is always the possibility that evidence which is presently held to be certain will be disconfirmed in the future. As a consequence, there is a need to accumulate as much perceptual evidence as possible in order to remain certain or to gain an even greater certainty. Such evidence becomes more adequate as more of it is amassed, as can be seen in the case of archeological excavations. In imagining, by contrast, there is no comparable process of collecting increasingly adequate evidence. Indeed, there is no process of collecting evidence in the first place. Imaginative evidence is acquired all at once and once for all. This all-or-nothing character suits the fleeting character of imaginative experience, which tends to occur in a flash and thus does not allow for the gradual accumulation of evidence of any kind.

Self-contained and self-evident, then, the experience of conscious imagining is in both respects a *self-sufficient* experience, an experience that takes place exclusively at the interface between the imaginer and his or her own imaginative activity. This experience is self-sufficient not only in the sense that it does not depend upon contributions from other types of experience, but also in the sense that it occurs solely within the field formed by the imaginer's own activity. This activity suffices for itself, being contained within its own self-prescribed limits and showing itself with pellucid self-evidence. As self-contained and self-evident, the act of conscious imagining is fully acquainted with itself at every moment of its duration. As such, it is an experience of supremely self-sufficient self-presence.

(c) *Indeterminacy and Pure Possibility.* Each of these last two essential features of imagining exhibits a straightforward trait-necessity. As contrasted with the trait-necessity of the previous pair of traits, however, in this instance the necessity does not qualify the phenomenon of imagination in both of its phases. The act-phase of imagining is neither indeterminate (in its occurrence it is as determinate as any other mental act) nor purely possible (qua act it is always already actual). But the entire object-phase of imagining is both indeterminate in character and purely possible in thetic status. We should also observe that the relationship between these two traits is different from that between the respective members of the foregoing pairs of traits. In the present case, the relation is not one of complementarity in which one term serves as the necessary condition of the other. Rather, the two terms in question are mutually facilitating. The appearance of either one enhances the likelihood of the other's appearance. Something that is indeterminate is more likely to be purely possible than it is to be actual; and something that is purely possible is more likely to be indeterminate than determinate.

(i) *indeterminacy.* Although only rarely singled out in previous psychological or philosophical treatments, indeterminacy is one of the most characteristic features of imagination. Inherently and unavoidably indeterminate in character, what we imagine is indefinite in a sense which does not allow for any considerable increase in definiteness, much less for the achievement of constant or perfect definiteness. Yet this is not to claim that what we imagine is *entirely* indeterminate: if this were the case, we could not be said to imagine certain things rather than others on a given occasion. Thus an imaginative presentation must possess a certain minimal definiteness.

This definiteness is found above all in the imagined content. Imagined objects and states of affairs are sufficiently distinct for us to be able to recognize, to interrelate, and even on occasion to name them. It is they which fulfill specific imaginative intentions and on which our conscious attention is explicitly focused. But this does not mean that they possess a determinateness comparable to that characterizing perceptual objects. In their fluctuating and fluid state, they lack the resistant character of the latter.[28] In particular, they lack determinate positions in a measurable space and time. More than anything else, it is the vague and shifting world-frame of imagined space and time which is responsible for the indeterminacy which infects even relatively definite imagined content.

Moreover, the image, or mode of presentation, is also fundamentally indeterminate. For example, the highest degree of clarity with which imagined content can be given never equals the limpid determinateness with which perceived objects and events are capable of presenting themselves. Nor is imagined texture ever as distinctly apprehended as perceived texture, or the directness of the imaginative presentation *as* direct as the directness with which what we perceive is given. Still, a certain amount of definiteness remains present in all of these cases. It is only the imaginal margin that is radically indeterminate—so indeterminate that, as we have seen, it cannot be given any definite description at all. It is the only part of the imaginative presentation that is utterly inchoate and that refuses any and all attempts at determination. In short, the imaginal margin is the indeterminate par excellence in imaginative experience. Nothing equivalent to this extreme degree of indeterminacy is found in perception. Although a given perceptual experience may be quite indistinct on occasion—as on a foggy evening—this indistinctness can usually be removed or obviated by means of appropriate actions on the part of the perceiver. But no such elimination of the nebulousness of the imaginal margin is possible. The indeterminacy of this margin is present as a permanent and unremovable feature of imaginative experience, giving to this experience its peculiarly beclouded aura.

(ii) *pure possibility.* This is the thetic character which is posited in the imaginative presentation, particularly in its objects and states of affairs. Corresponding to it is the belief-attitude of entertainment or sheer supposal. We entertain imagined content as purely possible—as something that *might be* in an unattenuated sense which involves no dependence upon, or reference to, the empirically real. Hence the term "pure possibility," that is, possibility that is free from reference or allusion to what is externally, intersubjectively the case on any given occasion. Pure possibility differs from hypothetical possibility in that the latter is posited as a means to a pre-existent end. Something which is posited as hypothetically possible is regarded *as if* it obtained for the sake of the particular situation at hand (as occurs, for instance, in pretending and in much everyday hypothesizing). A pure possibility, in contrast, plays no such mediatory, as-if role. When an imagined object or state of affairs is posited as purely possible, it is invested with an inherent, and not merely with an instrumental, interest or value. The object or state of affairs is envisaged as possible for its own sake—not for the sake of anything external to, or more final than, itself.

As purely possible, what we imagine merits our brief allegiance—our momentary glance—and yet is not accorded the existentially committed belief which is granted as a matter of course to perceptual objects or events (and even to the contents of hallucination). In fact, we do not strictly speaking *believe in* a given imaginative presentation; we just posit it as purely possible. Thus I do not believe that the hippogriff which I consciously imagine exists—not even in some sublimated form peculiar to imaginative experience—but only suppose that it *might* be. It is felt to be sheerly supposable, and I regard it as a purely possible denizen of my presently projected mini-world of imagination. No stronger existential claim is made or implied. Nor am I concerned with how such a beast relates to the rest of my experience or to the experiences of others. I am, in fact, merely entertaining or amusing myself by what I conjure by and for myself alone: I am entering a musing state of mind in which everything is experienced as a pure possibility. In sum, imagining is *entertaining oneself with what is purely possible.*

The descriptions of essential traits which have just been given in section B all point to the autonomy of conscious imagining. In closing, I wish to underline this autonomy, which must be established if we are not ourselves to fall prey to the two primary pitfalls of former theories—namely, confusion of imagination with other mental acts and a denial of its importance as an act in its own right. We have found that each of the first two pairs of essential traits exhibits a distinctive aspect of this autonomy. The autonomy manifested in imaginative spontaneity consists in the self-generativity of the imaginative act or presentation, which seems to bring *itself* forth rather than being caused to appear by some external agency. Controlledness, contrariwise, embodies the autonomy of the imaginer as he or she initiates, guides, and terminates the course of his or her own imagining. The self-containedness of imagination indicates that imagining is a self-insulating mental act which is basically discontinuous with other acts and is thus, in its essential solitude, free to follow its own devices. Imagination's self-evident character shows that imagining reveals itself without remainder and is valid for itself alone, involving its own evidential criteria. Together, self-containedness and self-evidence underscore imagination's autonomy as a self-sufficient, independently occurring mental act.

The last pair of traits to have been considered above forms no exception to this emerging pattern of self-motivating activity. The indeterminacy of the imaginative presentation reinforces its autonomy by allowing it to elude the confining determinateness of perceptual presentations: to be indeterminate in this manner is to be open to an endless elaboration in which no imaginable options are ruled out in advance. Everything becomes possible—or, more exactly, purely possible—in the realm of conscious imagining.[29] To be posited as purely possible is to be in a position to escape entangling alliances with both the actual and the necessary. It is to be liberated, however briefly, from the harsh constraints of perception, history, and inferential thinking—to be set free from *Anankē* in the largest sense.

Imagination's intentional structure as described earlier in section A further bears out the autonomy of this extraordinary mental act. With regard to the act-phase, the fact that we are able to range freely from imaging to imagining-that (of either a sensory or a nonsensory sort) and to imagining-how testifies to the self-directing character of conscious imagining, as does our capacity to imagine (strictly, to "image") in the sensory modality of our own choosing. Consequently, freedom of maneuver is everywhere present in the act-phase of imagining. In the object-phase, we confront aspects of imagination which are no less self-determining. Imagined content presents itself in terms of its own objects and /or states of affairs and within its own self-delimiting world-frame. Around this content and world-frame is found the imaginal margin, which in its obdurate indeterminacy resists outside manipulation and alteration: its very opaqueness to analysis serves to stress imagination's autonomy. And the image or mode of presentation, in its inherent variability, further contributes to the sense of open self-regulation which pervades the experience of conscious imagining in its entirety. Thus in both of its intentional phases imagination proves itself to be an actively self-legislative act.

It may be concluded that all six essential traits, taken together with imagination's bipolar intentional structure, demonstrate the unabashedly autonomous quality of imagining as it is consciously enacted and experienced. They suggest that such imagining is not only eidetically distinct from other kinds of mental acts—and hence not to be considered a mere mode or modification of some supposedly more basic mental activity—but is also a self-regulating act in its own right, with its own type of insight and thus with an intrinsic significance and value. In any event, it is toward a fuller recognition of the autonomous character of conscious imagining that the phenomenological descriptions outlined in this chapter are meant to contribute. This recognition is needed in order to secure for imagination, so long the pariah of the philosophy and psychology of mind, a place of its own on the map of essential mental powers.

1. Samuel Beckett, *Imagination Dead Imagine* (London: Calder and Boyars, 1965), p. 7; my italics.

2. Ludwig Wittgenstein, *Philosophical Investigations*, trans. G. E. M. Anscombe (Oxford: Blackwell, 1967), p. 207; his italics.

3. Herbert Marcuse, *Eros and Civilization* (Boston: Beacon Press, 1955), chap. 7–9.

4. On the associationist view of imagination, see Hippolyte Taine, *De L'Intelligence* (Paris, 1871), I, pp. 9 ff. For Sigmund Freud's view, see *The Standard Edition of the Complete Psychological Works,* 24 vols. (London: Hogarth Press, 1953–74), 1: 295 ff.; 5: 509–61; and 9: 144 f. C. G. Jung's most pertinent description of active imagination occurs in CW 14, ¶¶ 749 ff. For Jean Piaget's view, see *Play, Dreams, and Imitation in Childhood,* trans. C. Gattegno and F. M. Hodgson (New York: Norton, 1962), chap. 2–4. Cf. also Hans G. Furth, *Piaget and Knowledge* (Englewood Cliffs: Prentice Hall, 1969), pp. 68–106.

5. The quotation from Aristotle is to be found at *De Anima* 432 a 14; and the phrase quoted from Immanuel Kant is located at *Critique of Pure Reason* B 177 A 138.

6. Wittgenstein, *Philosophical Investigations,* p. 215.

7. Samuel Johnson, *Rambler,* no. 125 (1751).

8. Gilbert Ryle, *The Concept of Mind* (New York: Barnes and Noble, 1965), p. 272. For R. G. Collingwood's critique of an interpretation of imagination as make-believe, see *The Principles of Art* (Oxford: Oxford University Press, 1938), chap. 2–5 and especially the statement on p. 224: "The conceptions of past, future, the possible, the hypothetical, are as meaningless for imagination as they are for feeling."

9. Jean-Paul Sartre, *L'Imaginaire* (Paris: Gallimard, 1940), p. 146.

10. Ibid., p. 82: Sartre makes no essential distinction between knowing and thinking.

11. Edmund Husserl, *Ideen I* (The Hague: Nijhoff, 1950), sec. 133.

12. Ibid., sec. 111–12.

13. Wittgenstein, *Philosophical Investigations,* sec. 133.

14. Ryle, *The Concept of Mind,* p. 251. See also pp. 248 and 254.

15. See Maurice Merleau-Ponty, *Phenomenology of Perception,* trans. C. Smith (New York: Humanities Press, 1962), esp. Part Two. If there is any sense of building up in perception, it occurs precisely through imaging to ourselves how new or different aspects of the perceived object would appear if they were to be perceived, as when we anticipate an unseen side of a solid object standing before us. The difference remains, however, that what we imaginatively anticipate in the context of perception can be disconfirmed in the light of subsequent experience—while no such disconfirmation is possible in acts of pure imaging. For what we image is—insofar as this "is" has any existential force at all—as we imagine it to be and not some other way. It makes no sense to say of imaging that occurs in the context of imaginative experience proper that I can image something as appearing in one way, but that it may turn out to be or to appear differently from how I have thus imaged it.

16. David Hume's reduction is implicit in his entire treatment of imagination in *A Treatise of Human Nature,* ed. L. A. Selby-Bigge (Oxford: Oxford University Press, 1967), esp. pp. 10, 140, and 266 ff. Ryle states flatly that "imagining is always imagining that something is the case." (This statement is from Ryle's paper "Imaginary Objects," *Proceedings of the Aristotelian Society,* suppl. vol. XII (1933): 43. See also *The Concept of Mind,* p. 256.)

17. Sartre, *L'Imaginaire,* pp. 13 ff.

18. In this respect, we may agree with Ryle when he says that "roughly, imaging occurs, but images are not seen" (*The Concept of Mind,* p. 247).

19. Beckett, *Imagination Dead Imagine,* p. 7.

20. Here we may concur with Sartre when he says that "the image teaches nothing. Comprehension is realized *in* an image but not *by* the image" (*L'Imaginaire,* p. 136).

21. See Sören Kierkegaard, *Philosophical Fragments,* trans. D. F. Swenson and H. V. Hong (Princeton: Princeton University Press, 1962), esp. "Interlude."

22. Aristotle, *De Anima* 427 b 16–18.

23. Sartre, *L'Imaginaire,* pp. 20–21, 28, 171.

24. Neither does spontaneous imagining; but, contrary to Sartre's claim, it is at least capable of disconcerting us. (For Sartre's claim that we cannot be surprised by what we imagine, see *L'Imaginaire,* p. 170.)

25. It should be noted that, precisely because of its self-sufficiency, imaginative experience has *no need* for such relationships. It bodies forth a miniature plenum which, insubstantial and gossamer-like though it may seem to be, lacks nothing.

26. Thus we see that self-containedness is presupposed by self-evidence, forming a necessary condition for it: to be *self*-evident is to be given in such a self-contained way as to preclude the relevance of other kinds of evidence.

27. Blaise Pascal, *Pensées,* ed. L. Lafuma (Paris: Seuil, 1962), p. 54.

28. C. S. Peirce would say that they lack "Secondness." In Peirce's phaneroscopic analysis—which he sometimes called "phenomenology"—imaginative phenomena would be examples of sheer Firstness, that is, of undiluted qualitative immediacy. See *Collected Papers,* ed. P. Weiss and C. Hartshorne (Cambridge: Harvard University Press, 1931–35), esp. 1.25, 1.527 ff., 2.119, 3.63, 3.422–23, 5.66, and 5.194.

29. Here I would amend John Lilly's claim that "in the province of the mind, there are no limits" (*The Centre of the Cyclone* [London: Paladin, 1973], p. 19). Rather, we should say that in the province of conscious imagination, the limits that matter—i.e., those that are not merely logical or empirical—are those which the imaginer imposes on himself or herself.

Imagination as Intermediate

*. . . l'image, intermédiaire entre le concept et la
perception . . .*

—J.-P. SARTRE
L'Imaginaire

I

THE ROLE OF the intermediate in Western Philosophy has been of
critical, though strangely unnoticed, importance. This importance is
most evident in the twin fields of metaphysics and epistemology. In
metaphysics, the intermediate has played a decisive role ever since Plato
introduced the idea of a hierarchy of Forms, a hierarchy within which certain Forms (e.g., the "mathematicals") were conceived as distinctly intermediate in status. Thus was initiated a tradition which came to include
Plotinian Intellect as lying between the One and the Soul, the central
members of the Great Chain of Being in medieval thought, middle-range
Leibnizian monads, and Spinozan mediate infinite modes. Insofar as metaphysical thinking is itself hierarchical in character—and it might even be
said that this thinking is human hierarchicalizing activity par excellence—it
is forced to concern itself with intermediate stages or types of being. Within
given hierarchies, such stages or types play facilitating or mediating roles
by enabling transitions to be made between lower and higher strata. Because
of the inherent *nisus* within metaphysical thinking toward progressively
superior forms of being—i.e., because of its "onto-theological" character—
such intermediates are posited as links in an ever-ascending chain of entities.

If the role of the intermediate is thus crucial and sometimes even conspicuous in Western metaphysics, this does not appear to be the case in
Western epistemology, whose theories have often presupposed stratified
models of mind which remain merely implicit and unthematized. Yet once
these models are made explicit, they frequently show themselves to be just
as hierarchical as fully articulated metaphysical systems. Perhaps this
similarity of structure between epistemological and metaphysical theories

is not so surprising in view of the fact that it has been metaphysics which has to a considerable extent determined Western conceptions of the human subject, including his or her powers of knowing. But the directive force of metaphysics, whether innocent or insidious, has often been buried beneath the very claims for human cognitive capabilities which are so symptomatic of Western philosophers' "pursuit of the incorrigible."[1] Such claims typically stress the ability of the inquiring subject to come into direct and immediate contact with what he or she seeks, whether this contact takes place at the level of sensation or understanding—in other words, whether the directly evident has a sensible or a conceptual character. The immediacy of contact which is thereby posited as existing between knower and known is such as to obscure the inbuilt hierarchy of psychic operations which are considered to precede (in the case of understanding) or follow (in the case of sensation) the moment of contact.[2]

The presence of this epistemological hierarchy is assured by the fact that there must be a way of moving from sensation to understanding and vice versa, that is, from one kind of direct evidence to another. This movement can be accomplished only by traversing certain intermediate stages. And if we look carefully at Western epistemological theories since Plato, we find, however disguisedly, widespread recourse to just such middle-range factors. These factors ease, and indeed often make possible, transitions between two such disparate acts as sensation and understanding. In this manner there is instituted, within the human mind itself, a series of levels which is no less hierarchical than its metaphysical analogues. One need only think of the four stages of cognition in Plato's *Republic,* of Aristotle's analysis of the rational soul in the *De Anima,* of Plotinus's view of the human soul in the *Enneads,* of Locke's degrees of knowledge, Spinoza's three levels of cognition, Kant's complicated mental machinery in the A edition of the transcendental deduction, Hegel's theory of subjective mind, or even of Heidegger's notion of *Verstehen:* for all of these thinkers, the mind is conceived as structured into a stratification of acts.[3] In any such stratification, there have to be, in the very nature of the case, intermediate levels—levels which serve to mediate between divergent and otherwise irreconcilable mental powers. As Kant put it in the context of his own need for bringing sensibility and understanding together: "Obviously there must be some third thing, which is homogeneous on the one hand with the category, and on the other hand with the appearance, and which thus makes the application of the former to the latter possible."[4]

Still more remarkable than the pervasive presence, in so many Western epistemologies, of a hierarchical model of mind involving intermediate stages is the fact that a particular mental act has been singled out as the primary candidate for occupancy of the most central position in such a model. This act is the act of imagination. More than any other single mental activity, imagination has been regarded as the intermediate power of mind, as its essential midpoint. Thus Aristotle places *phantasia* squarely between *aisthēsis* and *noēsis;* Plotinus argues that *phantasia* must mediate between the senses and discursive reason; Descartes links imagination to mathematics and thereby gives it an intermediate position between sensation (which is concerned with secondary qualities) and understanding (which is occupied exclusively with imageless metaphysical truths); Hume, though not consistent, normally regards imagining as taking place midway between the passivity of receiving impressions and the activity of purely formal thinking; and Kant presents imagination in all of its forms as the essential third term between sensibility and understanding, terming the transcendental schema (the primary expression of productive imagination) a "mediating representation."[5]

To point to imagination's central position in Western epistemology is not to overlook the fact that philosophers have not been in complete accord as to imagination's intermediate status. There are significant exceptions, which fall into two groups. On the one hand, Plato attempts to subordinate imagining qua *eikasia* to perceiving insofar as the latter occurs at the level of *pistis*.[6] On the other hand, Schelling, Novalis, Coleridge, and other Romantics exalt imagination as the paramount or supreme mental power, the source even of perception: "the primary Imagination I hold to be the living power and prime agent of all human perception."[7] Nevertheless, following the explosion of the Romantic rebellion, and despite Baudelaire's and Breton's post-Romantic convictions as to imagination's supremacy, imagining was once again assigned its habitual locus midway between inferior and superior mental powers—as the above citation from Sartre indicates. In the twentieth century, this middle-range locus has been argued for most forcefully in the surprisingly similar epistemological theories of R. G. Collingwood and of Mikel Dufrenne. Collingwood, citing Aristotle and Kant as his predecessors in this regard, asserts that "imagination is a distinct level of experience intermediate between sensation and intellect."[8] Collingwood's entire epistemology is built around the central place occupied by imagination, not only in human knowledge but also (and above all) in aesthetic experience. So too Dufrenne envisages imagination as occupying a central position, and it does so within the same two domains of knowledge and art. In what follows, we shall take Collingwood's and Dufrenne's mutually illuminating theories of imagination as exemplary continuations of a whole tradition of thought in which imagination is regarded as intermediate in status. A brief review of these two theories will precede a critical discussion of their most controversial assumptions and consequences.

II

For Collingwood, there are two primary levels of mind: feeling and thought. Feeling is the "psychical level" at which we "experience sensations together with their peculiar emotional charge" (*PA*, p. 164). It is the necessary point of departure for all mental activity, even though it possesses an unstable and momentary character. Since thought in its developed form, i.e., as intellect, is concerned with relations between comparatively stable items of experience, there must be some agency for converting the flux of feeling into discriminable and persisting presentations. This agency, which is thought in its primary form, is called "consciousness" by Collingwood. Consciousness involves an act of attention whereby feelings (which correlate with Hume's "impressions") are transformed into imaginations (Hume's "ideas"). Imagining, then, is the end-result of this process of focusing on feeling.[9]

Yet the position of imagining within Collingwood's epistemology is not terminal but pivotal. As presented in *The Principles of Art*, imagination exists *between* sensation and intellect. Indeed, it is the betweenness per se of mind—that through which all mental activities come into contact with one another. To imagine is to hold contents of consciousness, whatever their ultimate origin or ontic status, before the mind so as to compare, contrast, or conjoin them—above all, to express them in language and art. It is in this way that Collingwood agrees with Kant that imagination is "a blind but indispensable faculty"—blind, because it cannot anticipate its own end-products, indispensable because of its consolidating function (cf. *PA*, p. 171).

In spite of its indispensability, however, imagination is not for Collingwood an autonomous power. Only consciousness is truly autonomous, and then only insofar as it remains free to focus on certain feelings and not on others. Imagining itself is a product of this very freedom and cannot break away from its moorings in feeling. It is an extension and refinement of feeling at another level, as the following crucial passage makes clear:

> From being impressions of sense, [feelings] become ideas of imagination. In this new capacity, as losing their power over us and becoming subject to our will, *they are still feelings, and feelings of the same kind as before;* but they have ceased to be mere sensations and have become what we call imaginations. . . .[10]

As a consequence, imagination's intermediary position consigns it to a distinctly secondary status. It is, in effect, "the modification of feeling by consciousness" (cf. *PA*, pp. 206–14). Its operation is limited to the domesticating of feeling and does not extend to changing it in any fundamental way. Therefore, feeling remains not only prior to imagination—prior both chronologically and logically—but also much more inclusive. Indeed, in Collingwood's view, imagination draws its entire content from feeling: we can imagine only what we have already felt or are presently in the process of feeling. At the same time, imagination is made subordinate to thought.

Since it is brought about by the activity of consciousness, which is conceived as thought in its primary function, imagination comes to be regarded as the presence of feeling at the level of thought. Consequently, imagination represents the point at which the two primary levels of mind merge. As essentially hybrid in character and role, it fails to achieve an independent status of its own. Informing the link between feeling or sensation and intellect, imagination loses the distinctive nature which Collingwood strives to procure for it: "I shall try to show that there is a special activity of mind [which] we generally call imagination, as distinct from sensation on the one hand and intellect on the other" (PA, p. 171). In the end, Collingwood does not succeed in showing this, but rather the very opposite—namely, the lack of clear demarcation between imagination and either of its two neighboring faculties. In place of distinctiveness, there is an overlapping and running together of mental activities; instead of differentiation, there is indistinguishability.

III

For Dufrenne, as much as for Collingwood, imagination is the intermediate human faculty par excellence. In Part II of his *Phénoménologie de l'expérience esthétique*, which contains Dufrenne's most complete consideration of epistemological issues, imagination is conceived as "the liaison between mind and body."[11] The image is said to be "a *metaxu* or middle term between the brute presence where the object is experienced and the thought where it becomes idea" (PAE, p. 345). Imagination is what ushers in representation, and representation stands midway between presence and reflection qua understanding. Dufrenne is quite explicit in his claim as to imagination's central position:

> Between imagination, which allows representation to come about, and understanding, which exercises judgment, there seems to be the same distance [as] . . . between presence and representation. (PAE, p. 370)

Although Dufrenne unequivocally places imagination precisely halfway between sensuous presence and understanding, his treatment of the relationships among these three levels of mind possesses an internal complexity which merits our attention. In particular, it is maintained that what is intermediate must, in order to act as a genuine liaison, itself be dual in character. Hence Dufrenne is driven to distinguish between two aspects or functions of imagination: transcendental and empirical. As transcendental, imagination opens up a spatio-temporal field within which appearances—and thus representations—may arise. In other words, imagination as transcendental creates "the distance within presence which constitutes representation" (*PAE,* p. 351). As empirical, imagination converts mere appearances into full-bodied objects. It fills out appearances by supplying them with additional dimensions and detail—thereby completing the process of representation. In so doing, empirical imagination draws upon implicit modes of knowledge (*les savoirs*) which are inherited from sensible presence.

Now, the two aspects of imagination distinguished by Dufrenne exhibit a parallel yet diverging structure. Just as the empirical aspect of imagining looks back to the plane of presence, so the transcendental aspect looks forward to understanding: "as soon as imagination is given so is understanding" (*PAE,* p. 371). To open up the field of appearances through the agency of transcendental imagination is to call for the eventual unification of this field in conceptual terms, much as filling out individual appearances gives rise to representations. As a consequence, Dufrenne's model of mind in *The Phenomenology of Aesthetic Experience* looks like this:

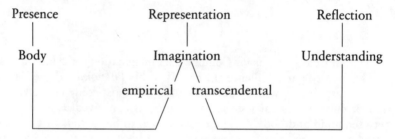

Such a schema may be compared with Collingwood's position in *The Principles of Art:*

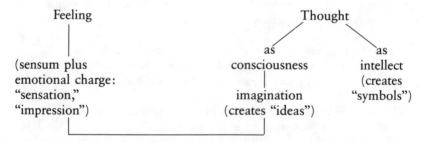

In this schema, it can be seen that imagination functions entirely as a transitional stage situated between feeling and thought. Indeed, it is itself a mode of thought—or, more exactly, it is an extension of consciousness, which in turn is thought in its primary form. Thus, despite Collingwood's efforts to stress the importance of imagination in art, it has no independent standing in the philosophy of mind upon which his aesthetics is supported.

Dufrenne's implicit model of mind may also be compared with a diagram of Kant's view as found in *The Critique of Pure Reason:*

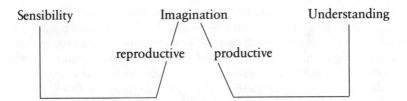

Sensibility   Imagination   Understanding

reproductive   productive

It is evident that for Kant imagination is the *sole* middle term between sensibility and understanding. Instead of being subsumed under another middle term such as "representation" or "consciousness," it is given recognition in its own right. Yet it remains the case that for Kant all three primary faculties—sensibility, imagination, and understanding—are conceived as modes of *Vorstellung,* that is, of representation in the most general sense. In this way, imagination is finally subsumed under representation at a higher level, thereby diminishing the relative autonomy which it enjoys at the level depicted in the diagram.

Similarly, for Dufrenne the three primary acts of mind—presence, representation, and reflection—are conceived as modes of "perception" in the broadest sense, and Part III of the *Phenomenology* is significantly entitled "Phenomenology of Aesthetic Perception." In terms of this ultimate epistemological horizon, representation does not occur until the second level, at which point there is a drawing back from the direct encounter with the sensible world that is achieved in presence. The result of this withdrawal is that at the level of representation the two primary forms which sensible presence takes are left behind: "presence to the world" and "presence to the body" (cf. *PAE,* pp. 335–45). In their place, there is only a "quasi-presence" (*PAE,* p. 351). Although this latter does not possess the concretely sensuous character of presence at the first level, it is not to be confused with absence or the unreal in Sartre's sense. Rather, imagination furnishes a kind of presence which is "nonconceptual and yet nonsensuous . . . an abstract and yet real presence *of* something sensuous which is adumbrated but not wholly given" (*PAE,* p. 349). Therefore, although imagination is ultimately a form of perception understood generically, it does possess its own mode of presence and is not to be confused with the other two primary kinds of perception. And this imaginal presence, as "an unsensed sensible," is emblematic of what Heidegger has called imagination's "remarkably ambiguous character."[12]

Imagination's ambiguity stems not only from its unique mode of presence. It also derives from its intrinsically intermediate position, as Dufrenne himself stresses: "imagination appears to possess at once the two faces of nature and mind (*esprit*)" (*PAE,* p. 351). As empirical, imagination can be considered as an extension of sensible presence; as transcendental, it is a prelude to understanding. But this basic ambiguity of imagination in its relation to sensible presence and understanding does not mean that imagining loses its self-identity in Dufrenne's conception. As compared with

Collingwood, who accords no separate position to imagination within his rigorously two-part theory of knowledge (feeling and thought are jointly exhaustive of human mental powers), Dufrenne attempts to reserve a special place for imagination within his general epistemology. Insofar as it is seen as occupying this place, imagining is not considered a mere aspect of sensible presence or understanding. Instead, its relation with each of these latter is (in Pradines's term) one of "reciprocal genesis": "whereby we oscillate from one term to another, confirming one by the other" (*PAE*, p. 352). Thus imagination is regarded as holding its own in relation to the surrounding acts of sensible presence and understanding, however intimately it is involved with these latter.

Not only does imagination hold its own in the Dufrennian perspective. In certain respects, it becomes even more fundamental than sensible presence and understanding. Much as Heidegger attempted to demonstrate that Kant's notion of productive imagination lay at the root of sensibility and understanding, so Dufrenne is tempted to consider imagination as prior to both of its neighboring acts. On the one hand, imagination in each of its aspects is necessary to the presentation of presence in perception, being "indispensable to both the advent and the richness of perception in general."[13] On the other hand, imagination is equally crucial for understanding, since imagining alone gives to appearances sufficient consistency to make them capable of exhibiting lawlike behavior: "understanding can do nothing without imagination" (*PAE*, p. 371).

Despite this dual priority of imagination, however, it remains the case that imagining is in certain other respects dependent upon sensible presence and understanding. Imagination needs sensible presence as its origin, as the specific source of its representations.[14] And it equally needs understanding as a restraining influence on its capricious tendencies.[15] Thus the principle of reciprocal genesis is reinstated and reaffirmed: in both of its primary relationships, imagination is an equal partner, not a *primus inter pares*. As Dufrenne says in summation:

> In short, between imagination and understanding there is the same ambiguous relation as between presence and imagination. Nature and mind, the lower and the higher, continue to unite and differentiate themselves within us. We do not cease to be one, even when we divide ourselves in order to subdue ourselves. . . . (*PAE*, p. 372)

What is the role of imagination in Dufrenne's view of aesthetic experience? Contrary to what one might have suspected and contrary to Collingwood's and Kant's explicit theories, imagination is *less* crucially operative here than in ordinary perception, for in the case of the aesthetic object, "appearance says everything" (*PAE*, p. 360). And since the aesthetic object suffices for itself, there is no need for empirical imagination to fill it out. In fact, "the work succeeds precisely when it restricts imagination within the work's limits, discouraging any further elaboration" (*PAE*, p. 366). Only in its transcendental dimension does imagination remain essential to aesthetic experience, i.e., insofar as it projects a spatio-temporal continuum in which the aesthetic object itself may appear. In this way, imagination may be said to be responsible for the relative detachment—the "psychic distance"— with which the aesthetic object presents itself to us. But once this distance has been established, imagining has no further function to perform.

There are two further and related reasons for the diminished role of imagination in aesthetic experience. First of all, the aesthetic object is conceived by Dufrenne as above all a (sensuously) *perceived* object. Precisely as perceived, it tends to exclude imagining as a concurrent or co-ordinate mental act. The being of the work is sensible, and its apprehension must therefore be perceptual in character. The work invites the spectator to perceive and not to imagine: "the work is a work only as perceived, and there can be no question of yielding only an image or idea of it."[16] But a second reason for the relatively repressed position of imagination in the experience of art is found in the fact that the work is not only perceived. In fact, the *world* of the work—especially this world in its expressive character—is not perceived at all; we do not grasp *it* at the level of sensible presence. Nor is it something we imagine by anticipation or by ap-presentation. Rather, as an expressive whole, the world of the aesthetic object is something the spectator *feels*. It is through feeling, and feeling alone, that we gain entry into this world, "a world which is not nourished by imagination or taken up by understanding but instead exists potentially in feeling" (*PAE*, p. 542). The aim of feeling in aesthetic experience is to read expression, and this act of reading cannot be accomplished at the level of imagination or of understanding. Summing up both of the above reasons, Dufrenne writes:

> Thus we can see what the proper function of art is. By allowing us to perceive an exemplary object whose whole reality consists in being sensuous, art invites us and trains us to read expression and to discover the atmosphere which is revealed only to feeling. (*PAE*, p. 542)

But where does feeling fit into Dufrenne's epistemological hierarchy, whose three main moments are presence, representation, and reflection? Although feeling involves "a new immediacy" (*PAE*, p. 418), this is not the immediacy of presence to the world or of presence to the body. It is the immediacy of a being-in-depth (*être-profond*), which belongs strictly speaking only to a subject or quasi-subject, that is, to a being who possesses genuine interiority. Just as feeling does not arise at the level of sensible presence, so it cannot be a function of representation in the form of imagination, which creates spatio-temporal distance and concerns itself exclusively with objects as discrete and separate from one another. Feeling arises, instead, at the level of reflection. This would seem to be an unlikely idea, except for the fact that Dufrenne distinguishes between two kinds of reflection: critical and sympathetic. *Critical* reflection is continuous with understanding; both are the direct heirs of imagination in its transcendental aspect because both concern themselves with objects in their lawlike character. In *sympathetic* reflection, in contrast, objects are replaced by intrinsically meaningful subjects or quasi-subjects, and appearances become aspects of an expressed world. As this latter reflection brings itself continually closer to the world of the work, it comes to realize a com-presence with this world. And precisely insofar as it seeks to read this world's expression, it becomes feeling. As a result, there is a tight dialectical relationship between sympathetic reflection and feeling, a relationship in which each factor aids the other to achieve fulfillment.[17] Feeling, as preceded and yet also ratified by sympathetic reflection, becomes the final stage of aesthetic experience: "aesthetic experience culminates in feeling as the reading of expression."[18] Through feeling, the spectator's depth comes to match the depth of the aesthetic object, and the "communion" which is the aim of all aesthetic experience and which expresses an ontological affinity between man and world is attained.[19]

The consequences of this culmination are decisive for the fate of imagination. Since feeling is concerned only with the reading of expression, it need not depend on the prior constitution of objects which is effected at the level of representation. This is why imagination is to be "repressed" in aesthetic experience: it keeps us within the limits of representation, limits which feeling need not acknowledge. While imagination must delineate objects on the basis of the corporeal *savoirs* inherited from sensible presence—and hence must operate in a mediated manner—feeling goes directly to expression: "I read a meaning or sense without passing through bodily knowledge which would have to be realized by imagination" (*PAE,* p. 384). Since this expressive meaning is given in its totality and without the necessity of mediation by objects, there is no longer any need for the constitutive work of imagination. In the experience of feeling, everything that matters is already given: "expression has said everything in a single stroke" (*PAE,* p. 386). Within this situation, imagination not only becomes useless; it is put out of play altogether, for expression "paralyzes imagination" (*PAE,* p. 385). In other words, imagination is not only *surpassed*— as it is in both critical and sympathetic reflection—it is also *suppressed* by feeling, which thus becomes the dominant term in the analysis of aesthetic experience. If imagination retains any function at all in art, it is only *après coup* and as an adjunct to feeling, that is, only when it has first been "released by feeling" (*PAE,* p. 438). Consequently, Dufrenne's phenomenology of aesthetic perception ends with an apotheosis of feeling and a corresponding demotion of imagination. However necessary imagination is in ordinary perception—where it remains of fundamental importance[20]—it becomes of secondary significance within aesthetic experience proper.

IV

Collingwood and Dufrenne, whom we have chosen as providing paradigmatic twentieth-century views of imagination, are in accord with regard to the following three general theses:

(1) Feeling is the primary level of aesthetic experience;

(2) Imagination is a second-order, object-oriented activity in comparison with feeling, which is pre-objective;

(3) Imagination is intermediate between two putatively more crucial levels of human experience.

Despite substantive agreement with regard to these three assertions, there remain important differences in the way in which each assertion would be supported. Thus, in maintaining thesis (1), Collingwood would consider feeling "primary" in the sense of the first, rather than the ultimate, level of aesthetic experience. Whereas for Dufrenne perception (qua sensible presence) and imagination are both epistemologically prior to feeling, for Collingwood feeling precedes specifications into either perception or imagination. Similarly, in affirming thesis (2), Collingwood would claim that imagining arises from feeling by an effort of attention on the part of consciousness. Thus imagination is a particular form assumed by feeling as this latter becomes the explicit focus of consciousness. For Dufrenne, in contrast, feeling arises at a stage which is posterior to imagination. Yet in its ability to grasp meaning directly, it harks back to a level of experience which is pre-representational, for the expression which it reads and the world which it comes to inhabit are pre-objective in character. In feeling, we have to do with what Dufrenne calls "the absolute experience of the affective" (PAE, p. 542), an experience which is radically indeterminate in character. Though indeterminate, such experience is nonetheless more insightful and revealing than experience at the level of imagination, whose comparatively greater definiteness is achieved at the price of a diminished richness of content—hence the secondary status of imagination in relation to feeling within aesthetic experience.

Finally, thesis (3) would be defended differently by these two authors. Collingwood considers imagination to be intermediate between the primordial level of feeling and the higher kind of thought termed "intellect." It is at the same time co-ordinate with consciousness, the lower kind of thought, as well as with expression and with language. As a consequence, Collingwood recognizes four simultaneous and correlative intermediate phenomena: imagination, consciousness, expression, and language. All of these exist midway between unrefined or "raw" feeling and the symbolic powers of intellect. Dufrenne, in comparison, links imagination exclusively with representation, which is itself situated precisely halfway between presence and reflection qua understanding. For Dufrenne, imagination is the *only* occupant of this intermediate position: representation is initiated by imagination, but it is also completed by imagination. Any further complexity at this level is internal to imagination itself and is found in its own two primary aspects: empirical and transcendental. The relationship between imagination and consciousness, expression, and language is not denied; but neither is it treated as such, and the unmistakable implication is that imagining (in both of its aspects) is the only intermediate psychic phenomenon of any decisive significance.

V

If we may thus take it for granted that a case can be made—and made in more than one way, as the above comparison between Collingwood and Dufrenne has suggested—for the thesis that imagination is an intermediate mental activity, we must now consider certain assumptions and consequences involved in holding this thesis. To what does it commit us concerning, first, the character of imagination itself and, second, the nature of mind as such? What does it mean, in short, to affirm that imagination is irrevocably a "mediatrix"?[21]

(1) *The Character of Imagination.* If imagination is a mental act of intermediate status in the overall hierarchy of mental functions, two major consequences follow forthwith. First, the person supporting this thesis cannot claim that imagination is *originative* in character. As intermediate, it cannot bring itself into being from its own resources alone. This is not to deny that, as Kant stressed, it may well be capable of producing new syntheses of elements: new Gestalten, new psychic situations, new insights. But if it is truly intermediate, it cannot bring forth *de novo* all of the elements of these syntheses. Some, if not all, of such elements must stem from a more primordial level of experience. This means that imagining depends— at least in part—upon this originary level, whether it be termed "sensibility," "feeling," or "presence." As Dufrenne himself admits, "representation comes about only through a preliminary experience of presence" (*PAE,* p. 384); and sensible presence, as we have seen, functions as an irreplaceable source for the implicit knowledge on which imagination continually draws its formative activities. Similarly, sensibility is for Kant the origin of spatialized and temporalized representations; and feeling, in Collingwood's view, furnishes the material impressions from which imaginative ideas derive. To assert this kind of epistemological dependency does not preclude questioning the very idea of origin or source and even suggesting that the idea of such an origin or source represents an illusion fostered by Western metaphysics. But this direction of inquiry, which both Kant and Dufrenne

pursue in advance of Derrida, does not replace a basic belief in imagination's dependent relation to something more fundamental, even if it proves to be itself dependent on a further origin. In brief, for a mental act to be intermediate in status, there must be some other act preceding or underlying it.

Imagination's intermediateness means, secondly, that imagining cannot be regarded as *ultimate* in status. It cannot be the final stage in a series of ascending stages, but must have at least one successor. This consequence has two concrete implications. (a) If intermediate, imagination is an activity which will be surpassed in any comprehensive deployment of mental powers. As penultimate, it cannot represent the most developed form of human mental activity. It is bound to be transcended at some point as this activity realizes its full potential. (b) By the same token, however, at least some of the products of imagining will be of relevance or use at subsequent levels. If imagination is genuinely intermediate, a legitimate "third thing," it has a function and value which transcend its own sphere of operation. As occupying a middle position, it is capable of passing on to its psychic successor certain results of its own functioning. Thus Dufrenne holds that imagination fashions objects between which understanding discovers lawlike relationships, and Collingwood maintains that ideas of imagination must first be established before intellect can discern stable patterns among them.[22] It is perhaps due to his recognition of this aspect of imagination's intermediate position that Kant was led to consider imagining as "indispensable." Aristotle put the point pithily: "The soul never thinks without an image."[23] Therefore, even if imagination as intermediate is neither originative nor ultimate, it is not thereby condemned to futility. It may still play a crucial, if delimited, role in the life of mind.

(2) *The Nature of Mind.* What does the notion of imagination as intermediate imply with regard to the nature of mind? It implies above all that the mind is susceptible of arrangement into a series of interlocking structures. Insofar as there is movement in this series from a preliminary to a final stage—i.e., from more basic to more advanced or refined modes of mentation—the series forms a hierarchy in which "lower" and "higher" stages are distinguishable.[24] The intermediate factor articulates what is lower with what is higher, mediating between levels or stages at least two of which must have no direct connection with one another. In this respect, the intermediate function provides a means of transition, a bridge, between disparate mental acts. In performing this role, it affords us an insight into a fundamental (if often covert) assumption concerning the structure of the human mind—namely, that it is inherently hierarchical. Within such a hierarchical model, it is the presence of an intermediate act or acts which ensures that there is communication between different levels of mind. Without an intermediate element, the differences in kind between different types of acts would be mutually exclusive differences, that is, differences not allowing for the overlapping of levels. That overlapping does in fact

somehow occur is evident from the basic observation that mind works as a whole, or not at all. Hence its various levels must be capable of forming effective liaisons with one another in order to allow for that spontaneity of mental activity of which Hobbes spoke when he said that "thought is quick."

Upon closer examination, the hierarchical model of mind is seen to be based on a further assumption concerning the nature of mind. This is that mental acts form a hierarchy not merely of eidetically different *kinds* of acts but of acts whose differences are at the same time differences of degree. The notion of difference of kind *cum* difference of degree allows for the construction of a scale of acts which are related to each other in a way that allows both for continuity between acts and for a progressive movement within the scale as a whole. Now, just such a scale underlies the models of mind which Dufrenne and Collingwood have proposed. In each model, those mental acts which occupy distinguishable places are related to one another as acts which are at once different in kind and different in degree.

Therefore, both of the models in question embody what Collingwood himself calls a "scale of forms."[25] A scale of forms possesses two closely related features. The first, on which we have just touched, is that all significant differences are simultaneously differences in degree and differences in kind: "differences of degree not merely entail, but actually are, differences of kind" (*EM*, p. 73). The reason for this coincidence of differences is that, although it is the case that (a) differences of kind represent specific forms (i.e., "species") of a common genus and that (b) differences in degree represent different expressions of a variable attribute of the genus, the variable itself is finally identical with the generic essence. Thus in Plato's hierarchy of forms of knowledge as given in Book VI of *The Republic,* each of the four main types of knowledge stands for a different degree of "truth," yet in the end truth is itself identical with knowledge. The second feature, which follows from the first, is that each form represents a progressively more adequate embodiment of the generic essence as one moves 'upward' in the hierarchy: "every form, so far as it is low in the scale, is to that extent an imperfect or inadequate specification of the generic essence, which is realized with progressive adequacy as the scale is ascended" (*EM,* p. 61). Hence *eikasia* stands for an extremely inadequate form of knowledge, while *pistis* and *dianoia* are comparatively more adequate. (It is clear from this example that the role of intermediates is crucial in a scale of forms. Indeed, in the scale of forms which Plato posits, the intermediates constitute the largest segment of the scale, which allows for a number of stages intermediate between sheer ignorance and fully realized *epistēmē*. In practice, that is, in terms of what is humanly experienceable, such a scale is in effect a scale *of* intermediates, since the two end-states are rarely, if ever, encountered as such.)

Returning to the special case of imagination, we can now see that to assign to imagining an intermediate role is to presume, however tacitly, a scalar view of mind. For as an intermediate form or type of mental activity, imagining differs both in degree and in kind from other mental acts, inferior and superior, within an implicit spectrum of acts of mind. That both kinds of difference are present within this spectrum is hinted at in Collingwood's own appraisal of imagination as "a *distinct* level of experience *intermediate* between sensation and intellect" (*PA*, p. 215; my italics). To be a "distinct" level of experience is to differ in kind from the other two levels. To be "intermediate" between sensation and intellect is to differ in degree from both of the latter.

This combination or coincidence between two sorts of difference is the crucial factor in any scalar epistemological theory, and it serves to link philosophies of mind as different as those of Aristotle and Plato, Locke and Kant, Collingwood and Dufrenne. For the presence of a common scale-structure is as important as the considerable divergences which otherwise serve to separate these philosophers. One of the most important of these divergences is found in the fact that the generic essence which is realized throughout the successive levels of a given hierarchy differs from case to case. For Aristotle, *aisthēsis, phantasia,* and *noēsis* are the three essential stages in the realization of rational soul; for Plato, the divided line symbolizes four stages of cognition or knowledge in the most comprehensive sense; and while knowledge also supplies the generic essence for Locke's "degrees of knowledge," here knowledge is construed in a sense that is closer to natural science—as it is in Kant's epistemology. For Collingwood, the generic essence is feeling, and the stages he describes in *The Principles of Art* can be considered successive forms of feeling. For Dufrenne, the significant epistemological stages are stages in the realization of "perception" in the largest sense. Such striking differences in the generic essences which are realized in specific cases do not, however, vitiate the basic similarity in structure exhibited by the epistemological hierarchies implicitly or explicitly espoused by all of these thinkers.

Within the framework of this structure, imagination occupies in each instance a pivotal position, being presented as a critical turning-point in the life of mind. Yet it is in precisely this respect that we must call into question the notion of imagination as *intermediary*. To be an intermediary stage is ipso facto to be a transitional phenomenon. And if so, this has two crucial consequences. (a) It is implied that the stages *between* which imagination qua intermediary mediates are somehow more fundamental than imagination itself. Thus one finds the assumption in most of the above theories that sensation and intellect (or their equivalents) are the two primordial psychic strata. Being primordial in distinctly different ways, they are not in direct communication with one another, and imagination is called upon to guarantee that they enter into contact (however indirectly). If imagination thereby becomes indispensable, it is only in this mediatory role, only in this connective function. But is this so? Is imagining always restricted to mediatory activity? Is not imagining on occasion active for its *own* sake and not merely for the sake of other mental acts? Is not imagination capable of achieving its own kind of insight and of bringing forth its own kind of creation, e.g., the free image? This is not the place to present a case for the autonomy of imagining; but if such autonomy could be established, it would undermine the reductionism implicit in the view of imagination as exclusively intermediary.[26]

(b) To be a strictly transitional stage is not only to lack autonomy. It is, in the end, to lack an independent status altogether. This is a matter not just of the endemic tendency to regard imagining as a mere mode of something held to be more basic such as sensation, but of a possible consequence of being an intermediary stage in a scalar model of mind. The consequence is that imagination may be reduced to a dimensionless and characterless point within this model. Surprisingly, Collingwood accepts and even endorses this consequence: imagination is said to be "the *point* at which the activity of thought makes contact with the merely psychical life of feeling."[27] This is stated even though, in his own earlier *Essay on Philosophical Method,* Collingwood had attempted to show that an intermediate stage in a scalar hierarchy can only be a point of transition between more enduring initial or terminal stages. Referring to any scale of forms, whether metaphysical or epistemological, he wrote:

> In such a system of specifications the two sets of differences [i.e., of kind and of degree] are so connected that whenever the variable [i.e., the difference in degree], increasing or decreasing, reaches *certain critical points* on the scale, one specific form [i.e., one kind] disappears and is replaced by another. (*EM,* p. 57; my italics)

Thus the point of transition, however "critical" it may be as the means of contact between diverse forms or levels, is itself only the place or moment where one of the "great kinds" (in Plato's term) is replaced by another of the great kinds. The critical point is not itself a specific *kind* of entity or activity which could compete or be on a par with the subvenient and supervenient items between which it stands. Therefore, when imagination is conceived as such a critical point, it is in effect reduced to strictly mediatory and transitory existence. Yet such a radical reduction, which is entailed by the very structure of a nested hierarchy of epistemological levels, fails to do justice to imagination as an activity in its own right, with its own unique content and modus operandi. In particular, the notion of imagining as a transitional point obscures imagination's intrinsic temporality, a temporality which refuses to be confined to punctiform instants. However fleeting it may seem to be, imagining possesses its own mode of duration, including its own kind of experiential continuity. Because of this distinctive temporal character, it would be mistaken to consider imagination as a mere moment of tension between more enduring stages.

What both of the above consequences suggest is that the nature of human mental activity is not adequately delineated in a model of mind that is strictly hierarchical or scalar. However attractive this model may be for reasons of elegance or economy, it fails to account for fundamental features of those mental acts which are forced into intermediary positions in given hierarchies. This failure is particularly conspicuous in the case of imagination, which resists reduction to what is merely momentary and transitional. As over against this reduction, which is entailed in nearly all Western theories of imagination as intermediate, the act of imagining asserts its autonomy. For it is an act with certain incomparable characteristics—characteristics which call for direct description and separate assessment. To claim this is not to deny that imagining may *also* play an intermediary role vis-à-vis other mental acts such as sensing or conceptual thinking. But such a role does not exhaust the powers of imagination, powers which exceed any merely mediatory or connective capacity. Possessing their own criteria of identification and achievement, these powers must be considered on their own merits.

We need another, more adequate model of mind. In place of a graduated hierarchy of mental acts arranged in terms of the degree to which a single generic essence is realized, we should look for a model which acknowledges the intrinsic pluralism and polyvalence of psychic powers. In such a model, each of these powers would be granted a genuinely distinctive character, and each would be given its own regional locus in the general geography of mind. Thus it is a matter of recognizing the essential multiplicity of the mental instead of stratifying mind into a series of successive stages, stages which differentially embody a monistic conception of mind in the form of feeling or perception or intellect. Maybe mind is in the end many things—so many sorts of things that no rigidly hierarchical model can pretend to capture or convey its innermost structure.

VI

It is perhaps precisely because Mikel Dufrenne came increasingly to realize the shortcomings of imagination as intermediate—and thus of the scalar model of mind which this view implies—that in more recent writings he has proposed new perspectives on the phenomenon. These perspectives tend to converge on two closely affiliated factors: the image and the imaginary. In closing, let us consider Dufrenne's treatments of each.

(1) *The Image.* In *Le Poétique* and in *Language and Philosophy*, stress is placed on the "great images" provided by the sky, night, earth, etc.[28] As contrasted with the domesticated images of reveries (which are only *images imaginées*), these great images do not invite us to enter a merely fictitious, unreal realm. On the contrary, they introduce us to the "prereal" through their ability to present the real in archetypal form and in advance

of its more attenuated appearances. Further, each great image possesses a limitless semantic depth which renders it strictly undefinable. Instead of possessing a single meaning, it "expands indefinitely into the dimensions of a world" (*P,* p. 233). But the revelation of a world is not, in contrast to what is maintained in his *Phenomenology,* the last step. Rather, *through* the world opened up by a great image, Nature expresses itself: "the intuition of Nature crystallizes into images of a world, and such a world is the cipher of Nature" (*P,* p. 235). A concrete consequence of the acknowledgment of Nature as ultimate is that the image is brought closer to perception; or, more exactly, Nature as perceived becomes the sole source of great images: "perception is always pregnant with images" (*P,* p. 194). Great images in turn become "intensely perceived objects," and as such they precede specific acts of imagining.[29] In this manner, Dufrenne tries to remove the phenomenon of imagination from a strictly subjective locus in the human mind: it is Nature, more than humankind, who imagines.[30]

Despite this displacement from the human subject to Nature—a shift called for by the polysemous character of poetry—it is to be noticed that two themes persist from Dufrenne's earlier treatment of imagination. (a) On the one hand, the role of imagination, insofar as it is an act of the poet or of the reader, remains repressed within the sphere of art. The great images may inspire the poet and (via poetry) his or her reader, but they do not liberate or even enlarge their imaginative experience as such. Rather than extending imaginative powers, the great images deepen perception: "great images are offered to us, and they invite perception to deepen itself as perception: such are aesthetic objects . . . which repress our imagination rather than put it into play" (*P,* p. 234). With regard to the reduced role of imagination in aesthetic experience, Dufrenne thus retains the same position that was put forth in his earlier work: in the realm of art, imagining possesses a distinctly subordinate role and is not to be given free rein. As a consequence, and also in keeping with the *Phenomenology,* feeling becomes a more crucial ingredient of aesthetic experience than imagination, for it is through feeling that we grasp the "affective visage" of the aesthetic object and of Nature itself.[31]

(b) On the other hand, the notion of imagination as intermediate in position is kept in spite of the new orientation of Dufrenne's thought in the direction of Nature and *le sauvage.* This intermediacy now stems from the fact that the great images mediate between humans and Nature, as becomes clear in Dufrenne's claim that "the image is only the correlate of an imaging consciousness; it is the announcement made to human beings by a *Natura Naturans*" (*P,* p. 234). In other words, one kind of intermediate status has been exchanged for another: instead of the original triad presence–imagination–understanding we now have human–image–Nature. And if the image (in the specific form of the great image) is only intermediary in status, it is subject to the same critical remarks which were made above in section v, since these remarks apply to *any* intermediary position in a hierarchy of levels, whether the position is occupied by imagination or by an affiliated phenomenon such as the image. In this regard, it does not matter whether the intermediary factor is intra-subjective or extra-subjective, for in either case it remains exposed to the danger of collapsing into a mere point of transition. Whatever the nature of the presiding *telos* or "generic essence," whether it be Nature or Perception, there is the same risk that the intermediate stage will be regarded merely as something to be surpassed and finally to be suppressed—in short, as ultimately dispensable. Hence, despite the considerably increased amplitude of *Le Poétique*— an amplitude which, in the form of a philosophy of Nature, serves to distinguish it from the more cautious metaphysical claims of the *Phenomenology*—the respective roles of imagination and the image are remarkably similar in the two works. In each instance, Dufrenne reserves for these roles a mediatory function which is "both docile and discrete" (*P,* p. 142).

(2) *The Imaginary.* In a still later essay, "L'Imaginaire," Dufrenne takes his later project a step further. Instead of stressing the great image as an intermediary between humans and Nature, he attempts to show that the imaginary is wholly *immanent in* Nature and thus situated within what is perceived: "the imaginary is anchored in perception."[32] It is anchored there not because it allows us to anticipate unapprehended aspects of perceived objects (this is, strictly speaking, a matter of *savoir*) but because it gives to these objects themselves a different allure. Thus it is by means of the imaginary that "the mountain is perceived as Titan, the spring as Nymph, the father as *Pater omnipotens,* the earth as Mother and the Mother as Earth" (ibid., p. 126). By implication, the kind of imagination which such an imaginary would require is (like Bachelard's material imagination) one which seeks to penetrate the perceived and to transform it *from within.* For such an imagination to become operative, it must function at a strictly pre-objective level of human experience. In contrast with the contentions of the *Phenomenology,* which situated imagination exclusively on the plane of representation, this deeper type of imagining would bring us back to the pre-representational, to a primordial level at which the perceived and the imagined are not yet distinguished. At this level, the subject would imagine not by representing Nature, but by re-establishing contact with it. For we have to do with "a subject still taken up in Nature" ("L'Imaginaire," p. 131). It is at this point that *"un imaginaire profond"* can root us in Nature, for here and here alone "the imaginary is in the thing" (ibid., p. 132).

This is a radical thesis which situates Dufrenne at the opposite end of the spectrum from Sartre's efforts to link the imaginary and the unreal. If this thesis is correct, the imaginary is capable of placing us squarely within the real, albeit a real which has been amplified enormously so as to become synonymous with Nature. If this line of thought were to be followed out, the act of imagination subtending such an imaginary would no longer be merely intermediary in status. It would be profoundly primordial, residing "above all in this origin in which human beings arise, in this kingdom of primary truth that is revealed to a brute perception" (ibid., p. 117). Imagination would finally be at one with perception and no longer confined to the task of taking up the latter in representation so as to subserve understanding.

Yet this extraordinary vision of the imaginary as nested within Nature remains at the periphery of Dufrenne's thought—as it does in the quite parallel reflections to be found in Merleau-Ponty's last major work.[33] And the crucial corollary that imagining is immanent in all perceiving—echoing Kant's claim that "imagination is a necessary ingredient of perception itself"[34]—is only hinted at and does not receive the careful consideration accorded to the earlier view of imagination in the *Phenomenology*. In fact, no comparable detailed treatment of any of the expanded notions of the image, the imaginary, or imagination itself is provided in Dufrenne's later work, where scintillating suggestion replaces elaborate exposition.

Moreover, the suspicion lingers that imagining in its ordinary, everyday avatars—that is, when it does *not* have to do with great images or with the imaginary in the extended sense sketched above—is no less intermediate than it was in the initial descriptions. Even if Dufrenne does establish the case for what Paracelsus would call an *Imaginatio vera*—i.e., for a kind of imagining which might undergird an entire philosophy of Nature—mundane imagining continues to populate the daytime world with its fickle fantasies. Since little more is said of this quotidian exercise of imagination, we must assume that it remains strictly subordinate both to sensible presence (as its immediate origin) and to reflection (whether as understanding or as feeling). In other words, imagining in its most familiar form stays suppressed, and Dufrenne can still say in *Le Poétique* that "imagination is thus *only a means* of perceiving and feeling" (*P*, p. 143; my italics). And even if the great images and the imaginary, understood as emanations from Nature, do not proceed from "an imaging subjectivity" (*P*, p. 183), nevertheless the majority of images and much of the imaginary remain rooted in this subjectivity. Although it is asserted that "imagination is source" (*P*, p. 184), it is in the end no more than a secondary or even tertiary source. For imagination is still dependent upon sensible perception as origin, and perception is in turn dependent upon Nature as the ultimate source.

Therefore, in the absence of further elucidation, we are left in fundamentally the same situation as before: imagination, at least in its aesthetic and everyday uses, continues to be considered as non-originary and non-ultimate. Changing the overall project from an epistemological to an ontological framework has not altered the fate of imagination. From being an intermezzo in the symphony of mind, it has become an intermission in the drama of Nature. The tendency to regard imagining as intermediate—a tendency which links Dufrenne's theorizing with the mainstream of the Western philosophical tradition—persists even within a philosophy stressing *le sauvage*. As a result, it becomes all the more imperative to clarify the consequences of this tendency. We have seen that one of the most important of these consequences is that imagination is denied any inherent autonomy of action, being condemned to second-order status. Here a series of questions poses itself: Why must imagination thus be seen as that which is to be transcended—whether toward understanding, feeling, or Nature? Why can we not take images, quotidian or archetypal, at their face value? Why should we not accord to the imaginary, whether conceived as unreal or as embedded in Nature, the same regard we bestow upon such supposedly more ultimate terms as the perceptual, the human, or the Natural? In sum, why do we not recognize imagination as a phenomenon in its own right and not merely as an intermediary between putatively more potent psychic agencies? As these questions indicate, much of the perplexing problematic presented by imagination remains unresolved.

1. "The pursuit of the incorrigible is one of the most venerable bugbears in the history of philosophy" (J. L. Austin, *Sense and Sensibilia*, ed. G. J. Warnock [Oxford: Oxford University Press, 1962], p. 104). Cf. also John Dewey, *The Quest for Certainty* (New York: Minton & Balch, 1929), passim.

2. It should be noted that the contact in question need not be actually attainable. It suffices that it be set forth as a regulative limit, as in C. S. Peirce's notion that truth is always only *approached* and never reached as such. Thus, even if Derrida is correct in arguing that the immediacy of presence will never be given, this does not make the *ideal* of immediacy any less compelling in epistemological contexts.

3. Of course, the hierarchical model is not limited to philosophy. It has been present in biology ever since Aristotle introduced the notion of a *scala naturae*. It is equally pervasive in psychology. Thus Sigmund Freud writes: "[the human] mind is not a simple thing; on the contrary, it is a hierarchy of superordinated and subordinated agencies. . ." (*The Standard Edition of the Complete Psychological Works*, ed. J. Strachey, 24 vols. [London: Hogarth Press, 1953–74], 17: 141).

4. Immanuel Kant, *Critique of Pure Reason*, trans. N. K. Smith (New York: Humanities Press, 1950), A 138 B 177, p. 181.

5. Of this "mediating representation" Kant says: "while it must in one respect be *intellectual*, it must in another be *sensible*" (ibid.). For Plotinus, "the imaginative faculty . . . passes on information received by the senses to the discursive reason . . . [and] is somehow the bond between the upper and the lower soul" (H. J. Blumenthal, *Plotinus' Psychology* [The Hague: Nijhoff, 1971], p. 89). Descartes wrote to Mersenne in 1639 that "the imagination, which is the part of the mind that most helps mathematics, is more of a hindrance than a help in metaphysical speculation."

6. I say "attempts" because imagination reappears at the intermediate level of *dianoia*, which involves the use of images as an aid to mathematical insight. Plato's conception of *dianoia* thus anticipates Descartes' linking of imagination and mathematics as cited in the letter to Mersenne quoted above in note 5.

7. S. T. Coleridge, *Biographia Literaria*, ed. John Shawcross (Oxford: Oxford University Press, 1907), vol. I, p. 202.

8.   R. G. Collingwood, *The Principles of Art* (Oxford: Oxford University Press, 1938), p. 215. (Hereafter *PA*.) See also ibid., p. 171 and the statement on p. 198: ". . . imagination forms a kind of link between sensation and intellect, as Aristotle and Kant agreed in maintaining."

9.   Failure to focus adequately results in "corruption of consciousness," which Collingwood regards as the *radix malorum* of mind, the basis not only of bad art but also of bad faith in general. See *PA*, pp. 282–85, for a discussion which anticipates Sartre's notion of *mauvaise foi.*

10.   *PA*, pp. 222–23; my italics. Collingwood continues: "From one point of view, imagination does not differ from sensation: what we imagine is the very same kinds of things (colours, etc.) which present themselves to us in mere sensation. From another point of view, it is very different through being . . . tamed or domesticated. That which tames it is the activity of consciousness. . . ."

11.   Mikel Dufrenne, *The Phenomenology of Aesthetic Experience*, trans. E. S. Casey et al. (Evanston: Northwestern University Press, 1973), p. 345. (Hereafter *PAE*.)

12.   Martin Heidegger, *Kant et le problème de métaphysique*, trans. A. de Waelhens and W. Biemal (Paris: Gallimard, 1953), p. 188.

13.   *PAE*, p. 358. Dufrenne even goes so far as to suggest, in a sentence which foreshadows Derrida, that "the experience of presence, far from being originary, is in fact secondary" (ibid., p. 352).

14.   "Indeed, to the extent that it nourishes representation, the experience of presence provides an originary source of all knowledge by acquaintance and even of all consciousness, a source on which we constantly draw" (*PAE*, p. 351). It is at this point that the gap between Dufrenne's and Derrida's perspectives becomes evident. For Dufrenne's own discussion of Derrida, see "Pour une philosophie non théologique" in *Le Poétique*, 2d ed. (Paris: Presses Universitaires de France, 1973), pp. 7–57, esp. pp. 39–41.

15.   "The function of understanding seems to be to correct imagination. To the extent that imagination is suspect, owing to its capacity for disorder, the mingling of the perceived and the imaginary must be continually undone" (*PAE*, p. 370).

16.   *PAE*, p. 39. Cf. also ibid., p. 366: "The genuine work of art spares us the expense of an exuberant imagination."

17.   As Dufrenne says: "reflection prepares the way for and then clarifies feeling. Conversely, feeling first appeals to and then guides reflection. This alternation between reflection and feeling designates a dialectical progress toward an increasingly complete comprehension of the aesthetic object" (*PAE*, p. 423).

18.   *PAE*, p. 437. Cf. also ibid., p. 49: "the very height of aesthetic perception is found in the feeling which reveals the expressiveness of the work."

19.   For the notion of communion, see *PAE*, p. 228; for the idea of feeling as "this reciprocity of two depths," see ibid., p. 483.

20.   "All perception is simultaneously imagination" (*PAE*, p. 541).

21.   Henri Corbin, *L'imagination créatrice dans le soufisme d'Ibn Arabi* (Paris: Flammarion, 1958), p. 161. The more complete statement is "Mais sous quelque aspect, à quelque degré ou phase que nous considérions l'Imagination, que ce soit . . . en sa fonction cosmique, ou que ce comme puissance imaginative dans l'homme, sa caractéristique est constante, et nous l'avons déjà relevée: c'est sa nature et fonction d'intermédiaire."

22.   Cf. *PAE*, pp. 369 ff.; *PA*, pp. 223–24.

23.   Aristotle, *De Anima* 431 a 16.

24.   Whether these stages are depicted in a horizontally or a vertically structured model is a matter of indifference. Normally, however, and especially in the two cases at hand, the model is implicitly vertical in its directionality.

25.   For Collingwood's presentation of this notion, see *An Essay on Philosophical Method* (Oxford: Oxford University Press, 1933), esp. Part III. (Hereafter *EM*.) It is a remarkable fact that Collingwood does not apply the scale of forms to his own scalar epistemology in *The Principles of Art*. For the historical development of the scale of forms, see Arthur Lovejoy,

The Great Chain of Being (Cambridge: Harvard University Press, 1953), esp. chap. 1–3. Lovejoy stresses its Greek and medieval origins.

26. On the question of imagination's autonomy, see my "Imagination: Imagining and the Image" (*Philosophy and Phenomenological Research* [1970]) and "Toward a Phenomenology of Imagination," in this volume.

27. *PA*, p. 171; my italics. As if to underline this punctiform nature of imagining, Collingwood repeats himself by speaking of imagination as "the point at which the life of thought makes contact with the life of purely psychical experience" (*PA*, p. 215).

28. On "great images" see esp. Mikel Dufrenne, *Language and Philosophy*, trans. H. B. Veatch (Bloomington: Indiana University Press, 1963), pp. 91 ff.; as well as *Le Poétique*, pp. 135, 186 ff., 233–37. (Hereafter *Le Poétique* will be referred to as *P*.) All subsequent translations from this work and others are my own.

29. *P*, p. 233. Dufrenne continues: "the perceived is an image through and through, yet without irrealizing the rest or converting it into the imaginary" (ibid.).

30. "Qui imagine, ici, sinon la Nature même?" (*P*, p. 234).

31. On the primacy of feeling over imagination, the following passage is crucial: "to avoid the particularity of the image, to do justice to the sensuous richness of the word and to the polyvalence of meaning, and also to express the proximity of what is evoked, I prefer another term: feeling" (*P*, p. 91).

32. Mikel Dufrenne, "L'imaginaire." This essay is published in Dufrenne's *Esthétique et Philosophie* (Paris: Klincksieck, 1976), vol. II, pp. 99–132.

33. See Maurice Merleau-Ponty, *Le visible et l'invisible* (Paris: Gallimard, 1964), pp. 49–51, 62, 298, 316, 320.

34. Kant, *Critique of Pure Reason*, p. 144 n.

Imagination, Fantasy, Hallucination,
and Memory

IT IS A QUITE remarkable fact that many previous philosophies and psychologies of mind, however perspicuous or profound they may be in other ways, have failed to provide adequate accounts of basic differences between imagining, remembering, hallucinating, and fantasying. Even the most elementary descriptions of such differences are often lacking. Perhaps it has been presumed that the four acts in question are so closely affiliated as not to need descriptive differentiation. In this vein, they are frequently regarded as sibling acts having the same progenitor: perception. Yet each of the acts is related to perception very differently, ranging from apparent replication (in hallucination) to distinct discontinuity (in imagination). It is not my present purpose, however, to delineate this particular series of relationships. Rather, in this chapter I shall concentrate on eidetic differences between imagining on the one hand and memory, hallucination, and fantasy on the other. Each of the latter three acts will be described in terms of its most salient features, features which serve to distinguish it from imagining in fundamental respects.[1] Thus the present project represents an exercise in the comparative phenomenology of mind—a neglected but important part of the eidetics of human experience.

I

Memory and imagination have long been regarded as psychical partners, as mates of the mind. Ever since Aristotle conjoined them under the common yoke of "experience,"[2] philosophers and psychologists have attempted to keep them together in a conjugal state by making two sorts of claim: either that the two acts are in fact one and the same act (though viewed from different perspectives) or that they differ in degree only. The first, more extreme, claim is made by Hobbes:

> This *decaying sense,* when wee should express the thing it self, (I mean *fancy* it selfe) wee call *Imagination.* . . . But when we would express the *decay,* and signifie that the Sense is fading, old, and past, it is called *Memory.* So that *Imagination* and *Memory* are but one thing, which for divers considerations hath diverse names.[3]

Imagination and memory "are but one thing" because both are immediate derivatives of "sense" or sensation, "The Originall of them all."[4] They differ only according to whether more stress is placed upon the *content* of decaying sense (i.e., "fancy it selfe") or upon the decay per se. Otherwise, they are identical—merely two aspects of the same thing. As Vico was to put it almost a century later: "Memory is the same as imagination" because imagination itself is "nothing but extended or compounded memory."[5] Yet what both Hobbes and Vico overlook are the felt differences that emerge in the actual experience of the two acts.

The second claim is more difficult to dispute. That memory and imagination differ only in degree is a thesis which has had perennial appeal. It informs the opinion of a contemporary psychologist, who writes that "the difference between [mental images] and memory images is one of degree and not absolute."[6] But the *locus classicus* is found in Hume's *Treatise of Human Nature,* where it is argued that "the ideas of the memory are much more lively and strong than those of the imagination."[7] Here a difference in vivacity—which is a difference in degree, being a matter of comparative sensory intensity—becomes the criterion for distinguishing imagination from memory. Yet Hume calls this very criterion into question by recognizing borderline cases in which relative vivacity is no longer an adequate basis for distinction:

> And as an idea of the memory, by losing its force and vivacity, may degenerate to such a degree, as to be taken for an idea of the imagination; so on the other hand an idea of the imagination may acquire such a force and vivacity, as to pass for an idea of the memory.[8]

If memory and imagination are not to be differentiated in terms of relative vivacity alone, how then do they differ? Are there more deep-going differences between the two acts which Hume and others overlook? To single out such differences is not to deny that imagining and remembering possess several features in common. Each act can occur in a spontaneous or in a controlled manner—as ordinary language indicates by distinguishing between "instant" or "involuntary" recall and the effort to "search one's memory."[9] Further, each act can alter, compound, or dissociate content that is borrowed initially from perception, though memory is largely restricted to modifying the sequence in which such content was originally experienced. There is, in addition, a similarity of act-forms: we can imagine or remember isolated objects and events, imagine or remember *that* a certain state of affairs took place, and even imagine or remember *how* something happened or was experienced. We should also notice that sensuous imagery is not any more essential to memory than it is to imagination; recollection can occur abstractly, as when I remember the "atmosphere" of a former situation or recall the answer to a problem in mathematics without summoning up any specific number-images.

Beyond these obvious similarities, however, there remain at least five fundamental differences between memory and imagination.

(i) *Rootedness in Perception.* Not only *can* memory borrow its content from perception; in most cases it *must* do so. To remember an object or event is almost always to summon back before the mind what was once in fact perceived. (In the relatively few instances when this is not the case, we recall a former fantasy or thought, although there is a tendency even here to remember the perceptual surroundings as well.) The prior perceptions upon which most remembering is founded influence not just its temporal direction (memory is exclusively past-oriented—see [ii]), but also its thetic character (see [v]), its corrigibility (recollection, like perception, can be correct or incorrect), and its ability to change its own content (an ability which is delimited by considerations of fidelity to what was originally perceived). All of these features of remembering reflect its basis in previous perceivings, and they represent distinctive divergences from imagining, which is less constricted and more maneuverable in regard to each such feature: we need not imagine what is past or real, and what we imagine is not subject to criteria of corrigibility or of fidelity to former experience.

(ii) *Link to the Past.* A crucial consequence of the close connection between memory and perception is to be found in the basic temporal character of memory. Just as perception has to do with the *in*-sistence of objects or events which appear or occur in the present, so memory has to do with the *per*-sistence of objects or events which first appeared or occurred in the past. Such persistence is in turn founded upon two factors. First, whatever persists as the specific content of memory must possess a certain minimal obduracy—a perseverance over time, even if this perseverance occurs solely in the mind. Secondly, the temporal field in which remembered content is presently given to one is ultimately continuous with the particular temporal field within which this content was first experienced at an earlier and precisely datable point. For both the original field of experience and the present field of recollection (which may resemble each other only insofar as it is the *same* object or event that is experienced-and-remembered) form part of a single temporal continuum. No matter how distant in time the two fields may be from each other, we are assured that intermediate fields serve to connect the original field with the one in which our remembering now occurs. The resulting continuum from past occurrence to present remembrance provides a unified foundation for the persistence of remembered material.

In imagining, there is a notable absence of both of these factors. Nothing, strictly speaking, persists in imaginative experience, whose content lacks the fixity and stability of remembered content. In their fluidity and fleetingness, imagined objects and events exhibit none of the obduracy or perseverance of the things we remember, and they are not datable and locatable in any measurably precise fashion. Further, there is nothing in imaginative experience that is meaningfully comparable to a perduring temporal field in which entities or events can arise, last, and be focused upon in an intersubjectively confirmable way. Consequently, a given imaginative experience does not necessarily intermesh with the imaginer's past experiences: in fact, it is normally quite discontinuous with the temporal fields in which these experiences took place. Yet, by the same token, precisely because what we imagine is not something that has persisted from the past and does not belong to a backward-reaching continuum of linked temporal fields, it is free to arise and develop in a less confined manner than is what we remember. In exercising memory we revert, implicitly or explicitly, to particular points of reference as factual-historical supports: I remember Jones standing on the dock, at such-and-such a time of day, etc. These referential points, which help to situate whatever it is that we recollect, *cannot be transposed* once they are established by the original appearance or occurrence of a given object or event. Imagined objects and events, in contrast, are not attached to any such fixed original positions and may be freely transported from one imaginative presentation to another.[10]

(iii) *Retentionality.* The term "retentionality" brings together two closely related features that are both inherent in the temporality of memory: retentiveness and the retentional fringe. Neither of these features has any counterpart in imagination. *Retentiveness* refers to the capacity to retain a former experience in mind (though not necessarily consciously in mind) so as to be able to recall it on subsequent occasions. Thus retentiveness is a "dispositional" term in the sense that it indicates what memory *puts at our disposition* through its powers of retention. These powers are considerable, and it has even been argued that in some sense we retain everything we have ever experienced. At the very least, we cannot fail to be struck by the way in which many of our prior experiences are preserved in a form that is, in Freud's phrase, "astonishingly intact."[11] At the same time, retentiveness makes possible the assimilation of cognitive, perceptual, and motor skills; once they are thoroughly learned, we need not recollect explicitly *how* we first learned them.[12] Retentiveness, we might say, is the means by which we hold the past ready for reactivation in the present. As such, it is the basis for all explicit recollection.[13]

The *retentional fringe,* on the other hand, is that element or phase of a just-past experience that lingers on in each successively new 'now'; it is the immediately preceding moment as it fades from focus. William James describes the retentional fringe as "the rearward portion of the present space of time,"[14] and Husserl (who terms it "retention" or "primary memory") likens it to "a comet's tail which clings onto the perception of the [present] moment."[15] The retentional fringe is essential to retentiveness, for an experience lacking a retentional fringe would not possess sufficient temporal density or distention to be retained for future recall. Moreover, far from being restricted to a role in retentiveness and recall, the retentional fringe shows itself to be operative in all areas of mental life: *every psychical phenomenon has its retentional fringe.* This fringe helps to constitute the felt continuity that is ingredient to some degree in all forms of human experience. For no single characteristic of imagining can a comparable universality be claimed. In fact, it is evident that imagining functions more as an alternative to, than as an accompaniment of, other mental acts. None of its essential features figures as an invariant dimension of other types of experience, while it is itself subject to retentionality in both senses of the term: a given imaginative experience is retained indefinitely and it possesses its own retentional fringe.

(iv) *Familiarity.* Another distinctive, but more delimited, trait of memory is familiarity, i.e., the fact that what we remember is always something with which we are already acquainted to some degree. Unless we were at least minimally familiar with the objects and events we recollect, we could not be said to re-member them—that is, to put them back together in a way that is faithful to the original experience, as well as becoming once more their contemporary (though now only via an intermediary act of recollection). In short, to be remembered something must form part of the rememberer's *own* past experience. As James puts it: "Memory requires more than mere dating of a fact in the past. It must be dated in *my* past. In other words, I must think that I, directly, experienced its occurrence."[16] The familiarity underlying memory thus involves a personal relationship with remembered content, a relationship characterized by what James calls "warmth and intimacy" and Russell "trust."[17]

Familiarity is closely related to retentionality as described above. First of all, familiarity presupposes retentiveness insofar as any object or event with which we are familiar is one whose acquaintance we have retained over a given period of time. Secondly, familiarity involves the retentional fringe because we could never have *become* familiar with a particular object or event in the first place unless the experience of this object or event had been allowed to linger ("sink down" into our mind, as Husserl says) long enough for familiarity to be established.

As a form of personal relationship with the content of past experience, familiarity decisively demarcates remembering from imagining. For familiarity is indispensable to memory but dispensable in imagination. I can imagine something with which I am not at all familiar (i.e., which has never been present in my experience), but I cannot remember anything with which I am not acquainted or familiar in some way and to some extent. It comes as no surprise, therefore, to discover that a number of philosophers "have regarded this same sense of familiarity as the feature which distinguishes memory from imagination."[18] All that needs qualification in this assertion is that familiarity is not the *only* feature that differentiates the one act from the other.

(v) *Belief.* By "belief" I refer to the characteristic thetic activity of remembering. In this usage, I follow Hume's lead: "The *belief* or *assent,* which always attends the memory and senses . . . alone distinguishes them from the imagination."[19] But if such belief, in line with the critical remarks made previously, is not to be reduced to what Hume calls the "vivacity of perceptions," in what does it consist? Is it only a matter, as James claims, of "feeling" or "emotion"?[20] Also, and more crucially, involved in mnemonic belief is a specific cognitive operation by which we attribute a particular thetic character to what we recall. When I remember an object or event, and whether I do so with effort or spontaneously, I take this object or event to be something that once actually appeared or occurred in my presence. I accept or take it as possessing the thetic quality of *having-been-part-of-my-past-experience.*

This thetic character is unique to memory and is intimately bound up with the four characteristics of remembering outlined in preceding sections. It is related, first of all, to prior perceptual experience, for to believe in the empirical existence of something requires that it be (or have been) perceived or at least perceivable. As Freud says laconically, "Belief in reality is bound up with perception through the senses."[21] Second, belief in the content of memory as having-been-part-of-my-past-experience carries with it the presumption that my present act of recollection is temporally continuous, through a series of interlacing time-fields, with the original experience I am now recalling; the absence of such continuity might lead me to doubt the authenticity of my memory. Third, belief in the past reality of what I remember presupposes retentionality; I believe that something actually has been because it has been "retained" in both of the primary meanings of this term. Finally, and perhaps most tellingly, I lend mnemonic credence to what I am familiar with through former (and perhaps continuing) acquaintance. To be familiar with the content of memory is to be in a position to posit this content as authentically having-been-part-of-my-past.

As Husserl recognized, the verb "to posit" (*setzen*) is of critical importance in any consideration of thetic activity. To say that I believe in the reality of what I recall is to say that I posit it, i.e., set it forth, as existent-in-my-past—just as I posit the content of anticipation as existent-in-my-future. Both forms of "positing presentification" (to use Husserl's technical term) are thus to be distinguished from the non-positing presentifications of imagining, picturing, and sign-activity.[22] This suggests a final formulation of the difference between memory and imagination in regard to their respective thetic activities. In remembering, I believe in, or posit, as existing in my personal past that which presents itself (or more exactly, that which is presentified) now in the present; in imagining, I do no such thing:

not only do I not posit imagined content as having-been, I do not posit it as existing in *any* sense or at *any* time.

Memory, we may conclude, is the *Janus bifrons* of mind. It gazes (and gazes most insistently) in one direction: toward the pole of perception, from which it derives the features of temporal order, familiarity, and belief that have been expounded in the pages above. But it also looks in a quite different direction: toward the pole of imagination, with which it shares such features as presentification, the option of spontaneity / controlledness, various act-forms, and the non-essentiality of imagery. This double directedness of memory appears graphically if we attempt to represent Husserl's classificatory system in a diagrammatic form:

positing acts	presentifying acts
memory perception	memory imagination

In contrast with perception and imagination, which are single placeholders, memory appears twice in this schema. It is at once positing and presentifying, just as it is at once reality-bound (in terms of its origin in prior perceptions) and reality-free (insofar as it does not actually present, but only presentifies, an experience of the real). Given such strict ambivalence, it is not surprising that memory has been forced into ambiguous alliances by philosophers and psychologists—being made to side sometimes with perception and sometimes (indeed, more frequently) with imagination. In view of the foregoing analysis, however, it should be recognized as distinct and distinguishable from perception and imagination alike.

II

Hallucination is an experience which presents itself as even more akin to perception than is memory. Many of those who have attempted to determine the nature of hallucinating consider it to be, in fact, a species of perception. "Perception without an object" has been a classical definition of hallucination, frequently found in the literature on the subject.[23] Freud remarks that hallucinatory dream-images are "more like perceptions than they are like mnemonic presentations," and he tries to demonstrate that these images are, in the final analysis, reactivated perceptions.[24] A representative recent pronouncement is that "a hallucination is an internal image

that seems as real, vivid, and external as the perception of an object."[25]
To bear this out, the author furnishes the following report of a full-blown
hallucination:

> I was staring off into space, then I saw my brother in the corner of the
> room. His mouth moved but I heard no words. I spoke to him and he
> didn't answer. He just stood there, about eight feet away from me. Then
> he kind of fogged up and disappeared.[26]

Such a statement helps us to understand why so many writers on the
subject have taken hallucinations to be forms of perception. For the report
indicates that the hallucinated brother-figure appeared in the hallucinator's
ordinary perceptual space ("in the corner of the room"), as if he occupied
a position along with, or in place of, everyday objects of perception; it
also disappeared from this same perceived area by "fogging up." Here what
is hallucinated and what is perceived are on a par, and seem to coexist,
with each other.

The perceptual or at least quasi-perceptual status of hallucinations is
at once their most striking and their most perplexing characteristic. It may
lead us to ask: How can something that is nonperceptual in nature be taken
as perceived? Fortunately, a phenomenological investigation need not
provide an answer to this question. All that such an investigation must
concern itself with is the fact *that* hallucinations present themselves as
perceptions. From this fact, which contrasts so vividly with the situation
in imagining (where nothing presents itself as perceptual), we may derive
the following five features of hallucinatory experience, none of which has
an exact counterpart in imaginative experience.

(i) *Paranormality.* The vast majority of hallucinations come tinged with
the pathological. It is clear that to hallucinate is not just to fall into perceptual *illusion,* which may be a natural and normal part of perceptual experience. It is to depart radically from the usual course of perceiving and
to enter into an experience which it is natural to consider abnormal vis-à-
vis the usual norms and practices of perception. To be more accurate,
though, we should call hallucinating a "paranormal" activity, where the
"para" stresses that the activity takes place "beside" normal perceptual activity. Hallucinations arise *alongside* ordinary perceptions, or they *replace*
them for the time being. When this occurs in waking life, the suspicion
of pathology is difficult to suppress, whether the hallucination is a positive
one (as in the case just cited) or a negative one (as when the Wolf Man
hallucinated that he had cut off one of his fingers).[27] Even hallucinatory
dream-images, which emerge every night in the lives of non-pathological
as well as pathological human subjects, are considered by Freud to be quite
analogous to "hallucinatory wish psychosis" and to furnish a paradigm
for psychoneurotic symptoms.[28]
Nevertheless, the paranormal character of hallucinating need not be

pathological in any strict clinical or nosological sense. There is a whole group of hallucinatory experiences which, while potentially disruptive, are not signs or symptoms of sickness of any kind. These include vivid entoptic images ("phosphenes"), after-images and eidetic images, hallucinations induced under hypnosis, déjà vu experiences, various synesthetic sensations, misreadings of written texts (these are often species of negative hallucination, as in imperfect proofreading), phantom limbs, imaginary companions, "dream scintillations," and religious visions.[29] None of these varied experiences is inherently pathological, and yet each is a genuine instance of hallucination inasmuch as its perceptual or quasi-perceptual nature is able to arrest our attention and divert it from absorption in present perceptual experience. By thus competing with ordinary perception, such experiences remain paranormal. From this we may conclude that, whether pathological or not, hallucinations differ distinctly from acts of imagining. The latter, lacking thetic commitment to the empirically real, typically do not interfere with or interrupt acts of perceiving. Imagined objects or events never appear as if existing in the perceptual world, much less as replacing actually perceived items in this world. Therefore, imagining cannot be considered paranormal, since it does not distort or divert perceiving or threaten to take its place. In its inherent innocence, imagination neither rivals nor replicates perception.

(ii) *Sensory Vivacity.* It follows from what has just been said that unless hallucinations achieve a certain sensory intensity they cannot be compared with, or substitute themselves for, perceptions. To invoke "intensity" and "vivacity" might seem to land us in the same difficulty in which Hume became ensnared when he tried to distinguish imagination from memory. But it is not here a question of establishing a *scale* of carefully graduated sensory intensities on which to locate various mental acts at different points. Rather, it is only a matter of attesting that *in a given situation* (and therefore allowing for differences from situation to situation) a hallucination must display sufficient vividness to allow it to enter into competition with our ongoing perceptual activity. It must be rich enough in sensory qualities to claim our committed awareness, to make us believe in it as a bona fide form of perception. Thus, a dream image need not be as sensuously vivid as a positive hallucination occurring in broad daylight. In the former case, the level of sensory vividness can be considerably diminished, thanks to what Freud called the "motor paralysis" of sleep. With our normal waking sensory channels mostly closed off, our mind is more easily attracted by a comparatively dim presentation. In the latter case, in contrast, the hallucination must appear vividly enough to be accepted as an actual or possible occupant of the daylight world.[30]

In imagining, there is no competition of any sort with perceiving. For one thing, we can imagine and perceive *concurrently*—so long as we are not attempting to imagine and perceive the same thing in the same respect.

Imagined content is not experienced as occupying part of our present perceptual field, much less as taking it over. Further, what we imagine need not be sensory in character. By imagining nonsensuously, we diminish still further the opportunity for any direct competition with perception. To imagine an abstract state of affairs as purely possible is ipso facto to leave the domain of perception—and any domain built upon, or analogous to, perception. Hallucinating, on the other hand, knows no such freedom from perceptual or quasi-perceptual domains. Hallucinations always appear in a specific sensory form, where the meaning of "sensory" includes reference to all of the following factors: "space, time, direction, distance, obtrusiveness, mineness, motion, measurability, and objectivity."[31] No such set of strictly perceptual parameters structures the mini-worlds of imagination.

(iii) *Projectedness.* Still another basic characteristic of hallucinations is that their contents are experienced as "out there," as projected presences existing externally to the hallucinator's consciousness. Thus Freud asserts that a dream (his prototype for all hallucinating) is "a *projection:* an externalization of an internal process."[32] Further, "dreams construct a *situation* out of [hallucinatory] images; they represent an event which is actually happening."[33] An event actually occurring in a situation takes place *outside* oneself as its observer; it is located externally to the perceiving self— as if arising *beyond* this self. Since a hallucinated event does *not* in fact occur in an actual situation, it has to be projected by the hallucinating subject as occurring there. "Projectedness" names the resulting pseudo-externality, which characterizes everything from the elaborate visual displays of LSD hallucinations to "autoscopic" observations of one's own body from an external point in space. What psychologists or physiologists would regard as located *inside* one's mind or body is projected outward until the equivalent of an authentically perceived object or event is felt to be present.[34]

Imaginative experience does not contain anything comparable to such thoroughgoing projectedness of content. We may speak of "projecting" possible objects and states of affairs in imagining, but such *possibilia* are not projected as constituents of actual situations external to the imaginer. Far from inhabiting a concrete setting, imagined possibilities are typically projected into a spatio-temporal limbo that is felt to be neither external nor internal to the imaginer. When I imagine how to row a boat (and even when I do so in sensory detail), the scene I summon up lacks the distinctive situatedness of something hallucinated. Even if I expressly attempt to project a state of affairs that is at some significant distance from myself— and perhaps even partly superimposed on an actual perceptual scene— what I imagine still lacks the sense of obdurate otherness that is found as a matter of course in hallucinated scenes. And I can always, by a further effort, overcome this imaginary distance and make myself one with the imaginatively projected situation—which I cannot do readily, if at all, in hallucinating the same situation.

(iv) *Involuntariness*. With rare exceptions, hallucinations arise without our express volition. This may happen in various circumstances—in psychopathological states or when hypnotized, asleep, drugged, etc.—but whatever the causes or conditions of hallucinations they tend to emerge spontaneously and beyond our conscious control. Indeed, they often appear so rapidly and with so little warning that we are astounded or shocked that any such thing could happen. (Contrast this reaction with the character-istically *mild* surprise that occurs in imagining.) Furthermore, our ability to control or terminate hallucinations once they have appeared is usually quite limited: witness the "voices" of the schizophrenic patient, auditory presences that mercilessly pursue and threaten.[35] Hallucinations may also recur with distressing and unpredictable frequency, as in Sartre's persisting hallucinations of crabs (occasioned by mescaline).[36] There is little, if anything, that the hallucinating subject can do to ward off these unwelcome *revenants*—in contrast with imaginative experience, where the obsessive recurrence of an imagined object can be dealt with much more effectively. In fact, as imaginers, we are normally able to terminate, once and for all, a given imaginative appearance; and even if we cannot do this, we can alter the subsequent course of this appearance.

(v) *Belief*. The involuntariness of hallucinatory experience reflects its predominant thetic activity—belief in the empirical reality of its content. Voltaire remarked that hallucinating "is not seeing in imagination: it is seeing in reality."[37] And "seeing in reality" entails believing that what one apprehends is present to one's senses as spatio-temporally existent. As Es-quirol said in 1833, "A man who has the inner conviction of a sensation actually perceived while no object fitting for its excitation is at the threshold of his senses, such a man is in a condition of hallucinating."[38] Or as Freud put it much more pithily, "Hallucination brings belief in reality with it."[39]

Hallucination involves belief in the empirically real precisely because of the vivid sensory quality of hallucinated content.[40] We adhere to the reality of what we hallucinate inasmuch as it appears to us not only as the sort of thing that *could be* perceived (this is true of many things we imagine) but as *actually* perceived. By "actually" is meant perceived *in the present* as an occupant of the very same spatio-temporal field in which one is situated oneself. In this way, the hallucinator's belief is to be distinguished from the sort of thetic activity that inheres in either memory or imagina-tion. In contrast with mnemonic belief, hallucinatory belief does not bear on realities in their pastness (i.e., as having-been-present-in-my-past) but on realities that appear (or *appear* to appear) at the present moment. As contrasted with what happens in imagining, in hallucinating we place credence in the existence of *some* presently appearing object or event; we do not suspend committed belief altogether and entertain pure possibilities. If we include anticipation in a schema for comparing different types of thetic character, we arrive at the following diagrammatic result:

Type of Act or Activity	(Empirical) Reality			Possibility
Thetic Character and Temporal Mode	present	past	future	omnitemporal
perception	X			
hallucination	X			
memory		X		
anticipation			X	
imagination				X

Does this mean, as the diagram suggests, that there is *no distinction* to be made between the belief-character of hallucination and that of perception? Here we are forced to recognize that there are in fact two forms of hallucinatory belief. The first is experientially indistinguishable from perceptual belief; occurring in what is called colloquially a "full-blown hallucination," it involves the same fully committed credence in empirical reality that characterizes ordinary perception. The second form of hallucinatory belief is less intensely committed in character; in this case, the hallucinator remains able to distinguish between what is hallucinated and what is actually perceived. The paradox is that the hallucinated content, even though distinguishable from what is genuinely perceived, is still regarded as real. The patient who does not confuse his recurrent hallucinations of a person dressed in a certain way and standing under his window with bona fide perceptions of just such a person actually standing under his window nevertheless maintains that both presences are real: "Yes, there is someone there, but it's someone else."[41] Qualitative distinctness does not preclude the belief that both forms of presence are empirically real, as we can also observe in many cases of "hearing voices": the hallucinated voices are experienced as real (i.e., encroaching on one's senses from the outside, occurring in the present, etc.) and at the same time as different from ordinary, authentically perceived human voices. Indeed, it may be this very difference that accounts for the frequently reported "eeriness" of numerous hallucinatory experiences. The implication, in any case, is that the thetic character of empirical reality possesses sufficient ambiguity or latitude to allow it to be the object of at least two different forms or modes of belief, one of which is common to perception and full-blown hallucination while the other is peculiar to a less intense type of hallucination.

No such overlap of belief-forms emerges when we compare hallucination or perception with imagination, which does not in any way involve belief in empirical reality. The imaginer remains content to posit pure possibilities. It is clear that the natural alliance between perceiving and hallucinating in this regard, and thus the basis for their mutual differentiation from imagining, is to be found in the fact that hallucination not only resembles perception but seems to provide a form of surrogate perceptual experience. This is why we are often tempted to term hallucinatory experience "quasi-perceptual," where the "quasi" indicates that the hallucinated content may in certain cases be taken as fully valid perceptual content. We might say that hallucination fashions a world *like* the perceptual world, and one that momentarily usurps its place, even though such a world is in fact no world at all. In this, the hallucinator departs widely from the imaginer, whose mentated mini-worlds neither resemble the perceptual world nor replace it with something quasi-real.

III

Of the various psychical phenomena with which imagination may be compared, fantasy is no doubt the most ambiguous and difficult to define. "Fantasy" is a polysemous word which in ordinary parlance denotes a variety of acts ranging from near-hallucinatory and quite involving experiences, through reveries and daydreams, to mere "passing fancies."[42] Because of this equivocality, attempts at strict definition are in danger of effecting premature foreclosure. Consider, for example, one recent attempt:

> Fantasy is defined as verbal reports of all mentation whose ideational products are not evaluated by the subject in terms of their usefulness in advancing some immediate goal extrinsic to the mentation itself.[43]

Conspicuous in this statement is its entirely negative character; we are told what fantasy is *not*, not what it is. Moreover, the single criterion mentioned—not evaluating results of mental activity in terms of usefulness—is so general as also to apply to imagining as well as to hallucination and even to memory. Greater specificity is clearly called for.

When we try to become more specific, however, we notice that the ambiguity of fantasy is not only verbal. It is also, and more importantly, *phenomenal*. For human experience includes a whole series of phenomena which can be considered types of fantasy, from children's "theories" about the adult world to the Walter Mitty daydreams of adults themselves. Compounding the problem is the fact that these phenomena are not always readily isolatable from each other. They tend to overlap in such a way as to make strict separation extremely difficult:

> There are many transitional forms. . . . Fantasying shades into remembering when it uses memories and when the inaccuracies of memory are fantasies. For corresponding reasons, fantasying shades into perceiving, anticipating, and planning.[44]

Nevertheless, fantasy tends to ally itself more with certain mental activities than with others; it is not indifferently connectable with all such activities. In particular, it has a tendency to border on *hallucination* on the one hand and on *imagination* on the other. In the former case, a fantasy becomes increasingly involving, dramatic, and sensuously vivid. It draws the subject into its grip in such a way that he or she is on the verge of losing control of the experience, which may then become fully hallucinatory.[45] But there is a second possibility as well—namely, the conversion of fantasy into imagination. Such a conversion typically occurs in daydreams or reveries, when what had been a full-fledged fantasy suddenly becomes an experience in which the autonomous action of the subject is much more prominent than in fantasy proper. The daydream or reverie ceases to be as engrossing as before and is experienced as something merely entertained (hence more easily controllable) by the now-imagining subject.

But here we must ask: What *is* fantasy if it is still distinguishable from hallucination and imagination? Even while admitting that fantasy is exceedingly difficult to pinpoint in its pure state (Sartre would call it "metastable"),[46] we may single out five distinctive characteristics.

(i) *Narrative Character.* Perhaps the single most striking feature of fantasies is their tendency to tell a story. This feature is based on their sequential structure, which contrasts with the fragmentariness of most hallucinating and imagining. In fantasy, individual episodes are woven together to realize a more or less coherent story line, instead of being allowed to appear in isolation. A representative fantasy is given in the following autobiographical account of Jerome Singer's:

> Within the format of [my] fantasied football games, Poppy Ott emerged as the super-star, the shifty-hipped, clever broken-field runner and accurate passer. As time passed the overt motor representation of an imagined game was no longer socially feasible and I began to draw the game on paper in cartoon form. I would visualize an entire league series, draw significant highlights from each game, occasionally write out play-by-play accounts of the games, and keep statistics on the various achievements of my fantasy players in the same way that the newspapers do for running or passing averages. As I grew into adolescence, Poppy Ott, who was supposedly a few years older than I was, grew up too. He left Tutter to play professional football and, after some well-documented setbacks, emerged as the greatest football player of all time on a Boston professional team of my own creation.[47]

Several significant aspects of this "Poppy Ott" fantasy should be noticed. First of all, it was initially inspired by Singer's boyhood reading of a series of children's books which featured Poppy Ott as one of the principal characters. Not only did Singer borrow the fictitious personage of Ott from these books, but also he placed Ott into fantasies which by their very form and structure continued the narrative mode of the original stories. It was as if the fantasies took over at the point where the stories left off. Secondly, in the early stages of his Ott fantasies, Singer depicted their content in dramatized actions, drawings, or in words. Only later did he turn to visualizing as the predominant mode in which to realize these fantasies. Moreover, the fantasies were not unrelated to actual events in Singer's life; for example, they appeared especially frequently during the football season. In all of these ways—i.e., by dramatization, drawing, and writing, and by correlation with actual events—Singer drew on resources which reinforced the inner continuity, sequential character, and general credibility of his fantasy experiences. The result was that "the entire fantasy sequence settled into a fairly circumscribed pattern. In high school and even into adult life I would deal with situations that were monotonous or dull by resorting consciously to playing out a particular game in which Poppy Ott starred."[48]

No such "circumscribed pattern" characterizes imaginative experiences, which lack the fundamental consistency and coherency of fantasies of the sort Singer describes. Indeed, it is even questionable whether we can be said to imagine the *same* object or event again and again, and any sense of a perduring spatial or temporal "field" in which a narrated action could take place is lacking in imaginative presentations. Thus, without any basis for recurrency or spatio-temporal stability, it is very difficult to superimpose a narrative form on what we imagine. For such a form to "take," a certain continuity in content and manner of presentation is required. In the absence of such continuity, isolated episodes may appear, but they will not fit together to constitute anything like a story. The result is that imaginings are inherently non-narrative in character; episodic at best (though often much more fleeting even than this), they disintegrate too quickly to possess a strictly narrative structure—"one glimpse and vanished."[49]

(ii) *Sense of Participation.* The tales that are told in fantasies differ from explicitly literary tales in two important regards. First, there is not a comparable concern with *form* in the two cases. Literary tales are fashioned with an eye to their formal perfection, and part of our pleasure in coming to know them stems from our apprehending their well-crafted formal qualities. Fantasies are, as it were, *purely narrative,* stories spun solely for the sake of their content—a content which is typically, as Freud observed, either erotic or ambitious in tenor.[50] At the same time, they often give the impression of "taking their own course," that is, proceeding without the express direction of the fantasist.

Secondly, fantasied stories always involve the fantasist himself or herself as a participant in their narrated scenes. This fantasist (who is none other than "His Majesty the Ego")[51] represents himself as partaking in the unfolding action of the fantasy in either of two ways. On the one hand, he may do so straightforwardly by depicting himself as present *in person* in the fantasy, as one of its *dramatis personae*—though the exact nature of this presence varies considerably from fantasy to fantasy. On the other hand, the fantasist may participate in the fantasied action *by proxy,* either by identifying himself with one of its presented personages (e.g., Poppy Ott) or by designating one of these personages as his delegate or representative (e.g., as when the fantasist thinks to himself, "That's my type of man").

A further and closely related phenomenon is found in what psycho-analysts call "reflective self representation," that is, a distinct sense of oneself as separate from the self that is represented (directly or indirectly) in the fantasied scenes. This peculiar self-consciousness is by no means constantly present—it tends to come and go—but it is always felt to be within reach: "the suspension of the reflective self representation is temporary or oscillating, or, in other terms, easily and effortlessly reversible."[52]

These aspects of participation in fantasy may be contrasted with what happens in imagining and hallucinating, especially the latter. In hallucinating, the subject typically feels himself or herself to be the passive recipient or victim of external forces over which he or she has no control (hence their frequently frightening character). Only rarely does one represent oneself as *participating,* in person or by proxy, in a hallucinated scene. In fact, one's sense of self-identity may be so weak that one feels that a dead or depersonalized self is being attacked by the threatening forces. The imaginer, on the other hand, normally retains a quite intact sense of self-identity. Indeed, his or her reflective self representation may be even more pronounced than that of the fantasist, particularly during experiences of controlled imagining: '*I* am imagining this,' one is implicitly saying to oneself at such moments. By the same token, and perhaps as a consequence of this secure self-consciousness, there is a tendency for the imaginer *not* to represent himself or herself as a participant in the imaginatively projected scene. This is not to deny that one may do so on occasion, especially when one imagines *how* it is to be in a certain imagined situation. Yet if imagining-how thereby requires one's participation, this is not the case with regard to simple visualizing or imagining *that* such-and-such obtains. These latter spread before the imaginer momentary scenes of which he or she is the mere witness, situated at their edge as it seems. In such instances, one does not depict himself as a participant in the ongoing action.

(iii) *Waywardness.* By this term, I refer to the specific character of control which the fantasist experiences vis-à-vis his or her fantasy. In contrast with both fantasy and imagination, hallucination allows for very little conscious control, arising as an externally imposed and often overwhelming experience. It is true that certain hallucinations may be elicited at will, but once having emerged even these have a way of taking over the whole of one's awareness and of vanishing unpredictably and independently of one's volition. Fantasies are subject to considerably more control throughout. The fantasist can encourage their initial appearance (coax them into being, as it were), exercise varying degrees of influence upon their development, and draw them to a close by merely diverting his or her attention. But we should not exaggerate the controlled character of fantasy. As was remarked earlier, fantasying tends to take its own course, not to the wild and bizarre extent of hallucinating, but nonetheless to the point of appearing to generate its own content. It is in this sense *wayward,* seeming to have a will of its own and spinning itself out. The fantasist is usually content to assume a position of engrossed awareness so as to follow the unfolding narrative. This contrasts with what is found in imagining, where the factor of control is much more prominent. In almost every case, the imaginer can imagine precisely as, how, and when he or she wishes to. No comparable controllability of content manifests itself in fantasies, most of which arise and proceed spontaneously. The point is not that such fantasies *cannot* be controlled (as is so often the case in hallucinating), but that they are in fact less frequently and thoroughly controlled than are imaginative experiences.

(iv) *Wish Fulfillment.* In a much-quoted statement, Freud asserted that "a happy person never phantasies, only an unsatisfied one. The motive forces of phantasies are unsatisfied wishes, and every single phantasy is the fulfillment of a wish, a correction of unsatisfying reality."[53] We need not posit wishes as "motive forces" in order to agree with Freud. Fantasies are experienced as wish-fulfilling, whatever the exact status of wishes may be in the total system of the psyche. Thus "wish-fulfilling" as used here refers to an actually experienced trait of fantasies, not to their general function. Fantasies set forth situations that, by their very nature, represent the fulfillment of wishes. The sense of fulfillment is itself based on the fact that fantasies present relatively complete depictions of their own content, and their narrative character aids immensely in presenting scenes which are complex enough (spatially, temporally, and in other ways) to be *scenes of satisfaction.*

The term "satisfaction" is important here. The primary affect attaching to fantasy experiences is that of pleasure. We find most fantasies pleasant to behold, and this is so even when the scenes they portray are sadistic or self-reproachful. It is no less enjoyable to witness the fulfillment of our own vengeful or self-critical thoughts than it is to project the fulfillment of altruistic or erotic impulses. In each instance, we derive satisfaction from seeing such impulses or thoughts enacted—but enacted precisely in fantasy. Where *actual* enactment might well bring consternation or horror, enactment in fantasy gives rise to pleasure. Much as in viewing movies, we know that the scenes fantasies proffer, however terrifying they might be if they were in fact present, are by no means real ones. There is a "willing suspension of disbelief," but by the same token there is the assurance that what we witness is not to be believed in as actually occurring.

The factor of wish-fulfillment brings fantasy closer to hallucination in one respect and to imagination in another. It is clear that fantasy and hallucination resemble each other to the extent that each projects entire scenes or situations; each thus provides a sufficient pictorial basis for representing the fulfillment of a wish by some particular action or set of actions. Imagining, in contrast, is often too scanty in its presentations to allow wish-fulfillment to be adequately represented. Nevertheless, in terms of affective quality, fantasy and imagination are closer to each other than either is to hallucination. Hallucination elicits fully and deeply felt emotions, often of an anxious or apprehensive nature, while the emotions associated with fantasying and imagining are comparatively tepid. Where a peculiarly self-indulgent pleasure is the main affect experienced in fantasying, a muted surprise or even an absence of overt emotion is characteristic of imagining.

(v) *Belief.* As in the case of several other basic traits of fantasy, its thetic activity situates itself *between* the corresponding activities of hallucinating and imagining. On the one hand, this activity differs from the sort of committed belief found in hallucination, since fantasied content is not posited as real or as competing with the real. As Freud formulates it, "daydreaming is never confused with reality"[54]—as opposed to nocturnal dreaming, where the confusion occurs constantly. Nothing in what we fantasy induces us to consider it as actually taking place before us. Indeed, the more attuned and open to fantasy we are, the more we rely upon a sure sense of the difference between what we experience in fantasy and what we experience in hallucination or in ordinary perception.

On the other hand, the thetic character of fantasy is to be distinguished from that of imagination insofar as what we fantasy is not experienced as purely possible. Thanks to its narrative form, fantasied content evokes in us a special allegiance—a conviction that what we are witnessing is, if not empirically or externally real, at least real *in mente.* Such content has a peculiar ability to persuade us that the scenes we are fantasying exist by right—by *psychological* right—if not in fact. As a consequence, we ascribe to them what Jung calls *"esse in anima"*[55] or what other psychoanalysts term variously "inner reality," "internal reality," and above all "psychical reality."[56] The scene being enacted in fantasy does not represent or even adumbrate what is empirically real or purely possible; it has a distinct form of psychological presence which calls forth neither the commitment of hallucination or perception nor the noncommittal attitude of imagining. In fact, the resulting sense of the psychically real involves a turning away from the extra-psychically (i.e., materially or socially) real.[57] Extra-psychical reality is replaced, not by a quasi-perceptual hallucinatory reality, but by a psychical reality that is of our own making.

A last remark is in order. It cannot be denied that important continuities and overlaps occur between the four acts which have been compared in this essay: memory may furnish the framework and even the details of hallucinating, fantasying, and imagining; fantasy can collapse into hallucination or be taken up into imagination; hallucination can be instigated and modified by all of the other acts, just as it may significantly influence them in turn; and imagining may draw on each of the others for its specific content, while also (though infrequently) lending content to them. But any such mutual impinging must be distinguished from epistemological dependency. For each of these four acts can occur independently of the others and in their absence, and none serves as a necessary condition for the rest. Moreover, each is eidetically differentiable from the others, possessing its own unique set of distinctive characteristics. Although resemblances exist between certain of these characteristics, distinctions are to be found even here: the controllability of fantasying and that of imagining, however similar, are not precisely the same; the positing activities of hallucination and of memory, though both bearing on empirical reality, do so in very different ways. We may conclude, therefore, that a descriptive analysis of memory, hallucination, and fantasy reveals these acts to be epistemologically and eidetically distinct not only from imagination but from each other as well.

1.   The structure of imagining itself is described in detail in my *Imagining: A Phenomenological Study* (Bloomington: Indiana University Press, 1976). The same work also contains a comparison of imagination and perception (cf. chap. 6 and 7) and a specification (in the Introduction) of the ways in which imagining, remembering, fantasying, and hallucinating have been inadequately distinguished from each other in Western psychology and philosophy.

2.   See Aristotle, *Metaphysics* I 980b 24–30. Cf. also Aristotle's explicit linking of memory and imagination in *De Memoria et Reminiscentia:* "Memory, even the memory of objects of thought, is not without an image. . . . And it is the objects of imagination that are remembered in their own right" (*Aristotle on Memory,* trans. R. Sorabji [London: Duckworth, 1972], p. 49).

3.   Thomas Hobbes, *Leviathan,* ed. C. B. Macpherson (London: Pelican, 1968), p. 89; his italics. Note that "fancy" and "imagination" are interchangeable for Hobbes.

4.   Ibid., p. 85. In Hobbes's proto-empiricist view, *all* mental acts stem from sensation: from it, "the rest are derived" (p. 85). But memory and imagination are more directly derived from sensation than are other acts.

5.   Giambattista Vico, *The New Science,* trans. T. G. Bergin and M. J. Fisch (Ithaca: Cornell University Press, 1968), pp. 75, 313. Cf. also p. 264: memory "is nothing but the springing up again of reminiscences." Such a view is not restricted to Hobbes or Vico. An eminent imagery researcher writes that "images are not merely imitations, *but memory fragments,* reconstructions, reinterpretations" (M. J. Horowitz, *Image Formation and Cognition* [New York: Appleton-Century Crofts, 1970], p. 4; my italics).

6.   Peter McKellar, *Imagination and Thinking* (New York: Basic Books, 1957), p. 23. Note that McKellar supports his position by invoking the same argument as Aristotle or Hobbes: "No imagination image can occur that is not composed of elements derived from actual perceptual experience" (ibid.).

7.   David Hume, *A Treatise of Human Nature,* ed. L. A. Selby-Bigge (Oxford: Claren-

don Press, 1967), p. 9. On the same page, Hume suggests another criterion for distinguishing between ideas of memory and ideas of imagination. The "order and form" of the former must conform to their "original impressions," while no such conformity is required of the latter. But Hume comes to reject this criterion when he acknowledges that it is "impossible to recall the past impressions, in order to compare them with our present ideas, and see whether their arrangement be exactly similar" (p. 85).

8. Ibid., p. 96.

9. In fact, the situation is more complex than this simple division implies. The generic term "memory" (active form: "remembering") subsumes spontaneous recall and labored recollection; but it also includes intermediate acts such as "reminiscing," which may be spontaneous *or* controlled.

10. As remembered, of course, my *act* of imagining possesses a determinate temporal position: I imagined x at time y, and this remains true indefinitely. But the *contents* of my act are neither positioned on an objective time-line nor located in a determinate spatial expanse. Rather, these contents exfoliate, at whim or at will, without regard to any precise point of origin in space or in time.

11. Sigmund Freud, *Standard Edition of the Complete Psychological Works*, 24 vols. (London: Hogarth Press, 1953–74), 2: 10. Freud also muses upon how "unexpectedly accurate memory can be" (p. 111) and is struck by the "hypermnesic" quality of dreams which reproduce earlier and long-forgotten situations (see *Standard Edition*, vol. 4, pp. 11–17).

12. On this point, see Brian Smith, *Memory* (London: Allen & Unwin, 1966), pp. 108 ff.

13. As William James says, "An object which is recollected, in the proper sense of that term, is one which has been absent from consciousness altogether, and now revives anew. It is brought back, recalled, fished up, so to speak, from a reservoir in which, with countless other objects, it lay buried and lost from view" (*Principles of Psychology* [New York: Dover, 1950], I, p. 646). Described thus, retentiveness cannot be restricted to specific skills we have learned; it applies to anything and everything which, having once been experienced, has now sedimented itself into our permanent stock of recallable material.

14. Ibid., p. 647.

15. Edmund Husserl, *The Phenomenology of Internal Time-Consciousness*, trans. J. Churchill (Bloomington: Indiana University Press, 1962), sec. 14.

16. James, *Principles of Psychology*, I, p. 650; his italics.

17. Ibid.; Bertrand Russell, *Analysis of Mind* (London: Allen & Unwin, 1921), p. 161 (the "characteristic by which we distinguish the [memory] images we trust is the feeling of familiarity that accompanies them").

18. Smith, *Memory*, p. 20. For Smith's own reservations as to this thesis, see pp. 42, 96.

19. Hume, *A Treatise of Human Nature*, p. 86; his italics.

20. "Memory is then the feeling of belief in a peculiar complex object. . . . The object of memory is only an object imagined in the past . . . to which the emotion of belief adheres" (James, *Principles of Psychology*, I, p. 652).

21. Freud, *Standard Edition*, vol. 14, p. 230. Cf. also Hume: "To believe is . . . to feel an intimate impression of the senses, or a repetition of that impression in the memory" (*A Treatise of Human Nature*, p. 86). Aristotle agrees: "Belief will have as [its] object nothing else but that which, if it exists, is the object of the perception" (*De Anima* 428a 28–30).

22. See Husserl, *The Phenomenology of Internal Time-Consciousness*, sec. 16–28 and Appendices I and II. Cf. also Husserl, *Ideas*, trans. W. R. Boyce Gibson (London: Allen & Unwin, 1958), sec. 43, 99–101, and 111. My two essays "Imagination and Repetition in Literature" (*Yale French Studies* [Spring, 1976]) and "The Image / Sign Relation in Husserl and Freud" (*Review of Metaphysics* [December, 1976]) discuss Husserl's classification in more detail than can be attempted above.

23. See, for example, Pierre Quercy, *L'Hallucination* (Paris: Alcan, 1930), II, esp. pp. 112 and 559; and Jean Lhermitte, *Les hallucinations* (Paris: Doin, 1951), p. 25. For a critique of this definition see Erwin Straus, "Phenomenology of Hallucinations," in Straus's *Phenomenological Psychology* (New York: Basic Books, 1966), pp. 277–89.

24.   See Freud, *Standard Edition*, vol. 4, p. 50. See also vol. 5, pp. 544–46, 598 ff.; and vol. 19, p. 20. These passages make it clear that, although the formation of dream-images specifically involves the cathexis of memory traces, the memory that is thereby revived is of a former *perception*.

25.   Horowitz, *Image Formation and Cognition*, p. 8.

26.   Ibid.

27.   See Freud, *Standard Edition*, vol. 17, pp. 85–86.

28.   See ibid., vol. 14, pp. 222–35, esp. p. 230: "One might speak quite generally of a 'hallucinatory wishful psychosis', and attribute it equally to dreams and amentia." On the dream as a prototype of neurotic symptoms, see ibid., vol. 4, pp. xxiii. On the relation between dreams and insanity, see ibid., pp. 88–92.

29.   For a comprehensive overview of such non-pathological paranormal experiences, see Horowitz, *Image Formation and Cognition*, chap. 1.

30.   I say "actual *or possible*" because of the fact that many hallucinators do not believe that what they hallucinate is actually present before them. They assume what Lhermitte calls a "critical" attitude even as they are hallucinating. Cf. Lhermitte, *Les hallucinations*, p. 26 f. and section (v) below.

31.   Straus, "Phenomenology of Hallucinations," p. 284. Note the detailed chart on p. 285.

32.   Freud, *Standard Edition*, vol. 14, p. 233; his italics. Such projection is then analogized to the projection that occurs in hysterical phobia and paranoia (ibid., pp. 223–24).

33.   Ibid., vol. 4, p. 50; his italics.

34.   That there is a link between sensory vivacity and projectedness is suggested in Lord Brain's definition of hallucinations as "mental impressions of sensory vividness occurring without external stimulus, but appearing to be located outside the subject" (W. R. Brain, *Diseases of the Nervous System* [London: Oxford University Press, 1962], p. 828).

35.   As Straus observes, such voices are all the more insidious and uncontrollable for being disembodied: "eluding all limits and boundaries and not hindered by walls or distances, such voices are overwhelming and irresistible in their power. The patient is helpless!" ("Phenomenology of Hallucinations," p. 286). Evident here is the close link between the externality of hallucinatory phenomena and their involuntariness.

36.   For a brief account of Sartre's hallucinations, see M. Contat and M. Rybalka, *Les écrits de Sartre* (Paris: Gallimard, 1970), p. 26. The technical term for hallucinatory persistence is "flashback" or "throwback."

37.   Quoted by T. R. Sarbin and J. B. Juhasz, "The Historical Background of the Concept of Hallucination," *Journal of the History of the Behavioral Sciences* 3 (1967): 348.

38.   Quoted from Esquirol's *Observations on the Illusions of the Insane* by Straus, "Phenomenology of Hallucinations," pp. 288–89.

39.   Freud, *Standard Edition*, vol. 14, p. 230.

40.   As Straus observes, "sensory experiencing and experiencing the real are one and the same" ("Aesthesiology and Hallucination," in Rollo May et al., eds., *Existence* [New York: Basic Books, 1958], p. 162).

41.   See Maurice Merleau-Ponty's discussion of this case in *Phenomenology of Perception*, trans. C. Smith (New York: Humanities Press, 1962), pp. 334 ff. Striking instances of hallucinatory voices are given in Joanne Greenberg, *I Never Promised You a Rose Garden* (New York: Signet, 1964), esp. chap. 6–8. It is misleading to term either of these experiences a "pseudo-hallucination" (cf. Horowitz, *Image Formation and Cognition*, p. 9). There is nothing *experientially* "pseudo" about such experiences; indeed, their sense of reality is such as to be able to cause considerable consternation. Not to be fully believable is not necessarily not to be believable at all.

42.   Actually, the ambiguity of "fantasy" is even more extensive than this. As Charles Rycroft has written, "At present the word is used to mean (i) a general mental activity, (ii) a particular, neurotic form of this activity, (iii) a state of mind arising from it, and (iv) the fictive realm in which it occurs" (*Imagination and Reality* [London: Hogarth, 1968], p. 52).

43.   Eric Klinger, *Structure and Functions of Fantasy* (New York: Wiley, 1971), pp. 9–10.

44.   Roy Schafer, *Aspects of Internalization* (New York: International Universities Press, 1968), pp. 37–38.

45.   As Schafer writes, "Although fantasying is recognized (or recognizable) for what it is by the subject, through regression it can succumb to the primary process and lose its index of being 'in the imagination'; in that case, it turns into a delusion or hallucination, and it is coped with by the subject as though it existed in the immediate outer world" (*Aspects of Internalization*, p. 38).

46.   The term "metastable" is used by Jean-Paul Sartre in *Being and Nothingness* to describe constantly changing and transitional modes of activity. See especially Part I, chap. 2 and Part II, chap. 1 of *Being and Nothingness,* trans. H. Barnes (New York: Washington Square Press, 1975).

47.   Jerome Singer, *Daydreaming* (New York: Random House, 1966), p. 19. Singer records other examples on pp. 20 ff. See also the instances of elaborate children's fantasies cited by Anna Freud in *The Ego and the Mechanisms of Defense* (New York: International Universities Press, 1967), pp. 73 ff.

48.   Singer, *Daydreaming,* pp. 19–20.

49.   Samuel Beckett, *Imagination Dead Imagine* (London: Calder and Boyars, 1965), p. 7. My claim concerning the narrative character of fantasies does not mean that all fantasies must be as intricate and quasi-literary as Singer's. The point is rather that there is a strong tendency toward a full narrative form—i.e., the stringing together of episodes into a single story—even if this form is realized only imperfectly on given occasions. As Schafer says, fantasy "has a narrative aspect. In some instances, however, its content is an isolated static representation, the remainder of the narrative being blocked from development, and, thus, only implied. In these instances, fantasy overlaps idle, odd, or obsessive thoughts. In other instances, the fantasy's narrative *organization* is minimally developed; then, fantasy and stream of consciousness overlap" (*Aspects of Internalization,* p. 38; his italics).

50.   Freud, *Standard Edition,* vol. 9, p. 147.

51.   "We can immediately recognize His Majesty the Ego, the hero alike of every daydream and of every story" (Freud, *Standard Edition,* vol. 9, p. 150).

52.   Schafer, *Aspects of Internalization,* p. 94.

53.   Freud, *Standard Edition,* vol. 9, p. 146.

54.   Freud, *Standard Edition,* vol. 4, p. 50.

55.   Cf. C. G. Jung, *Collected Works,* 20 vols. (Princeton: Princeton University Press, 1947–75), 6: 45.

56.   D. W. Winnicott writes, "Fantasy is part of the individual's effort to deal with inner reality" (*Collected Papers* [New York: Basic Books, 1958], p. 130). Heinz Hartmann avers that fantasies "open internal reality" to the individual (*Ego Psychology and the Problem of Adaptation,* trans. D. Rapaport [New York: International Universities Press, 1961], p. 373). Freud first proposed the use of "psychical reality" in *Standard Edition,* vol. 5, pp. 613, 620.

57.   Thus Hartmann writes, "Fantasy always implies an initial turning away from a real situation" (*Ego Psychology and the Problem of Adaptation,* p. 373). And in Eugen Bleuler's classic description, "What is usually called fantasy disregards one or more aspects of reality, replacing them by arbitrary presuppositions; it is autistic" ("Autistic Thinking," in D. Rapaport, ed., *Organization and Pathology of Thought* [New York: Columbia University Press, 1951], p. 416). But to turn away from or disregard empirical reality is not necessarily to *deny* this reality, as Anna Freud implies when she writes that little Hans "denied reality by means of his fantasy" (*The Ego and the Mechanisms of Defense,* p. 73).

Between Imagination and Memory

Image and Memory in Bachelard and Bergson

I

IMAGE *and memory,* Bachelard *and Bergson*: isn't this going too far already? Surely sufficient unto the day would be a treatment of Bachelard alone on the image alone: this is an enormous task in itself. Nevertheless, flying in the face of good sense, I shall pursue this double juxtaposition.

The juxtaposition readily subdivides into two pairs of terms: image / memory, Bachelard / Bergson. By a logic of ratios, the immediate implication might seem to be that image is to Bachelard as memory is to Bergson.

$$\frac{\text{image}}{\text{Bachelard}} :: \frac{\text{memory}}{\text{Bergson}}$$

This would not be false insofar as each author rather conspicuously neglects what the other stresses most: Bachelard says as precious little about memory as Bergson does about imagination. In fact, each can even be construed as an archetypal advocate of that which the other downplays. Who in the last century has written so eloquently about memory as has Bergson, and who can match Bachelard's elucidations of the image? But to say this is also to keep the terms of comparison in neat dyadic packages: Bergson as the mailman of memory, Bachelard as the postman of polymorphic images. (I remind you that Bachelard was in fact an employee of the French postal service from 1903 to 1913!)

A step away from dyadicity is taken when we consider that one member of each pair of terms can be considered plausibly as the covert foil of the other term. Bergson is certainly a foil for Bachelard, who struggles in his writings in the 1930s to dissociate himself from Bergson, the regnant French philosopher of the period. To Bergson's passion for continuity (especially at the level of life), Bachelard will oppose his own commitment to discontinuity (especially at the level of the psyche). So too we might easily be tempted to take memory as a foil for image, its back-ground. Doesn't memory embody depth and pastness—sedimentation in short—in contrast with the way the image is a primary phenomenon of present consciousness, shimmering on the *superficies* of the self (it is, says Bachelard himself, "a sudden salience on the surface of the psyche").[1] Perhaps so: this is easily claimed and not incorrect. More importantly, it begins to put into question the initial dualisms from which we began: we all know that one of the major ways of dealing with the anxiety of influence is by incorporating the influence itself (thus Bergsonian *élan* will survive in Bachelardian *essor*). Foil leads to counterfoil: memory finds itself reflected in image as its inseam and not just as its external other.

But we can go further yet. In the end, image and memory, Bachelard and Bergson, will prove co-essential to each other. We cannot understand one term of each pair without having reflected on the other. Bergson's *durée* is seen in its true viscosity—as the sticky stuff it is—only when illuminated by the lambency of Bachelard's ascensional images of air and light. The horizontality of the molasses-like movement of duration calls for the verticality of a soaring imagination—and vice-versa. Image and memory prove co-essential as well, once we appreciate the materiality of images and the fickleness of memory. And it is precisely by pondering the work of Bergson and Bachelard themselves that any such reassessment of the relationship between imagination and memory becomes possible, thereby illustrating the complex co-implication of all four terms of comparison. These become finally a veritable fourfold of significance, a genuine *quadrivium* for those who are engaged in the matter of mind in its soulful dimensions.

II

Matter and Memory: it is only appropriate that we begin with this classic early work of Bergson's, first published in 1896 (the same year in which the term "psychoanalysis" was coined by Freud). For the sake of brevity I shall restrict consideration to this much-neglected book, which approaches memory so very differently from Freud. Beyond a psychological dimension, memory possesses metaphysical moorings because it takes us directly into questions of body and soul, image and matter.[2] Much as the poetic image moves Bachelard into metaphysical speculation—"poetry is an instantaneous metaphysics"[3] he wrote in 1939—so Bergson is convinced that memory images require reflection on the nature of matter.

In fact, the internal link between image and matter—a link forged precisely by memory as their most intimate and revealing point of connection—is deep, so deep that we can find in Bergson a pre-poetic *materialization of the image*. In contrast with the Cartesian paradigm wherein 'image' is merely one form of representation within *res cogitans,* and 'matter' an inert residuum of res extensa,[4] Bergson conceives them as continuous with each other. Thus matter itself is said to be nothing but "an aggregate of 'images' " (MM, p. xi) while an image for its part is "an existence placed half-way between the 'thing' and the 'representation' [of the thing]" (ibid.). More radically still, "we can only grasp things in the form of images" (MM, p. 10). This means that what we call the perceived world could be called "the image world" (MM, p. 6) and that, more generally, the 'material world' is to be considered a "system of images" (MM, p. 44). Hence, wherever I am and whatever I am doing, I can always say about myself: "here I am in the presence of images" (MM, p. 1; my italics).

Here I am indeed—in a world in which nothing is not image, including my own body and brain (cf. ibid., pp. 3 ff.). Since body and brain constitute the last bastion of reductive materialism, it is evident that Bergson has landed us squarely in a full-blown imagism. As he says at the outset, "we must state the problem [of matter] in terms of images, and of images alone" (MM, p. 10). If this is beginning to sound Bachelardian already, I would enter two cautionary questions before we are tempted to a premature rapprochement.

(i) Is "material image" (MM, p. 224) for Bergson the same thing as image of matter for Bachelard?

(ii) If not, does not Bachelard offer a third way between the two sorts of material image recognized by Bergson, namely, between those "wherein each image, related only to itself, possesses an absolute value" (MM, p. 10) and those "wherein all the images depend on a central image, our body" (ibid.)—roughly, between the kinds of images studied in natural science and those experienced by an individual consciousness? (To anticipate: in poetic revery, images are neither absolute nor separate nor dependent on the imaginer's own body. Here Bachelard helps to overcome an incipient dualism of Bergson's own devising.)

But let us move rapidly to memory, which is itself a mediational third term in the Bergsonian nexus—and in this role strictly analogous to poetic revery on Bachelard's account. Memory occurs at "precisely the intersection of mind [esprit: spirit rather than soul] and matter" (MM, pp. xv). Or we might say that memory is the difference that mind makes to matter—just as poetic imagination is the difference that soul makes with matter. (Here we cannot help asking a very basic question even if we cannot possibly resolve it at this preliminary point: does not memory move irremediably in the realm of spirit, while imagination pulls us down into the domain of soul? Does memory mediate by spiritualizing, whereas imagination does so by making soul?)

It is critical to recognize that Bergson distinguishes between two fundamental kinds of memory (not at all unlike the two sorts of imagination, material and formal, which Bachelard discerns).

(i) *Habit Memory*: Acquired by sheer repetition, it decomposes with disuse—only to be recomposed as a whole upon the proper solicitation; non-representational, it consists wholly in a bodily action constituted by automatic, successive movements of prescribed duration; here the past merges entirely into the present.

(ii) *Recollective Memory*: This does not require repetition for its formation. It is representational in status; that is, it utilizes memory-images in representing a past that is distinct from the present moment of recollection, which "I may lengthen or shorten at will" (*MM*, p. 69). These images bear a distinct place and date and thus depict unique events.[5]

Although habit memory is of great interest to psychologists and physiologists and although it is the very acting of the past in the present,[6] only recollective memory is "memory *par excellence*" (*MM*, p. 72). In the end, the first sort of remembering is "habit rather than memory; it acts our past experience but does not call up its image. The [second form] is the true memory" (*MM*, p. 144). Where habit memory is condemned to repeating the past, recollective memory actively imagines it.[7] But otherwise (and most revealingly): "it is necessary, and for similar reasons, that the past should be *acted* by matter, *imagined* by mind" (*MM*, p. 220; his italics).

Notice what has happened here. Images, which in their generic role bring together mind and matter, serve in their specific role of *memory*-images to drive mind and matter apart. When memory is examined closely and found to have two species of its own, body and action (with which again images in general are continuous) get tied to habit memory, while mind and its activity (presumably contemplation) become exclusively affiliated with recollective or "true" memory. And only the latter operates via images, conceived as means of representing the past. Indeed, the only thing that distinguishes recollective memory from imagining proper is the former's retro-reference to past place and date. Otherwise, recollection is an activity of "mingling dream with reality" (*MM*, p. 73), and its "dream-images" (p. 74) are at once "evanescent" (p. 75) and "spontaneous" (pp. 75, 77). It is evident that just here—where memory is taken in its recollective, fully imagistic mode—the connection is closest to Bachelard's conception of imagination, to which the very same terms ("dream," "evanescent," "spontaneous") would equally apply. This would suggest that the diremption between memory and imagination may not be so drastic as we first suspected.

But if this latter dualism begins to be bridged by the notion of memory-images, it is at the cost of an increasing dualism between mind and matter themselves. Not only is it the case that, by the end of *Matter and Memory*, the past is said to be acted by matter and imagined by mind or spirit (*MM*, p. 220), but, as if to cinch the dualism, a *"pure* memory" has been distinguished from recollective memory itself. This pure memory is wholly virtual[8] in status—so virtual that it does not even consist in images, which have a definiteness reminiscent of sensation.[9] The polar opposite of such memory is perception, now no longer merged or mergeable with memory because of its status as at once material and actualized.[10] Continuity has given way to discontinuity; and memory, instead of being the hinge-point between mind and matter, has retreated into a pristine realm of its own— so much so that Bergson can claim in the closing pages of *Matter and Memory* that "pure memory is a spiritual manifestation. With memory we are in very truth in the domain of spirit [*esprit*]" (*MM*, p. 237). And if pure memory is the epitome of spirit, pure perception is the emblem of matter: "it is [also] in very truth within matter that pure perception places us" (*MM*, p. 174). As purified, memory and perception place us therefore back into the very dichotomy of mind and matter which it was Bergson's anti-Cartesian motive to overcome.

Purified of what? *Of images.* Images continue to call the mind/matter dichotomy into question—even in the recrudescent form it takes in the last parts of *Matter and Memory.* If it is true that *pure* memory is "absolutely independent of matter" (*MM*, p. 171) and is "in no degree an emanation [from it]" (p. 176)—hence Bergson's ongoing critique of the cerebral localization of memories[11]—recollective memory remains in touch with matter via perception. More than that, memory-images, by being situated *between* pure memory and pure perception,[12] are on the way to the actualization of the virtual that reaches an apogee in habit memory, itself a material mode of memory at one with the rhythms of the body and the lures of perception. This is why Bergson can talk about the "continuous progress [by which] the past tends to reconquer, in actualizing itself, the influence it had lost."[13] The progress is so continuous and so insistent that we can even speak of a kind of emanationism at work: not mind being extruded from matter (as in epiphenomenalist theories) but matter itself emanating from mind—not by an idealism of concept but by the productivity of image. For when Bergson asserts that "matter, as grasped in concrete perception that always occupies a certain duration, is in great part the work of memory" (*MM*, p. 176), he means memory of the middle realm, the imagistic memory of recollection. Memory-images have just the right concreteness to allow for the progressive actualization of pure memory (abstract remembering-that in my nomenclature) on the one hand and to impregnate[14] concrete perception itself on the other: "personal memory-images . . . picture all past events with their outline, their color and their place in time" (*MM*, p. 77). The result is a definitive overturn of dualism, following an initial rhetorical affirmation of continuism and despite a late temptation to antithetical extremism. "It is impossible to say," writes

Bergson midway through *Matter and Memory,* "precisely where one of the terms ends and another begins" (*MM*, p. 126). It is a matter, in short, of "the continuity of becoming" (ibid.). This continuity is nowhere more eloquently expressed than in the final sentence of the book:

> Spirit borrows from matter the perceptions on which it feeds, and restores them to matter in the form of movements which it has stamped with its own freedom. (*MM*, p. 246)

The free movements at issue are movements of images, which effect the continuity of becoming that is realized in the dialectic of mind and matter, a dialectic which is the work of memory in its recollective mode.

III

But what if images, including memory-images, are *not* continuous in character? What if they are in fact deeply discontinuous? Just this is Bachelard's most persistent philosophical intuition from the beginning to the end of his writing career. It emerges most forcefully in the two books of his mid-career devoted precisely to a critique of Bergsonian philosophy: *L'intuition de l'instant* (1932) and *La dialectique de la durée* (1936). Each book is designed to prove "the absolutely discontinuous character of time" (*II*, p. 38) by arguing that time's "truly specific character" (*II*, p. 23), its ultimate unit, is the instant. Indeed, that which Bergson holds finally responsible for the continuity of becoming—namely, "duration" (*la durée*)—is itself constituted entirely from strictly punctiform instants, from "the active and polymorphic grouping of realizing instants."[15] The consequence is what we could call a *pointillism of the psyche and of time.* In what does this consist?

When Bachelard writes that "we accept nearly everything in Bergsonism except continuity" (*DD*, p. 7), he is saying that he cannot accept the Parmenidian premise on which all of Bergson's metaphysics depends. This is that being is a plenum in which there are no gaps: the first sentence of *La dialectique de la durée* is that "the philosophy of Mr. Bergson is a philosophy of fullness (*du plein*) and his psychology is a psychology of plenitude" (*DD*, p. 1). Bachelard's first task, in a chapter entitled intriguingly "Détente et Néant," is to remind the reader that there are several lacunae in duration (itself conceived in the concrete and unique temporal form of plenitude): to wit, astonishment, novelty, repose, spatial points—and instants.[16] If there is in fact "a fundamental dialectic of being and non-being" (*DD*, p. 9), then time will manifest itself as discontinuous—as "a series of ruptures" (*DD*, p. 34). The continuity of being is therefore at best a metaphor[17] and is in any case *constructed,* not given (cf. *DD*, pp. 7–8).

What *is* given then? If we persist in calling it "duration," it has such a "prodigious heterogeneity"[18] that we shall have to speak of *many* durations, each of which is intrinsically polymorphic.[19] But to speak of many polymorphic durations is no longer to speak of Bergsonian *durée*, which is all-encompassing and as such singular.[20] The monolithic durational block of Bergson has been pulverized into a "dust of instants" (*II*, p. 33). Rather than being confronted with the world as "continuous in itself," we "are always only face to face with the discontinuousness of our experience" (*II*, p. 42). The basis of this discontinuity is nothing other than the instant, which is therefore the true (and sole) given of experience. Not only is it the case that "we notice time only in instants" (*II*, p. 33) but more generally "the present instant is the only domain in which reality is experienced" (*II*, p. 14). The instant is at once indispensable and irreducible.

Moreover, if the instant is the source of discontinuity, it cannot be a merely nugatory entity, much less a non-entity. In particular, it cannot be what Bergson had taken it to be: "an abstraction," "an artificial demarcation (*coupure*) that aids the geometer's schematic thought" (*II*, pp. 25, 17). It is itself a positive power, capable of a creativity that manifests itself as freedom (*II*, p. 27) and continual newness: "novelty is obviously always instantaneous" (*II*, p. 37). Its "absolutely punctiform" character implies the strict arithmetizability of time.[21] It also implies the essential solitude of the instant as experienced: "the instant is already solitude . . . by a sort of creative violence, time limited to the instant isolates us not only from others but from ourselves, since it breaks with our most cherished past" (*II*, p. 13).

Does this break mean that the instant is a form of "counter-memory" (to adopt a term of Foucault's)? In fact it is incompatible only with habit memory, wherein the past continually ingresses into the present in the form of preprogrammed bodily action. Otherwise, even Bergson's "pure memory" cannot begin to be actualized except as "an image taken in its isolation" (*II*, p. 34). Further, without an instant that is more than a "false caesura" (*II*, p. 18), there would be no way to keep past and future as distinct temporal domains. Not only is the past always experienced *as past* in a present moment (*DD*, p. 33), but we recall only past instants, not duration as such.[22] Although we might like to recount our past as if it were continuous, we keep "only the memory of events that have created us in decisive instants of our past. . . . all these events are reduced to their rooting in an instant" (*DD*, p. 34). Even in relation to the past, then, there is only "une poussière d'instants," and non-habitual memory consists in the re-collection of one set of instants in another set of instants. That which correlates the two sets and serves as their mediator: what can it be but memory-images, themselves instantaneous?

In this way Bachelard comes to the support of Bergson's theory of memory even as he attempts to demolish its metaphysical foundation. In one respect, however, the two diverge decisively in matters of memory. Where Bergson had spoken all too vaguely of recollection as supplying "date and place"[23] to an otherwise dreamlike presentation, Bachelard (drawing on Pierre Janet)[24] develops a notion of the *encadrement* or framing of our memories. We frame them by narrating[25] them and thus projecting a temporal vacuum around them, fixating them in their very narrativity: "we retain only what has been dramatized by language. . . . without spoken, expressed, dramatized fixation, memory cannot be related to its frames" (*DD*, p. 47). Narrativizing is schematizing—as Gerard Genette has shown so elegantly in his *Narrative Discourse*—and we can conclude in the present context that

> every act of remembering [i.e., recollectively] is inseparable from a schematization which, in dating events, isolates them. It empties them of their duration to give them a precise place. (*DD*, p. 48)

"A precise place" is a point in space or an instant in time: either way, the content of memories is pulverized, since what Bergson had called their "continuity of becoming" dissolves into discontinuous parts and moments. Instead of progressive actualization, recollective remembering realizes abrupt punctuations. As in the case of duration itself, memories are not so much given as constructed—"organized into an artificial system—a rational or social system—which provides them with meaning and a date" (*DD*, p. 50).

Despite their shared respect for the role of memory-images as essential go-betweens, Bachelard and Bergson begin to part ways, therefore, when it is a question of the basic action of remembering. This action is "spontaneous" for Bergson; it is "perfect from the onset; time can add nothing to its image without distinguishing it; it retains in memory its place and date" (*MM*, p. 72). The lack of a theory of active *encadrement* goes hand in hand with the view that recollective memory "*leaves* to each fact, to each gesture, its place and date" (*MM*, p. 69; my italics): nothing need be added. Whereas for Bachelard recollection is a labor of construction (or reconstruction): "one must *compose* one's past" (*DD*, p. 49; his italics); and "memory is an often difficult work (*ouvrage*)" (ibid., p. 50).

From this contrast between an activist and passivist[26] conception of memory, there follow two consequences of immediate import. (a) First, while Bergson retains a connection between memory and matter (however attenuated this may be in the case of pure memory), Bachelard severs this connection (only to restore it later in the realm of imagination). For the latter, recollection is in the end a "rational or social system" (*DD*, p. 50), and here "no image can emerge without a reason" (ibid.). (Whereas, within a few years, Bachelard will find that no properly *poetic* image can emerge *with* a reason!) So too in his distinction between the two "axes" of "superimposed time"—which strikingly anticipate his eventual differentiation between formal and material imagination—Bachelard links the "horizontal" axis of "transitive" time to the world and to matter without any sign of concern or interest, concentrating instead on the "vertical" axis of "imma-nent" time. This latter "is an axis where the self can develop a formal ac-tivity. One explores it in evoking the *matter* of the self . . . its historical experience" (*DD*, p. 98; my italics). Only by pursuing the vertical axis can we realize how deeply discontinuous time is (e.g., in allowing for four superimposed temporalities of the *cogito*).[27] We are also led thereby to a "pure aesthetics" (*DD*, p. 101) in which "everything scintillates" (*DD*, p. 145). (Whereas again several years later in *Water and Dreams*, Bachelard will find formal imagination, with its focus on surface forms, inadequate for a more complete aesthetics;[28] and he will consign verticalizing movements to a material imagination of air in *Air and Dreams*.[29] In these two books and others in the series on the imagination of elements, Bachelard will redeem the importance of the horizontal axis of matter which he so con-spicuously neglects in *La dialectique de la durée*, dismissing it with the peremptory statement that "time is certainly vertical" [*DD*, p. 98].)[30]

(b) Second, and still more significant, is something that follows directly from Bachelard's seemingly innocent remark that without the *encadrement* of memories in place and date we would have "revery mixed with illusions" (*DD*, p. 46). Without the fixation and isolation effected by reconstructive narrative, there would be an untethered content of the mind. Having no such temporal substructure, "the image of revery is gratuitous."[31] What is a deficiency in regard to memory—to be "incomplete, undated" (*DD*, p. 51)—is precisely a virtue in respect to imagination. Nothing distinguishes Bachelard in mid-career more dramatically from Bergson than this Janu-sian situation. For the latter, memory and revery are not only compatible and continuous but indissociable:

> To call up the past in the form of an image [i.e., in recollection], we must be able to withdraw ourselves from the action of the moment, we must have the power to value the useless, we must have the *will to dream*. (*MM*, p. 71; my italics)

It is not surprising that not having attended expressly to *encadrement* Bergson considers the memorial and the oneiric to be so closely allied. Nor is it surprising either that, not distinguishing these two dimensions clearly, he would not pursue imagination as a topic of any special significance, remaining enmeshed in the paradigm of duration that guides *Matter and Memory*, a book wherein images refer us back to and down to matter. Bachelard, in vivid contrast, frees images from memory—insofar as they are unframed and open—and from duration—insofar as they are instan-taneous and punctiform. No wonder he finds the vertical axis of time— an axis of instantaneous, non-extended realization—so tempting as a model for escaping the horizontal viscosity of duration. No wonder too that in *La dialectique de la durée* Bachelard extracts himself so fully from Bergson's own philosophical viscosity, coming into his own precisely by developing a model of memory that sets it decisively apart from revery, the dream, and imagination—as from matter, which will henceforth be linked with these latter. Small wonder either, then, that this book, which marks Bachelard's most fateful *rite de passage* as he passes from the anxiety of Bergson's influence to his own most original direction of work, finishes by proposing an "Orpheus complex" as an antithesis to the Oedipus complex (talk about "antithetical criticism" à la Bloom!). In the new complex, what matters most is not rivalrous influence but "active, vibrant repose," "an always possible childhood," and that "lyrical state"[32] which consists in "letting images succeed images" (*DD,* p. 150) and which is best realized in *poetry*. Looking forward auspiciously to what lies ahead, this pivotal book of 1936, turning as it does from memory to revery, from duration to the instant, and from matter to the image of matter, ends with these two sentences:

> Poetry, thus liberated from habitual involvements, becomes again a model of rhythmatized life and thought. It [is] thus the most appropriate means for . . . returning to the mind the mastery of the dialectics of duration. (*DD,* p. 150)

IV

It is time to draw back, reconnoiter, and reflect a bit after this rather rapid confrontation. If we take Bergson and Bachelard in isolation from each other, it might seem that we have traced out practically antithetical movements of thought. Bergson was seen to move in *Matter and Memory* from a position of pan-imagism, an immanence of the image ("Here I am in the presence of images" [*MM,* p. 1]) wherein mind and matter are at one, to a complex dialectic of three terms (pure memory, pure perception, and memory-images) in which the third, imagistic term serves to mediate the previous two otherwise irreconcilable terms. Yet it was precisely memory in its imagistic-recollective mode that set it apart from matter, with which non-imagistic habit memory alone is continuous. Bachelard, on the other hand, was observed to *begin* with the conviction that images of all kinds are strictly discontinuous with matter—where matter implies (as it certainly does imply for Bergson) the continuity of becoming within the actions of *élan vital*. In their punctiform appearance, their very instantaneity of being, images are the antithesis of the magma-like movement that characterizes duration. All the more, then, does recollective memory declare its independence of *devenir* and *durée,* since its framing operations require it to construct and project an imaged space and time as scenes for remembered actions.

Yet, despite starting from a discontinuist position which is even more radical than that with which Bergson ends (for Bachelard leaves little room for mediation of any kind), Bachelard changes perceptibly in the very course of acting out his Orpheus (or is it a Prometheus?)[33] complex vis-à-vis Bergson himself. He turns increasingly to the imagination of matter in poetry as a basis for all significant imagining, even the formal imagining in which such high confidence was placed as late as his book on Lautréamont. And in the oneiric-alchemical opus of material imagination, everything becomes immanent to matter, including forms, instants, memories, and images of all kinds. In this way Bachelard ends with an even more extreme imagism than that with which Bergson began in *Matter and Memory*. The image, or more exactly "the imaginary,"[34] comes to encompass all; all transcendence of the imaginary is either a false and self-deceived transcendence or itself a mode of material imagination (the latter being the object lesson of *Air and Dreams,* which subsumes the very verticalizing movements that had earlier been the epitome of formal imagining under the aegis of the material imagining of air).[35]

If it is true that Bachelard ends where Bergson began via a curious crisscrossing of itineraries, it is not a simple matter of the return of the repressed. In the end, the two thinkers do not blend into a single concoction, smooth and sippable, a kind of philosophical 'B & B.' Or, more exactly, they are at once farther apart *and* closer together than I have been able to indicate. *Farther apart*: for the "matter" with which Bergson commences is of course very different from that with which Bachelard terminates. The former is solidly and stolidly perceptual, felt in and through the body (and thus mainly through habit memory). True, it is not inert; it is not *res extensa;* it is animated; but it is not *res imaginans* either. It is not animated by a soul that imagines but by a massive, prepersonal *élan.* In contrast, Bachelardian matter is the substance not of perception but of revery, the revery of the solitary reader of poetry whose solitude is strangely reminiscent of Descartes—both figures meditating their otherwise so disparate thoughts beside a fire. Matter for Bachelard is essentially oneiric matter; its images have the same flickering, lambent character as does *La flamme d'une chandelle;* they are discontinuous and discordant and are truly the objects of "l'intuition de l'instant." Only when we conjure up something non-instantaneous, "a stable and completed image," do we have the equivalent of a "present perception"; but just such an image, which might well be paradigmatic for Bergson (who tries to analogize memory-images, despite their virtuality, to images of sensation),[36] "clips the wings of imagination"[37] for Bachelard. Both thinkers would certainly agree that "we can only grasp the problem in terms of images and of images alone" (ibid.). But what different images are at stake here!

Closer together: nevertheless, and now strangely indeed, the two compatriots conjoin in lasting and striking ways. Some of these are merely surprising matters of overlap. For example, both agree that habit has a broader compass than recollective memory, that it supplies continuity to isolated instants, that it is tied as much to the future as to the past, and that it

has an especially close link with (non-oneiric) matter: Bachelard's statement that "matter is thus the most uniformly realized habitude of being"
(*II*, p. 69) might well have been uttered by Bergson.[38] We could even say
that just as memory and the image allow us to appreciate the divergences
between the two philosophers, habit lets us see them in their sameness.

Another area of striking overlap is found in the two-dimensional,
ultimately Cartesian model of vertical and horizontal axes which are
perpendicular to each other. We know how important this model is for
Bachelard from *La dialectique de la durée* (where it is first formally proposed) through "Instant poétique et instant métaphysique" (where it is applied forthrightly to poetry) and finally to *Water and Dreams* (whose very
first sentence reads "the image-making powers of our mind develop around
two very different axes" [*WD*, p. 1]). What has not been brought out is
the fact that the model first appears in *Matter and Memory* as an explicit
diagram of the way that recollections (represented as residing on the vertical axis) bear upon perceptions of objects (represented on the horizontal
axis).[39] The vertical axis is that of time, the horizontal that of space—
with the implication that while recollections succeed each other, perceptions are of simultaneously given objects:

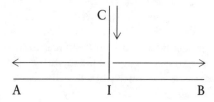

Apart from the fact that the movement of the vertical axis is *downward*
for Bergson (since the past of recollections impinges on the present of
perceptions), it is clearly the case that for him as for Bachelard the vertical
axis is reserved for images (memorial or imaginative), while matter (perceptual or oneiric) inhabits the horizontal axis for both thinkers.[40] Specific
differences in the treatment of imagination and memory are incorporated
in the double directionality of a diagram, a geometric image, to which they
both subscribe. Does this not portend a deeper affiliation?

It does indeed. For all their manifold and manifest discrepancies, the
B Brothers teach us a basic lesson in common: memory, "true" memory,
occurs in and through images, *as* images. If the relation between matter
and memory is moot, images are the authentic matter of memory itself,
its essential vehicle, its very substance. Pure memory, important as it may
be to posit as a pole of sheer virtuality, does not become operative until
it invests itself in the *lingua franca* of the image—just as pure perception
is orphaned of its own past if it fails to make connection with the images
which it has itself helped to spawn. Everything in matters of memory con-
verges on the image—even if memory as a whole, any more than imagina-

tion itself, cannot be contained there altogether.[41] Likewise, in Bachelard's early conception of *encadrement* we discern the indispensability of images for memory; the framings of past places and dates are imagings. So too are the much less explicit embodiments of the past which we have come to suspect form part of the covert content of a bounteous material imagination, which retains the past in depth even as it seeks novelty on the surface. Everywhere, and in every imaginable way, the past is forcefully and effectively remembered in images. We reach the past, just as we may reach matter, through their essential agency.

If this is so, it points to yet another deep affinity. Bachelard and Bergson are both telling us that in order to be the purveyors of matter and memory images cannot be merely pictographic in their mode of operation. Images not only *represent* the past and matter; they actively *imagine* both.[42] In order to do so, they must be capable of a special action that exceeds isomorphically based depiction. This is *resonance* or *reverberation*. In images the past *and* matter and the past *of* matter come to resound—to reverberate beyond any of the frames in which they may have been set by a mind concerned with exact location. It is revealing to find Bachelard and Bergson once more in accord on this point. Thus Bergson says expressly that the primary function of memory is

> . . . to evoke [not to picture] all these past perceptions which are analogous to the present perception . . . so that the memory of a living being appears indeed to measure, above all, its power of action upon things and to be only the intellectual reverberation of this power. (*MM*, p. 224)

Bachelard is still more insistent on this score: "the value of an image is measured by the extent of its imaginary radiance (*son auréole imaginaire*)" (*AS*, p. 7). The openness of open imagination itself has very much to do with such radiance, which cannot be reduced to efficient-causal effect: "very often, then, it is in the opposite of causality, that is, in *reverberation* . . . that I think we find the real measure of the being of a poetic image" (*PS*, p. xii; his italics). The same holds true of a memory image: "through the brilliance of an image, the distant past resounds with echoes, and it is hard to know at what depth these echoes will reverberate and die away" (ibid).

As this last statement is made in a discussion of the poetic image in *The Poetics of Space*, it is evident that by this late point (1957) in his career, Bachelard was able to assimilate memory-images and poetic images to each other thanks to the factor of resonance, with the result that every poetic image harbors a past within it even as it surprises us by its newness.[43] This is an inference which Bergson did *not* make—just as he did not follow Bachelard in tracing the ontological consequences of resonance, namely, that an image ultimately resonates with a *world*, which is what it evokes.[44] And if memory images in particular reverberate with a world, then the past they convey cannot be a "phantom" or merely "empty"—as Bachelard was tempted to believe at the time of writing *L'intuition de l'instant*.[45] Here the two thinkers rejoin once more, since for Bergson the past conveyed by a memory image is not a mode of absence; it is a form of presence, albeit virtual and not amounting to an entire world; and it can only be evoked by the rich *retentissement* of an image.

Let me draw to a close by picking out two general lessons to be learned from our running confrontation of Bachelard and Bergson. (1) The first is that we are henceforth cautioned against thinking of images as fickle and frothy only—as products of a formal imagination alone—and of memories as deadweight ballasts, heavy replicas, of a closed past. Images, at least those generated by a material imagination, "have weight; they constitute a heart" (*WD*, p. 1). They include memory-images, which come to us with their own specific gravity and as having a life of their own not entirely dependent on their origins in personal or collective history. Such images not only become immixed with "imagined images":[46] this is something we have known since Freud identified 'screen memories' one year after the publication of *Matter and Memory*. They may belong to material imagination as part of its repertoire of producing reverberating psychic events. Or else, more modestly (and following Bergson rather than Bachelard), they may be on their way to the materiality of perception, wherein their virtuality will be actualized. In either case, the line between memory-images and other images becomes increasingly difficult to draw— as does the line between memory and image simpliciter. Just as we have seen Bachelard and Bergson, archetypal and irreconcilable opponents when it is a question of the nature of time, quietly embrace in an *entente cordiale* when we examine them more closely, so imagination and memory, those traditionally antagonistic powers of mind, come to share more than one might at first have thought possible—allowing us to discern a memorial dimension to *all* images and to appreciate the unique value of a resonating imagistic component of memories. The very term "memory-image," in its ambiguous and bivalent format, says it all: *memory/image*. How to choose? Where to cut? Who can say? Perhaps image and memory are as indissociable as Bachelard and Bergson themselves have come to appear to us to be.

(2) Still, despite such equitable and equalitarian trade-offs between image and memory, the one term that survives all the sea-changes is *image*. It is the memory-*image* that, precisely as an image (i.e., having materiality in the form of sensuous specificity), makes possible a continuous transition from pure memory to pure perception, otherwise unredeemably dirempt from each other in *Matter and Memory*. And it is also the image, now taken in its instantaneous upsurge (not at all incomparable with its sensuousness), that empowered Bachelard to effect his critique of Bergsonian continuity, including that belonging to memory itself. But it was the poetic image that first alerted Bachelard to the full formal powers of imagining (its transformative ability, later renamed "pure sublimation"[47]).

It was also the poetic image that led Bachelard to suspect the material and even the cosmic dimensions of a genuinely pure or open imagination. He discovered both dimensions[48] in the process of writing *Water and Dreams;* and it seems only fitting that I should end by citing the last sentence of the Introduction to this fabulous work:

> The images born in us, that live in our dreams and are filled with a dense and rich oneiric matter—[thus furnishing] inexhaustible food for material imagination—must be pursued. (*WD*, p. 18)

1. Gaston Bachelard, *The Poetics of Space*, trans. M. Jolas (New York: Orion Press, 1964), p. xxi. (Hereafter *PS*.)
2. On this theme, see Henri Bergson, *Matter and Memory*, trans. N. M. Paul and W. S. Palmer (New York: Anchor, 1959), pp. xvii–xviii. (Hereafter *MM*.)
3. "Instant poétique et instant métaphysique" in Gaston Bachelard, *L'intuition de l'instant* (Paris: Gonthier, 1932), p. 103. (Hereafter *II*.)
4. Matter is "half-way between the place to which Descartes had driven it and that to which Berkeley drew it back [i.e., into pure mind]" (*MM*, p. xiii).
5. The most thorough discussion of the two kinds of memory occurs at *MM*, pp. 67–74.
6. See ibid., pp. 76, 144, 220.
7. "Of these two memories . . . the one *imagines* and the other *repeats*" (*MM*, p. 70; his italics).
8. "In this virtual state pure memory consists" (*MM*, p. 236).
9. Thus empiricists "perceive memory only in the form of an image, that is to say, already embodied in nascent sensations" (*MM*, p. 132).
10. On the difference between memory and perception, see *MM*, pp. 235 ff.
11. On this, see *MM*, pp. 98 ff., 116–23, 140 ff., 170–71, 233.
12. As is made clear in the diagram at *MM*, p. 125.
13. *MM*, p. 123. Cf. also pp. 126, 132, 173, 221.
14. Perception is "impregnated with memory-images which complete it as they interpret it" (*MM*, p. 125).
15. *La dialectique de la durée*, 2d ed. (Paris: PUF, 1950), p. 42. (Hereafter referred to as *DD*.)
16. Cf. *DD*, pp. 7 ff.
17. See chap. 7 of *DD:* "Les métaphores de la durée."
18. "We shall never overcome the prodigious heterogeneity of duration" (*II*, p. 32).
19. "Every veritable duration is essentially polymorphic" (*DD*, p. viii).
20. On this point, see *II*, p. 29: Bergson "showed us objectively that we were solidary with one single *élan*, all of us being carried away by one and the same flow."
21. On this notion, see *II*, p. 38.
22. On this last point, see *DD*, p. 35.
23. Speaking of recollection, Bergson says that "its essence is to bear a date" (*MM*, p. 68), but he never suggests what the mechanism of this date-bearing consists in.
24. Bachelard was much taken by Janet's *L'évolution de la mémoire et de la notion de temps* (Paris: Vrin, 1928) and builds on it extensively in chap. 2 of *La dialectique de la durée*.
25. On narrative versus recitation, see *DD*, pp. 48–50.
26. Notice that habit memory is even more passive in operation: "it is stored up in a mechanism which is set in motion as a whole by an initial impulse, in a closed system of automatic movements" (*MM*, p. 68).
27. See *DD*, pp. 98 ff.

28. Cf. *Water and Dreams*, trans. Edith Farrell (Dallas: Pegasus, 1983), pp. 1–5. (Hereafter *WD*.)

29. See *L'air et les songes* (Paris: Corti, 1943), passim. (Hereafter *AS*.) Available in English as *Air and Dreams: An Essay on the Imagination of Movement*, trans. Edith R. and C. Frederick Farrell (Dallas: The Dallas Institute Publications, 1988).

30. Three years later, in 1939, Bachelard will still be able to say that "le temps de la poésie est vertical" ("L'instant poétique et l'instant métaphysique" in *II*, p. 104).

31. *DD*, p. 51. The full statement is revealing: ". . . veritable memory possesses a temporal substructure which is lacking in revery. The image of revery is gratuitous. It is not a pure memory because it is an incomplete, undated memory. There is no date or duration where there is no construction" (ibid.).

32. The foregoing phrases are from *DD*, pp. 148–149.

33. In addition to contrasting the Orpheus with the Oedipus complex at the end of *DD* (pp. 148–49), Bachelard also asserts that "the Promethean complex is the Oedipus complex of intellectual life" (*La psychanalyse du feu* [Paris: Presses Universitaires de France, 1949], p. 27; hereafter *PF*).

34. "The fundamental word corresponding to imagination is not *image*, but *imaginary*" (*AS*, p. 7; his italics).

35. See *AS*, esp. chap. 2, 5, 6.

36. A memory image is "a perception in process of birth" (*MM*, p. 126). On the virtuality of memory images, see ibid., pp. 126–32.

37. All the citations from Bachelard in this sentence are from *AS*, p. 8. The last phrase is in italics in the text.

38. For Bergson's view of habit as it impinges on memory, see *MM*, pp. 67 ff.; on Bachelard's convergent (but not coinciding) view, see *II*, pp. 59–83.

39. For Bergson's diagram and its discussion, see *MM*, pp. 135 ff.

40. We can also construe the diagram as prophetic of Bachelard's own development: from a concern with time in the form of instants (the vertical axis) in *II* and *DD* to a consuming passion for matter (in the series on the elements) and space (in *PS*) as these are sheltered by the horizontal axis. The latter axis is certainly suggested by "the constancy and lovely monotony of matter" (*WD*, p. 2) or by the "intimate immensity" of space (cf. *PS*, chap. 8).

41. Just as habit memory (and other modes such as commemoration and reminiscence) exceeds the confines of recollection, so the imaginary exceeds its own explicit contents: "undoubtedly, the imaginary lays down images during its prodigious life, but it always appears to exist beyond the images, it is always a little more than its images" (*AS*, p. 8).

42. It remains true that neither figure attempts any rigorous distinction between representing and imagining the past. These latter acts are even conflated by Bergson if we compare statements made at *MM*, p. 70 with those at *MM*, p. 220. I am not ignoring the fact that Bergson is convinced that the past is acted in matter (i.e., in concrete habits) even as it is imagined in mind (cf. *MM*, pp. 220–21). On the other hand, we should notice Bergson's critique of views that make perception or memory "the useless duplicate of an external reality" (*MM*, p. 223).

43. Bachelard cautions, however, that "the poet does not confer the past of his image upon me, and yet his image immediately takes root in me" (*PS*, p. xiii). This is so despite "the wholly unexpected nature of the new image" (ibid.).

44. On the cosmological aspects of the poetic image, see *WD*, pp. 160 ff.; *AS*, p. 22; and *The Poetics of Reverie*, trans. Daniel Russell (Boston: Beacon Press, 1969), pp. 187–90. As early as *PF*, Bachelard has said that "the object designates us more than we designate it" (p. 9).

45. The two descriptive terms cited are from *II*, p. 5, and *II*, p. 48, respectively.

46. This phrase occurs in *La terre et les rêveries de la volonté* (Paris: Corti, 1948), p. 3.

47. At *PS*, pp. xxvi–xxviii. Cf. "dialectical sublimation" at *PF*, pp. 164 ff.

48. The cosmic dimension is explored under the heading of "cosmic narcissism": cf. *WD*, pp. 24 ff. It is fully savored in *PS* and *The Poetics of Reverie*.

How Important Are Images for Memory?

L ET ME BEGIN with an image—in this case a dream image:

> I was wearing a white shirt of thick and rough texture. Red wine I was
> drinking spilled onto the shirt. In attempting to remove the wine stains,
> I found the shirt suddenly transformed into a polychromatic garment.

A simple enough image—a shirt of many colors as the transfiguration of
a shirt of one color alone (a color which, nonetheless, contains all the other
colors implicitly). Simple but compelling: like all images, whether these
be dream images, eidetic images, or memory images.

Of these three sorts of image I would contend that the memory image
constitutes the most encompassing class. This can be seen in the case of
my dream: built on prior memory images (I own just such a shirt; I was
drinking red wine the night before), it has become for me a memory image that still resonates with significance down to this day (the dream occurred more than six months ago). How can this be? How can anything
so innocuous as a mere image have such significance? How is memory so
pervasive, of images as of life itself? How are images so important for
memory?

The Greeks have given us a hint that may cast a provisional light on
such questions. They named the Mother of the Muses "Memory":
Mnēmosynē. Memory gives rise to the arts. This happens, moreover, only
by means of the image. For in the Greek view all the arts are imitative in
origin, matters of *mimēsis* in the generous sense of non-reproductive, playful
miming of what is or was the case. Our word "image" derives from the
Latin *imago, imaginem*—which derives in turn from *mimos*, mime.

A mime moves in space and portends more than he or she gestures. In
this way miming—which is precisely *not* imitating in a strictly repetitive
manner—*creates images* and, in instances of excellent performance,
employs *creative images* as well. Every art attempts to do the same thing—

to bring forth transformative images just as dreaming does effortlessly each night. My dream of a transfigured shirt could be taken as an image itself—an oneiric miming—of what all images that aspire to more than repetition-of-the-same accomplish. And if the Greeks were right, this accomplishment occurs in the arts through the procreative agency of Memory. This agency is at work, I will suggest, beyond the arts as well, not only in dreams, but also in everyday, garden-variety remembering. And this happens, as I shall also attempt to trace, through the intervention of space—the space of psychic miming that is at once the medium and the reality of memory. In order to make this case, I shall be drawing on several Greek thinkers—Aristotle, Simonides, and above all Plato—who will serve as our muses in the face of certain modern modes of thinking that act to undermine the importance of images for memory.

I

First of all, however, let me hasten to admit that I am in the somewhat embarrassing position of having proposed a theory of mental imagery which, if true, might render the present essay futile from the start. In *Imagining* I explored the thesis that images enjoy a peculiar kind of "thin autonomy" which makes them exemplary of the human mind in its fullest freedom. This freedom seems difficult to reconcile with the concrete and dense demands of memory, which is forever tying us down—to the past, to matters of fact, to *what has been the case*. When not actually bogging us down (e.g., in the pathos of nostalgia or in a futile memory search), remembering might realize at best a "thick autonomy"—a certain capacity for creatively reshaping the past rather than merely reflecting it in what Kant called euphemistically but tellingly "reproductive imagination."

But precisely when imagination is *not* being reproductive, it moves in ways that are apparently inimical to memory. As "etherealizing" and "verticalizing"—descriptive terms which I could not resist in my earlier descriptions—imagining concerns itself with pure possibilities, with *what might be the case*. Where memory characteristically moves back to quite determinate and already realized possibilities, imagination moves out to the radically indeterminate and not yet (and perhaps never to be) realized: "here freedom is the freedom of never having to come to a pre-established or peremptory end."[1]

If indeterminacy and pure possibility—two of the major traits of all imagining—are thus singularly unpropitious when it comes to understanding matters of memory, so are the other central descriptive terms which I singled out in my earlier book. The "self-containedness" of much imagining—its tendency toward encapsulation and auto-iconicity—contrasts with memory's proclivity to pervade our lives utterly and to refer beyond its own dateable origins. So too what I called the "self-evidence" of imagining, that is, its striking lack of need for supplementary evidence of any kind, stands in opposition to the frequently felt need to fill out (and sometimes to contravene) evidence for the events that we remember. Even the descriptive dyad entitled "spontaneity/controlledness," though ostensibly applicable to memory as well, ends by misrepresenting it. Whereas in imagining we experience as a matter of course rather pure cases of spontaneity and control—think only of the complementary role of images in poetic inspiration and production—remembering lacks sheer spontaneity (i.e., to the extent that it is a mode of repetition) just as it resists being completely controlled (thanks to having its own historical roots—roots not to be manipulated *post facto*).

Thus it appears that if I am right about imagining I will not have much to say about remembering. But is this really so? I trust not—at least if the term "memory image" is to live up to its own name. As everyone might easily grant, images are centrally important to memory; and images, after all, *are* images—which means that they must share certain features in common with "imagination images" (as products of free imagining are called in an irritating pleonasm). And surely there are basic ways in which memory images may be, after all, spontaneous and controlled (the past does "rise before us" in imagistic form, and we can control its unfolding in memory by acts of selective attention or by hybridizations of various sorts), self-contained and self-evident (both of these thanks to the transparency of remembered contents), and even sometimes indeterminate and concerned with the purely possible (consider only how diffuse memory images can be, and how some of them bear on *what might have been* but was not).

But enough of comparative phenomenology! I am tempted into it at this beginning point only because the sheer plausibility of applying categories ingredient in imagined images to memory images – an application that by its very imperfection stops short of claiming equivalence of structure between the two kinds of images – belies any temptation to adopt either of two extreme positions when it comes to the role of images in memory:

(a) that such images are dispensable, indifferent, even detrimental to memory, or

(b) that they are essential – so much so that remembering of *all* kinds depends on them desperately and would not occur without them.

The first, literally iconoclastic position is familiar to us from the days of classical behaviorism, which found memory images to be useless *impedimenta*—entities multiplied beyond necessity—and to be extirpated as such. More recently, Zeno Pylyshyn has argued that no mental image can be considered a "primitive explanatory construct,"[2] where the corollary is that memory images are dispensable in theory even if they are undeniably part of memorial experience per se. The second position, equally radical, is implicit in the classical empiricist view that memory is (in James Mill's words) "more like the sensation, than anything else can be; so like, that I call it a copy, an image of sensation; sometimes, a representation, or trace of the sensation."[3] The mention of "trace" reminds us that the very notion of memory trace—insofar as "trace" is isomorphic with the experience of which it is a trace—entails the indispensability of memory images in many modern neurophysiological accounts.

It is clear that we must avoid both extremes. On the one hand, images are manifestly valuable—and often invaluable—for remembering; and this is true not only empirically (for example, in situations of reminding) but theoretically as well (where if not explanatory, as would be a physical mechanism, memory images are fully legitimate theoretical entities—as much so as eidetic images proper). On the other hand, it would be exaggerated to claim that all memory literally *requires* an image. My own current research has been focusing on modes of remembrance which are not representational in any strictly isomorphic manner and which need not employ memory images in their performance: such as many forms of body memory, a large selection of place memories, and various kinds of commemorative action. Body and place in particular are underconstrued when forced into a representational format; as they exceed this format, they also exceed the memory images by which they can come to be represented in the mind.

At stake here is very much the mind—or, more exactly, the *mentalism* which subtends so many theories of memory images. It would be too vast a matter indeed to provide an adequate critique of mentalism on this occasion—especially in the wake of the groundbreaking efforts of such diverse figures as Wittgenstein, Merleau-Ponty, and Richard Rorty—but it is crucial to keep in mind both the mentalistic biases of much thinking about memory images (e.g., in assumptions about their privacy, their derivation from perceptions, their picturelikeness, etc.) and the fact that a great deal of significant remembering does not proceed imagistically at all (as is found in purely "semantic" or "factual" memory of the sorts which have been explored by Endel Tulving and Norman Malcolm). In fact, I am committed to the possibly perverse view that imagination itself need not occur in or by images—one more valid overlap with memory; but in this case remembering far exceeds imagining in the kinds and forms of non-imagistic realization, which is in turn probably a reflection of the fact that memory pervades our lives more thoroughly and more definitively than does imagination in the first place. We may well be able to create the new and to recreate the old by imagining; but it is ineluctably true that we are created by our memories, our very destiny and identity depending on them in direct and drastic ways for which there is no precise parallel in sheer imaginings. In memory images, however, *both imagining and remember-*

ing are operative at once; and it is accordingly to these strange entities themselves that we must turn at this point.

II

Memory images are mysterious. Perhaps the major mystery is this: if they are in fact dispensable on many occasions, why are they nonetheless so important in our ongoing lives? Why do we keep on retaining experiences in the form of images when memory images themselves can be so manifestly clumsy, vague, and even actively misleading? Think only of how difficult it is to identify positive features in detail from a given memory image: short of hypermnesia, there is a curious but stubborn resistance to such specification. (Ask yourself only this: what exact shade of color is my friend JoAnne's hair, what is the precise configuration of her hand, how to describe her gait, etc.? None of these features is simply there in the memory image of my friend to be read off in splendid isolation.) Moreover, even in instances of hypermnesia itself, there is nothing like inbuilt trustworthiness, much less guaranteed truth—as we have come to realize recently in the controversies surrounding hypnotically induced memories used as testimony in court. A revealing analogue to our increasing skepticism in this area is found in Freud's movement away from an ideal of psychotherapy based precisely on hypermnesia—i.e., fully "abreactive" or cathartic recollections of childhood trauma—to a psychotherapeutic model founded on a respect for non-recollective modes of remembering such as occur in transference and even in "acting out." The term "hypermnesia" itself does not recur in Freud's writings after his use of it to describe memory images in vividly sensory dream-scenes in *The Interpretation of Dreams* (1900); by 1909 he had already begun to speak of the radical "untrustworthiness" of memory in general and thus of memory images in particular.

The mystery only deepens: despite such misgivings on the part of Freud and contemporary judges when it comes to claims for hyper-memory—and on our own part when we examine the quotidian offerings of ordinary recollection—we continue to search for and to value memory images. It is as if the flip side of their very dubitability and dispensability was their high desirability as well as an abiding conviction that we cannot do without them after all. This is precisely what Bertrand Russell claims when he states that "memory demands an image."[4] "Demands an image"? How can this be? Desirability is one thing: an easy case can be built for this by stressing the aesthetic or mnemonic virtues of anything pictorial in character, including representational painting and pictographic writing as well as dreams and memories themselves. But the idea of requirement is something else again: why ought we to move to images when we remember?

One false answer is that which Russell would give out of allegiance to his bedrock empiricism: namely, that to every sensation *must* correspond an image. This is simply circular, since "images" (including memory images) are nothing but copies of sensations on the empiricist view. A more promising answer is provided by Henri Bergson, himself a trenchant critic of empiricism:

> From the moment that it becomes image, the past leaves the state of pure memory and coincides with a certain part of my present. . . . The image is a present state, and its sole share in the past is the memory whence it arose.[5]

Here is a valuable clue: short of becoming an image, a given memory must be regarded as "pure," that is, as suspended in a state of sheer virtuality which belongs to the past and the past alone. Unlike such a virtual entity— whose neurological correlate would be a memory trace held in a state of readiness to be activated upon the proper electro-chemical signal—an image has nothing merely virtual or even ready about it: it belongs ineluctably to the present and as such can only be actual in status. In contrast with the state of mind or brain which makes it possible (and which ensures that it will be available again on future occasions), a memory image is *actually present, actualized as present*—indeed, cannot be otherwise and still be an image.

Now this is not a mere matter of definition—or else we would be back in Russell's vicious circle! Memory images are wholly hypothetical unless and until they are experienced as items occurring in present consciousness. In fact, they are themselves a paradigm of what consciousness craves in the present: something intuitively given, that is to say, given as unmediated by words or other signs. Just *why* consciousness should crave such a thing is itself still another major mystery: I suspect that the reason lies in a profound and even metaphysical hunger for the presentation of something sheerly spatial in our experience, something free from the confinement of the developmental diachrony which verbal language (and other comparable sign systems) imposes upon us by its very nature. When Bergson says that "the image is a present *state*," I believe that he is pointing in this same direction despite the temporal qualification of the "present." The paradox is that it is only in the present and as the present that anything like an experience of unmediated spatiality can occur; as Aristotle says in his *Physics* (217 b 35–36), the past is "no longer" and the future is "not yet," leaving the present as the sole opportunity for confronting that which *is*—i.e., is actual, exists actually now rather than formerly or to come. Memory images, in spite of their undeniable moorings in the past and their equally undeniable effects upon the future, exist pre-eminently *now*—right now and at no other time. As such, they are especially well suited not just for bringing the past to bear on contemporary concerns (this can be done in other equally effective ways) but for achieving a manner of "presentational immediacy" not otherwise accessible in human experience. In such immediacy we are invited to enjoy spectacles of space (and vistas of time) from which we are normally debarred in the rest of our experience. Both the space and the time—the time in which the space is presented to us— are special, so special that we are loathe to give them up for other, more mediated if more exact, (re)presentations.

III

One very basic way of regarding the role of images in memory is in terms of the contrasting pair *passivism/activism*. Do memory images serve as the mere replicative replay of the past—subordinate to the past experiences they repeat as to form and content alike—or are they creatively reconstructive of such experiences, transforming them actively in the present? It is tempting indeed to put the question in such dichotomous terms as those of passivity and activity. As a philosopher, I feel obliged to remind you that these are the very terms which have been operative in Western thinking on the subject since Aristotle. Not only was Aristotle the first to focus on the exact place of images in memory—Plato having found images qua likenesses (*eikonēs*) incompatible with the deliverance of an exalted Recollection (*anamnēsis*) of Forms—but Aristotle also conceived memory images to be *copies* of their originals. In his view recollection becomes "a search in something bodily for an image" (*De Memoria et Reminiscentia* 453 a 15–16)—where "image" itself is defined as "a copy of that of which it is an image" (451 a 15–16). Thus was launched an entire tradition of thought about the nature of memory images—a tradition which we may entitle "passivist" and which attained its apogee in classical British empiricism of the seventeenth and eighteenth centuries. For Hume, who epitomizes this tradition, memory images are direct, unmediated copies of discrete sensory impressions, less vivid than these impressions but constrained to the same succession of contents (unlike purely imaginary images, which are unconstrained in this regard). Although the heritage of Aristotle and Hume continued in force in the associationism that was such a dominant factor in nineteenth-century psychology and philosophy (the two fields were not yet fully distinct) and still appears today in certain paradigms of paired-associate learning situations, it was decisively challenged by Kant at the end of the eighteenth century when he proposed that, in addition to a strictly associative memory that is bound to reproduce its experiential antecedents (this he called "reproductive imagination" in its *empirical* guise), there is also a transcendental memory that is as much creative as re-creative. It was such a conception of memory that can be said to have sanctioned Romanticism as it arose soon after in England and Germany: Wordsworth's *Prelude,* like Goethe's *Faust,* is unimaginable without Kant's bold move toward an activism of memory images. According to this activism, memory brings forth images that, instead of merely reflecting or repeating previous experience, reshape it in ways that cannot be attributed to any sheer association of prior contents. Rather than being the simple mirror of these contents, the image is now allowed to take the lead in memory, not just as source of inspiration (as it certainly was for many Romantic poets) but as constitutive of what we remember, intrinsic to its very content.

Whatever may have been the fate of Kant's own formulation of the matter, his decidedly anti-passivist position shows up more recently in Piaget's and Bartlett's common stress on the actively structuring role of schemata in remembering (the term "schema" is itself Kantian in origin, referring in *The Critique of Pure Reason* to the way in which the deliverances of "sensibility" gain temporal specificity—and thus aptness for being remembered). In fact, one way of understanding the current state of memory theory in cognitive psychology and in neurology—as well as in philosophy proper—is to view it as an open battlefield between those who continue to adhere to passivism (via such notions as "rehearsal" or "retrieval," both of which imply the mere manipulation of a predetermined content) and those who espouse activism (if not through schematizing, then through such notions as holograms or "levels of processing"—each entailing that images actively guide remembering).

If such a sketch of the matter is at all accurate—if it is the case that from Aristotle into the present we have been given a forced option between passivism and activism when it comes to the nature and function of memory images—then we must look more carefully at this option itself. Are we indeed forced to make such a choice? Is passivism incompatible with activism as has so often been assumed? Not at all! There is no exclusive choice to be made between activism and passivism, nor are they incompatible with each other. Aristotle might have suspected this himself had he paid closer attention to Plato's claim that time is "the *moving image* of eternity" (*Timaeus* 37 d), for this clearly implies that the images of memory (which are eminently timelike and timebound) are actively moving agencies while still being cast in the image of their source. Indeed, Aristotle should have paid closer attention to some of his *own* teachings, since he also claims in his treatise on memory that there is an "active" relation between the memory image and its object (*De Memoria et Reminiscentia* 450 b 29); and in his *Metaphysics* (980 a 28–b 30) he even attributes to memory the quite creative role of producing coherent "experiences" out of sundry sensations. If this is the first time that a covert activism accompanies a professed passivism, it is by no means the last. Even Hume accords to memory images an organizing role in the very midst of their passive status as mere copies of impressions; and much the same moral could be drawn from Hume's heirs among the associationists and behaviorists of the last two centuries.

IV

But let me concentrate on two concrete cases in order to exhibit the striking way in which an ostensible passivism shows itself to be in an unsuspected alliance with a concerted activism. (1) The first example is the celebrated circumstance of "involuntary memory" as this term was understood by Marcel Proust. It might seem as if there could be nothing more passive than the experience of Proust, who upon tasting the famous madeleine dipped in a tea infusion was brought back so dramatically to an earlier scene of attending his bed-ridden Aunt Leonie at Combray. To say "brought back" is already to insinuate that he was the passive victim of his own released memory image—that he was somehow confined and limited in this return to the past. And yet a close reading of Proust reveals that the precipitating sensation in the present, far from eliciting an image that would be the mere copy or repetition of the relevant past sensation, is held to be *identical with* the latter and to be efficacious precisely as such and without evoking any replicative images. Moreover, the memory image that *is* evoked with genuinely hypermnesic intensity—here the image of being at the bedside of Aunt Leonie—serves to *open up* the experience with which it is associated. Indeed, it opens up an entire world as well, that of Combray as-a-whole, which had formerly been closed off to the narrator's remembrance. I cite a well-known passage from *Remembrance of Things Past:*

> And as in the game wherein the Japanese amuse themselves by filling a porcelain bowl with water and steeping in it little pieces of paper which until then are without character or form, but, the moment they become wet, stretch and twist and take on colour and distinctive shape, become flowers or houses or people, solid and recognizable, so in that moment [of tasting the madeleine] all the flowers in our garden and in M. Swann's park, and the water-lilies on the Vivonne and the good folk of the village and their dwellings and the parish church and the whole of Combray and its surroundings, taking shape and solidity, sprang into being, town and gardens alike, from my cup of tea. (Vol. 1, p. 51; Moncrieff and Kilmartin translation)

The paradox is that what seems initially a purely passive matter—shocked submission to a sensation that connects mutely with a prior sensation—turns out to be, thanks precisely to the initial sensation and its associated image, a resolutely active affair, so active that the rest of the remembering in *Remembrance of Things Past* flows forth from this exponentially expanding memory image. The sensation-*cum*-image, far from being the dead *décalque* of a settled past, actively affords entry into a world otherwise inaccessible.[6] The activism not only lurks in the passivism that makes it possible but surmounts it in the end.

(2) Lest you think that this is merely an anomalous or simply a "literary" case, let me turn to an arena of memory at once ancient in vintage and contemporary in significance, an arena that is accessible to all of us with but a minimum of practice. I refer of course to the method of *loci* or "places" as this is found in the mnemotechnique that was supposedly invented by Simonides, a fellow countryman of Aristotle and Plato who lived in the sixth century B.C. No better description of the method of places has been given than that by Frances Yates in *The Art of Memory*:

> The first step was to imprint on the memory a series of *loci* or places. The commonest, though not the only, type of mnemonic place system used was the architectural type. The clearest description of the process is that given by Quintilian. In order to form a series of places in memory, he says, a building is to be remembered, as the living room, bedroom, and parlors, not omitting statues and other ornaments with which the rooms are decorated. The images by which the speech is to be remembered . . . are then placed in imagination on the places which have been memorized in the building. This done, as soon as the memory of the facts requires to be revived, all these places are visited in turn and the various deposits demanded or their custodians. . . . The method ensures that the points are remembered in the right order, since the order is fixed by the sequence of places in the building.[7]

Although this method was held by Cicero and others to be the quintessence of "artificial memory" (in contrast with a "natural" memory that requires no training), in fact it can arise spontaneously and without instruction— as occurred in the notorious case of Luria's subject "S.," who employed Gorki Street in Moscow as the basic grid of places rather than a house as recommended by Quintilian.

What is most important to notice for our purposes is the fact that the grid itself represents the passive moment in this technique, while the images placed upon it—images of the things to be remembered, or symbolic of them—serve as active elements. The grid is passive insofar as it is (a) based on a fixed and invariant setting of origin, whether real or imaginary; (b) strictly memorized so as to sediment it intact into our minds; (c) traversed in a certain order of succession (though the direction can be reversed). In short, the grid is laid down as a given—much as the pegword jingle is also laid down in advance ("one is a bun, two is a shoe," etc.). Onto this base are superimposed singular images of the items to be recalled, and all ancient writers are in accord that such images need to be salient: "visual impressions of almost incredible intensity," says Yates. Thus it is not surprising to find that these images were termed *imagines agentes* ("active images") by the anonymous author of the Latin treatise entitled *Ad Herennium*:

We ought, then, to set up images of a kind that can adhere longest in memory. And we shall do so if we establish similitudes as striking as possible; if we set up images that are not many or vague but active (*imagines agentes*); if we assign to them exceptional beauty or singular ugliness; if we ornament some of them, as with crowns or purple cloaks, so that the similitude may be more distinct to us; or if we somehow disfigure them, as by introducing one stained with blood or soiled with mud or smeared with red paint, so that its form is more striking, or by assigning certain comic effects to our images, for that, too, will ensure our remembering them more readily. (*Ad Herennium*, III, xxii; cited by Yates, p. 10)

Yates comments that the active images are of "human figures dramatically engaged in some activity—*doing something*" (p. 10; my italics). She cites from the *Ad Herennium* an image of a defendant in a legal case seated at the bedside of his accuser, "holding in his right hand a cup, in his left, tablets, and on the fourth finger, a ram's testicles. . . . The cup would remind of the poisoning, the tablets of the will or inheritance, and the testicles of the ram through verbal similarity with *testes*—of the witnesses" (p. 11).[8]

Even with this much minimal description it is evident that the method of places, like Proust's involuntary memory, combines passivist and activist components. Indeed, it is effective *only* as combining both: the grid supports the active images, and the vivacity of the images bedecks the monotony of the places. It is a strictly tandem operation, each component being essential to the other: the images would be unanchored and lack order without the ordering effect of places, while the places themselves provide only the template and not the content for given acts of remembering. But it is important to remind ourselves that *both the grid and its content are present as images*. The experience is imageful through and through, indicating that images are able to occupy both ends of the spectrum whose poles are sheer passivity (say, in the grid-image of a house one knows well already) and pure activity (as in the most grotesque or surreal of conjured figures). Not only this but the special mnemonic effect—an effect which cannot be doubted as anyone can discover today for himself or herself, even if we might fall somewhat short of "S." or Seneca the Elder (who could repeat two thousand names in the order in which they were offered)—is a function of the two aspects of imagery in co-ordination with each other: the active being merely frenetic without the sobriety of the passive, the passive being merely orderly and dull without the active.

V

In brief, mnemonic effectiveness is a matter of the *interaction* between active and passive dimensions of mental imagery. As Yates puts it without explicit references to these dimensions, "the manipulation of images in memory must always to some extent involve the psyche as a whole" (*The Art of Memory*, p. xi). If so, it is wrong to attribute the efficacity of memory imagery to the active element alone—as did Quintilian, who gave the credit to the fact that the active images have to be "invented," and Cicero, who said that "images which are active . . . have the power of speedily encountering and penetrating the psyche" (ibid., pp. 17–18; Quintilian cited at p. 23). Precisely because of the flamboyance of the *imagines agentes* it is tempting to make them into the exclusive bearers of positive memorial effects. But the mainly passive grid of places which subtends them—or any other comparable means of implacement, including the pegword jingle—*also* possesses the power of "encountering and penetrating the psyche"—if not so "speedily," then (in compensation) more lastingly.

To claim this much is at once to connect up with an earlier point in this essay and with a situation in contemporary research in cognitive psychology. The earlier point was that memory images are effective in their capacity to bring the past resolutely into the present. Now we can re-interpret this proposal to mean that the sheer passivity of the past—its ever-receding and over-and-done-with character—enters into alliance with the activism of the present (the excitement of its happening *now*); and this occurs in and through the life of even the most ordinary memory images, which at once represent the past *and* precipitate it into the present, thereby bringing together an activism and passivism of time in one single moment and movement—the moment and movement of remembering itself.

The mention of "even the most ordinary memory images" brings us to the situation of contemporary research. This research has established fairly definitively that the mnemonically effective factor in the method of places—indeed, in *any* use of imagery for purposes of memorizing or remembering—is *not* the "bizarreness," the saliency or unusualness per se of the images which are employed.[9] The crucial study here is that of Wollen, Weber, and Lowry (1972), who set up a circumstance with two main variants: bizarreness of images (a cigar and a piano subject to grotesque distortion) and the combination of these images (whether bizarrely depicted or not). The result was clear: bizarreness alone did not benefit recall, whether the two images were initially conjoined or not; whereas the interaction of the images, bizarre or not, produced remembering that was nearly twice as effective as non-interacting images (again bizarre or not). In other words, it is almost two times as easy to remember an image of a cigar placed on a piano—even if both are straightforwardly represented—than of a cigar situated separately from the piano (even if both are gro-tesquely represented).[10] The overall lesson is as clear as the result: the ef-fective ingredient is the interaction of images, not their specific content or configuration.

VI

In other words, could it be that the reason (or at least the main reason) why images are so beneficial for memory is due to their capacity for drawing together dimensions and regions of human experience otherwise unassimilated and held apart: passivity and activity, bizarreness and non-bizarreness, past and present, body and mind? This capacity is so considerable that it remains undaunted even when the item to be remembered is presented as *concealed* in an image; the interaction continues despite the hiddenness of the item. I refer here to the celebrated study of Neisser and Kerr (1973), who offered three situations to their subjects as specified in the following sentences:

"a harp is hidden inside the torch held by the Statue of Liberty";

"a harp is sitting on top of the torch held by the Statue of Liberty";

"looking from one window you see the Statue of Liberty; from a window on another wall you see a harp."

Correct recall of the response "Statue of Liberty" given the stimulus word "harp" occurs just as frequently in the concealed condition (with the harp hidden) as in the fully explicit pictorial condition (with the harp exposed); and both forms of recall are once again vastly superior to that which arises in the condition of separation (when the harp and the Statue of Liberty are represented in distinctly different places).[11]

An important finding reported in the same experiment concerns the factor of vividness of images. It is natural to assume that what Hume called the "force and vivacity" of mental images contributes directly to their mnemonic effectiveness; such was doubtless the presumption behind the ancient instruction in the *ars memorativa* to make the active images as "striking" as possible. Nevertheless, Neisser and Kerr discovered that there is no significant positive correlation between the vividness and the memorability of images: the exposed or "pictorial" condition which depicted a harp sitting on top of the torch held by the Statue of Liberty was rated as decidedly more vivid than the concealed condition and yet was recalled with no greater correctness; and the concealed and separate conditions possessed the same vivacity but were remembered with considerable differences in accuracy. As Robert Crowder comments, "across conditions . . . there was a lack of correlation between vividness of images and their helpfulness in facilitating memory."[12] From this negative correlation two things of more general import are to be learned. First, any remaining belief that memory images are, or should be, snapshotlike—

that they ought to be the mental analogues of photographs—is here decisively expunged, since something that would not appear in any photograph (namely, the concealed harp) is remembered without prejudice.[13] Second, the spatiality which is operative in memory imagery cannot be reduced to strictly visual properties alone; it is not pictographic in nature, since it may include items not pictured at all; and with this recognition comes a definitive realization that memory images cannot any longer be conceived as direct copies of anything pre-existing in visual space.

Supporting this last line of consideration is the fact that congenitally blind subjects have been shown to be at no disadvantage when instructed to employ mental imagery as a way of better remembering strings of concrete nouns.[14] This points to their ability to draw on an intact sense of spatiality which is not at all dependent on the input of specific visual givens. We can speculate that it is precisely this abiding spatial sense that, in its independence of any particular sensory modality, offers an encompassing ambiance for the various forms of interaction which we have seen to be so intrinsic to memory imagery generally. One is reminded here of Plato's notion of space as *chōra,* that is, a common matrix in which particular properties and relations appear and disappear and in which connections between shapes and substances of all kinds are made. May we not infer that memory imagery requires the psychical equivalent of this cosmological medium?

We may take a further clue from Plato, whom we bypassed too rapidly earlier. In the *Timaeus* he links space (described as "the Receptacle of Becoming") to Necessity, and he claims that as such it precedes Time in the creation of the universe (cf. *Timaeus* 47e–48e). Following this line of reasoning, could it be that one of the reasons—perhaps even the major reason—why images are so important for memory is that they are the proper occupants of a layer of our mentation that is at once necessary and pretemporal (perhaps even a condition for our experience of time)? If this is so, it would accord well with one of the most influential models in cognitive psychology of the last twenty years: to wit, Allan Paivio's "dual coding" or "dual trace" hypothesis. As set forth in Paivio's *Imagery and Verbal Processes,* this is the view that we have two encoding systems at our disposal: one is sequential or "serial" in its mode of processing and thus favors verbal material; the other operates by "parallel" processing of simultaneously given items and thus favors images.[15] The diachrony or successiveness of the former, the "logogen" system—its timelike character— stands in contrast with the *totum simul* nature, the all-at-onceness, of the latter "imagen" system: its spacelike character. The special value of parallel processing is immediately evident. On the one hand, many items of information can be taken in at a single cognitive glance (as when viewing a painting we apprehend a synthetic whole and not a mere succession of parts); on the other hand, the items thus taken in together in one spatial display will be in a most propitious position for interaction. In particular, the two items which we conventionally label "stimulus" and "response" in a given experimental situation—indeed, any paired-associate learning circumstance—will be given a maximum opportunity to merge: to become "fused into a single entity, one part of which can be elicited by the other."[16]

In view of this two-fold advantage of parallel or spatial processing, is it adequate to say (as did Paivio himself) that "memory performance increases directly with the number of alternative memory codes available for an item."[17] This is the "coding redundancy hypothesis," which amounts in practice to saying that the effects of encoding in verbal and spatial terms are "additive" in nature, producing impressive mnemonic results when both codes are at work (e.g., in the case of concrete nouns or other easily imageable items). Such effects are real and have been replicated many times; but does the notion of mere *addition* adequately capture the matter at hand? I think not; nor does the compromise position (adopted by Gordon Bower) of a "common coding" underlying verbal and spatial codes. We should remember Plato once more: space may be necessary in that it underlies and precedes time. Translated into contemporary terms, this would mean that the parallel processing of images takes precedence over the serial processing of words—that the former is both necessary and prior to the latter. And the reason for the necessity and priority would lie precisely in the decided facilitation of interaction which imagery of all kinds, including mental imagery, accomplishes.

If this is indeed the case, it would support the quite general finding in countless experiments of the last thirty years that it is not "the encoding of individual items" but "the formation of relational associations" which is the truly effective factor in remembering of every sort.[18] For imagery is especially adept in creating such associations, given its operation within a spatial field which (however implicit or tacit it may be in certain cases) serves to bring together the most disparate items in one common embrace. Where diachronic time tends to "disperse subsistence" (in a phrase from Aristotle's *Physics*) by emphasizing possibilities of decay and replacement— think only of how each 'now' takes the place of its immediate predecessor, shoving the latter into oblivion—synchronic space allows for the retaining of the subsistent in the face of time's dispersal itself. And if remembering is quintessentially an activity of keeping—"keeping," says Heidegger, "is the fundamental nature and essence of memory"[19]—then it is not at all surprising that the spatializing movements of images are essential to remembering and promote its improvement and its very well-being.

VII

How important are images for memory? We should rather ask: how can they *fail* to be important? It is beginning to emerge that images are potentially *all*-important for memory; and they are this thanks to their inherent spatiality, their extraordinary capacity for being inclusive and interconnective. These are especially important properties to have in the teeth of time's disintegrative action: memory is, after all, the ultimate holding action in human existence, holding our lives together in a fused whole which time continually threatens to take apart. As an integrating force, memory relies on its own most "natural resources" as these are given by images. It is hardly surprising that imagery is at work in the most forceful and lasting kinds of remembering—from hypermnesia (where the images are eidetic) to facial recognition—as well as in the most momentary forms of echoic and primary memory. As Richardson observes laconically, "mental imagery not only improves memory performance, but also makes the stored material less vulnerable to forgetting."[20]

At the same time, we become less startled to observe the original success and the remarkable tenacity of the place method of memorizing. This method may be considered an almost literal embodiment of the general truth that space provides a baseline for remembering of many kinds, acting as a steady "receptacle" for the implacement of active images that denote, embody, or symbolize specific things-to-be-recalled. The matrix formed by the concatenation of *loci* in the "art of memory" is itself a concretization of the interfusing nature of memory in its spatial being.

We begin to suspect that the very "passivity" of the place method— namely, its underlying grid system—may be the hidden source of its effectiveness. The same would be true for the pegword method—indeed, for every mnemonically efficacious device or circumstance. What we had taken to be a mere precondition or a matter of rote learning (e.g., in memorizing the successive locations within a house as recommended by Quintilian) may turn out to be the truly potent factor: more potent in any case than the gaudily decorated "active images" which are placed on these locations. If so, we would find ourselves in agreement with a basic claim of Edmund Husserl, the founder of phenomenology:

> [there is] a passivity which is truly objectivating, namely, one which
> thematizes or cothematizes objects; [this] is a passivity which belongs
> to the act, not as a base but as act, a kind of *passivity in activity.*[21]

The radicality of this claim is that it challenges the very distinction between passivity and activity on which so much of Western philosophy and psychology has been founded—and on which I have been drawing myself earlier in this chapter. If there is such a thing as "passivity in activity" (and thus its converse, activity in passivity), then it was always presumptuous to assume that all of the passivity could be contained in images and all the activity in sensation (as on the classical empiricist view) or that, as in the place method, all the passivity could be kept on the side of the grid while allotting all the activity to the images of things to be remembered. Just as the ancient art of memory reminds us that images can be active on their own, so we must remind ourselves that its own tendency to take the underlying system of places as a passive given betrays the role of space in memory. This role is one that we can now characterize as active *in its very passivity*. Thus, even to speak (as I spoke myself a while ago) of the spatial medium as a "baseline" is to betray the basic insight that (in Husserl's words once again) space operates "not as a base but *as act*."

Space as act: this is far indeed from any conception of space as neutral medium or mere setting for action—as on the model that we inherit from Newtonian physics, which sought exact, "simple locations" within an undifferentiated infinite container. It is also far from the view that we have as a legacy from Kant, who makes space into an a priori condition of experience, including temporal experience. I believe that this Kantian conception is true, but it still does not capture fully the radicality of the model of space which was first suggested by Plato and then refined by Husserl. And yet it is this very model which is most apposite for understanding the importance of images for memory. For images—and images alone—activate spatiality at a level of experience which is simultaneously passive and active: active in its own apparent passivity and thus all the more effective in matters of memory, since memory often works best precisely by indirection and not by voluntary effort, as Proust demonstrated so eloquently.

If "memory demands an image"—if, beyond exceptional moments and any particular mnemotechnique, we find ourselves spontaneously relying on images in remembering—then we are beginning at last to comprehend why such images are required, even if we do not yet know exactly how they operate in given cases. They are called for (and fortunately they often arise unbidden) as exemplars and representatives of space-in-act. Memory images certainly convey the past into the present, but they do so as figured in space—which is to say, in an active-passive embrace that is unique to spatial configurations. The passivity of inclusion and location is conjoined with the activity of compression and comprehension. Is this not just what memory images of every sort, ranging from the hyper- to the hypomnesiac, do for us in ways that language on its own cannot achieve?

To speak of "space-as-act" is to come close to talking of an *enacted space.* Coming full cycle, I refer here to the aesthetic and specifically the dramaturgical potential of images for memory. A case in point is that dream of mine with which this chapter began. Itself compounded of prior memory images and now a re-enacted memory image, the scene of my wine-stained shirt turning polychromatic exemplifies the actively passive properties of space-in-act. How else—how better—than in an image could such a scene of transfiguration take place? Factors of implacement (the shirt as a field of polychromatic presentation) combine in a single fused whole that we call simply "the dream image." In this particular case—which is perhaps not otherwise remarkable—I would venture to say that the dream image is itself an image of a memory outside the special context of dreams themselves. It testifies to the capacity of memory images to capture and to transfigure memorial content—to refer back and to refer forward, to sum up and to move on. It is human spatiality that makes this possible. More than a basis for action, such spatiality *is* action, and above all when it is enacted in images of such a sort as this—and of many other sorts too.

In my opening remarks above, I invoked the figure of Mnēmosynē, the mythic Mother of the Muses—she who operates through the conjoint action of images in all the arts. Memory is the generative force in (and of) the arts—thanks precisely to the role of images in the arts, images that transcend their own origins in imitation. Two of the arts—and thus two of the Muses—brought forth are lyric poetry and the dance, presided over by Euterpe and Terpsichore respectively. Let me close with a few lines from T. S. Eliot's "Burnt Norton," lines which in their lyricism invoke the dance in the setting of space (and "Terpsichore" means literally 'to delight-in-space'):

At the still point of the turning world. Neither flesh nor fleshless;
Neither from nor towards; at the still point, there the dance is,
But neither arrest nor movement. And do not call it fixity,
Where past and future are gathered. Neither movement from nor towards,
Neither ascent nor decline. Except for the point, the still point,
There would be no dance, and there is only the dance.

I can only say, *there* we have been; but I cannot say where.
And I cannot say, how long, for that is to place it in time. . . .

Images, we may conclude, take us there in memory: a there that need not possess exact location or date. Memory images are thus important still points of the turning world: passive-active gatherings of past and future in the present of the dance that is always already *now*.

1.   Edward S. Casey, *Imagining: A Phenomenological Study* (Bloomington, IN.: Indiana University Press, 1976), p. 199.

2.   Z. E. Pylyshyn, "What the Mind's Eye Tells the Mind's Brain: A Critique of Mental Imagery," *Psychological Bulletin* 80 (1973): 1–24.

3.   James Mill, *An Analysis of the Phenomena of the Human Mind*, I, pp. 51–52. Cited by Norman Malcolm, *Memory and Mind* (Ithaca, N.Y.: Cornell University Press, 1977), p. 121.

4.   Bertrand Russell, *The Analysis of Mind* (London: Allen & Unwin, 1921), p. 186.

5.   Henri Bergson, *Matter and Memory*, trans. N. M. Paul and W. S. Palmer (New York: Anchor, 1959), p. 133.

6.   On this point, see Mary C. Rawlinson, "Proust's Impressionism," *L'Espirit Créateur* (Fall, 1984): 80–91.

7.   Frances A. Yates, *The Art of Memory* (London: Routledge and Kegan Paul, 1966), p. 3.

8.   *Testes* means equally 'testicles' or 'witnesses.'

9.   Two possible exceptions need to be mentioned. There are certain genuinely positive

effects of bizarre imagery after a delay of twenty-four hours or more, as well as in those cases where subjects rank the bizarreness of their images at the moment of initial presentation. See the studies cited by J. T. E. Richardson on p. 73 of his *Mental Imagery and Human Memory* (New York: St. Martin's, 1980).

10. See K. A. Wollen, A. Weber and D. Lowry, "Bizarreness versus Interaction of Mental Images as Determinants of Learning," *Cognitive Psychology* 3 (1973): 518–23.

11. See U. Neisser and N. Kerr, "Spatial and Mnemonic Properties of Visual Images," *Cognitive Psychology* 5 (1973): 138–50. For a critique of Neisser and Kerr, however, see Richardson, *Mental Imagery and Human Memory*, p. 75; but Richardson admits that the experiment nonetheless "supports the general idea of the mnemonic effectiveness of interactive imagery" (ibid.).

12. Robert G. Crowder, *Principles of Learning and Memory* (Hillsdale, N.J.: Erlbaum, 1976), p. 129.

13. On this point, see ibid., pp. 129–30.

14. Cf. J. Jonides, R. Kahn, and P. Rozin, "Imagery Instruction Improves Memory in Blind Subjects," *Bulletin of the Psychonomic Society* 5 (1975): 424–26.

15. See Allan Paivio, *Imagery and Verbal Processes* (New York: Holt, Rinehart & Winston, 1971).

16. Crowder, *Principles of Learning and Memory*, p. 125.

17. Richardson, commenting on Paivio, in *Mental Imagery and Human Memory*, p. 62.

18. Richardson, *Mental Imagery and Human Memory*. p. 75, with reference to G. H. Bower, "Imagery as a Relational Organizer in Associative Learning," *Journal of Verbal Learning and Verbal Behavior* 9 (1970): 529–33.

19. Martin Heidegger, *What Is Called Thinking?*, trans. J. Glenn Gray (New York: Harper & Row, 1968), p. 151.

20. Richardson, *Mental Imagery and Human Memory*, p. 72. Cf. also ibid., p. 61: such imagery "gives rise to a distinctive and highly efficient means of storing information."

21. Edmund Husserl, *Experience and Judgment*, trans. J. S. Churchill and K. Ameriks (Evanston: Northwestern University Press, 1973), p. 108; his italics.

Imagining and Remembering

I

IMAGINING AND REMEMBERING, two of the most frequent and fundamental acts of mind, have long been unwelcome guests in most of the many mansions of philosophy. When not simply ignored or overlooked, they have been considered only to be dismissed. This is above all true of imagination, as first becomes evident in Plato's view that the art of making exact images (*eikastikē*) tends to degenerate into the making of mere semblances (*phantastikē*). Kant, despite the importance he gives to imagination in the first edition of *The Critique of Pure Reason,* nevertheless considers images to be lowly "monograms" that are unruly and thus untrustworthy. In more recent times, Sartre, who is nearly as ambivalent as Kant on the subject, has stressed imagination's "essential poverty"—its character as "debased thought"—while Ryle, in covert counterpoint, has attempted to conceive imagining as parody and pretense—as mere make-believe.[1]

In all such questioning of the legitimacy and cognitive value of imagination, memory is willy-nilly implicated as well. This is not only because memory is so frequently confined to a passively reproductive function of low epistemic status. It is also because remembering is held to be intrinsically imagistic in nature; it takes place, according to a widely accepted view, by the animation of what are significantly called "memory *images.*" As Aristotle said, launching a whole tradition, remembering is "the having of an image regarded as a copy of that of which it is an image."[2] Quite apart from the special problems arising from a copy theory of memory, what is striking in Aristotle's position is the way in which he thrusts imagining and remembering together: "it is the objects of imagination that are remembered in their own right."[3] After Aristotle, the conception of imagination and memory as twin faculties, as the Dioscuri of mind, became a commonplace of medieval and Renaissance thought, and Hobbes could even claim that "*Imagination* and *Memory* are but one thing, which for divers considerations hath divers names."[4] This statement is certainly false, but it is also highly revealing: imagination and memory *might as well be the same thing* in the eyes of an entire philosophical tradition which has imperialistically considered them as mere outposts or offshoots of some more primordial act.

Perception, sensory perception in particular, has characteristically been regarded as this more primordial act—as the act of acts, from which all other acts of mind are seen to stem. The primacy of perception is a basic tenet of Western philosophy—at many points *the* basic tenet—and when Aristotle observes nonchalantly that "it is apparent, then, to which part of the soul memory belongs, namely, the same [primary perceptual] part as that to which imagination belongs,"[5] he is only foreshadowing Merleau-Ponty's view that imagining and—a fortiori—remembering are forms of "teleperception," that is, diluted and extended modes of perceiving.[6] Hume, in this context a close cousin of both Aristotle and Merleau-Ponty, holds that imagination and memory are to be distinguished mainly by their relative "vivacity," a criterion itself borrowed from the analysis of sensory perception. And the latter is said to be the origin and exclusive source of imagination and memory alike: "both these faculties borrow their simple ideas from impressions, and can never go beyond these original perceptions."[7]

We may take this familiar statement of Hume's as emblematic of what many mainstream Western philosophers have maintained, implicitly or explicitly, concerning the proper place of imagining and remembering within the mind. The gist of their thinking may be summed up in two closely correlated propositions:

Proposition 1: Imagining and remembering have approximately or even exactly equivalent standing in the mind; if they are not in fact the same act viewed in different respects, they are at least comparable in epistemic status and in their basic operations.

Proposition 2: Both are strictly derivative from sensory perception, which provides them with all of their content.

The two propositions are closely linked because to assert that imagining and remembering stem straight from perception is ipso facto to give the two acts an equivalent and equally subordinate position vis-à-vis their parent act. If each is a direct derivative of perception, each may be regarded as a form of what Hobbes called "decaying sense." To differentiate them further becomes a matter of nuance, depending merely on whether we wish to stress the factor of "decay" or not.[8]

Just here a series of questions arises. What if the two acts are neither directly derivative from perception nor basically similar to each other? What if, on the contrary, they are essentially *dis*similar in structure and operation and quite distinguishable from perception as well? And what if, despite their dissimilarity (and perhaps even because of it), they prove to be part of the very fabric of human experience—including perceptual experience itself? It is to these questions that I wish to address myself in this essay.

II

First of all, is it the case that, as Proposition 2 asserts, imagining and remembering are "strictly derivative from sensory perception, which provides them with all of their content"? This is doubtful. It is one thing to argue that perception is *presupposed* by other cognitive activities and quite another to claim that the latter ineluctably draw their entire content from previous perceiving. It may certainly be admitted that perception is a general precondition of other, perhaps even of all, acts of mind: if we were not perceivers, we could not also be imaginers, rememberers, or even thinkers. To be-in-the-world at all, even in the most minimally responsive way, is to be there as perceivers, as differentially sentient beings.

But to grant the basic indispensability of perception—its sine qua non status in human experience—is not thereby to be committed to the much more extreme claim set forth in proposition 2. On closer inspection, this claim breaks down into two sub-theses: (a) perception is the *specific cause* of "postperceptual" acts such as imagining and remembering (this is implicit in the notion of derivation itself); (b) perception is the *unique source* of content for these two acts. Let us examine each of these sub-theses briefly and with special reference to imagining and remembering. To find them problematic will be to question the fundamental assumption of the primacy of perception on which they are ultimately based.

(a) To hold that an act of perception is the specific cause of another act is to maintain either that the perceptual act is the first member of a series of causally concatenated acts giving rise to the other act or that it is the precipitating factor immediately preceding the latter. But we must ask here: Is one or the other of these two forms of causal precedence always at work in actual instances of imagining and remembering? Surely I can imagine or remember in such a way and at such a time that my act is *not* precipitated by some particular perceptual experience either directly or through a series of intermediary causal links. Indeed, even when I *am* able to trace my present imagining or remembering back to an initial perception, this perception does not necessarily serve as a *cause* of my contemporary experience: it may only set the stage for it by establishing its context or primary parameters.

(b) It is even more manifest that former perceptions are not the sole source of content for acts of imagining and remembering. Sometimes, of course, they are such a source (just as they are also sometimes causally efficacious in their regard): for example, in imagining a classically conceived centaur on the basis of illustrations in mythology books or in remembering what one's childhood home looked like. At other times, however, this is simply not so: I can imagine a creature I have never perceived before, and not merely as a composite of already perceived parts (as on the empiricist model); likewise, I can remember such non-perceptual items as a former thought, an emotion, even a prior memory. Given this essential independence of imagined and remembered contents from previously perceived content, it is mistaken to claim, as does Hume, that all imagining (and, consequently, all remembering) "amounts to no more than the materials afforded us by the senses and experience."[9] Hume himself cites a critical exception to his rule of strict derivation—the famous missing shade of blue[10]—and if this single exception is allowed many more are possible. Thus the second of the sub-theses of proposition 2 survives scrutiny no better than the first, and we are forced to reject the proposition as a whole.[11]

III

If imagining and remembering are therefore to be regarded as noncontinuous with perceiving in terms of causation and content, how are they to be viewed vis-à-vis one another? So far, we have lumped them together much as the tradition has done, as if to endorse Vico's bald Hobbesian declaration that "memory is the same as imagination."[12] To espouse such a view is to subscribe to proposition 1. In questioning this claim, we need not go to the opposite extreme and concur with William Blake that "imagination has *nothing* to do with memory."[13] But we do need to acknowledge some of the fundamental differences between the two acts— differences that prevent us from altogether assimilating one to the other. Four such differences merit mention here.[14]

First of all, in remembering proper or "recollection," we normally proceed by *positing* the former existence or occurrence of whatever it is that we are recalling: we impute to what we recollect a unique (though not necessarily specified) temporal position in the past. No such positing activity is intrinsic to imagining, in which we may entertain what we imagine as something that indifferently might appear, arise, or happen at *any* given time or place—or even at *no* given time or place at all. Imagining is in this respect non-positing in nature and involves an attitude of sheer supposal that contrasts with the committed character of remembering— committed precisely to stationing its content at some particular point in past experience.

A second and closely related difference between imagining and remembering is found in the factor of *familiarity*. Basic to remembering, but not to imagining, is the sense of being already acquainted with what we remember. The content of memory not only forms part of *the* past but part of *our own* past; and as such it is something with which we are familiar, however partially or imperfectly. In contrast with this, we are able to imagine objects and situations with which we are quite unfamiliar. The Romantics and the surrealists, for all their excesses, were right in this regard: imagining may herald the advent of the genuinely new in our experience, of what has never before been projected or contemplated by us.

Thirdly, memories are inherently *corrigible*; they may present as having happened what did not in fact happen (or happened differently); they can deny that something happened when in fact it did and in still other ways mislead us concerning our own previous experience. Imagining, on the other hand, is incapable of misleading us in this respect; not purporting to depict something as it really is or was (though often projecting what might be or might have been), it cannot be called to account for *mis*depicting it either. Imagining is thus, and to this extent, non-corrigible.

Finally, imagining and remembering diverge from each other with regard to their fundamental *act-forms*. Imagining, as I have attempted to show elsewhere,[15] has three basic forms: imaging (in which quasi-sensuous content is entertained in the guise of simple objects or events), imagining-that (in which states of affairs, quasi-sensuous or not sensuous at all, are envisioned), and imagining-how (wherein we project a situation in which we are ourselves actively involved). Remembering, contrastingly, has more than three major forms. There is, to begin with, remembering in the form of contemplating a simple object or event as past (this corresponds to imaging), and there are also frequent instances of remembering-how (something was done or experienced) and/or remembering-that (such and such occurred). But in addition we can remember *to* do X or Y (including remembering to remember), and we can also remember *on the occasion of* (my birthday, my return home, etc.). None of these latter forms of activity has a direct analogue in imaginative experience, which is in this respect at least a less luxuriant phenomenon. It is almost as if the intrinsically limited content of memory (limited precisely to experiences posited as past) has led, by way of compensation, to a greater multiplicity of act-forms by which to diversify the presentation of this content.

IV

Now that imagining and remembering have been seen to be more than mere extensions or modalities of perception and to be demonstrably distinct from each other, we must turn to the still more urgent task of demonstrating that the two acts are fundamental, and not merely adventitious, forms of mental life. To show this is to call into question the widespread tendency, evident in philosophical theorizing and in common sense alike, that seeks to belittle the significance of imagination and memory—to trivialize them by supposing that they perform easily eliminable or transferable roles within the economy of mentation: we were "just imagining" or "only reminisc-ing," we sometimes say, as if we were not doing anything of any real consequence.

Against such a disparaging view, it would not be difficult to cite various ways in which imagining and remembering, taken separately, are each of importance in human experience. On the one hand, what Dewey called "dramatic rehearsal in imagination"[16] is crucial to such diverse activities as artistic creation and ethical reflection (in both of which the possible results of actions need to be foreseen). On the other hand, remembering is essential to our very sense of personal identity—of persistence over time as continuously the same person or self.[17] But instead of discussing such familiar instances, I want to consider a comparatively neglected set of cases. In these, the two acts acquire significance not in isolation from each other but precisely in their *conjoint* action. In other words, I shall take the "and" in the title of this essay quite seriously by inquiring into various ways in which imagining-*and*-remembering functions as a single (though often in-ternally complex) unit of mental activity.

We may begin by distinguishing between two different sorts of cases in point: contingent and non-contingent collaboration. In contingent col-laboration, the conjunction of imagining and remembering is a possible but not an inherent or required feature. Everyday examples are found in the mixed modes of consciousness wherein we spontaneously combine im-agining and remembering to form an aggregate act, as when I remember myself as a small boy imagining how delightful it would be to be an adult—for you could then stop the car wherever you desired and collect roadside rocks to your heart's content. Here an act of imagining becomes the con-tent of an act of remembering. The converse is also possible, since I can very well imagine myself remembering any number of things, including remembering to imagine myself remembering . . . to imagine myself remembering. And so on.

Such contingent (and often quite trivial) combinations nevertheless make manifest the mutual inclusiveness and co-iterability of the two acts, their inbuilt co-operativeness. On many occasions, moreover, one act seems designed to solicit the other—to call the other to its aid. What we cannot remember we can try to imagine, and what we cannot imagine we can try to summon up in memory as an analogue from the past. A striking case of such reciprocal solicitation, but one that is no longer contingent in status, is found in the historian's activity of reconstructing past events. It is just because the historian cannot, from her own experience and resources alone, imagine a given past event in full detail that she seeks out the testimony of those who once witnessed it—which is to say, she seeks their remember-ings in lieu of her own. Yet precisely because these rememberings are notoriously untrustworthy (frequently being based on what still others remembered or were reported to remember), the historian must correct and supplement them by her own imaginings in the present. Indeed, her imaginings are needed even when her sources *are* to be trusted. For no amount of historical evidence, however copious or firsthand it may be, can restore the past event itself as seen from every significant perspective. It cannot, in particular, incorporate the historian's *own* perspectival position, which has to be imagined *into* the original event. And, still more generally, the historian must imagine how the event as a whole held together and was experienced as a single, datable happening. In the end, what Collingwood terms "the web of imaginative construction"[18] extends to the entirety of each epoch or period studied by the historian and is not limited to her interpolations between attested facts: the "facts" themselves, as reconstructed in her mind, are compounded of imagined and remembered elements, and necessarily so. Even if the historian writes as if she were herself remembering the events recounted, such quasi-remembering is highly imaginified; it is in fact the product of an extensive collaboration between imagination and memory.

V

Historical reconstruction represents a relatively conspicuous instance of non-contingent collaboration between imagining and remembering. In this kind of collaboration, the respective roles of the two acts are not only difficult to disentangle but, more crucially, each proves to be uneliminable. Or more exactly: each act is indispensable *in its collaboration with the other*. Each is not just essential but *co*-essential, essential in its very coordination with the other. I want now to take up three less obvious but even more exemplary cases of non-contingent collaboration.[19] Two of these, screen memories and dreaming, emerge from a reading of Freud; the third, time-consciousness, is based on the writings of Husserl.

Like historical reconstruction, screen memories concern the past—but this time the remote past of the individual himself or herself. They are those vivid, recurrent, and apparently innocent memories which we seem to recall from earliest childhood. In fact, however, they are not simple, straightforward recollections, but complex combinations of imagined and remembered components in which what we recall (or appear to recall) cloaks phantasies whose naked expression in full consciousness is disallowed. These phantasies are imaginings of scenes of satisfaction which did *not* occur at the time of the remembered event, though they were (and still are) ardently wished for. In Freud's own autobiographical example, the screen memory of stealing flowers from a younger female cousin in a country meadow concealed his longing to "deflower" a peasant girl whom he had met when he returned as an adolescent to the small Moravian town in which he had spent the first few years of his life. It also screened his wish that his family had remained in Moravia, where life seemed easier and simpler than in teeming Vienna.[20] A screen memory such as this is a vehicle for the fulfillment of phantasy, yet only as covertly contained in a memory. As Freud says, the screen memory "offers phantasy a point of contact— comes, as it were, half way to meet it."[21] The result is a compromise for- mation in which the interests of memory and imaginative phantasy alike receive satisfaction. And they do so precisely by colluding with each other. On the one hand, the childhood memory would not have such vivacity, or be so recurrent, were it not for the festering phantasy that has singled it out for special stress. On the other hand, the phantasy in turn needs the memory as a cover (hence the *Deck-* of *Deckerinnerung*), as a concrete representation that, precisely because of its ostensibly historical character, lends credibility and substance to what is otherwise mere wish, mere im- agining. The interaction extends still further. For the memory may itself be modified and even falsified in order to suit the phantasy, retaining just enough of its original content to present itself plausibly as an actual scene from childhood. Thus Freud can conclude in a highly skeptical vein that "it may indeed be questioned whether we have any memories at all *from* our childhood: memories *relating to* our childhood may be all that we possess."[22] If this is so, it is due to an intimate and often undetected liaison between imagination and memory, a liaison which serves to reshape con- tinually the apprehension of our personal past.

Dreams Freud regarded as comparable to screen memories in important respects.[23] Just as a screen memory is an ambiguous amalgam of actual memories and phantasies, so a dream combines the same two constituents in still another compromise formation. But in dreaming the situation is further complicated by the fact that imagination and memory conjoin on two distinctively different levels, latent and manifest, thereby producing a *double* commixture of imagistic and remembered elements—much as the full dream is also doubly articulated with regard to its imagistic and signifying elements. A dream is therefore imagined-and-remembered twice over, just as it is also always a twice-told tale. How is this so?

At the latent level of dreams, that of basic wishes or "dream-thoughts," memory enters in the form of imprints or "traces" left over from experiences of need and its satisfaction in earliest infancy, that is, in a period predating even the origin of screen memories. Freud invokes the questionable notion of memory-trace because he wants to emphasize that we do not remember these archaic experiences as such, in their explicit, fully detailed content; we remember them only engrammatically—schematically, as it were. It is just because of such schematicalness that we must, as adults, *imagine* something specific enough to convert empty traces into the images of an experience of satisfaction repeating, or patterned on, an archaic experience. Such imaginative filling out of memory-traces occurs at the latent level in the form of unconscious phantasy—which is why Freud can say that "the unconscious activity of the imagination has a large share in the construc- tion of the [latent] dream-thoughts."[24]

The full expression of such activity is accomplished, however, only at the manifest level, i.e., in the "dream scene" that we explicitly experience and recount. Like a screen memory or a neurotic symptom, the manifest dream must manage to bring about the satisfaction of a suppressed wish while at the same time concealing it *as* satisfaction. The means by which this delicate, self-deceiving operation is performed are again both imaginative and mnemonic in character. While the dream scene itself is vividly imagistic, even to the point of hallucinatory intensity,[25] much of the detailed content of the manifest imagery of dreams derives from the "day's residues," that is, from the short-term memory of miscellaneous objects and events encountered in the last twenty-four hours or so. Because of their topical and often trivial nature, the day's residues furnish an ideal mode of disguise for latent wishes whose satisfaction cannot be expressly represented. Thus one form of residue, the most recent, serves to conceal another form, the original memory-trace underlying unconscious wishes; and the two residues are conjoined by the activity of imagination, first in the guise of unconscious phantasy and then as that type of imagining which shapes the day's residues into the finished facade of the dream. The result is a unique dual collaboration between imagination and memory, which rejoin each other at both latent and manifest levels.

Therefore, when Freud concludes that "our experience in dreams is only a modified kind of imagining made possible by the conditions of the state of sleep,"[26] he might well have added: and also a modified kind of remembering qua trace and day residue. Dreaming is a modified and redoubled activity of imagining and remembering—of imagining *by* remembering and of remembering *by* imagining. As Freud's frequently used compound term *Erinnerungsbild*, "mnemic image," suggests, dreaming is a composite act of imagining-*cum*-remembering. But it is a composite act raised to the second power. Without two-tiered memories, dreams would lack both sensory intensity and any basis for drawing upon the dreamer's recent and distant past; and without a shaping and synthesizing imagination at work at both levels of their formation, they would lapse into a mere mishmash of rememberings.

VI

When we come to time-consciousness, we encounter a collaboration between imagining and remembering that is not only non-contingent but continuously operative. Our sense of being in time and of time's passing is not merely episodic or intermittent—as are occurrences of screen memories or dreams. It is pervasively present and gives to our lives their most cohesive and recurrent structure; as such, it is the source of what Dilthey called *"der Zusammenhang des Lebens."* Time binds—even if it does not always heal.

Our consciousness of time manifests itself in a series of closely related and often overlapping phases which we conventionally label "past," "present," and "future." Let us begin with the present, which is in many respects the most problematic because of the tendency (especially noticeable in Aristotle, Augustine, and Descartes) to reduce it to an instantaneous point, an extensionless now. An entire countertendency, led by Bergson and James, has resisted this reduction, arguing that the notion of a punctiform present fails to represent our actual experience of time. With this objection one cannot help but agree from a descriptive or phenomenological point of view. What the upholders of the prolonged present leave unresolved, however, is the question as to how the present's prolongation is effected. What, in James's celebrated terms, turns the knife-edge into a saddle-back?[27] What makes it the case that, as Husserl says, "it belongs to the essence of lived experiences to have to be spread out in such a way that there is never an isolated punctual phase"?[28]

It is Husserl's own analysis of internal time-consciousness, perhaps the most subtle such analysis ever performed, that points the way to an answer. Punctiformity is overcome in one direction by a continuous streaming backward of every new experience—a streaming which is to be likened to the tail of a comet. Husserl's technical term for this tail is "retention," a penumbral phase or continuum of phases actively shadowing the ever-changing contents of consciousness, holding them in mind even as they lapse from explicit impressional awareness. As modified in retention, these contents sink back or down in consciousness until they reach imperceptibility. In so doing, they stretch out the initial moment of perception regarded as the "now-point" or "source-point" and thereby create what James calls "the rearward portion of the present space of time."[29]

The activity underlying this whole process of retentional *Herabsinken* is designated as "primary memory" by Husserl. It is a form of *memory* because it involves the consciousness of something as having already happened, and it is *primary* because it concerns itself with the immediate past, with what has *just* happened. In fact, the past of primary memory is a past that, paradoxically, is still part of the present: it is the present-as-just-past, the present in the very process of *becoming* past. Primary memory, through the agency of retentions, allows the merely momentary to linger as the just-having-been, the *soeben gewesen*.

But the punctiform present or now-point is extended in a second way as well. In addition to being drawn back in retention, it is also drawn forward in a prospective direction by "protentions," which give to the present its aura of immediate futurity. Without this aura, we would arrive at the end of experienced time, for we would lack any sense of what is about-to-be, any sense of onward movement. Protentions bring about this consciousness of forward flow, of intercepting the future in the making. What does the protending is what I would like to term "primary imagination"—not "primary expectation" as Husserl calls it.[30] Expectation implies an attitude of anxious awaiting, an expectancy, which is foreign to the spontaneity of protending. This spontaneity is a spontaneity of projecting the proximal future in acts of primary imagining. Just as in primary memory we grasp what has just-come-to-be, so in primary imagination we glimpse what is just-coming-to-be in the very process of its coming to be; and this is the case even if we do not explicitly intuit what is *not yet* or the future proper. Among mental acts, imagining is best suited for engendering a protentional consciousness of this sort. For the single most characteristic operation of imagination consists in projecting possibilities, among which are those possibilities predelineated on the growing edge of the present. To protend such possibilities is what is *primary* imagining, which thus allows the present to move forward and to become an ongoing, never-fully-concluded enterprise.

Primary memory and primary imagination combine forces in the generation of what Husserl calls the "living present," a temporal expanse sedimented with the immediate past in retentions and alive with the immediate future through protentions. Retentions and protentions may also be considered the "primitive" or "first" forms of the past and the future.[31] But if so, they do not constitute the past or future proper. For these latter are not mere extensions of the living present; they are temporal domains in their own right and call for separate analysis. The past proper is that part of experienced time which has become so thoroughly dissociated from the present that it can *only* be recalled or recollected—called *back* to consciousness from the waters of Lethe in which all retentions are eventually immersed. James, who influenced Husserl's analysis of time so profoundly, put it this way:

> An object which is recollected, in the proper sense of the term, is one which has been absent from the consciousness altogether, and now revives anew. It is brought back, recalled, fished up, so to speak, from a reservoir in which, with countless other objects, it lay buried and lost from view.[32]

As "*Wiedererinnerung,*" one of the several German words for recollection, intimates, recollecting is remembering *again* and involves a "secondary" memory pursuant upon (and also dependent upon) primary memory. In secondary remembering, we re-collect[33] a previous present (as constituted by its retentions and protentions) from the standpoint of our *present* present, that is, the present of the act of recollection itself, which of course has its own retentions and protentions and is likewise subject to subsequent recollection. Such remembering is secondary, therefore, not in its overall importance but in its necessary posteriority to, and discontinuity with, the experience we are recalling. It is a way of giving that experience a second chance, a second life.[34]

Secondary memory thus operates by means of revival: by the *re-*

presentation, the experiencing again, of an original experience, not "just as it was" but as it can now be reconstituted in recollection. This recollective re-experiencing is made possible by the fact that the experience being recalled, lacking fresh retentions and protentions (indeed, having had all of its protentions turned into now-fixed retentions), has gained the compression and closure required for becoming the content of secondary memory. What we recollect has not only sunk down in consciousness but has contracted in such a way as to acquire what Husserl calls "the unity of the remembered."[35] We remember discrete objects and events which, *precisely as discrete*, can be given determinate positions in a continuum of past experiences and thereby be posited as actualities in the specific temporal mode of "once-having been." (This is what enables us to say that "the past rises up before us"; it does so not by auto-resurrection but by having gained sufficient unity to be remembered as such.)

The future proper, by way of contrast, lacks the contractedness, the felt density, of the recollected past. Although it does momentarily assume a determinate guise in prophetic visions (visions which we often distrust just because of their specificity), normally it is quite indeterminate in content and its exact form is left in suspense.[36] For the most part, we leave future time *open*—open for the appearance of what must, from the perspective of the present, be merely projected there: put there as a possibility. This is so even when we try to tie down the future by means of calculation and planning; as we know, the best-laid plans often dissolve into the pointless or the irrelevant when the planned-for future itself arrives.

The future proper is projected by a form of imagining which, rather than prolonging the present into what is about-to-happen (as in primary imagining), ranges freely over the more remote reaches of the not yet. Such specifically *secondary* imagining concerns itself with possibilities beyond those already predelineated in the present or already realized in the past. They are to this extent *pure* possibilities, possibilities untethered to any particular point in time or to any particular event or set of events. Even the probabilities which are sometimes imputed to future events represent a subset of the purely possible. For to project any event (however highly probable) as taking place in the future we must *imagine* it as being there; and this is necessarily to place it under the sign of the purely possible: which is to say, still possibly quite different from what we may presently anticipate. The future, not yet being (being still open, being unanticipatable), does not, in contrast with the past, deliver itself to us in closed wholes. Rarely being exactly what we expect it to be (concerning it we must, as Heraclitus said, "expect the unexpected"[37]), it has to be actively projected, projected as purely possible, by acts of secondary imagining.[38]

In sum, there are two fundamental levels of collaboration between imagining and remembering in the structure of time-consciousness. At one level, the two acts are jointly responsible for extending our experience of the present beyond the purely punctiform. Here the collaboration consists in a bi-directional action of distension backward on the part of the retentions of primary memory and of distension forward by the protentions of primary imagination. At another level, of which we are usually more explicitly aware, imagining and remembering serve to demarcate whole regions of time—regions which are discontinuous with the living present of the first level. These regions, the past and future proper, are never experienced in their entirety, but only in fragmentary form, through partial perspectives. Such perspectives are opened up and maintained by secondary memory when we seek to reillumine already expired experiences, and by secondary imagination when we attempt to light up possible experiences to come. Again there is movement in opposite directions, but this time as beginning from a fully constituted present (the present precisely of the act of imagining or remembering itself) and aiming at a strictly non-present period of time. The farther this period is from the immediate present of the imaginer or rememberer, the more requisite is his or her activity. Events distant enough from this present (that is to say, out of the range of retentional and protentional consciousness) can in fact *only* be imagined or remembered; and when they are extremely remote, as in the case of ancient history or early childhood, they are often attainable only by a complex and covert commingling of secondary remembering and secondary imagining such as we have seen in historical reconstruction and screen memories. There is no temptation here to consider imagining and remembering as forms of perception (as Husserl was tempted to do in the case of retentions and protentions),[39] for in their secondary forms memory and imagination *take the place* of perception, of a perception which we no longer have or do not yet have. The two acts serve to summon up the absent, the not-now-existent, and thus precisely what eludes present perception.

It should also be stressed that the very distinctness of secondary imagining and remembering from each other—in terms of their respective conditions and modes of operation, their experiential sense and resulting products, and in other ways indicated earlier such as corrigibility and familiarity—makes their collaboration all the more intricate and variegated. We do not need to claim equivalence or even similarity between the two acts to make out a case for their collaborative capabilities. They co-operate precisely by being directed to the possible and to the actual respectively; by the crossing-over of one into the domain of the other (as when imagining fills in the gaps in imperfectly remembered material or when remembering offers an explicit basis for the projection of the future); and, more generally, by the fact that each effects what the other cannot—and yet needs as complementary to its own activity. The re-presentation of a stably situated past and the pro-jection of an unsituated future call for each other as equally requisite epicenters of a time-consciousness whose moving center is the living present.[40]

VII

Imagining and remembering have shown themselves to be essential, and not merely contingent, co-ingredients in four separate cases: historical reconstruction, screen memories, dreams, and time-consciousness. If I have lingered longest over time-consciousness, this is not only because it exhibits the collaboration, indeed the *double* collaboration, between the two acts in its most convincing and complete form. It is also because time-consciousness is a much less isolated instance than the others. Where we suspect that the first three examples of non-contingent combination are of largely local significance—each having its own discrete realm of application, e.g., in selected stretches of the past, in early childhood, and in the REM periods of sleep—we are no longer bound to any such special regionality in our consciousness of time, which is so intrinsic to human experience that no part of it is without some tinge of the temporal.

To point to such panchronicity is hardly to say anything unfamiliar in the context of the preoccupation with time so characteristic of this century's physics, philosophy, psychology, and literature. What may be less familiar, however, is the inference implicit in the discussion of the last section: if time-consciousness is so deeply pervasive a phenomenon and if imagination and memory are indispensable parts of it, then these latter must *themselves be pervasive features of human experience.* Their intimate involvement (or, better, their *inter*-involvement, in Merleau-Ponty's term) in the constitution of time-consciousness is necessarily an involvement in the constitution of all experience as we know it.

But there is another, more controversial contention which I want to consider in closing and which takes us back to this chapter's point of departure: namely, that imagining and remembering are co-constituents of *perception.* This is implied by the close link between perception and time-consciousness itself, a link stressed by Kant to the point of virtual identity.[41] I would not want to claim identity—especially not if it requires recourse to an elaborate apparatus of mediating temporal schemata—but I do want to underline the following ways in which imagining and remembering reveal themselves to be equally essential constituents of the very structure of perceptual experience.

1. Turning first to immediate perception in the present, we find that what we perceive is given as (a) already *consolidated* to some degree as a form of sensuous presence, and as (b) *adumbrating* more of itself than has hitherto been given, i.e., as still-to-be-given. The consolidation, I would propose, is the work of the same kind of activity that we have seen to be operative in time-consciousness under the heading of "primary memory." For what we perceive gains its consistency and coherence mainly through the amassing of aspects which have been perceived in earlier viewings. These aspects are held in mind and as such sediment themselves into our ongo-

ing perceiving as already belonging to what we perceive. Adumbration, in contrast, concerns what we are about to perceive, thanks to a spontaneous projection of possible parts and profiles suggested by present and past perceiving. This projection is effected by what I have termed "primary imagination," since it is a matter of following out possibilities predelineated by what has come before in the phase of consolidation. That we are tempted to call such adumbration "protentional," just as we are also inclined to call consolidation "retentional," comes as no surprise. It is by means of the same basic activities of primary remembering and primary imagining that, on the one hand, our sense of the plenary present arises and that, on the other, the felt objectivity, the robust well-roundedness, of what we perceive within this present is constituted.

2. But the objectivity of what we perceive is not restricted to what is immediately felt or purely palpable. Consolidation and adumbration bear only on the object of my current perception—what I am now perceiving in the distended present described above. Yet for anything to be fully an *object of perception*—where "object" has its full Kantian sense of "object of experience"—it must possess at least three additional characteristics which are the direct concern of secondary memory and secondary imagination. I shall confine myself to the briefest of indications as to how this is so.

(a) First of all, perceived objects must possess a minimum *recognizability*—if not as unique individuals (as this particular house, which I may never have seen before), then at least as objects of a certain type (as a house or as houselike). All such recognizability implies secondary memory, that is, the possibility of the recollective consciousness that I have perceived this very house, or objects significantly similar to it, before. That the activity of memory is often only implicit in perceptual recognition—that it is frequently a matter of what I could recall rather than of what I do recall on a given occasion—renders it not any the less important. For the status of secondary memory is here de jure and not de facto, which means that it must be possible, at some point and in favorable circumstances, to effect the relevant recollection.

(b) Secondary memory is even more closely bound up with the trait of *repeatability*. A fully constituted perceptual object is an object which can be re-encountered, if not again in perception (for it may cease to exist in the meanwhile), then in a subsequent recollection. This is more than a matter of reidentifiability or selfsameness over time, in which primary and secondary memory are both involved. If I could never remember, at any time or under any circumstances, what I now perceive in the present, it would not count as a perceived object in the first place: to be an object of perception is necessarily to be rememorable as having once been perceived. Such subsequent remembering is a form of repetition, and thus we can say that perceptual objectivity requires repeatability in secondary memory.[42]

(c) *Projectability* refers to a final crucial feature of the objectivity of perceptual objects: they must be such as are capable of being envisioned in a future state. Not to be envisageable in the future at all is to lack an essential dimension of being perceivable; and this is true even of presently perceived objects on the verge of extinction: their future is precisely *not* to figure into the future that I populate projectively with other, non-extinct objects and yet also to be positable as having-once-existed from the standpoint of this projected future. What does the envisaging or projecting is secondary imagination, which we have seen to be equal to this very task because of its predilection for the purely possible—for what *might be* in contrast with what is, was, or must be. It should be evident that I am not claiming that, on every occasion of perceiving, we do in fact imagine what the future state of the object we perceive will be. Rather, it is that we must be able to project such a state as possible if what we perceive is to be a fully objective *perceptum*. Perhaps this is what Kant had in mind when he said in an aside that "imagination is a necessary ingredient of perception itself."[43] To this we need only add that so too is memory—and that each is necessary in its primary as well as its secondary form.

VIII

By the foregoing remarks, I do not mean to suggest that perception is wholly engendered by, or even adequately understood in terms of, the structures I have singled out for emphasis. I only want to underscore the fact that imagination and memory are ineluctably involved in the total operation of perception, that they are involved *together* as essentially different from (and complementary to) each other, and that their relationship within perceptual experience is remarkably analogous to their relationship in time-consciousness since there is a matching or pairing of their respective functions in each instance. In perception as in time-consciousness—as indeed in dreams, screen memories, and historical reconstruction as well, though in structurally divergent ways in these latter cases—imagining and remembering are continually conjoining in non-contingent forms.

If this is true, and especially if it is true that imagining and remembering are essential components of perceptual experience, one conclusion is inescapable, a conclusion that controverts the traditionalist position examined above in section II. Imagining and remembering are not the mere offshoots or pale replicas of perception, for *we cannot regard as derivative from perception what is constitutive of perception itself.* And if the two acts are not forms of "decaying sense" but are ingredient in sense itself, a second conclusion also presents itself: imagining and remembering, far from being the mere marginalia of mind, its *disjecta membra*, emerge as absolutely central in any appraisal that attempts to do justice to human experience in its full variety and ramifying richness. Or more exactly, they are con-centric in such an appraisal, since what I have tried to demonstrate is that, rather than eccentric extensions, they are co-essential members of mind, basic in their very collusiveness and complementarity to its own most basic activities and functions.

1. See Plato, *Republic* 595a–602b, and *Sophist* 235d–236c, 264b–d; Immanuel Kant, *The Critique of Pure Reason*, A 570–B 598; Jean-Paul Sartre, *Psychology of Imagination* (New York: Washington Square Press, 1966), pp. 11, 19, 143–53, and 170; Gilbert Ryle, *The Concept of Mind* (New York: Barnes and Noble, 1949), pp. 245–79.

2. Aristotle, *De Memoria et Reminiscentia* 451 a 15–16; see also 450 a 11: "Memory, even the memory of objects of thought, is not without an image." Here and below I use Richard Sorabji's translation in his *Aristotle on Memory* (Providence: Brown University Press, 1972).

3. Ibid., 450 a 24–25.

4. Thomas Hobbes, *Leviathan*, ed. C. B. Macpherson (Gretna, LA.: Pelican, 1968), p. 89; his italics.

5. Aristotle, *De Memoria et Reminiscentia* 450 a 22. Cf. also ibid., 451 a 17–18 and *De Anima* 428 b 32–33. (The term "primary perceptual part" is Aristotle's own.)

6. Maurice Merleau-Ponty, *Le visible et l'invisible* (Paris: Gallimard, 1964), p. 311.

7. David Hume, *A Treatise of Human Nature*, ed. L. A. Selby-Bigge (Oxford: Oxford University Press, 1955), p. 85. At pp. 8–9, Hume proposes another basis of distinction between imagination and memory, to wit, that the "order and form" of the original impressions are retained in memory alone; but he rejects this criterion later on p. 85.

8. Cf. Hobbes, *Leviathan*, p. 89; "this *decaying sense*, when wee would express the thing it self . . . wee call *Imagination*. . . . *But* when wee would express the *decay* and signifie that the Sense is fading, old, and past, it is called *Memory*" (his italics). Hume discusses the factor of decay in the *Treatise* on pp. 85–86.

9. David Hume, *An Inquiry Concerning Human Understanding*, ed. C. W. Hendel (Indianapolis: Bobbs-Merrill, 1955), p. 27.

10. Hume, *A Treatise of Human Nature*, p. 6.

11. Nor can we adopt the milder version of this proposition, according to which we always imagine or remember things which, if not actually perceived before, *could have been*. For we can very well imagine how to think a certain thought or remember how it was to feel in such and such a way, where in neither case is the content we imagine or remember the sort of thing that is even in principle subject to sensory perception.

12. Giambattista Vico, *The New Science*, trans. T. G. Bergin and M. H. Fisch (Ithaca: Cornell University Press, 1968), p. 313. Cf. also p. 75 ("imagination is nothing but extended or compounded memory") and p. 264 ("imagination is nothing but the springing up again of reminiscences").

13. Quoted in Crabb Robinson's diary as reprinted in Arthur Symons, *William Blake* (New York: Dutton, 1907), p. 301; my italics.

14. For a more complete discussion, see my "Imagination, Fantasy, Hallucination, and Memory" in this volume.

15. Edward S. Casey, *Imagining: A Phenomenological Study* (Bloomington: Indiana University Press, 1976), chap. 2.

16. John Dewey, *Human Nature and Conduct* (New York: Random House, 1957), pp. 190–91.

17. On the relationship between memory and personal identity, see R. S. Benjamin, "Remembering," in D. F. Gustafson, ed., *Essays in Philosophical Psychology* (Garden City, N.Y.: Anchor Press/Doubleday, 1964), pp. 171–72 and John Perry, ed., *Personal Identity* (Berkeley: University of California Press, 1975), especially Parts I and II.

18. R. G. Collingwood, *The Idea of History* (Oxford: Oxford University Press, 1956),

p. 244: "The web of imaginative construction is something far more solid and powerful than we have hitherto realized."

19.   Still another case is found in the ancient "art of memory." Its mnemotechnical method brought together imagination and memory by the use of a set sequence of "places" (e.g., the rooms of a large imaginary building), which were memorized in advance as a basic grid and to which were affixed mental images signifying the items to be remembered. As Frances Yates writes in commentary on Quintilian, "we have to think of the ancient orator as *moving in imagination through his memory building*, drawing from the memorized places the images he has placed on them" (*The Art of Memory* [London: Routledge and Kegan Paul, 1966], p. 3; my italics). Thus the art of memory involved "the use of imagination as a duty" (p. 104), i.e., in a required relationship of the non-contingent sort to be described below. In this relationship, images serve as more than a mere *aide-mémoire;* they are the very foundation of systematic remembering.

20.   I have simplified Freud's account by omitting mention of another part of the same screen memory in which a peasant woman offers a piece of delicious black bread to Freud and his playmates. In Freud's analysis, the bread symbolizes the bucolic and secure existence which he wished to regain as a young man. See Sigmund Freud, *The Standard Edition of the Complete Psychological Works*, ed. James Strachey, 24 vols. (London: Hogarth Press, 1953–74), 3: 309–20. (Hereinafter cited as *SE.*)

21.   Ibid., p. 318.

22.   Ibid., p. 322; his italics. Freud continues: "our childhood memories show us our earliest years not as they were but as they appeared at the later periods when the memories were aroused. In these periods of arousal, the childhood memories did not, as people are accustomed to say, *emerge*; they were *formed* at that time." See also *SE*, vol. 17, p. 51.

23.   Cf. Freud, *SE*, vol. 12, p. 148: screen memories "represent the forgotten years of childhood as adequately as the manifest content of a dream represents the dream-thoughts."

24.   Freud, *SE*, vol. 5, p. 592.

25.   "What are truly characteristic of dreams are only those elements of their [manifest] content which behave like images . . . dreams *hallucinate* . . . they replace thoughts by hallucinations" (Freud, *SE*, vol. 4, pp. 49–50; his italics).

26.   Freud, *SE*, vol. 15, p. 130.

27.   "The practically cognized present is no knife-edge, but a saddle-back, with a certain breadth of its own on which we look in two directions into time" (William James, *The Principles of Psychology* [New York: Dover, 1950], vol. 1, p. 609; hereinafter *PP*).

28.   Edmund Husserl, *The Phenomenology of Internal Time-Consciousness*, trans. James S. Churchill (Bloomington: Indiana University Press, 1964), p. 70. Here as elsewhere I have modified Churchill's translation, hereinafter referred to as *PIT*.

29.   James, *PP*, vol. 1, p. 647. Husserl's main discussion of retention is in sec. 8–13 of *PIT*. The analogy of the comet's tail is on p. 52.

30.   See Husserl, *PIT*, sec. 16, 24, and 26. William James also contrasts "memory" with "expectation" as respectively "the retrospective and the prospective sense of time" (*PP*, vol. 1, p. 606).

31.   "Retentions and protentions are the primitive, the first and fundamental, forms of the past and the future" (Edmund Husserl, *Analysen zur Passiven Synthesis* [The Hague: Nijhoff, 1966], p. 326).

32.   James, *PP*, vol. 1, p. 646. See also Aristotle, *De Memoria et Reminiscentia* 451 a 31–451 b 4.

33.   I hyphenate this word to indicate that a full act of recollection involves the apprehension of a *setting* for the remembered event. On this point, see James, *PP*, pp. 654–58.

34.   Husserl warns, however, that even if "I can re-live the present . . . it can never be given again" (*PIT*, p. 66)—i.e., given again as a pristine present.

35.   Husserl, *PIT*, p. 75: *"die Einheit des Erinnerten."*

36.   For Husserl's discussion of prophetic visions, see *PIT*, p. 80.

37.   Heraclitus, Fragment 19. The full statement is "Unless you expect the unexpected,

you will never find [truth], for it is hard to discover and hard to attain" (Philip Wheelwright's translation in *Heraclitus* [New York: Atheneum, 1968], p. 20).

38.   This is not to say that all possibilities entertained by such imagining are situated in the future. Although there is a natural affinity between the purely possible and the futural, my point is only that our consciousness of the future involves a special use of secondary imagining. The latter is consequently more free-ranging than secondary memory, which remains confined to the past proper; we can imagine pure possibilities as situated in the past, but we cannot remember the future.

39.   See Husserl, *PIT*, sec. 14, 16, 17.

40.   The same point applies to primary remembering and primary imagining. While it is true that these acts realize a basically symmetrical co-action of elongation, the elongation itself proceeds in two different directions and is realized by retentions which are always already full and by protentions which are essentially empty.

41.   I have especially in mind Kant's position in the Second Analogy, where he writes that "it is a necessary law of our sensibility, and therefore a *formal condition* of all perceptions, that the preceding time necessarily determines the succeeding" (A 199; his italics), and that "only insofar as our representations are necessitated in a certain order as regards their time-relations do they acquire objective meaning" (B 243, where "objective" means reference to an object of perception).

42.   Again, the point is not that I must actually recall my prior perception but that I must be able to do so in principle. Moreover, that the recollection is here situated in the future does not diminish in any way its indispensability.

43.   Kant, *The Critique of Pure Reason*, A 120 n.

REMEMBERING

Memory, Time, and Soul

Out of memory, and within memory, the soul . . .
pours forth its wealth of images—of visions envi-
sioning the soul itself.
> —MARTIN HEIDEGGER
> *What Is Called Thinking?*

Out of the beginning all things are, and towards
it all revert.
> —PROCLUS
> *Elements of Theology*

Whatever is in memory is also in the soul.
> —ST. AUGUSTINE
> *Confessions*

I

TIME IS NOT only perceived, imagined, and conceived, but remembered
as well. Time remembered is time past, past time—though remembering itself is no mere pastime in view of the difficulty and the painfulness
it may occasion. In fact, memory is so rooted in the past that it may become
mired there, much like T. S. Eliot's garlic and sapphires stuck in the mud
of desire. In contrast with imagination's alleviating and refreshing projection
of the future-as-possible, remembering encourages us to lose ourselves in
the past-as-actualized, to indulge our antiquarian interests. Freud spoke
in this connection of his "predilection for the prehistoric."[1] Unlike imagining's proclivity for the purely possible, in remembering we return home
to the heartland of the already known, the already-having-happened. Hence
the nostalgia in which we become so easily immersed in recollection: despite
the pain (the *algos*), the *nostos* or homecoming is too heartening to do

without. There is also something slightly sticky about remembering, an entrapment or engulfment which we find difficult to resist. All remembering, as Husserl reminds us, begins in a movement of "sinking back or away"—back or away from the full-bodied present—so as to sink eventually into a morass of memories from which retrieval may no longer be possible.[2]

If memory is this morassive movement in arrears—this *contretemps*[3] of time viewed puer-wise as progressing ever onward—it is a most disconcerting fact to find that those who would seem to have a vested interest in its detailed pursuit are surprisingly stingy in their actual assessment of it. Immanuel Kant, for example, was passionately concerned with the origins of knowledge, its roots in the knowing subject (and, incidentally, reintroduced the word "archetype" into the modern vocabulary by distinguishing between *archetypal* and *ectypal*, ideal and image);[4] and yet he strangely neglects memory. There is only a handful of references of any kind to memory in all of his works. Imagination, in which one would expect Kant to be much less interested, takes the lion's share of credit for human cognition in the crucial First Edition of the *Critique of Pure Reason,* where memory is not even so much as named, its place being taken by what Kant calls euphemistically "reproductive imagination."

If we turn to psychology, we meet with a still more paradoxical situation. Those who *have* paid special attention to memory are precisely those devoted to a strictly scientific study of mind. From Ebbinghaus to the most recent research in cognitive psychology (where memory is most frequently viewed as a form of information-processing), there has been a proliferation of experimental laboratory studies that is little short of astonishing by standards of sheer ingenuity and productivity.[5] In many respects, these studies have stolen the show when it comes to matters of memory. Depth psychology (and this is the other side of the paradox), just where one would have anticipated the greatest activity because of the profound link between psyche, depth, and memory, has largely dismissed remembering, preferring (as in the analogous case of Kant) to place the stress on imagination or fantasy instead.

Take, for instance, the now classic case of Freud's turn-about of 1897. Before then, Freud had indeed credited memory with a great deal, both in the *Studies on Hysteria* (with its dictum that "hysterics suffer mainly from reminiscences," its conception of the hysteric symptom as a "mnemic symbol," and its model of the mind as composed of concentric layers of memories)[6] and in the abortive "Project for a Scientific Psychology" (in which Freud remarks that "a psychological theory deserving any consideration must furnish an explanation of memory").[7] However, as is well known, Freud's disenchantment with the validity of his patients' ostensible memories of seduction by their parents led him to question memory as the main pillar upon which to build psychoanalysis as a therapy or as a theory. By 21 September 1897 (barely a year after the very name "psychoanalysis" had been coined), Freud felt impelled to write to Wilhelm Fliess:

I will confide to you the great secret that has been slowly dawning on me in the last few months. I no longer believe in my *neurotica*. . . . [Two of the reasons that Freud goes on to give are:] [First,] the certain discovery that there are no indications of reality in the unconscious, so that one cannot distinguish between the [historical, remembered] truth and fiction that is cathected with affect [i.e., fantasy that is independent of memory]. [Second,] the reflection that [even] in the most deep-going psychosis the unconscious memory does not break through, so that the secret of the childhood experiences is not betrayed even in the most confused delirium.[8]

Hence, neither consciously entertained memories nor even those residing in the unconscious itself (where less opportunity for distortion is found) can be counted on any longer.

By default or elimination, the fundamental term becomes fantasy—and *has remained so ever since in depth psychology.* By 1911, in his paper on "Two Principles of Mental Functioning" (a definitive metapsychological summing-up of the mind's development) Freud will devote just one brief sentence to memory.[9]

1911—the year during which the break between Jung and Freud became imminent and the very year during which Jung wrote the original version of *Transformations and Symbols of the Libido.* Despite the break and the revolutionary thinking that was beginning to manifest itself in his work, Jung still supported Freud on the fantasmatic origin of childhood memories: "the golden haze of childhood memories arises not so much from the objective facts as from the admixture of magical images which are more intuited than actually conscious."[10] These "magical images" are fantasies; they are not yet those "primordial images" which are the bearers of archetypes and which are "condensed expressions of the psychic situation as a whole."[11] Moreover, even the notion of *imago*, one of Jung's most seminal contributions to early psychoanalytic theory, is not confined to its strictly mnemonic components. Although the imagos of one's father and mother may be considered "unique and imperishable"[12] in the individual (and to this extent are forms of constant memory), they too are essentially fantasmatic in status: "they are not concerned anymore with the real father and mother but with subjective and often very much distorted images of them which lead a shadowy, but nonetheless potent existence in the mind of the patient."[13] As in Freud's case, we detect a distinct distrust of memory on Jung's part. He speaks at one point in *Transformations and Symbols of the Libido* of "submersion in the abyss of memory"[14] as if this were to be avoided at all costs; and he takes both himself and Freud to task in his Fordham lectures of 1912 for having made the past into a fateful determinant of the present: "we had [mistakenly] allowed ourselves to be guided by the tendency of the patient to revert to the past, following the direction of his introverted libido."[15] The link between introversion and memory is a very close one for Jung; introversion, and especially the involuntary introversion of regression, is precisely to a memory:

> If the libido is partially or totally introverted, it invests to a greater or lesser degree areas of memory, with the result that [the ensuing] reminiscences acquire a vitality that no longer properly belongs to them.[16]

"A vitality that no longer properly belongs to them"! It is as if memories were essentially moribund entities with no life (no *after*-life) of their own. It is thus not surprising to find that in his subsequent publications Jung rarely refers to memory as such. There are, for example, no indexical entries whatsoever under "memory" or "remembering" in *Psychology and Alchemy* and *Mysterium Coniunctionis*, which I consider to be his two most valuable later works. Even in *Psychological Types*, that profoundly important transitional book, memory merits no entry of its own in chapter 11 ("Definitions"), and it is given only a begrudging and backhanded acknowledgment in the critical definition of "primordial images":

> *From the scientific, causal standpoint* [that is, the very standpoint Jung would *not* ultimately endorse] the primordial image can be conceived as a mnemic deposit, an imprint or engram . . . which has arisen through the condensation of countless processes of a similar kind. In this respect it is a precipitate and, therefore, a typical basic form of certain ever-recurring psychic experiences.[17]

By allowing himself to employ (however skeptically) the mechanistic-physiological language of "deposit," "imprint," "engram," and "precipitate," Jung (much like Freud, who persisted in speaking similarly of memory "traces") underscores his premise that memories are in themselves lifeless, the mere results of ongoing processes in relation to which the individual is presented as quite passive. In this view, which pervades the thinking not only of Jung and of Freud but of many contemporary cognitive psychologists as well, memories are mainly records or registrations. Hence one's chief concern is with their accuracy: and if we discover, as Freud and Jung did, that they may be systematically *in*accurate, it becomes a natural temptation to discredit them and to focus instead on what does the distorting, namely, fantasy or imagination.

In Jung's instance, one of the most revealing consequences of this whole way of thinking is found in the fact that, whereas he distinguishes rigorously between passive and active fantasy (and even makes the latter the main avenue to archetypal experience), he draws no such distinction between a passive and an active memory.[18] Indeed, all remembering, whether voluntary or involuntary, is essentially passive, a matter of participation in something so organically predetermined—so much a matter of matter—that any talk of activity, much less of creativity, seems wholly beside the point.

I am aware that Jung's total stance regarding memory is far from un-equivocal. On two counts, he comes close to acknowledging its deeper significance. First, he does give to memory a role in enlivening our con-sciousness of archetypes, which can be "so enriched with individual memories through the introversion of libido as to become perceptible to the conscious mind, in much the same way as the crystalline structure la-tent in the saturated solution takes visible shape from the aggregation of molecules."[19] How this enriching takes place, however, is never spelled out; and in any case it is made subservient to gaining consciousness of archetypes themselves. Second, Jung attributes to primordial images an "archaic" character which roots them in the past—that very distant past of "time immemorial" which is also expressed in mythological motifs:

> I call the image *primordial* when it possesses an *archaic* character. I speak
> of its archaic character when the image is in striking accord with familiar
> mythological motifs. It then expresses material primarily derived from
> the *collective unconscious*. [Note the transition from "primordial" to "ar-
> chaic" to "mythological" to "collective": an important conceptual *quater-
> nity*.] The primordial image is an inherited organization of psychic energy,
> an ingrained system. . . . It shows how the energic process has run its
> unvarying course from time immemorial, while simultaneously allowing
> a perpetual repetition of it by means of an apprehension or psychic grasp
> of situations so that life can continue into the future.[20]

These pronouncements are certainly insightful, but they do not answer the need to pinpoint the role of memory as such, that is, as it is specified in finite acts of remembering. Instead, the emphasis is shifted away from such acts to a basis of activity (the collective unconscious) and a period of time (the archaic, "time immemorial") in which such acts no longer have a relevant role to play. It is not even clear that the "perpetual repetition" is effected by remembering at all, just as the link between myth and memory is left unclarified and only suggested.

From the foregoing forays into the depth psychologies of Freud and Jung, three basic areas of questioning emerge as particularly pertinent to the aims of the present chapter:

(i) Is there not an active remembering which is just as psychically signifi-cant as active fantasying (including the specific technique of active im-agination, which is designed to foster and extend active fantasy itself)?

(ii) Are not memories, individual and collective, far from being a mere imprinting on neural matter, rather themselves a *prima materia* for a geniunely archetypal psychology?

(iii) Is not memory, in short, a royal road to soul with as much right, and as much psychical power, as fantasy and imagination? Do not memory-images belong along with fantasy-images to the psychological alchemist's "intermediate realm of subtle bodies"?[21] If depth psychology is truly to plumb the depths as it promises to do, must it not perforce go into the depths of memory as well?

II

Before we can even begin to answer such encompassing questions, we must attend carefully to how remembering in fact operates in our daily lives. Here I shall start by singling out four of its basic operations or traits insofar as these bear on the constitution and consciousness of time.

(1) First, there is the way in which remembering brings about our *sense of the past* itself. As I said, the past is the realm of that which has already happened, whether it continues to reverberate in the present or not. Past happenings can be physical, psychical, or psychophysical; they can be events of feeling as of thought, of intuition as of sensation. Once past, a given happening becomes accessible to us mainly in and through memory, except in those cases where still perceivable marks or records of it have been preserved. But the lived quality of the happening, what it was to experience it in the first person, is available to us only in personal memory. This is so even if we cannot, strictly speaking, ever reconfront it again as such— in its pristine first-time-ness. What we can do is to re-experience it in a way that brings back enough of its qualitative immediacy to convince us that we have "been there" before. This "before" always has a felt familiarity about it, so that an effect, however minimal, of recognition or "return home" is achieved (here is one basis of the nostalgia spoken of earlier); and the same "before" is usually datable within certain large limits as well: if not by hour or day, at least by period-in-our-life. (The perplexing quality of undated memories, which may drive us to considerable lengths to find their correct date, itself indicates how much we have come to expect datability.)[22]

Now all of this (and much else besides—especially the building up of a secure stock of memories forming the basis of our life history and indeed our personal identity) is the accomplishment of "secondary memory" as James and Husserl both call it: of "recollection" or "recall" as we usually term it in English. But beyond secondary memory (with which we too facilely identify all remembering), there is also a primary memory, which captures the past in the very process of its formation. Or, more exactly, such memory *is* the past in the course of its creation; it is the holding-in-mind of that which has *just* happened and is now beginning to "sink back" into the dimness. We hold on to this fast-receding content by means of "retentions"—not to be confused with after-shocks or reverberations in the musculature or brain. For it is evident that both secondary and primary memory are strictly psychical processes, mental events experienced by the psyche. Together, the two kinds of remembering constitute the personal past—which is very close to being, or making, the person per se.

We should notice, however, that the role of remembering in these two forms is not to be restricted to the production of such a past or even of pastness generally. Just as imagination in its primary and secondary forms ranges over more than the future proper, so memory is active (and I stress "active" in face of the passivist tendency cited just above) in the constitution of our sense of the future and of the present: of the future, as a basis for anticipating what is to come (both in the short term and the long), and of the present, as the foundation for all the acts of identification that take place there. What emerges from any such analysis—the merest outlines of which I sketch here—is an appreciation of the manyness of memory's constitutive roles in time-consciousness:[23] even at this bare descriptive level, a proliferation of types and subtypes presents itself, preventing us from taking refuge in monolithic models. Still more radically, we may begin to wonder if the customary division of time into its three *modi* of past, present, and future can any longer be regarded as adequate: do we not have to recognize a multiplicity in the very dimensionality of time itself if we are to do justice to the diverse activities of imagining and remembering alike in the generation of our sense of being in time?[24] *We are in time—as we are in soul—in many ways.*

(2) *Expansion* is a second basic operation of memory. Here it is a matter of the way in which remembering effects a *distentio animi* (in Augustine's term), an extendedness of the soul in two directions at once. On the one hand, there is an expansion backward toward previously experienced events. In most cases, these latter have been "out of mind," and so effectively and completely that until remembered they have been non-existent for us— less than ghosts even, since as forgotten or unthought-of they have not even been haunting us. And when they *do* haunt us, it is often in such an indeterminate way that we cannot always say for certain that a particular memory or group of memories is doing the haunting; rather, there is only the vague sense of a lack or void: a missing name, a faded image, a lapsed state of affairs which we cannot quite get back or get back to. This curious state of non-knowledge—whether total (as in genuine amnesia) or partial (as in the instances just cited)—is quickly dispelled, however, when we do succeed in remembering a given item. We suddenly link up with the past and in so doing distend the contracted present (contracted in ignorance, in concentration on the now, in dalliances and distractions). The present is thereby opened up, freed temporarily of its burden of sheer presentation—opened *out* into the past, the particular past of the memory at stake. By the same token, a counter-movement is realized: the past itself is extended by being revived in memory. It is expanded precisely into the present of remembering, allowed to relive there on lien or loan; it is given a second life, a second chance. This exfoliation of the past is part of the

expansionism of all remembering: revival is survival, where the "sur" expresses added or extra life. Remembering always brings with it a surplus, something extra: either the extra of a memory added to present desires or interests or the extra involved in the very resuscitation of the memory itself. Expansion occurs on both counts, backward in the one case, forward in the other; and each happens simultaneously, in the one sudden stroke of remembering.

(3) Closely correlated with expansion is a third trait: *encapsulment*, by which I mean the way in which so many memories come to us in a pre-packaged, condensed, and schematical format. Let us look briefly at each of these subtraits.

(a) First, memories arrive in consciousness pre-packaged not just in the sense that they have a life of their own (though it is a strangely uneven half-life continually revived) but especially insofar as they are usually already fully formed. We do not create or devise our memories *ad libitum*—in contrast with many of our imaginings. We certainly do pursue memories, and we can clarify them to some degree. Yet our powers of pursuit and clarification are notoriously weak: however strenuous my efforts, I can become only so clear, and no clearer, as to the exact structure of my Aunt Leone's face (which I last saw when I was eight years old); and as for the actual occasion on which I last viewed this face, my mind is even more unredeemably dim. There is pre-packaging here but of such a sort as to render the contents accessible only through a glass darkly.

(b) What does arrive in this variously displayed form is often highly condensed. Such condensation is the very heart of encapsulment, the strict meaning of the term. Think of almost any memory you may now have in mind and notice how much is compressed into just a few movements, a few traits, a few figures: say, my memory of having once been in Dallas for Christmas some forty years ago, this entire experience being now condensed into a few fleeting images of the bedroom in which I anxiously and fitfully slept. It is relatively rare that we replay an event in memory in any considerable detail. Detailed recollection is usually restricted to very recent events or to stand-out events of a traumatic or otherwise compelling nature (and even here there is a tendency to reduce the event to its barest bones). Such condensation is not to be attributed exclusively to economic considerations or to fading memory traces. It is, rather, an *intrinsic feature* of remembering: we remember in abbreviation, and it is therefore usually quite in vain that we attempt to recapture the past *in toto*. The past is never going to yield itself up to us altogether—in memory or in any other way. Part of what being past means is precisely *not* to be retrievable in its original state; the past in this state has always already passed out of our present experience, even if it can pass back in precisely in the condensed versions which remembering it provides. Condensation in memory, then, comes as both the condition and the cost of readmittance to consciousness.

(c) The schematicalness of much remembering is an ally of condensa-

tion; or, more exactly, it is the specific means by which mnemonic condensation is most frequently carried out. The exact nature of memory
schemata was first suggested by Bartlett and then sophisticated by Piaget.[25]
Suffice it to say for now that it consists in an assimilating action by which
the essential, or at least the characteristic, features of a given phenomenon
are singled out, amalgamated, and made to stand for the event being thus
remembered in reduced format.

(4) A final descriptive trait of remembering I shall baptize with the word
"ruminescence," a combination of reminiscence and rumination. To consider ruminescence is to focus on the act phase of remembering rather than
on the object phase as has been done so far. The act of remembering can
take various forms: simple imagistic recall (in which a single object or event
rises before us), remembering-that (such-and-such a state of affairs
obtained), remembering-how (to do skilled and now habitual actions),
remembering-as ("I remember him as an angry young man"), remembering on-the-occasion-of (your birthday, etc.). To each of these will correspond as a full intentional correlate a mnemonic presentation (composed
of the specific content remembered and of the memory-frame of space and
time within which it is set) and its "aura," that indefinite margin that rings
around memories as if it were some primal mist. But in addition to such
structural items there is the factor of affect or attitude—how we experience
our own remembering. This emotive aspect of the act phase is very often
characterizable as *ruminescent*. What is this?

On the reminiscent side, there is an entire galaxy of feelings, not all of
which emerge distinctly (or at all: they may remain quite subliminal), ranging from deep remorse to wan wistfulness. To be in a reminiscent mood
is to partake in such emotions, which move us precisely because of our
realization that what we remember is *no more* and is at best capable of
merely momentary resuscitation in mind or soul. The sheer fact of transience, in other words, calls out these past-affiliated emotions. On the
ruminative side, we observe the quite different factor of the deliberativeness
with which we experience so many memories. Memories are matters, even
prime matters, for reflection, that is, for turning back to what went before,
deliberating on it, ruminating it in reflection. There is a peculiar steadiness
in our absorption in memories which contrasts with the flightiness of imagining, whose mercurial character may even rule over our rumination.
And when this ruminative steadiness is combined with the emotions of
reminiscence, we find ourselves in that ruminescent state which remembering alone can induce.

III

Thus far we have been considering various ways in which the past—the
personal past—gets constituted in and through memory in its several roles

and capacities. Not only constituted by, but shaped, tamed, and even dominated by it. Part of remembering in its everydayness has to do with putting the past in its place. Even when the past is allowed to expand into the present, or vice versa, it is rarely permitted to overwhelm us: by entering the present precisely *as past*—by bearing the temporal index "pastness"—it is kept out of direct competition with that which is going on in the present. Its encapsulated quality expressly subserves this state of comparative captivity. So too does ruminescence, another way of keeping the past in thrall. Remembering in its mundane manifestations seems to have a stake in making the past into a borderline condition.

But Hermes, god of the borderline, is also (and for this very reason) the god who transgresses borders and boundaries in his capacity as messenger of the gods and as archetypal trickster. As Rafael López-Pedraza has written in his remarkable book *Hermes and His Children,* "Hermes permeates the whole world because of his [capacity for] making connections, his commerce with, and constellation of, the other Gods [in] his borderline [movements]. He is *the connection-maker.*"[26] Hermes guides remembering too— "protects"[27] it by enabling it to make a connection, and connection not only with a casual and contingent past, encapsulated and personal (encapsulated as personal), but with a past that is at once necessary and transpersonal. This past we cannot contain so easily and so well; it refuses to submit to the deeply domineering tendencies of the ego, since the ego is itself one of its own expressions, even one of its properties. Just as character is in Freud's definition "a precipitate of abandoned object-cathexes,"[28] so the ego, the seat of character as of anxiety, is a sedimented formation— precipitated not only from particular object-choices, but also from archetypal dominants that dominate the ego itself, making it into one part only of what Jung called the "paleopsyche." These dominants infiltrate and infuse the present in manners that resist encapsulation of any ordinary sort. Like Hermes, the archetypal past moves in fast, with swift-sandaled feet, tricking us at every turn.

What can we do vis-à-vis such an undomesticatable past, which invades us so unwittingly and often so unwillingly and even overwhelmingly?[29] One thing we can do is to *revert* to it. "Reversion" is no simple counter-action of the sort we take when we try actively to obliterate a past that is burdening or obsessing us (e.g., by "burying" it, censoring it, substituting new demands in the present for it: all of these being forms of what Nietzsche calls "active forgetfulness"). Nor is it a matter of passive submission either, as when we allow ourselves to be crushed by the past as incubus, regarding it as fated (and yet lacking the saving grace of *amor fati*): here would be a truly "passive memory" comparable to Jung's passive fantasy. Rather, just as Hermes is a perpetually paradoxical blend of opposites,[30] so reversion as I shall construe this term is a curious merging of activity and passivity. It is, indeed, passive to the extent of acknowledging (and not denying, evading, or trying to displace) the past's invasive power, its more or less complete permeation of our lives; no part of us is not, always already, past; although it is no consolation to know it, living humanly is inexorably "passifying." Reversion to the past is active, however, insofar as an action of some sort is taken: but what kind of action can this be?

There are four primary forms of the mercurial action of reversion, which like quicksilver flows very rapidly through our accustomed conceptual nets. Let us call these *re-verting, re-connecting, re-versioning,* and *re-visioning.* The multiple resonances of the "re-" resound through these closely affiliated terms—as in so many other phenomena of memory and the past: re-turn, re-currence, *ri-corso* (as in Vico's repetitive cycles of history), re-call, re-collection, re-dolent (as when we say "redolent of the past"), and of course re-membering itself (one of the most suggestive words of all with its connotation of a ritual re-memberment after a Dionysian dis-memberment). It needs noting that the prefix "re-" signifies not only "again" (in the sense of re-peated action) but also "back," as is explicitly designated in "re-verse" movement, a backwards (but not necessarily backward!) movement back to a given starting-point.

Let us look more closely at the four forms in question, which will occupy most of the remainder of this chapter.

(1) *Re-verting.* This I take to be the basic action of *looking back* by bending our mental or psychical gaze back to an origin, whether this origin be conceived simply as a first experience of something, as the dynamic source of all that has issued from it, as a prototype of other experiences like it, or even as an abyss of the forgotten and not remembered. Implicit in this *re*-gard (*regard*, in French, means precisely look, glance, gaze) is a re-fraction of our attention in the literal sense of a di-version or de-flection from a particular course, a passing obliquely from one medium into another of different density. The diversion is from the world of our current or future concerns; a deflection from this world is equivalent to a re-flection on(to) the past, a re-turning there by our very (mental) look. This differs from ordinary remembering by the peculiar intensity with which we gaze back— the way we focus on, and even fixate, the past event to which we thus revert and which becomes a genuine *focus memorius* and not only a *focus imaginarius* (in Kant's term). What we revert to is taken as re-memorable in its own right; we are drawn to it on this basis, whatever our subsequent assessment of it may be. In this respect it is like any adversion of attention; but it differs from others in that we are being drawn by something specifically *past*, something for which this particular temporal predicate is constitutive. We can only revert to what has already happened, already passed by and passed on—something on which the shadow of transience has now fallen—and we revert as much to this shadow, in its adumbration of finitude, as to its substance (that is, to the memory's specific content).

(2) *Re-connecting.* Reverting, however, would be a lifeless or soulless exercise—a mere turning back—if it could not re-connect with that to which it returns. More than Janus's fixed stare backwards is involved in

a reversion that is more than re-verting. *The gaze must meet with matters to which connections can be made.* Thus Proclus says that "reversion is a communion and conjunction."[31] In the present context such communion or conjunction is at once historical and psychological—and the one *because* of the other. It might be helpful to consider examples of such re-connections at this point.

(a) We can re-connect through remembrance (conscious or not) with more than our personal past history. Another kind of history with which we meaningfully re-connect is the history of our family, our city, our gender identity, etc. In each case we realize distinctive continuities with the more than merely personal (though not yet, strictly speaking, with the transpersonal). Thus I re-connect vividly with my great uncle Emmett, who died many years before I was born but many of whose interests (and even whose photographed physiognomy) resemble mine uncannily. A different kind of extra-personal re-connection can occur in the case of another historical epoch—with the Romantic period, say, or more distantly with the Renaissance. This latter case is in many ways paradigmatic, as the very name *Renaissance* signifies. For here we re-connect with a period that is itself founded on re-connection—re-connection with antiquity. Re-connection to the second power! Little wonder then that the Renaissance becomes for archetypal psychology a pivotal point in which the historical and the psychological fructify and enliven each other. As Hillman writes in *Re-Visioning Psychology:*

> We have *reverted* . . . to the Renaissance in order to find a vision of the psyche which might also provide a background for a re-vision of psychology. By looking backward to that "creative breakdown" called the Renaissance we are better able to see the psyche now as it goes through similar processes. [Thus we can use] history as a means to psychologize the present.[32]

The most basic process in all this is re-connection—re-linking with that extraordinary time when the human psyche was so lambent and alive that our contemporary souls are re-enlivened by the very remembrance of it in the present.

(b) But we may re-connect with an even more distant and primal past. This occurs in ritualistically or mythically determined actions which repeat, with variations, a primordial event—one which is not at all dated in historical time, whether personal or cultural, but in a time before this-worldly time, a cosmogonic *Ur-zeit* of creation and founding events. Eliade, of course, has been a main explorer of these matters, and I can do no better than to quote him here:

> To assure the reality and the enduringness of a [rite of] construction [e.g., in the construction rites dictated by the legend of Master Manole], there

is a repetition of the divine art of perfect construction: the Creation of the worlds and of man. . . . Through the paradox of rite, the time of any ritual coincides with the mythical time of the "beginning." Through repetition of the cosmogonic act, concrete time, in which the construction takes place, is projected into mythical time, *in illo tempore* ["in that time"] when the foundation of the world occurred.[33]

A strange sort of remembrance this! It does not involve memory at all in any conventional sense. In the conventional or ordinary sense we cannot in remembering perfectly coincide with, and thus "repeat," what we are recollecting. The very act of calling something back to mind is an addition to—is distinguishably different from—that which we are re-calling. But now the remembrance adds nothing; re-connection is effected by repetition alone.

The difference between ordinary remembrance or "recollection" and memory as repetition ("commemoration" as Eliade sometimes calls it) can be represented in formal terms as follows:

$$R [E_X - (E_V)]$$

R = act of remembering
E_X = experience of an event
E_V = event remembered

And this can be reiterated in memories of memories:

$$R_2(E_{X2} - \{R_1[E_{X1} - (E_V)]\})$$

Eliade is proposing quite a different formulation:

$$R_i \cong E_{VO}$$

R_i = present ritual
E_{VO} = original event
$\cong$ = repetition

How then can we claim that we still have to do with memory here? Will it do to posit, as does Eliade, an *"ahistorical memory"* which belongs to the collectivity alone"?[34] The difficulty with this idea—which is formally parallel to Jung's notion of the "collective unconscious"—is that it eliminates from the content of such memory those very aspects which invite psychological re-connection. As Eliade himself admits, a collective-ahistorical memory "cannot accept what is individual and preserves only what is exemplary. [There is] a reduction of events to categories and of individuals to archetypes. . . ."[35] But the categories are *in* the events, and the archetypes *in* the individuals that emerge in personified images, including memory-images actively entertained. We re-connect with an archetypal past, in short, by the active remembering of which the psyche is uniquely capable.

This is not to say that repetition per se, even in the cosmic coincidence which is the focus of Eliade's analysis, is excluded in such remembering—after all, the metempsychosis and re-incarnation of soul, its "eternal return," involve the notion of repetitive cycles and thus an "archaic ontology" in Eliade's term.[36] What *is* excluded is the kind of repetition in which the oddities and veerings of soul are dissolved in sameness, in which the particular and the peculiar are lost in the exemplary and the eternal. If cosmogonic repetition indeed entails the regeneration of the soul itself[37] and if the gods are involved as well[38] (that is, beings who are intrinsically multiple and self-differentiating), then the repetition involved in ahistoric reversion cannot be a matter of strict coincidence, that is, of the attainment of a collective or ontological unity.

There is a larger lesson looming in this brief excursus into Eliade's model. In coming to grips with ahistorical, extra-personal remembering of the sort at which the psyche is so adept, we need to replace the logic of "instead of"—"categories *instead of* events, archetypes *instead of* historical personages"[39]—by the psychological logic of "this too": categories and events *too*, archetypes and history *also*. The point applies crucially to memory and time themselves. It is not a question of collective versus personal memory, or of profane *contra* sacred time. In particular, the enactment of one side of each dichotomy does not require the elimination or suspension of the other, as Eliade asserts.[40] Why not collective *and* personal—collective *as* personal—and why not profane *and* sacred: profane *as* sacred, sacred *as* profane? Why keep on keeping apart what may belong together—at least psychically? In the psyche, after all, it is always a matter of mixture (of same and different, odd and even, like and unlike) as well as a mixture of matters (aqueous, telluric, sulfuric, and the like).

(3) *Re-versioning*. A third, and quite crucial, form of reversion (especially for archetypal psychology) is found in re-versioning in memory. "Re-versioning" means, strictly, giving another version; but the question immediately arises: another version of what? Of the present in which the re-versioning activity is taking place or of the past which provides the original version? The answer, in keeping with the foregoing psycho-logic, is *both*. How this is so can be seen from the following familiar scenario.

(a) A person arrives in psychotherapy suffering and complaining of a set of finite and ego-centered particulars: e.g., an inability to start writing a thesis, to relate to certain other people freely and openly, etc. Such so-called "symptoms," inhering in and directly afflicting the ego, form the point of departure: "the symptom is on the agenda";[41]

(b) discussion of these afflictions allows a certain coherent pattern to emerge, often constellated around primary figures in the patient's life; a personal story or "tale," if not yet a myth, begins to coalesce as this chronicle is told and re-told time and again;

(c) it is at this critical juncture that a genuine *mythos* may begin to come forth as the analyst or the patient (or, best, both) come to see in the tale a mythical substrate, analogue, parallel, or what have you: the exact form does not matter here; what does matter is that something of mythical proportion is apprehended or sensed;

(d) although any number of courses of action then become available, one possible course is the following:

(i) reversion to an explicit myth or mythical figure: to Apollo, to Hermes, etc., along with his exploits, actions, maneuvers;

(ii) re-reading (re-interpreting) of the patient's symptoms-and-tale as somehow exemplifying the myth or mythical figure thus evoked— this providing elucidation and deepening, if not cure as such.

Notice what has happened in this not unusual sequence of events in a Jungian-style analysis, which I am not taking to be invariant or even necessarily typical. On the one hand, and most obviously, there has been a re-versioning of the patient's initial setting or "personal myth" by recourse to a pre-existing myth: in short, amplification has taken place. This first re-versioning is itself two-fold: the present tale is seen to be a version *of* an older story, illustrating it, bodying it forth, and so on; and this tale, once interpreted in the light of the antecedent myth, is itself re-versioned, given a different, a deeper, dimension than it possessed at first. On the other hand, and less obviously, the proto-myth is also re-versioned, and once more in two fashions: first, by being re-told or at least mentally rehearsed and thus recast, however subtly (e.g., by the inflection or mood with which it is re-told, if not by an explicit change in wording); second, by the very act of being brought into proximity with the patient's tale— which cannot fail to illuminate the proto-myth itself or at least to put it into a different light. Thus re-versioning works both ways: *in* and *of* the present and *of* and *by* the past. It is two-fold, if not in fact four-fold. In such a situation, it is manifest that nothing remains un-re-versioned.

Now the remarkable thing is that this radical re-versioning can go on— and often does, albeit unconsciously—*everywhere* and not only in therapy, which only provides a microcosm for the "everywhere." And not only in relation to, or by means of, myth in its explicit form. It occurs in the pondering of present perplexity in the light of past prototypes, including ancestors, figures of our childhood, former teachers and friends, and so forth. And not only previously known or heard-of persons, but events and experiences of all imaginable sorts—not excluding fictions, fantasies, and dreams— are grist for the mill of re-versioning. Each can contribute, and contribute richly, to the process; each is a valid *prima materia* for re-versioning; and this is so even if none is expressly recollected in its original state: the ur-version is no less an origin for not being explicitly called back to mind in its precise primal form or shape. Moreover, all such re-versioning can re-version itself by means of indefinite self-reiteration. Indeed, this is just what often occurs in psychotherapy itself: the myth, both personal and prototypical, moves on into other modalities and modulations, other versions, of itself: expanding in and through the indefinite expansiveness of soul-time, the kind of time in which all archetypally significant re-versioning takes place and in which there is always time for yet another re-writing of the psyche's self-inscription.

Here we must pause to consider a matter that is at once logical and psychological. This is the *necessity of origin*. Logically, there must be some prior version of a memory or a myth if re-versioning is to take place at all. This strictly logical point is at the same time psychological. For in psychologizing too (whether in therapy or outside it) I need to posit an origin for my re-versioning: something I can count on as already there, as at least semi-stably situated in the past. Of course, such an origin can be an occasion for nostalgia and regret; but however it is actually experienced or felt, it remains a fundamental need. I need to believe in an earlier version of myself of which my present self is an extension or outgrowth, a later version: this is stressed as much by Bachelard (e.g., in *The Poetics of Reverie*) as by Freud. In soul-making of all sorts (where the personal past is less at stake), I have the same insistent need to posit the prior as the origin of the current—the immemorial before the narrowly memorial. But the "before" means neither that which merely precedes in historical or cosmic time nor that which authorizes by its sheer priority—nor even that which lends credence by its facticity as past—but rather that which validates by deepening.

What sort of deepening is this? Re-versioning as we have come to understand it cannot be reduced simply to giving another version, however effectual or eloquent the new version may be. It is much more a matter of *shifting levels*: retelling the tale, indeed—but at, or in view of, another level of meaning, another stratum of significance. Now, I need not be present *at* the origin to make use *of* the origin in this shifting of levels. Deepening can occur just as effectively in the absence of presence—provided that re-versioning takes place in some significant form. But the presence of origin must be presumed even if it need not be experienced as such. Origins give bases and bottoms, lower limits, to what otherwise would be baseless and bottomless: baseless fabrication, bottomless abyss.

In sum: re-versioning in myth and by myth (and in dream and by myth)—and in life and by myth—is a basic way in which we practice active remembering. It is also a major mode wherein soul lives its time—makes it and distends it. Re-versioning takes time; and since time (as Augustine tells us) is "an extendedness of soul itself," the expanding and shifting going on in re-versioning is an extending of time in the soul—and of soul in time as well. Just as we must resist the idea of time as perfectly circular—

made in the image of eternity, an image that is itself consequently one of circular motion for the Greeks[42] and that still shows up in clock faces—so we now have to resist the reduction of re-versioning to a repetition of the same: to coincidence with re-presence to, or co-presence at, the origin (as again on Eliade's view). But if re-versioning is not strict repetition, it is also not radical re-casting of the kind that occurs when a story is passed on in whispers among the guests at a table, ending as a wholly different story once the circuit is made. Re-versioning happens when the story is told out loud—when the guests speak freely and openly to one another. Changes certainly do arise in this procedure; the line, the story-line, is not straight, much less circular; versions get told; but likeness remains, enough of it and of sufficient strength for the variant versions to be recognized as genuine re-versionings of something recognizably self-alike.

(4) *Re-visioning.* Likeness in fact emerges as a central theme in psychical memory of an active sort. Proclus tells us that likeness is basic to reversion of every kind and not to re-versioning alone. Let me cite in full Proposition 32 from the *Elements of Theology:*

> *All reversion is accomplished through a likeness of the reverting terms to the goal of reversion.* For that which reverts endeavors to be conjoined in every part with every part of its cause, and desires to have communion in it and be bound to it. But all things are bound together by likeness, and by unlikeness they are distinguished and severed. If, then, reversion is a communion and conjunction, and all communion and conjunction is through likeness, it follows that all reversion must be accomplished through likeness.[43]

"Likeness" renders the Greek word *homoiotēs,* recalling the Anaxagorean "homoeomereity," the principle of universal homogenization of things: all-things-in-all. But likeness also recalls copy—and thus *image,* whose Latin etymon (*imago*) means precisely copy or imitation. I think that we would all agree that "image" in art or psychology—indeed, in advertising or politics as well—has come to mean more than copy. But does it signify more than *likeness*? It does signify more than likeness in the restricted sense of exact, or even proportionate, resemblance; if it did not, it could not convey that sense of the novel and the startling which is intrinsic to our experience of the image as (in Bachelard's phrase) "a sudden salience on the surface of the psyche."[44] Moreover, such newness is not incompatible with a likening to something which we might once have known but have now forgotten. So too noetic insights according to Plato strike the knower as new—as "sparks" in the benighted ignorance of this life—but are in fact likenings of the soul to what it already knows, albeit from previous lives.[45] Now Plato himself calls this noetic likening *anamnēsis,* "recollection" or "reminiscence"; and I would like to extend Plato's point by proposing that all likening in mind or soul is a form of remembering—not, of course, of things from our personal past only but of things that exceed the person by their very nature. Such likening, then, is ineluctably memorious in character; it is a truly active remembering: re / membering, putting things together again, shoring up fragments from the past. Nietzsche says in *Beyond Good and Evil:*

> Thinking is, in fact, far less a discovery than a recognition, a remembering, a return and a homecoming to a remote, primordial, and inclusive household of the soul. . . .[46]

What Nietzsche asserts of thinking I would want to claim concerning remembering as well. It too is a homecoming, one that is effected precisely by the action of *homoiotēs*: by likening (and continual re-likening) of present to past and of past to present.

Such an action is essential to the re-visioning which a richly reversionary remembering accomplishes. To re-vision our remembered past we must make, and have, adequate likenesses of it. These likenesses must be genuinely visionary images: in Plato's distinction, they must be products of *phantastikē technē* ("semblance-making") and not merely of *eikastikē technē* ("resemblance-making").[47] An *eikon* requires exact replication of features, dimensions, qualities; it is indeed a copy, an "after-image" of the very sort that empiricist and engrammatic theories of memory both call for. A semblance, on the other hand, allows for alteration of proportions in the interest of achieving particular effects, aesthetic or rhetorical: hence even *dis*semblance comes within its purview (e.g., in the subtle manipulation of the width of the columns at the Parthenon which dissemble as to estimated breadth). Visionary images are matters of semblance and sometimes of dissemblance as well; when they are images of the past as such— "memory-images" as they are often termed reductively—they are more, or other, than strict resemblances to it. They are likenings to it; they convey it rather than copy it.

Re-visioning is a matter of just this kind of conveyance by semblance. The semblance is all in the image—in the "primordial image" as Jung would term it.[48] When we recall that it is in and through primordial images that archetypal presences are in turn conveyed, we realize something truly visionary is at work here. *Eidos,* the proper object of *anamnēsis* for Plato, means "visual aspect" in its original acceptation; "Form," by which it is usually translated into English, still retains the sense of something beheld, albeit noetically and not perceptually. Can it be contingent that Jung, in so many ways a natural neo-Platonist, defines archetypes as "pre-existent forms" and as "thought-forms"?[49] *Eidos* and archetype—*eidos* and *typos,* after all, both connote "kind"—rejoin as ultimate objects of a visionary state of soul. Or more exactly, of a *re*-visionary state, since it is Plato's explicit argument that knowledge of the Forms entails having been acquainted with them in a pre-existent life: how else can we account for the sense of recogni-

tion (of noetic déjà vu) which attends their apprehension and for the closely
related fact that we do not learn them from inductions based on our present life? Noetic knowing is, then, a matter of re-visioning: *getting the vision
again;* and the same is true of archetypal insight, which is equally an affair of reacquaintance and re-visioning—now mediated by primordial images, for which Plato has no proper place.

If we attempt to be less exalted in our vision of re-visioning by descend-
ing from the expressly transpersonal realm of the eidetic and the archetypal
to the domain of our own personal past (not that the two can be kept an-
tiseptically separate!), we discover that re-visioning consists in the following actions.

(a) *Re-viewing.* Letting our remembered lives "pass in review" before us,
this is more than a reverting to the past since it means letting it parade
and unfold in its own time and at its own tempo; the kind of remembering at work here is more akin to revery than to effortful recall of past
fact; it is a matter of an absorptive, a re-absorbed, state in which such
concerted activities as dating and evaluating play a minor role;

(b) *Re-visualizing.* This is a decidedly more active mode in which we
attempt to summon up scenes which are not coming back in involuntary revery; it is not limited to "filling in the gaps in memory"[50] (as Freud
calls it), that is, supplying missing details of various sorts; for it may
also occur in an attempt at clarifying what has come forth from memory
spontaneously—seeing it more vividly, perhaps more vividly than we
experienced it at the moment of origin;

(c) *Re-envisioning.* This is the most active, encompassing mode of all,
since we now have to do with "visions envisioning the soul itself" (in
the words of the epigram from Heidegger cited at the beginning of this
essay); once our lives have been adequately re-viewed and re-visualized,
we can begin to envision them again in a more psychically sensitive way,
one that takes account more fully of all that we have been and done
of significance; it is what an authentic autobiography of one's own psyche
would uncover, whether at a micro- or a macro-level of our lives; and
it would almost certainly not be restricted to the past in the manner of
(a) and (b), but would actively involve the present in which the envisioning is done; for the re-envisioning is of one's psyche as a whole, and
an important part of this very psychical totality is temporal in character,
hence including all three ecstases of past, present, and future;[51] no matter how capacious the envisioning may be, it takes place in the form of
a visionary image—of imaginative semblance rather than reduplicative
resemblance. This is the point at which imagining and remembering
realize maximal overlap, as can be seen in the general formula for re-
envisionment: "how I could be . . . different from what I have been"

(where the "could be" is the imaginal moment and the "have been" is memorial in nature).

These three modes of re-visioning represent progressively more active forms of remembering, that is, forms for which we not merely take increased responsibility (e.g., because of the more concerted or voluntary character of the actions undertaken) but which themselves may lead to specifications beyond remembering proper. If these latter are in fact based on memory, however, they can be considered "revisions" of our lives: modifications of it due to the work of remembering. They would be akin to those "revised editions" by which Freud characterized the effects of transference.[52] But the revision in question here is more than a palpable change in lifestyle or life goals; it is also a *re-vision*, a new or renewed vision of the direction and significance of one's life up to the present and beyond.

It is evident that re-visioning, when grasped in its full scope, involves an active remembering that defies passive models of memory. It does so more completely than does re-verting (with its fixation on the turned-to object), re-connecting (which requires an already existing and still stable past with which to connect), and even re-versioning (wherein the role of the past as original, as ur-version, is uneliminable, albeit immensely variable). In re-visioning, we witness an activism no longer beholden to origins, points of connection, adverted objects: indeed, no longer beholden even to the past per se.

Remembering has here truly come into its own. It achieves a freedom of movement whose only adequate analogy is that of active imagination. Just as the latter enables us "to dream the myth onwards" (in Jung's classic phrase), so active remembering allows us to take our lives onwards into new depths. It does so precisely by revivifying old depths, especially by re-visioning them in more psychically ramified ways. There is no danger of exhausting such depths, for it remains true (as Heraclitus said) that "you could not discover the limits of soul, even if you traveled every road to do so; such is the depth of its meaning."[53] But one main road into soul remains remembering itself, above all in its active modes, modes that belie the attempt to confine remembrance to registration or to reduplicative replay of the past.

IV

In making such claims, I am in effect answering affirmatively the first question raised early in this chapter: Is there an active remembering which is just as psychically significant as active fantasying? Further, I have suggested the lines of positive responses to the second and third questions as well:

Are not memories a *prima materia* for archetypal psychology? Is not memory a means to soul with as much right, and as much psychical power, as fantasy and imagination? In closing I want to sketch out more satisfying answers to these last two questions by considering briefly six areas in which the primordiality of active remembering shows itself.

(1) It is all the more striking that, even when we are not concerned with memory at the highest, noetic level, images continue to rest on memories as if they were the more basic term. In the ancient art of memory as brought to our attention so brilliantly by Frances Yates, we find the following advice on mnemotechnics ("how to improve your memory") offered by Quintilian: "The images by which the [orator's] speech is to be remembered . . . are placed in imagination on the places which have been memorized [in advance]."[54] A grid of places (*loci*) is committed to memory so that on each successive position of the grid an image of the item-to-be-remembered can be deposited—and then retrieved at the proper moment later on. In this practice, memory literally *stands under* imagination, giving to the latter a coherence and order which it might lack if left on its own; and imagining, thus structured, subserves remembering in turn by aiding in the ordinary, non-noetic recollection of a series of discrete items. The sequence at work here is *memorizing-imagining-remembering,* thereby putting imagination in the middle as "mediatrix," just where Aristotle and Kant, Corbin and Jung have all placed it.[55]

(2) But imagining refuses to be cabined, cribbed, and confined—even by remembering in this pragmatic, robust mode. It has an ascensional aspect, a verticalizing tendency that seeks to soar—to sublime and sublate itself. "He who cannot fly cannot imagine," writes Bachelard in *L'air et les songes.* "Imagining begins with wings," as Hillman has said.[56] Yet just this etherealizing activity of imagination calls for memory, both as point of departure (e.g., in those reveries of childhood so much stressed by Bachelard) and as counterweight to imagining's inconstancy—as the basis of all reversion, as that which gives resonance, body and echo, to what might otherwise be sheerly sublime.

(3) Closely related to all this is imagining's proclivity for the variable and the variegated. "Free variation in imagination" is the very name of one of Husserl's fundamental techniques in phenomenology—a technique closely akin to Jung's active imagination.[57] Yet both imaginotechnics require a compensating mnemotechnic if something geniunely *in*variant is to be attained. This invariant is the archetype for Jung and the essence for Husserl. We have seen how memory as reversion—especially as re-connecting and re-versioning—is indispensable to the achievement of an archetypally alive consciousness, alive in myths not entirely of its own making but re-membered from parts of the personal and, more particularly, the transpersonal past. Similarly, Husserl acknowledges that the exercise of free variation demands the explicit retaining-in-grasp (*im-Griff-behalten*)

of earlier variants—that is, their being held in memory—in order to attain insight into the essence (Jung would prefer to say the "dominant") of all the variations taken together.[58]

(4) In Hades "essence stands out"[59]—and thus the necessary and the invariant—and we must move at last to the underworld, where remembering finds its natural home. Imagining, as I have stressed on other occasions, is primarily possibilizing in its activity.[60] In the ethereal realm, everything is possible; down below, *nothing* is—any longer. Where imagining is itself no longer possible—much less perceiving, also strictly excluded—*remembering remains*. What remains, our psychically saving remnant, remains in memory. There may well be a specifically telluric imagination belonging to the earth and to its goddess Gaia; not *all* imagining is aerian, despite a powerful propensity in this direction. But there is no strictly Stygian imagination, no imagination belonging properly to Chthon. The chthonic realm is the realm of *memoria*—of com-memoration and re-memoration. Plotinus tells us that "[A] 'shade', being the characteristically human part, *remembers* all the action and experience of [its] life."[61] What else is it to do now that this life is over—wholly "passified," made past entirely? What different activity could a shade exhibit other than recalling its past time (especially in face of the forgetfulness which it has been led to imbibe at the waters of Lethe)? It is *past time* that we recognize that soul, which is always already dying—always already chthonian—is memorial through and through.

(5) Yet even if we do not wish to make such a precipitous descent, preferring to stay on *terra firma*, we cannot help noticing two final ways in which remembering remains essential. The first is found in the constitution of time-consciousness. Our being in time does not arise from an indifferently equalitarian mixture of remembering (the past), perceiving (the present), and imagining (the future). Important as imagining and perceiving are in this regard, remembering is still more crucial. It is hardly accidental that Augustine and Husserl, who have provided the most profound analyses of our experience of being in time, both accord a primacy to memory over imagination and perception: Augustine by stressing the "fields and dens and caverns [of *memoria*] . . . innumerably full of innumerable kinds of things"[62] and Husserl by devoting by far the largest portions of his seminal 1904–05 lectures on internal time-consciousness to primary and secondary memory.[63] The basis for this imputed primacy lies in the straightforward observation that unless we were aware of time's having already passed we could not perceive its passing in the present or imagine its coming to pass in the future. Only on the basis of the primary or secondary memory of *some* time having gone by are we in a position to consider *further* time going by. And it is precisely by our appreciation of the elapsing of time as registered in memory that we are impressed by that transiency so fundamental to time in the soul: "trans" after all means "across, beyond, through, to the other side"—to the other side of the present, indeed, but

also to the other side of life: death. Once more, remembering has to do with what remains over from the present or from life. *Remembering is re-maindering.*

(6) But still remaining on earth—earthings we are, as well as deathlings and timelings—what remains for us to do? Many things, of course, but one of these and one of the most essential is to re-member our lives psychologically. A most effective way of doing so, according to archetypal psychology, is to revert to the gods in all of the senses of reversion examined earlier or, to put it another way, to *liken our lives to theirs* and *theirs to ours.* This reciprocal likening is tantamount to a re-collection which is the ultimate source of all deepgoing likeness in the soul. The recollection is of the gods, who ask less to be imagined than recalled. As Hillman has put it, "what the Gods notoriously want is remembrance of them, not choice among them."[64] The want, though, should not be notorious if it is truly a matter of psychological necessity. The gods have no other way of surviving than by being revived in memory. They have not flown insofar as they remain in the only place in which they can remain—in memory—*revenants* from the realm of souls and rekindlers of it.

In short, I am calling for a return to memory as more than mere mental "flotsam"[65]—as more than a mere engrammatic inscription of the left-overs, the rags and tatters, of our lives. Remembering, rather, is soul-making, is its very basis. As such, remembering needs itself to be remembered— just as soul itself needs to be remembered in this soulless time of ours. Moreover, remembering needs a re-recognition, a recognition not accorded to it since the Greeks, who made Mnēmosynē one of the original Titans, the Mother of the Muses, and a partner of Hermes himself.[66] Depth psychology in particular needs to re-vision its assessment of memory, too often subjugated to fantasy and imagination viewed as exclusive inroads to psychical reality—whereas in fact the right rich remembering is an equiprimordial entrance to the soul's depths. If it is true that "archetypal psychology searches for the *archai,* the governing principles or root metaphors,"[67] then it must be realized that memory is one of these very *archai,* indeed in many ways the taproot of the rhizomatic structure of the soul itself. The archaic in its fullest and most resonant sense is, after all, the proper province of remembering.[68] Or, rather, remembering has no province proper to itself alone. As an activity of re-membering, it extends into all the parts of soul, continually putting them into relation with each other—reverting each to the other, so that finally each is a likening, a mutually memorious image, of the other. As Frances Yates reminds us, "the manipulation of images in memory must always to some extent involve the psyche as a whole."⁶⁹ As in the ancient art of memory, imagining and remembering come together *in memory*—which is to say, *in soul*, a soul as memorial as it is imaginal in its being and in its being in time.

Soul-making, we can conclude, is ineluctably a remembering, while remembering is itself a main means of reversion to soul. For we see into the depths of the psyche by the re-verting, re-connecting, re-versioning, and re-visioning which remembering in depth alone makes possible. Beyond the pandaemonium of imagining, and the pantheon of the gods, we need to recognize as well the panpsychism of such remembering. Then memory, time, and soul will be seen as three equally valid facets of the same multiplex truth.

1.   Letter of 30 January 1899 to Wilhelm Fliess: "My predilection for the prehistoric in all its human forms remains the same. . . ."

2.   See Edmund Husserl, *The Phenomenology of Internal Time-Consciousness,* trans. J. S. Churchill (Bloomington: Indiana University Press, 1964), sec. 8–12.

3.   *"Contretemps"* means "1. wrong time; 2. piece of ill luck; 3. syncopation"; and *"à contretemps"* means "inopportunely, out of time" (*The Concise Oxford French Dictionary*).

4.   Immanuel Kant, *Critique of Pure Reason,* trans. N. K. Smith (New York: St. Martin's Press, 1965), p. 492. Cf. also ibid., pp. 310 ff., 486 ff. Descartes, in the third *Meditation,* wrote that "we must finally reach a first idea, the cause of which is like an archetype or source."

5.   For a survey of this work *in extenso,* see Robert G. Crowder, *Principles of Learning and Memory* (Hillsdale, N.J.: Erlbaum, 1976), passim.

6.   On these notions, see J. Breuer and S. Freud, *Studies on Hysteria* (London: Hogarth, 1955), pp. 7, 172–81, 295 ff.

7.   Sigmund Freud, "Project for a Scientific Psychology" in vol. 1 of the *Standard Edition of the Complete Psychological Works of Sigmund Freud* (London: Hogarth, 1966), p. 299. One class of neurons is said to be "the vehicle of memory, *and so probably of psychical processes in general*" (ibid., p. 300; my italics): here memory is made fundamental to psyche itself.

8.   Ibid., pp. 259–60 (letter of 21 October 1897 to Fliess).

9.   ". . . a system of *notation* was introduced whose task it was to lay down the results of this periodical activity of consciousness—a part of what we call *memory*" ("Formulations on the Two Principles of Mental Functioning" in Freud, *Standard Edition* [London: Hogarth, 1958], vol. 12, pp. 220–21; his italics).

10.   C. G. Jung, *Symbols of Transformation,* trans. R. F. C. Hull (Princeton: Princeton University Press, 1976), p. 408. Cf. also Jung, *Critique of Psychoanalysis,* trans. R. F. C. Hull (Princeton: Princeton University Press, 1975), p. 93: "in tracing the libido's regression, the analysis does not always follow the exact path marked out by the historical development, but often that of a subsequently formed fantasy, based only in part on former realities."

11.   C. G. Jung, *Psychological Types,* trans. H. G. Baynes and R. F. C. Hull (Princeton: Princeton University Press, 1971), p. 442.

12.   Jung, *Symbols of Transformation,* p. 89.

13.   Jung, *Critique of Psychoanalysis,* p. 52. This statement is from Jung, "The Theory of Psychoanalysis," originally delivered at Fordham University as lectures in 1912.

14.   Jung, *Symbols of Transformation,* p. 407.

15.   Jung, *Critique of Psychoanalysis,* p. 53.

16.   Ibid., pp. 51–52. Jung adds: "the patients then live more or less entirely in the world of the past."

17. Jung, *Psychological Types,* pp. 443–44; my italics. Cf. also Jung, *The Structure and Dynamics of the Psyche,* trans. R. F. C. Hull (Princeton: Princeton University Press, 1972), p. 349: the unconscious contains "the accumulated deposits from the lives of our ancestors."

18. On this point, see my "Toward an Archetypal Imagination," in this volume.

19. Jung, *Symbols of Transformation,* p. 293. Notice the analogy from crystallography: this may be a more dramatic or effective analogy than that of the engram, but it is just as physicalistic.

20. Jung, *Psychological Types,* pp. 443, 447; his italics. Cf. also Jung, *Two Essays on Analytical Psychology,* trans. R. F. C. Hull (New York: Meridian, 1970), pp. 74–76.

21. C. G. Jung, *Psychology and Alchemy,* trans. R. F. C. Hull (Princeton: Princeton University Press, 1970), p. 279.

22. For further discussion of datability, see Martin Heidegger, *Being and Time,* trans. J. Macquarrie and E. Robinson (New York: Harper & Row, 1962), sec. 79, as well as William James, *The Principles of Psychology* (New York: Dover, 1950), vol. 1, pp. 610, 622–23, 631, 647, 650, 655.

23. More constitutive even than imagination, if we are to believe Husserl himself: *The Phenomenology of Internal Time-Consciousness* concentrates almost entirely on memory, mentioning imagination only incidentally and in passing.

24. See Eugène Minkowski, *Lived Time,* trans. N. Metzel (Evanston: Northwestern University Press, 1970), Part One, for a discussion of seven distinct zones of experienced time.

25. See F. C. Bartlett, *Remembering* (Cambridge: Cambridge University Press, 1964), pp. 197 ff., 208 ff.; Jean Piaget and Bärbel Inhelder, *Memory and Intelligence,* trans. A. J. Pomerans (New York: Basic Books, 1973), pp. 23 ff., 382 ff., 403.

26. Rafael López-Pedraza, *Hermes and His Children* (Spring Publications, 1977), p. 8; my italics.

27. Cf. ibid., pp. 4–5.

28. Sigmund Freud, *The Ego and the Id,* trans. J. Strachey (New York: Norton, 1960), p. 29. Freud adds that character also "contains the *history* of these object-choices" (ibid.; my italics).

29. On invasions as a feature of the "endopsyche," see C. G. Jung, *Analytical Psychology: Its Theory and Practice* (New York: Random House, 1968), pp. 24, 34–35, 37, 47.

30. On this point, see López-Pedraza, *Hermes and His Children,* pp. 10–11.

31. Proclus, *Elements of Theology,* trans. E. R. Dodds (Oxford: Oxford University Press, 1933), Proposition 32. Cf. also Proposition 35: "if it should proceed without reversion or immanence, it will be without sympathy with its cause, since it will have no communion with it."

32. James Hillman, *Re-Visioning Psychology* (New York: Harper & Row, 1975), p. 218; my italics.

33. Mircea Eliade, *Cosmos and History* (New York: Harper & Row, 1959), p. 20.

34. Cf. ibid., pp. 37 ff.; my italics.

35. Ibid., p. 44.

36. Ibid.

37. "Nothing can endure if it is not, 'animated', if it is not, through a sacrifice, endowed with a 'soul' " (ibid., p. 20).

38. Eliade cites the Satapatha Brahmana: "We must do what the gods did in the beginning" and comments that "this Indian adage summarizes all the theory underlying rituals in all countries" (ibid., p. 21).

39. Ibid., p. 43; my italics.

40. "Through the paradox of rite, profane time and duration are suspended . . . there is an implicit abolition of profane time, of duration, of 'history' " (ibid., p. 35).

41. Breuer and Freud, *Studies on Hysteria,* p. 297. To this statement the authors add the significant phrase "all the time" (ibid.)—which is precisely what is being contested here.

42. On this and related themes, see my "Time in the Soul," in this volume.

43. Proclus, *Elements of Theology;* my italics.
44. Gaston Bachelard, *The Poetics of Space,* trans. M. Jolas (New York: Orion, 1964), p. xi.
45. Plotinus sums up this Platonic line of thought by saying that "all knowing comes by likeness" (*The Enneads,* I, 8, 1; cited by Hillman, *Re-Visioning Psychology,* p. 99).
46. Friedrich Nietzsche, *Beyond Good and Evil,* trans. M. Cowan (Chicago: Regnery, 1955), sec. 20.
47. See Plato, *Sophist* 235d–236c.
48. See Jung, *Psychological Types,* pp. 442–47.
49. C. G. Jung, *The Archetypes and the Collective Unconscious* (Princeton: Princeton University Press, 1968), pp. 3–4; Jung, *Two Essays on Analytical Psychology,* p. 76.
50. Cf. Freud, "Remembering, Repeating, and Working-Through" (*Standard Edition* [London: Hogarth, 1968], vol. 12, p. 148).
51. Indeed, we can very well re-envision our lives in terms of the future as the pivotal point of concern, e.g., in a situation of impending difficulty, such as the onset of a major disease. But an at least oblique reference to the past would remain operative even in this circumstance.
52. Freud, "Fragment of an Analysis of a Case of Hysteria" (in *Standard Edition* [London: Hogarth, 1953], vol. 7): "What are transferences? They are new editions or facsimiles of the impulses and phantasies which are aroused and made conscious during the progress of the analysis. . . . [Some] are more ingeniously constructed. . . . These, then, will no longer be new impressions, but revised editions" (p. 116).
53. Heraclitus, Fragment 423, in Philip Wheelwright's translation: *Heraclitus* (New York: Atheneum, 1968), p. 58.
54. Frances A. Yates, *The Art of Memory* (London: Routledge and Kegan Paul, 1966), p. 3.
55. On this placing-in-the-middle, see my "Imagination as Intermediate" in *Vers une esthétique sans entrave,* ed. G. Lascault (Paris: Union Générale d'Editions, 1975); translated and reprinted in this volume.
56. Remark made at the first Institute on Archetypal Psychology, University of Notre Dame, June 1978.
57. For a treatment of this parallel, see Edward S. Casey, *Imagining: A Phenomenological Study* (Bloomington: Indiana University Press, 1976), pp. 212–17.
58. On retaining-in-grasp, see Edmund Husserl, *Experience and Judgment,* trans J. S. Churchill and K. Ameriks (Evanston: Northwestern University Press, 1973), pp. 342–43.
59. James Hillman, *The Dream and the Underworld* (New York: Harper & Row, 1979), p. 30. Cf. also ibid., p. 121: "Hades has a hidden connection with *eidos* and *eidolon*."
60. See Casey, *Imagining,* chap. 5 ("Indeterminacy and Pure Possibility").
61. *Enneads* I, 1, 12; my italics. Cited by Hillman in *The Dream and the Underworld,* p. 56, where Hillman comments that a "shade remembers all the actions of our Herculean life and its physical perspective."
62. Augustine, *Confessions,* Book 10, chap. 17.
63. See Husserl, *The Phenomenology of Internal Time-Consciousness,* esp. sec. 15–30.
64. Hillman, *Re-Visioning Psychology,* p. 139.
65. Ibid., p. xi: "the flotsam of memory."
66. "The tribute the [Homeric] *Hymn* pays to Hermes as a god of music, culminating in the claim that Hermes is a consort of Mnemosyne, the Mother of the Muses, is unique in Greek literature" (N. O. Brown, *Hermes the Thief* [Madison: University of Wisconsin Press, 1947], p. 122).
67. Hillman, *Re-Visioning Psychology,* p. 99.
68. For Jung's comments on the archaic aspects of memory, see *Psychological Types,* pp. 443, 447.
69. Yates, *The Art of Memory,* p. xi.

Remembering and Perceiving

*The subject of the human mind being so copious
and various, I shall here take advantage of this
vulgar and specious division, that I may proceed
with the greater order.*

—DAVID HUME
A Treatise of Human Nature

I

THE FATES OF perceiving and remembering have been inextricably intertwined in Western philosophy and psychology. It has been asserted
from Plato's *Theaetetus* onward that there can be no remembering without
perceiving and, though much less frequently, no perceiving without
remembering of some sort. Just how either of these forms of interdepend-
ency occurs, however, has given rise to continual controversy. Little discernible progress has been made since Plato first proposed, in the
Theaetetus, a model of the mind as an aviary in which individual memories
wait like captive birds to be plucked from the cage of recollection in order
to aid in the identification of present perceptions. The elaborate and ingenious character of this memory machine—elaborate and ingenious in
comparison with the simpler model of the wax tablet also proposed in
the *Theaetetus*[1]—was to prove prophetic, since later treatments of perception often invoke memory as a deus ex machina brought in to resolve
ambiguities and perplexities of perceptual experience.

Consider, for example, Berkeley's celebrated theory of vision, especially
its explanation of how we perceive objects at a distance or in depth. Insofar as we have visual cues alone, that is, "light and colors," we have to
do with something highly ambiguous—ambiguous because, with such
evidence alone available, it seems inexplicable that we could distinguish
an object ten feet away from an object of exactly equivalent color and shape

but twice as large and twenty feet away.[2] In this predicament, *something else,* something other than the direct deliverances of the eye, is called upon to explain how it is that we nevertheless do pass correct judgments about the distance of such perceived objects from our position as their observer. According to Berkeley, this something else is memory and in particular the memory of the kinesthetic and tactile sensations generated in the bodily traversing of just such distances in the past.

> Looking at an object, I perceive a certain visible figure and color, with some degree of faintness and other circumstances, which from what I have formerly observed, determine me to think, that if I advance forward so many paces or miles, I shall be affected with such and such ideas of touch. . . . What [one] sees only suggests to his understanding, that after having passed a certain distance, to be measured by the motion of his body, which is perceivable by touch, he shall come to perceive such and such tangible ideas which have been usually connected with such and such visible ideas.[3]

Now this claim is certainly not true and can be disputed on any number of grounds, factual and theoretical alike.[4] But what is of crucial concern at this point is not so much its empirical truth or falsity as its basic strategy. This strategy consists in an appeal to memory (in the convenient euphemism of experience) as an ultimate *explanans:* "And these same means, which suggest the magnitude of tangible things, do also suggest their distance, and in the same manner, that is to say, *by experience alone.*"[5] That is to say, by past, now-remembered, or rememberable experience alone.

Such a strategy is by no means isolated or unusual in treatments of perception. It is also found, for instance, in numerous attempted explanations of the so-called "perceptual constancies," that is, the penchant human beings have for perceiving things as retaining the same shape, size, color, degree of brightness, rate of motion, etc., even though each of these features has in fact changed in some objectively detectable manner during the course of the perception.[6] In accordance with a recurrently popular model, itself stemming from the empiricist methodology first fully espoused by Locke and Berkeley, these constancies are routinely attributed to "familiarity"—which is to say, to memory, the basis and source of the sense of the familiar. Once again, the explanation is dubious—the perceptual constancies can be shown to obtain even with quite unfamiliar objects—but strategically significant. It tries to resolve a problem in perception by invoking memory as a ready-to-hand and infinitely resourceful solvent, as if its very difference from a putatively "pure" perception with no resources of its own enabled it to be perception's savior. Just as evasive and flighty birds are caught and held in an aviary, so the slippery ambiguities of pure perceiving are caught and held in the catchall captivity of remembering. As any bird keeper knows, however, the least loosening of the cage door allows for escape—

that is, in the present context, for the reappearance of problems that cannot be contained in any such artifact of explanation.

It is also evident that, unless the nature of memory itself is clarified, all such recourse to it is a form of explaining the obscure by the still more obscure—of "explaining up to the explanation," as Kierkegaard put it.[7] Moreover, this recourse is circular and question-begging, imputing to memory the very things which perceptual experience, taken as "pure," supposedly lacks. In Merleau-Ponty's words:

> Before any contribution by memory, what is [perceived] must at the present moment so organize itself as to present a picture to me in which I can recognize my former experiences. Thus the appeal to memory presupposes what it is supposed to explain: the patterning of data, the imposition of meaning on a chaos of sense-data. No sooner is the recollection of memories made possible than it becomes superfluous, since the work it is being asked to do is already done [i.e., already done within perception itself].[8]

To claim this is not to deny the importance or the influence of memory; instead, it is to situate this importance and influence somewhere else than has been the case traditionally—rather than in an abstract aviary of intellect or in some covert cul-de-sac of mind, within perceiving itself, "arrayed in present consciousness itself," as Merleau-Ponty adds.[9]

Before we can begin to determine what forms this arraying takes—what forms of immanent unity between perception and memory are to be found in human experience—we must consider a further aspect of the relationship between perception and memory as it has been treated in Western thought. Of the two two-way relations mentioned above—no remembering without perceiving, no perceiving without remembering—the latter relation, especially as it is found in the perception of distance and in the perceptual constancies, has been of considerable strategic value in certain epistemological discussions; but as with so many such strategies, it possesses more rhetorical than philosophical substance. In contrast, the former relation—i.e., no remembering without perceiving—has been set forth straightforwardly and unrhetorically as a claim of substance, even as an undeniable claim. What is at stake in such a claim is no less than the primacy of perception as a proper and ultimate foundation of human experience. Merleau-Ponty is himself an outspoken advocate of this very primacy, which he defines in the following well-known formulation:

> The perceived world is the always presupposed foundation of all rationality, all value, and all existence. This thesis does not destroy either rationality or the absolute. It only tries to bring them down to earth.[10]

Noteworthy here is Merleau-Ponty's active espousal of the *arche*-concept of "foundation" and his somewhat defensive denial that he is trying to destroy "rationality or the absolute." On the contrary! He is passionately supporting them and supporting them in one of the most traditional manners—by reversion to perception as the foundational act, the act of acts, the act necessarily preceding all other acts (including the act of remembering), the "simple," "basic" act, as Husserl, another proponent of the primacy of perception, called it.[11] We shall have to ask, however: Is this ur-act not contaminated by the presence of remembering, supposedly its own offspring, from the very beginning? Is not perception, however basic it is in human experience, always already sullied by memory—mixed with it, much as memory itself is mixed with desire, from the start?

II

The answer to both of these questions is affirmative, as I shall try to show shortly. Previous to this, though, we need to become clear as to the differences between the two acts: before continuity can be rightfully claimed, distinctive discontinuities must be acknowledged. This is all the more needed in view of the widespread tendency (itself an expression of the belief in the primacy of perception) to regard memory as a mere extension or mode of perception, a tendency as prominent in Aristotle and Hume as it is in those contemporary cognitive psychologists who persist in positing "memory traces" of perceptions as the exclusive bases of remembering.[12] Inherent in this tendency is the demeaning notion that memory can only be derivative from perception and is, to this extent, its mere replica and replay. Remembering, in such a view, is *the continuation of perceiving by other means*—means, moreover, suspiciously like, or even the same as, those employed in perception itself considered as the primary act.

Now this is just not so. To remember is not to go on perceiving, as if to carry on the work of perceiving in some quasi- or para-perceptual way. It is to do something distinctively different. To begin with, it is simply not true that what we remember is in every case something we have once perceived, as F. C. Bartlett, among many others, has maintained: "it is obvious that nothing can be recognized or recalled which has not first been perceived."[13] In fact, I can very well remember having felt a certain emotion or having had a certain thought, where the content of the emotion or the thought is recalled quite independently of the perceptual context in which it first occurred. So too I can remember former imaginings and rememberings—as well as my present remembering of the same acts at some future point. The reiterability of many cognitive and emotive acts in recollection renders questionable any attempt to reduce these acts to avatars of perception. Nor can it be correctly claimed that perceivings are always or necessarily the cause—either the initial or the precipitating cause—of my present rememberings, which may arise apart from any instigation by perception. Indeed, the return of some memories is actually facilitated by a *lack* of perceptual vivacity in one's present experience, as has been shown in sensory deprivation experiments and as occurs daily in psychoanalysis (where the analyst's *not* being perceived helps to elicit memories otherwise difficult to retrieve). Thus, neither in terms of causation nor of content is it the case that remembering is a continuation of perceiving.[14]

Another, and still more decisive line of consideration, concerns those memories that do derive, directly or indirectly, from previous perceptions. Even here we cannot speak of a *repetition* of the latter in the former, as does Hume.[15] Taken in any strict sense, repetition is ruled out in the nature of the case, since the only complete repetition of a perception would be a *re-perception*, not a memory at all. Yet even when meant more loosely, repetition of a perception cannot be considered a continuation of it. For there are many ways of repeating—of "going over"—a prior perception in memory, only one of which would exhibit the same order and deliver the same ostensible content as did the original perception.[16] These variant modes of going over a perceived object or event in memory include the diverse possibilities of: (1) reversing the order in which the different parts of the perceived object or event appeared on the original occasion; (2) focusing more on myself as the perceiver than on what was perceived, or vice-versa; (3) thematizing things only collaterally or marginally given in the progenitor experience, e.g., the seedling which stood inconspicuously beside the oak I vividly remember playing under in my front yard; (4) recalling an object or event hurriedly as a whole, *totum simul* and as a vague totalized Gestalt; (5) in contrast with this last procedure, recalling something *partes extra partes,* lingering in memory over each separate portion; (6) infusing later perceptions of the same object or event into my memory of first perceiving it, thereby allowing remembering to be re-influenced by perceiving; (7) conversely, letting later memories, or still other acts of mind, affect a pristine "first" memory; and (8) exploring in memory aspects of an object or event which were not explored at all in originally perceiving it—of which, indeed, one may not even have been explicitly aware at the time. This last possibility is of special significance in the context of the present discussion, for it demonstrates decisively that the memory of what we perceive, far from being constrained by the original experience, can range beyond its consciously registered content by picking out features not expressly noted in this experience itself. We are even entitled, I believe, to speak of discovery in memory, for remembering sometimes represents a more acute and sensitive form of apprehension than the perceiving from which it stems. In any event, just because something has been presented originally in perception does not mean that its fate as remembered is forever sealed, although we may admit that the limits of what can be correctly recalled are indeed predetermined by the initial perception.

Let us now turn to a consideration of four eidetic or intrinsic differences between perceiving and remembering.

(1) First, and perhaps most obviously, there is a difference in temporal index. What we perceive is taken as appearing or existing in the present, as stationed irrevocably there no matter how broad or narrow our conception of the present itself may be. What we remember, in contrast, is posited precisely as appearing or existing in the past—or, more precisely, posited as once-having-been-present. As there is no way in which to make the formerly extant present re-extant, a literally de-cisive gap separates the temporality of perceived and remembered things; and this is so even though we are always assured that a continuum of intermediary temporal fields links the past of that which is recalled to the present moment of recall. Indeed, it is by means of this continuum itself (whether regarded as real or only as ideally constructible) that the gap in question is established and becomes measurable. To put this first difference in its most succinct form: if perceived, then occurring in the present; if remembered, then occurring at some point prior to the present, that is, in the past.

(2) A second difference concerns what we may call "the face of familiarity." That which we recollect we have experienced before and in the first person: it is my own experience even if I do not at first recognize this to be so.[17] There are no transferred memories; I cannot remember for you, or you for me, despite the illusion of doing so in situations of reminiscing.[18] Even if I have forgotten an experience for a long time, when I do manage to remember it, it presents itself as at least minimally familiar to me, as having happened in my immediate ambience. (This is not, of course, to say that a sense of familiarity guarantees the validity of the memory; cases of déjà vu involve apparent familiarity while lacking easily demonstrable validity.) A given perceptual experience, on the other hand, may be utterly novel insofar as I have never been engaged in this particular experience before, not even ostensibly. If so, it lacks the face of familiarity and may be deeply challenging or disturbing for this very reason. And yet, paradoxically and in contrast with the experience of remembering, I may genuinely co-perceive the objects of this experience along with others who are present at the time.

(3) A third, and closely related, difference between the two acts arises from the essentially closed character of remembering in opposition to the open-endedness of perceiving. What is remembered is something which in and by itself has become, if not ossified altogether (for it always remains subject to re-exploration and re-interpretation), at least fixed in several ways: in temporal position (i.e., in having a determinate relation to events both before and after it), primary structural features (in contrast with those secondary features that may, as stressed above, become thematic only on a subsequent occasion of remembering), internal dynamism (that is, possibilities of further development as predelineated in the original experience), and a certain inherent obduracy as a coherently recollected content (giving to it a characteristic contraction or compression). What brings about the closure is above all the fact that what is remembered comes packaged

in a tightly knit nexus of prior apprehensions and anticipations of consciousness, almost all of which have now faded or been fulfilled irrevocably. Contrast this fact with the situation obtaining when an act of perception takes place in the present. On the one hand, there is an ongoing lapsing from whatever temporal point one is at; newly elapsed phases of the perception continually modify older ones forming with these latter new series of just past perceptions, and so on ad infinitum. On the other hand, a stream of anticipations, all more or less unfulfilled, leads off from the same present point; these in particular provide perceptual experience with its sense of the open-ended, of not yet being a closed chapter. Since there is no definite "after" yet (this will be determined precisely by the fulfilling of anticipations), there is the sense of something still expanding as the perceiving continues on its uncharted course.

(4) "Every experience has its horizon,"[19] writes Husserl, and mnemonic experience is no exception. The horizonal structure of memories is in fact two-fold. (a) The first form of horizon, which we might term the "mnemonic frame," unifies each memory from within, providing it with an identity as a single discrete whole. This frame consists of several factors: the remembered content itself (furnishing a core of sameness), the fact that this content is presented to the rememberer in an internally coherent sequence with its own beginning and ending, and an adhesion of the rememberer to the object or event remembered by virtue of being the same person who once enacted or witnessed it. (b) In addition to this self-unifying horizon, there is a purely locatory or positional horizon serving to situate the memory, thus unified by the memory frame, in relation to other experiences of the subject himself or herself. This horizon is not always expressly manifest in the form of a date or any other assigned position within what Heidegger calls "world time." But it is always operative to some extent, e.g., when I place a recollected event as having happened "after starting kindergarten" but "before fourth grade." In contradistinction to both the internal and the external horizons of perception,[20] such a horizon as this is lacunary and hence not amenable to continuous exploration or filling-in: I may be able to recall *nothing else* between kindergarten and fourth grade, and yet my memory is no less legitimate for being thus cast adrift in my stream of experiences. It remains part of this stream and internal to it, even if it does not occupy a determinate stretch of it.[21]

III

If we grant these four fundamental differences between remembering and perceiving, we must go on to consider the more problematic and more fateful question of how they nevertheless, despite such differences (and perhaps even thanks to them in part), do manage to communicate and co-operate with each other—how they *both* become "arrayed in present consciousness" and arrayed *together* there in an indissoluble unity. As is so often the case in a descriptive project, after distinction comes reunification—after *dia-krisis, syn-krisis.* In our case, it is a matter of seeking forms of inherent unification between perceiving and remembering.

By saying "forms of *inherent* unification," I have in mind those modes of combination that are *non-contingent.* Contingent combinations between the two acts abound, occurring in such instances as those sudden recollections which are precipitated by perceptions but which possess no discernible link with the latter; situations of paired-associate learning in which the re-perception of the first member of a pair of items leads to the recall of the second member apart from any connection of content or form;[22] those experiences of hallucination in which perceived and remembered components commingle in varying ratios;[23] and so on. This list could be extended almost indefinitely—as in the precisely parallel case of contingent combinations of imagining and remembering.[24] Considerably more interest, however, attaches to non-contingent combinations, by which I mean cases in which the respective roles of the two acts are strictly co-essential. Such combinations in turn fall into two types: those in which the collaboration between perceiving and remembering is of a conspicuous and more or less readily analyzable nature and those in which it is much less evident.

A. *Conspicuous Collaboration.* Under this heading I find three closely related instances: recognizing, reconstructing, and reminding. In the interest of brevity, I shall mostly neglect recognition and reconstruction, concentrating instead on the somewhat more revealing case of reminding.

Unlike recognition, reminding normally involves a separation between the perceptual component ("the reminder") and the mnemonic component ("the remindand"), which are not in a relation of coincidence or *suffusion* as they are in recognition. Unlike reconstruction (with which it shares, however, a separateness of perceptual and mnemonic factors), the relation between reminder and remindand is not *indexical* in character; it does not consist in anything like evidence pointing beyond itself to a to-be-reconstructed past. Rather, I take the relation in question to be one of *adumbration* wherein the perceptual[25] component of the reminder adumbrates the non-perceived (because past or still future) remindand. What is adumbrated or "shadowed-forth" is an action which the reminder is charged with helping us to remember to undertake on the present or a future occasion— or a past action which is being "called back to mind" again (as in commemorative reminders). Notice, however, that the reminder, though designed to elicit an act of recollection, is not instituted for the sake of recollection as such but for the sake of the action which the recollecting is supposed to precipitate or to commemorate. In this respect, the recollection summoned forth by the reminder acts as an intermediary—a sort of second or "shadow" reminder—between the perceived reminder and the remindand proper. For example, I may tie a string around my finger (the reminder per se) so as to recall later in the evening (the act of recollection) to turn the heat down before going to bed (the remindand or action-which-I-shall-be-reminded-to-do). Indeed, the chain of reminders may be extended almost indefinitely, as when one memorandum refers to another and this latter to still another and so on: whole bureaucracies are based on this cycle of remindful reference, so elaborate in the end that few may be able to remember what is to be done or even where the reminders themselves are![26]

Given the indistinctness of the adumbrative relation inherent in reminding,[27] it might seem as if we have to do with something as amorphous as the suffusion that is ingredient in experiences of recognition. In the case of suffusion, however, the original experience so fully interpenetrates the presently perceived particular as to coincide or merge with it altogether; losing its identity as an experience stemming from a particular part of the past, it lends itself entirely to the present experience of recognition, making this latter possible by its very unobtrusiveness, its sheer immanence within it. Almost exactly the opposite obtains in reconstruction, where the past has characteristically fled or vanished from what we can now perceive, leaving us with the task of putting the surviving fragments together into a coherent "picture" of this past. In the case of reminding, there is neither a total inherence of the past in the present—of the remembered in the perceived—nor their disjunction from each other. Instead, in most situations of reminding something instituted in the past (the reminder) adumbrates something to be remembered now so as to be undertaken (as remindand) in the present or the future. Thus, in contrast with recognition, in reminding the perceptual and mnemonic components are kept distinct—the action is not *in* the reminder, only its adumbration is found there—yet not so distinct from one another as in reconstruction.

B. *Nonconspicuous Collaboration.* Conspicuous cases of collusion between perceiving and remembering arise frequently and in a well-marked manner in everyday existence. Now, however, we must consider a series of three cases in which the relation between perceiving and remembering is much less perspicuous. In these instances, we cannot appeal conveniently to already existing demarcations, verbal or nonverbal, or to unambiguous evidence from daily experience. Indeed, much of the difficulty in description arising at this point stems from the fact that the phenomena to be described are so deeply ingredient in this very experience, so radically constitutive of it, that they are not easily isolable as singular traits.

(1) *Consolidation.* Unless what we experience were consolidated to some degree—unless it had some minimal cohesion and unity—it could not be considered an *object* of experience in the first place. This holds for all types of experience, from acts of slow rumination to mercurial imaginings; but it is particularly true of perception in view of the latter's tendency to affix itself to discrete objects as its points of focus. The object-hunger of perceiving is such that what it does direct itself to must possess sufficient consolidation to serve as a focal point; it must be something sensuously

graspable to which we can attach our attention, however fleeting it may be. In what does such consolidation of the perceived object consist?

Let us take an example from ordinary perceptual experience—a porcelain-based table-lamp which is situated opposite me on the heavy wooden table on which I am presently writing. My attention is drawn immediately to the mesh shade, especially to its lower rim with its curiously reversed presentation of sides: I can see both the front side of the front side and the "front" (i.e., facing-me) side of the back side, though not the back side of either. In fact, I notice that my freely wandering eye is led forward toward precisely those parts of the lamp which are *not* given at the time, including the so far unseen back sides of the porcelain base of the lamp. This forward-tending aspect of perception has been discussed by Aron Gurwitsch under the heading of "perceptual implication":

> In speaking of perceptual implications we wish to indicate components and constituents which, though essential to the noematic structure [of perception], are not yet unfolded, unravelled, and articulated, and which contribute to that structure in, so to speak, a silent way.[28]

These thus far unperceived components and constituents form, together with those that have already been perceived, a complete "noematic system" of the object in question—a system in which the parts, taken together, constitute what Gurwitsch calls a "Gestalt contexture," that is, a whole in which each part is implied by all the others and is what it is perceived to be only in reference to these others.[29]

It is disconcerting that Gurwitsch, who is committed in principle to the idea of the "*mutual* qualification and *inter*-determination of the constituents by one another,"[30] nevertheless emphasizes in practice the forward-looking element in a given Gestalt contexture—even to the point of considering it (under the rubric of "perceptual adumbration") the "fundamental phenomenon" of perception and a necessary "point of departure" for any phenomenological theory of perception.[31] Yet it is *only* a point of departure and should not be conceived as somehow representative of *all* forms of perceptual implication. Over-insistence on it leads in particular to a neglect of the critical role of consolidation, in which a quite different kind of implication is involved.

Let us return to my perception of the lamp. Despite the admittedly impelling way in which my eye was drawn around the already given sides toward those not yet given, equally impelling is the fact that I could not have been so lured had I not begun from, and continued to count on as still present, something already consolidated—already steadily in view and to this extent steadfast in my experience. This is the case not only in regard to the middle or the last members of a series of perceptions of the same object—where consolidation appears in the form of an actual accumulation of prior perceptions of this object—but even of *the very first member,* as in my first glance at the lamp in question. In this first look (and, a fortiori, in any subsequent look) there are three basic ways in which consolidation may already be at work: (i) there may be an embedding of perceptions of this same object from previous perceivings—perceivings which establish a specific pre-acquaintance such that the object presents itself as this particular already perceived object and no other; (ii) in the absence of already existing familiarity with this given object, there may nonetheless be a pre-acquaintance with the *kind* of object being perceived—say, table-lamps rather than floor-lamps; even if I had never before laid eyes on the lamp just described, I would still not encounter it as wholly alien or inassimilable to my present perceptual experience;[32] (iii) quite apart from these two modes of consolidation—one based on specification, the other on typification—there is the spontaneous constitution of any perceived object, previously known or not, as an-object-being-perceived-from-a-particular-side (or sides); this occurs so spontaneously in fact that it presents itself to the perceiver as a *fait accompli*—as always already effected, always already a feature of the perceptual situation, part of its very structure.

Each of these three basic forms of perceptual consolidation is the work of *memory*. Not, of course, of recollection or "secondary memory" as both James and Husserl termed it: in no instance is it a matter of invoking particular recollections of my table-lamp in states that are now altogether past. Rather, remembering is at work here in its specifically "primary" form as this was first described by James:

> an object of primary memory is not . . . brought back [i.e., from oblivion, as in secondary memory]; it never was lost; its date was never cut off in consciousness from that of the immediately present moment. In fact it comes to us as belonging to the rearward portion of the present space of time. . . .[33]

What is primary in primary memory is not just its being antecedent to secondary memory as its progenitor but also its unique modus operandi, which is cognitively and not only temporally prior. This mode of operation serves to consolidate perceptual experience from the very start by providing it with what James called a "vaguely vanishing backward fringe."[34] This fringe is what gives to the perceived object, even as immediately perceived, its felt density—its sense of being *an* object, sufficiently consolidated to be the focus of present and future perceptions.

Each of the three forms of consolidation specified above is indebted to primary memory. On the one hand, thanks to its character as "sinking back" (*zurücksinken* in Husserl's term), it enables previous experiences to bear upon the present situation by prolonging the perception of an object in such a way that immediately precedent perceptions of it, or perceptions of like objects, can function as horizons of pre-acquaintance. On the other hand, primary memory allows for the constitution of the object as a

perceivable whole with aspects and perspectival features of many kinds—
something that would not be possible if consciousness were strictly punctiform and lacked the connectiveness contributed by primary memory,
which draws out the merely momentary into a genuine span of duration,
a span wherein a given perceived object can present itself as a multiplex
particular, a consolidated *concretum*.

Perceptual experience is thus not exclusively, or even predominantly,
forward-looking. This experience is also, and just as importantly, backward-
tending. As Augustine was the first to state expressly, and as James and
Husserl were to re-emphasize, perception is interwoven with expectation
and memory and is therefore an inherently bi-directional phenomenon,
a *Janus bifrons* which looks in two opposite directions at once while nevertheless occupying the center-stage of the present. We must not affirm the
anticipatory aspect of perception at the cost of failing to recognize its matrix
in memory—and particularly in primary memory.

(2) *Still-Retaining-in-Grasp.* Freud's view of memory, like Bergson's,
stresses its enormously retentive powers. On the model of the laying-down
of permanent memory-traces, *every* perceptual experience is registered in
a memory, and not only once but "several times over."[35] This is so despite
those obstacles to complete recall which begin to interpose themselves early
in life and which lead to the deviations and falsifications of memories
(especially in the form of screen memories) that fascinated Freud in his
clinical practice. In fact, such subterranean influence of past perceptions
presupposes their continuing retention, albeit in a distorted and quite unconscious form. They are retained in the system of the unconscious but
not retained *in grasp*—in the grasp of conscious mind.

Husserl, whose doubts concerning unconscious mentation are well-
known and whose primary efforts in phenomenology were directed at
elucidating the structures of consciousness, termed one of these structures
"still-retaining-in-grasp" (*noch-im-Griff-behalten*). Still-retaining-in-grasp
is to be distinguished from retentiveness not only insofar as it is carried
out consciously or preconsciously but also insofar as it is an activity over
which the human agent maintains a considerable degree of control—in
contrast with the automaticity of retentiveness, which tends to follow its
own course independently of the human subject's designs. It is on much
the same grounds that we must also distinguish still-retaining-in-grasp from
what Husserl calls technically "retention," that is, the gradual sinking back
or down into dimness of whatever we have just experienced in the "now."
Retention, considered by Husserl to be the specific form always (and
uniquely) assumed by primary memory, is itself a purely passive affair, since
it represents an absolutely *invariant* modification of each successive experience and occurs apart from any intervention by the experiencer. Thus,
no more than retentiveness can retention be taken to be an act or activity
of the remembering subject; it is always a dependent moment of an already
engendered act or activity of this subject.[36]

What then *is* still-retaining-in-grasp? It is an activity so common and pervasive that we rarely notice it at all; yet it is absolutely essential to the constitution of human experience as we know it, and above all to perceptual experience. Each time I perceive something for more than a brief instant (and so long as I am not utterly distracted at the time), I actively hold in mind aspects already perceived as my glance moves on to other aspects. The former aspects (e.g., colors, shapes, surfaces, various kinds of interaction with other objects) are retained in grasp not merely in the sense that they are still in view along with the presentation of the new aspects. Whether they are still in view or not, I maintain them in my awareness: *I keep them in mind* as I turn to the perception of what succeeds them. This keeping-in-mind is what is essential here, and it can be analyzed into a set of three closely co-ordinated factors or moments.

(i) *holding-together.* In its minimal form this first constitutive moment amounts to keeping within one apprehensive grasp (a) an aspect just-before perceived; (b) an aspect which I am now, at this very point in time, perceiving. Such a dyadic unit held within apprehension is a case of what Husserl might term "associative pairing";[37] but unlike most forms of primordial association it need not be based on similarity or likeness—or, for that matter, on simultaneity or causality either. For the paired terms held together may bear no sensuous or structural resemblance to each other and can very well be successively perceived as qualitatively discontinuous with each other—as when I suddenly perceive a different side of an object, a side with an altogether different color or shape from that so far perceived. Despite the discontinuity in perceptual content, I do not hesitate to align the new side with the old, holding the two together in a temporally distended and yet unitary span of apprehension. Onto this primordial pair I can add still other members—up to the limit of my apprehensive powers.

(ii) *partial coincidence.* The discontinuity just mentioned is also not incompatible with a second basic feature of still-retaining-in-grasp: the partial or "overlapping"[38] coincidence between the members of the dyad or polyad being kept in mind. Such coincidence is neither temporal nor qualitative but a coincidence at the level of the object (or group of objects) that is being retained in grasp. That which is brought together is brought together *on,* or *in,* a substratum of some sort, whether this is itself a single perceived object such as my table-lamp or an entire complex of perceived objects such as my-lamp-now-situated-on-a-table, which is in turn in-my-study, etc. The moments and properties coincide via the substratum or substrata as the abiding ground of coincidence. This coincidence, however, remains partial since complete coincidence (e.g., of the sort that occurs in recognition) entails indistinguishability and thus lacks a basis for keeping-in-mind: we keep in mind only that which is somehow distinguishably different from that with which it is being paired.

(iii) *running-through.* This is a moment expressly singled out by Kant as well as by Husserl, both of whom designate it with the same verb: *"durch-*

laufen." For Kant, it represents the basic action of "synopsis," the lowest-level synthesis of the sensible manifold as effected by apprehension.[39] For Husserl, too, it is a quite preliminary stage—arising, strictly speaking, *before* still-retaining-in-grasp in his own use of the term.[40] Both are mistaken if the model I am proposing here is correct; for on this model, only that which has first (logically and chronologically first) been brought and held together and made to coincide partially can be run through, whether in perception, memory, or imagination. There must be something placed before apprehension that is already sufficiently preconstituted *to be* run through—to be traversed in successive steps. By the same token, once something *has been* run through and is still present in mind, still-retaining-in-grasp has ipso facto occurred. This last moment of the phenomenon brings it to completion and yet is often the only moment of which we are explicitly aware. Hence the natural tendency to identify running-through with still-retaining-in-grasp as a whole, a *pars pro toto* error that overlooks the equally constitutive role of holding-together and of partial coincidence.

From the above discussion there emerge two conclusions of immediate consequence for this study of perceiving and remembering. The first is that still-retaining-in-grasp is a complex combination of activity *and* (as we must now aver) passivity. Or, to be more precise, we must say that just as it cannot be understood as purely passive in the manner of retention and retentiveness—or even of consolidation, in which the perceived object presents itself as constituting *itself* as a self-unified whole—so it cannot be understood as wholly active either. Rather, it is a form of *passivity in activity,* a higher passivity in which the perceiver is at least partly responsible for the constitution of the perceived object. In Husserl's words, it is "a passivity which is truly objectivating, namely, one which thematizes or co-thematizes objects."[41] Rather than referring to thematizing activity, I would prefer to speak of holding-together and running-through as the active moments (since they entail the activity of the perceiving subject) and of partial coincidence as the passive moment (passive because the coincidence depends strictly on the given characteristics of the preconstituted object).[42]

A second conclusion is that in the phenomenon of still-retaining-in-grasp we encounter a unique mode of memory which is unusually well-suited for collaboration with perception. To begin with, each of the three constituent moments I have isolated can be said with equal justice to belong to either of the two acts—and indeed, finally, to *both.* We can hold items together in remembering as well as in perceiving; there can be partial coincidence in the case of perceived as well as remembered objects; and running-through can be just as much perceptual as mnemonic in nature. Because of this bivalency throughout, possibilities of collusion are, as it were, built into the very structure of the phenomenon.

(3) *Time-Consciousness as Ultimate Unifier.* To speak of still-retaining-in-grasp is already necessarily to allude to time-consciousness, whose

single most crucial characteristic is its pervasively unifying nature. It is that form of experiential unification which includes—and makes possible—all others. Not only is it "the original seat of the constitution of the unity of identity in general"[43] (i.e., the unity of that which is self-identical whether perceived or remembered or imagined), but its own unity is the basis and measure of all other particular unities in human experience:

> As far as originally constituted time extends, thus far extends the originally
> . . . constituted unity of a possible objectivity, which is either a single
> individual or a plurality of co-existing independent individuals.[44]

According to Husserl, there are three basic forms of "associative unification," the most thorough-going unification of which the mind is capable: of like with like ("homogeneous" unification), of unlike with unlike ("heterogeneous" unification), and of the present with the not present—where "*Präsent*" can be either spatial or temporal.[45] Most importantly, the paradigm case of the unification of the temporally present with the temporally non-present is for Husserl precisely the unification of perception with memory—of "the presently perceived with remote memories separated from it."[46] The question thus becomes: In what specific unities does this unification of perception and memory in time realize itself? Four such unities may be singled out for brief discussion.

(i) *unity through primary memory or retention*. This is found most notably in the case of consolidation, where primary memory is mainly responsible for the presentation of perceived objects (or groups of such objects) as coherent, self-given wholes. But it is at least implicitly present as well in all the other conjunctions between perceiving and remembering which we have considered inasmuch as *every* psychical phenomenon, whether specifiable in terms of one mental act or two such acts ("coadunate" acts as they might be called), has its retentional fringe and has it necessarily. This fringe unifies a given perception with what has just preceded it in time.

(ii) *unity through secondary memory or recollection*. Where primary memory unifies what is perceived—or a particular coadunation of the remembered-*cum*-perceived—within a continuous but vanishing interval of time (being in fact the very vanishing of items from explicit consciousness), secondary memory unifies quite discontinuous and often long-since lapsed moments of time, its task being precisely to *re*-present to mind what is no longer available to the senses in a pristine, first-time-through form.[47] Reconstruction of a distant past is only the most striking instance of this re-presentational activity, which is not to say *representational* activity, since there can very well be non-imagistic recollection. But secondary memory is also operative in cases of what I would call "continuation," in which earlier perceptions are conjoined to present perceptions so as to form a concatenated series—as is seen strikingly in various types of sedimentation of past experience in present experience. Such sedimentation, especially in its specifically unconscious form, reminds us that the role of secondary memory need not be explicit but may proceed at a quite latent or tacit level.[48]

All such operations of secondary memory, tacit or explicit, and active as well in still-retaining-in-grasp, recognizing, reconstructing, and reminding, are made possible by the assumption of a gapless continuum of moments stretching between the original event remembered and the present moment. The presence of this continuum is presumed by time-consciousness, one of whose major tasks is so to structure experience that the not-now, the past now, of secondary memory is brought into rapport with—in fact, brought into the very content of—the present now of perception and of recollection itself. Unless this importation of the past via an intervening continuum could be effected, secondary memory could lay no claim to reviving the past—to presenting it again in the present. And whenever it does occur, a unity between the recollected and the perceived is realized, a unity normally designated by the single basic term "remembering." Indeed, every time I say "I remember," "I recall," or "that comes back to me now" on the occasion of perceiving, this unity is spontaneously achieved in one fell swoop.

(iii) *longitudinal unity.* If we consider primary and secondary memory *together,* as co-operating precisely insofar as they co-constitute the memory of *the same thing,* then memory and perception accomplish a peculiar longitudinal unity. By this I refer to the following, frequently illustrated, course of events: a perception occurs, sinks back in primary memory, and thereafter becomes available in secondary memory.[49] When such a sequence of events occurs, a genuine longitudinal unity of perception and memory is brought about, a unity based on the sameness of their intentional objects. This unity is temporal, since one and the same object, first perceived and then remembered, is posited as having two determinate (or at least determinable) positions in a single spread of world-time to which they both belong. The object-as-perceived occupies a first position in this spread, while the object-as-remembered occupies another; but it is the selfsame object which takes up these two positions in a well-ordered temporal series.[50] In this way the otherwise quite disparate acts of perceiving and remembering are unified by the identity of their respective intentional objects insofar as these latter are both situated in a common continuum of time.

(iv) *unity of simultaneous acts.* This brings us to a last, and somewhat more complex, unification of perception and memory in time. Thus far, we have been considering the relationship of these two acts exclusively in terms of the order of succession. Now we must reflect on the way in which they may become related to each other in accordance with the other great Leibnizian temporal axis—the order of co-existence or co-occurrence. When perceiving and remembering arise *at the same time,* they do not exhibit a unity of becoming or duration that is inherently longitudinal; they

exhibit instead an intuitive unity involving the co-presentation of singu-
larities, some of which are perceived and some remembered.

Let us return for a last time to the porcelain table-lamp examined earlier.
Suppose that, in addition to perceiving this lamp, I recall another, quite
different lamp, a bronze lamp I owned over a decade ago. I can place this
remembered lamp (and it can *only* be remembered now that it has vanished
from my life altogether) alongside my now-perceived porcelain lamp in such
a way as to enjoy a simultaneous presentation of both. I am speaking here
of a strictly visual memory of my old lamp, and I am assuming a certain
power of imaginative projection on my part. Rarely as we may engage in
such projection in everyday existence, when it does occur we are confronted
with a special unity of the perceived and the remembered within a single
time-frame: the two lamps co-exist equanimously, even if not on exactly
equal terms, within the same durational present. What are we to make of
this puzzling situation?

Such an experience of the perceived-*cum*-remembered—seemingly impossible on the view of space as objective and three-dimensional only (and
thus as incapable of "containing" anything as unobjective and subject-
dependent as a mere memory) and of time as consisting in a sheer succession of punctiform instants, each excluding the next in turn—is rendered
possible not just because such notions of space and time are unduly constrictive in accounting for human experience but also because the acts of
perceiving and remembering are securely anchored in the temporality of
the subject. I remember and perceive in the same present—in one single
stretch of duration which is my own—even if the things which I remember
and perceive relate to each other uneasily in my present perceptual space.[51]
The problem of space apart, what is crucial is the fact that two diverse
objects having distinctly different histories in time can nevertheless appear
together in a single temporal unit, that subtending my present experience
of them. On the one hand, they are the objects of various acts of apprehension which, though scattered in terms of world-time, are still *my* acts, that
is, acts belonging to my own immanent temporality, events in my history;
it is in the selfsame *me* that the objects in question make contact.[52] On
the other hand, at the present time they are the intentional objects of just
one (though double-rayed) apprehension, having its unique position both
in my immanent temporality *and* in world-time.[53] In short, perceiving and
remembering realize a meaningful unity in the problematic case before us
through a peculiar dual rooting in a present both immanent and worldly.
In this regard *they come together in time twice over:* in the immanence
of the subject and in his or her world.

If we were to pursue the point to its transcendental limit, we would have
to say that time is not only a bond of unity between perceiving and remembering on the diverse occasions, successive and simultaneous, which
we have been considering under the heading of "nonconspicuous collaboration" between the two acts. It is the very condition of possibility—"the

first and fundamental form, the form of all forms"[54]—for establishing unity of *all* kinds in *all* combinations between perceiving and remembering, that in which and by which they become conjoinable at all, whatever the particular shape of their conjunction may be on a given occasion. It is in this regard that time-consciousness can be said to serve as their ultimate unifier.

IV

Were there but world enough and time (and in particular more world-time!), we could pursue the question of time itself further. Instead, respecting George Eliot's observations that "every day is a hurrying march of crowded Time,"[55] let me hasten to draw some conclusions in the form of three minimalist remarks, followed by three maximal or more hazardous ones.

(1) The ongoing interaction between perceiving and remembering within human experience is more multiform and more subtle than mechanistic models convey, especially those (such as the recent model of memory as a form of information processing) that are based directly or ultimately on an empiricist view of memory as the mere replication or complication of perception (albeit in fainter tones and colors, in more elegant and discerning categories)—thus as ineluctably second-order in status, condemned to mimic and to repeat perception as the privileged first-order act. As Husserl said in 1905, in memory "everything may resemble perception . . . and yet is not itself perception."[56] Resemblance of content, or even of mode of operation, does not prove perception's primacy. In particular, it does not demonstrate the validity of an implicitly or explicitly hierarchical framework within which perception is depicted as standing under and supporting memory as if it were an ailing stepchild. Nor does it justify the equally hierarchical notion (found in Plato and Berkeley) according to which memory somehow swoops down from on high to resolve the paradoxes and problems arising within perceiving proper. Our examination of the relationship between the two acts, especially in their less conspicuous combinations, has revealed that they often co-operate on the *same* ground level of experience. Their relationship on this level is a non-stratified one; it is a relation of partners in a common cognitive enterprise in which we would be ill-advised to designate either partner as topmost or as bottommost.

(2) The partnership in question takes the following specific forms in which each activity proves to be complementary to the other, thereby manifesting a matchingness that is founded as much on the distinctive differences between the two acts as on their likenesses. On the one hand, perception construed as "self-giving" serves as a fertile "source-point"[57] within which objects and events are continually encountered and presented in human awareness. It is by no means the only such source—I have argued elsewhere that imagination brings forth its own content independently of

perception and memory[58]—and it is certainly not best understood in terms of the reception of "impressions," as both Hume and Husserl presume.[59] But it is an ever-changing source of new experiences given in various sensory and intersensory modalities, experiences which cannot derive from memory alone or from imagination alone and which in their novelty and plurality, alterity and closely-wrought sensuousness, are unparalleled and irreplaceable by anything in remembering or imagining. On the other hand, these very characteristics of perception are complemented by various features of memory and imagination. Restricting ourselves to memory, it is evident that it provides a peculiar temporal *depth* lacking almost altogether in perception. The plenary but non-enduring present of perceiving is drawn out in primary memory into an elongated *moment* (an *Augenblick* in Kierkegaard's and Heidegger's term), while being extended still further by secondary memory into the reiterable content of recollection. What I called earlier the "mnemonic frame" deepens perceptions still further by providing for them a position in an immanent experiential stream—in this way creating a "horizon of the past"[60] within which they become apprehensible as ever-receding. Thanks to these activities of primary and secondary memory, "each now is changed into a past [now], and . . . moves uniformly 'downward' into the depths of the past."[61] Yet it so moves not as a mere point (as Husserl persisted in thinking), a point which can eventually vanish from view altogether, but as having its own identity and substantiality, allowing us to retrieve it intact in later moments of our experience.[62] Losing the ephemeral newness of the now, it gains the unity of the remembered.

(3) Another kind of unity gained is *the unity of perceiving and remembering themselves,* the elusive unity I have been pursuing throughout this chapter. This is a unity of the "living present" of perception and the "no longer living worlds"[63] of memory, and it has exhibited itself at each stage in my analysis of the ways in which the two acts collaborate with each other. Among conspicuous modes of collaboration, recognition is the most manifest case of an experience that, despite its double origin in perception and memory, occurs as a single experiential unit—as is indicated when we say that we recognize someone "in a flash." Among nonconspicuous modes, it is in terms of time-consciousness (particularly when both immanent time and world-time are considered) that the unity of perceiving and remembering presents itself in its most encompassing and rigorous form. But distinctive modes of unification occur in each of the other cases of collaboration as well. In every instance, we can observe a *unio mentalis* in which the two acts conjoin to form a unitary, even if sometimes a momentary, whole. Therefore, we can say of all the collaborative modes— and there are doubtless many more than I have traced out here—what Husserl says in *Experience and Judgment* concerning the divergent worlds of perception and memory: "nevertheless, despite [their] separation, there

is still a *unity* here, and *relations of unity* based on it."[64] The divergences, far from being diremptive or disruptive, themselves contribute to the continuing unification of mental life from within.

(4) Recall the two mottoes from which we took our departure: no remembering without perceiving (a substantive even if mistaken claim); no perceiving without remembering (seemingly a largely rhetorical assertion). By now, however, the latter claim can be seen to be right and substantive—and not just rhetorical—if it is understood in the following form: *no object or event can count as fully perceivable unless it is also rememberable.* Unless I could subsequently recall that which I now perceive, what I apprehend in the present would lack a crucial component of its very perceptualness, a certain essential perdurability which allows me to say that I am really *perceiving* something. To maintain this is not to hold that I must in fact subsequently remember it—only that I must *in principle* be able to do so, that is, given the right circumstances, assuming no impairment of my faculties, etc. But it remains a stronger claim than that which asserts merely that a rememberable past precedes, or is presupposed by, every present perception—namely, the past of previous perceptions of this particular, or of some similar, object. For the point is that my present perception must *itself be rememberable* on some future occasion if it is to be considered a full-fledged perceptual act. It must, in short, be reiterable in secondary memory, and this *de jure* reiterability is a constituent feature of its very status as a fully formed (though not necessarily veridical) act of perceiving in the present.[65]

(5) When we reflect, further, that this very present in which perception takes place is dependent upon primary memory for its constitution as a spanned duration, we begin to envision the still more intriguingly heterodox thesis that, far from being the mere continuation of perception by other means, memory is *indispensable to the very accomplishment of perception itself.* Not only is it "arrayed in present consciousness" *along with* perception, it is arrayed *in perception itself,* ingredient in its very being. If this is so, then it cannot be valid to claim, as an entire tradition stretching from Aristotle to Merleau-Ponty has claimed, that perception represents a point or stage occurring (in Merleau-Ponty's words cited earlier) "before any contribution by memory." There cannot be any such point or stage if perception is mixed with memory—mired in it, we might say— from the beginning.

Such a state of immixture does not mean, of course, that the respective roles of these two acts in human experience are indistinguishable. These roles are certainly distinguishable from each other, and even eidetically so, as I attempted to demonstrate in section II above. But perceiving and remembering remain *inseparable* within experience itself—not only as complementary to but as reliant upon one another: dependent equals, as it were.

(6) Still, vis-à-vis perception, memory taken in both its primary and its secondary forms is something of a *primus inter pares,* a first among equals.

"The present," said Husserl, "is always born *out of the past*."[66] By this he did not mean that it arises from a fixed fund or stock of memories: to think this would only be to reverse the terms of the classical sequence of "*first* perception—*then* memory" by positing a primacy of memory over perception. Rather, Husserl is suggesting that we shall never discover a pure, uncontaminated perception, a perception which is not always already in the process of becoming a primary memory and on its way as well to becoming the content of a secondary memory. Not only do perception and primary memory "continually pass over into one another,"[67] but there is no detectable (that is, non-idealized, non-punctiform) moment at which a given perception has not already passed over into primary memory. Thus it becomes plausible to assert with Husserl that "if we call perception the act in which all 'origination' [*Ursprung*] lies, which constitutes originarily, then primary memory is perception."[68] Or rather: perception is primary memory—is never not infused with it, sullied by it through and through. And since primary memory is itself preserved in secondary memory—"what is given as just having been [i.e., in primary memory] turns out to be identical with what is recollected"[69]—then perception is also, and in this very way, secondary memory: it finds its fate there, it has no other fate, such is its character. This is why Husserl can add thirty years later that "the actual connection of all perceptions of an ego, present and past, [is established] in the unity of one memory . . . [in] an intuitive unity of the remembered."[70]

Remembering unifies not just itself but perceiving as well—or, better, both together in the one intrepid stream of lived experience:

> If a consciousness is actually given (or [is even] represented as given in possibility) and if it necessarily continues to flow on, then the possibility exists that recollections of consciousness [will] arise which lead to a stream of consciousness unified in memory.[71]

Consciousness does flow on, and flowing as it does it comes to oneness in remembering out of the manyness of perceiving. If it is true (as Heraclitus was the first in the West to affirm) that "you cannot step twice into the same river, for other waters are continually flowing on,"[72] you can nevertheless *remember* the water which has now flowed on and been replaced by other waters—by other perceptions. And if it is also true (as Heraclitus said as well) that "everything flows and nothing abides; everything gives way and nothing stays fixed,"[73] it is nonetheless the case that *experience remains in memory*. Remembering fixes the flow of perceiving and makes it into an abiding possession of mind.

1. For both models, see Plato, *Theaetetus* 190e–199c.
2. From the standpoint of sensory psychophysics, one would speak of the ambiguity

of "a stationary monocular retinal image" which is produced by the fact that "since the proximal stimulus pattern for the eye is two-dimensional, an infinite number of different tridimensional spatial arrangements will produce the same pattern at the eye" (Julian Hochberg, *Perception* [Englewood Cliffs: Prentice-Hall, 1964], p. 37).

3.   George Berkeley, *An Essay Towards a New Theory of Vision* (London: Dent, 1934), pp. 32–33.

4.   It is disputable on empirical grounds because very young children (and chickens!) will perceive and correctly interpret depth cues in the absence of previous kinesthetic or tactile experience. (Cf. the classic experiments of Gibson and Walk dealing with the "visual cliff" and Thorndike's experiment with chickens, especially as discussed by Hochberg, *Perception*, p. 48.) Berkeley's theory is unsound theoretically insofar as it privileges, without adequate justification, kinesthetic and tactile sensations over visual sensations, giving to the latter a secondary status.

5.   George Berkeley, *The Theory of Vision* (London: Macmillan, 1860), pp. 108–09; my italics.

6.   On the perceptual constancies, see C. M. Wyburn, R. W. Pickford, and R. J. Hirst, *Human Senses and Perception* (Toronto: University of Toronto Press, 1964), chap. 7.

7.   Sören Kierkegaard, *The Concept of Dread,* trans. Walter Lowrie (Princeton: Princeton University Press, 1957), p. 35: "psychology . . . can only explain up to the explanation, and above all must guard against seeming to explain what no science explains."

8.   Maurice Merleau-Ponty, *Phenomenology of Perception,* trans. Colin Smith (New York: Humanities Press, 1962), p. 19.

9.   Ibid.

10.   Maurice Merleau-Ponty, *The Primacy of Perception,* ed. James Edie (Evanston: Northwestern University Press, 1964), p. 13.

11.   Cf. Edmund Husserl, *Logical Investigations,* trans. J. N. Findlay, 2 vols. (New York: Humanities Press, 1970), esp. Investigation 5, chap. 3–5, and Investigation 6, chap. 6.

12.   Aristotle's celebrated position is summed up thus: "By nature animals are born with the faculty of sensation, and from sensation memory is produced in some of them, though not in others" (*Metaphysics* Book Alpha, 980a28–30; W. D. Ross translation). For Hume, memory is tied to the reproduction of the "order" and the "position" of the original impressions; hence its content can differ from the content of perception only in degree or vivacity—a difference which may be very slight indeed insofar as a memory "retains a considerable degree of [the] first vivacity [i.e., of perception]": *A Treatise of Human Nature,* ed. Selby-Bigge (Oxford: Oxford University Press, 1967), p. 8. On memory-traces as a premise of psychological theories of memory, see Deborah A. Rosen, "An Argument for the Logical Notion of a Memory Trace," *Philosophy of Science* 13 (March 1975): 1–10, and Norman Malcolm's discussion of Rosen in his *Memory and Mind* (Ithaca: Cornell University Press, 1977), pp. 181–82.

13.   F. C. Bartlett, *Remembering: A Study in Experimental and Social Psychology* (Cambridge: Cambridge University Press, 1964), p. 187.

14.   For a more complete statement of this point, see my essay "Imagining and Remembering" in this volume.

15.   Cf. Hume, *A Treatise of Human Nature,* p. 86: "the belief or assent, which always attends the memory and senses, is nothing but the vivacity of the perceptions they present . . . to believe is in this case to feel an immediate impression of the senses, or a *repetition of that impression in the memory*" (my italics).

16.   I say "ostensible" content, for even if the content-as-remembered would yield the same verbal description—e.g., "the large oak tree in front of my childhood home"—as the content-as-once-perceived, there is an undeniable felt difference between the oak tree as it was presented to my senses and the same object (if we can still speak of "same" here) as it is now presentified in memory. This difference is not one of vivacity alone, but includes other factors to be detailed below.

17.   As William James says, "memory requires more than mere dating of a fact in the

past. It must be dated in *my* past. In other words, I must think that I, directly, experienced its content" (*The Principles of Psychology* [New York: Dover, 1950], vol. 1, p. 650; his italics).

18.   I say "illusion" because reminiscences, though sometimes stemming from shared experiences, nevertheless remain personal and not interpersonal in character: each is based on the unique perspective of the person who relates its specific content.

19.   Edmund Husserl, *Experience and Judgment,* trans. James S. Churchill and Karl Ameriks (Evanston: Northwestern University Press, 1973), p. 132. (Hereinafter cited as *EJ.*)

20.   On these horizons, see Husserl, *EJ,* pp. 149 ff. and pp. 360–61.

21.   It should be noticed that memories of perceived objects may contain a counterpart of the internal horizon, albeit a fragmentary one. Whereas in actual perception I can scrutinize an internal horizon *ad libitum,* I often encounter gaps in memory that prevent my full specification of its internal horizon: e.g., what was the color of the reverse side of the colored ball I am now remembering? I may be unable to answer this question, and if so I am left without recourse of the sort that is readily available in perception (turning the ball over, etc.). The same observation applies, *mutatis mutandis,* to the external horizon.

22.   On the subject of paired-associate learning, see Robert G. Crowder, *Principles of Learning and Memory* (Hillsdale, N.J.: Lawrence Erlbaum, 1976), esp. chap. 1, 8, and 9.

23.   I mean that even if the exact origin, perceptual or mnemonic, of a given hallucination could be determined, this would not alter one's actual experience of it in view of its compelling character.

24.   On this point, see Casey, "Imagining and Remembering," sec. 4, in this volume.

25.   I am restricting consideration to cases of perceptual reminders without denying in any way that there are non-perceived reminders as well: e.g., those that occur in the situation of "taking mental notes."

26.   The relation of reminding, in being thus easily reiterable, stands in contrast with both recognizing and reconstructing, each of which tends to settle more decisively on an end-product as a *terminus ad quem.*

27.   In understanding this special mode of reference, I have found it useful to invoke Piaget's distinction between *schema* and *scheme.* The reminder, being sensuous ("figurative" in Piaget's own term), serves as a schema, directing us to a particular action. The action, or remindand proper, is adumbrated by this figurative-schematic presentation thanks to the working of the scheme of the action foreshadowed. This scheme, of which we are not explicitly conscious, is nonetheless active in tacitly organizing the reminder's figurative properties so as to signify the remindand. For a reminder to be a reminder *of* an action, it must elicit the scheme of this action by its figuration—a figuration which operates by allusion or by suggestion. Reminders function, then, by a combination of figurative format (designed to attract our attention amid distracting tasks) and of sub rosa allusiveness via a scheme of the action which they are designed to put us in mind of. (On the distinction between schema and scheme, see Hans G. Furth, *Piaget and Knowledge* [Englewood Cliffs: Prentice-Hall, 1969], pp. 95 and 102.)

28.   Aron Gurwitsch, "Perceptual Implications," in P. Tibbetts, ed., *Perception* (Chicago: Quadrangle, 1969), p. 252.

29.   See ibid., pp. 252–57, for the full discussion.

30.   Ibid., p. 254; my italics.

31.   Ibid., p. 249.

32.   On the question of "typical pre-acquaintance," see Husserl, *EJ,* p. 150. The result of such pre-acquaintance is that "the object is present from the very first with a character of familiarity" (ibid., p. 113).

33.   James, *Principles of Psychology,* vol. 1, pp. 646–47.

34.   Ibid., p. 643.

35.   Sigmund Freud, *Standard Edition of the Complete Psychological Works,* ed. J. Strachey, 24 vols. (London: Hogarth Press, 1953–74), 1: 233: "what is essentially new about

my theory is the thesis that memory is present not once but several times over, that it is laid down in various species of indications."

36. On retention, see Edmund Husserl, *Phenomenology of Internal Time-Consciousness*, trans. James S. Churchill (Bloomington: Indiana University Press, 1964), sec. 10–13 and Appendix 1. (Hereinafter designated as *PIT*.) For an explicit comparison between retention and still-retaining-in-grasp, see Husserl, *EJ*, pp. 109–12.

37. On this phenomenon, see Husserl, *EJ*, pp. 74–76.

38. On *"überschiebender Deckung"* see ibid., pp. 190 and 343.

39. Cf. Immanuel Kant, *Critique of Pure Reason*, trans. N. K. Smith (New York: Humanities Press, 1950), A 99; also A 94–95.

40. See Husserl, *EJ*, p. 343, where a sequence of "running-through—still-retaining-in-grasp—overlapping coincidence" is suggested. In my view, this complicates the situation needlessly and puts moments of the process on the same level as the process itself.

41. Ibid., p. 108. The term "passivity in activity" is found here as well.

42. But I can certainly agree with Husserl's own conclusion concerning the result of still-retaining-in-grasp: "[it is] only on the basis of this active-passive retaining-in-grasp that [something] can be apprehended in a simple perception as an enduring object, as one which not only is now but which was also the same just before and will be in the next now" (*EJ*, p. 109).

43. Ibid., p. 73.

44. Ibid., p. 158.

45. See ibid., pp. 74–76. Strictly speaking, the association is of like *or similar,* and of unlike *or dissimilar,* with their respective counterparts, since Husserl distinguishes between likeness and similarity.

46. Ibid., p. 177. Cf. also ibid., p. 156.

47. On this point, see Husserl, *PIT,* p. 66.

48. That is, at the level of what Husserl calls " 'obscure' recollections of the similar" (*EJ*, p. 150). Cf. also ibid., p. 162: "everything perceived 'reminds' one of something past that is similar or like even though temporally separated [from it]."

49. In the ideal case, this is what *always* occurs: "each perception has its retentional horizon and provides the possibility of entering into this horizon and of developing it in [secondary] memories" (Husserl, *EJ*, p. 166). In a given instance, however, an easy unbroken sequence such as this may not take place: we may not be able to prolong the initial perception-*cum*-retention into an accessible recollection.

50. The series is well-ordered insofar as all of the intermediate positions in this same series are in principle determinable as moments of perceiving or remembering the same thing.

51. This unease drives Husserl to posit an "apparent space" nested in actual space to explain a case such as this. Cf. *EJ*, pp. 181–83.

52. Cf. ibid., p. 162: "I am led back into my own past, this past is precisely *my* own, the past of this same subject who is present and living" (his italics).

53. After all, another person can say about me, as I can say about myself, that I perceived-and-remembered the two lamps at, e.g., 10:01 A.M. on 28 March 1978.

54. Husserl, *EJ*, p. 164. Time is also described as a "common form" at ibid.

55. George Eliot, *Daniel Deronda*, chap. 50.

56. The full statement is "Everything [in secondary memory] thus resembles perception and primary memory and yet is not itself perception and primary memory" (Husserl, *PIT,* p. 58).

57. On the now of perception as a self-giving source-point, see Husserl, *PIT,* sec. 10–11.

58. Cf. Edward S. Casey, *Imagining: A Phenomenological Study* (Bloomington: Indiana University Press, 1976), chap. 7–8.

59. For Husserl's view of "impressional" consciousness, see *PIT,* pp. 51 ff. Hume's view is most fully presented in *A Treatise of Human Nature,* part 1, sec. 1–3; part 3, sec. 5–6.

60. This term occurs in Husserl's chart at *PIT,* p. 49.

61. Ibid., p. 50.

62.   It is of interest that Berkeley's theory of vision is based on the premise that the "line of sight" eventuates in a *point* of the eye: "distance being a line directed end-wise to the eye, it projects only one point in the fund of the eye" (*An Essay Towards a New Theory of Vision,* p. 13).

63.   Husserl uses this phrase both at *PIT,* p. 75 and at *EJ,* p. 180.

64.   Husserl, *EJ,* p. 162; his italics.

65.   I explore this point further in "Imagining and Remembering," sec. 7 in this volume. Husserl hints at it in the context of a discussion of evidence: "I can 'always return' to the itself-beheld actuality [of perception] . . . in a series of intuitive recollections": *Cartesian Meditations,* trans. D. Cairns (The Hague: Nijhoff, 1960), p. 60.

66.   Husserl, *PIT,* p. 140; my italics.

67.   Ibid., p. 62.

68.   Ibid., p. 64; in italics in original.

69.   Ibid., p. 60.

70.   Husserl, *EJ,* p. 180.

71.   Ibid., p. 167.

72.   Heraclitus, Fragment 21 in Philip Wheelwright's numbering and translation: *Heraclitus* (New York: Atheneum, 1968), p. 29.

73.   Fragment 20 in ibid., p. 29.

The Memorability of the Filmic Image

I

IMAGES MEMORABLE? How could anything so diaphanous, so transparently thin, so reduced in format and domesticated in dimension be worthy of remembrance? Of images generally, Samuel Beckett says, "one glimpse and vanished."[1] One might think that this is true of mental images only, mere "monograms" of imagination as Kant called them. For mental images do indeed seem inconstant and fickle. They pass, or appear to pass, haphazardly through the haze of the mind's meanderings, emerging barely long enough to be noticed at all, only to vanish into the misty margins of mentation.

Even when the images of things are themselves *things*—"external images," in Sartre's phrase, or "icons" in an earlier nomenclature—it is difficult to conceive of them as intrinsically memorable. In the classical Platonic conception, to be an image *of* something is to be some lesser thing, diminished both epistemologically and metaphysically in comparison with the original, of which it is the mere reflection (hence *eikon* connotes reflection, shadow, offcast being). This conception is still very much with us, in particular in the conviction that the original—the original experience or thing—is to be preferred to its replication. On the premise that first in the order of existence means first in other orders as well, it ascribes most of the values and most of the rights to the first-order thing or experience: *it*, not its image, has the right to be enjoyed, known, and remembered.

But we need look no further than film experience to find any such assumption placed into question from the very beginning. For what we care most about, value most highly, in the case of film is precisely *the presented image*, not its original. It is this image which is memorable if anything about the experience is memorable at all. Without denying its origin in an actual sequence of events in world-time (the shooting of the film itself, its financing, editing, etc.), as moviegoers we find our attention and concern going to the filmic image in an almost exclusive and nearly irrevocable fashion; and our remembering goes back to it as well. It is this image which, in captivating us, has the rights and priority otherwise ascribable to its historical origin. The same is true, *mutatis mutandis*, of other external images in other arts—say, a painting or a piece of sculpture. It is these images, not their sources, which we seek to experience and which we find ourselves remembering.

Moreover, such images are not just place-fillers of an already overstocked long-term or "secondary" memory—as if they were mere memorial embellishments of some supposedly more primordial stratum of remembering (e.g., that in which our personal identity is constituted). Works of art regarded as images are eminently recollectable. They contribute forcefully to our entire memorial life, including our sense of personal identity: who is ever quite the same again after viewing *The Rules of the Game*? Such works work their way into our lives both as external images and as memory images proper: Renoir's film is impactful not just on each actual occasion of presentation but in its insistent return between such occasions via particular memory images. In every case, whether the image is within or without our viewing body, memory is at work—in its "primary" form on the actual occasions, which would not cohere as discrete occasions in the first place if they were not unified by the activity of short-term memory, and in its "secondary" form later on when parts of what was experienced on these occasions come to mind again.

In other words, the whole experience of viewing works of art, from start to finish, is memorial in character; it is steeped in memory throughout; it is massively memorious. "Memorious," a word that still exists in larger dictionaries, means 'memorable' as well as 'mindful of.' We might say then that works of art, at least those that move us psychically, make us mindful of them in being memorable, where "memorable" takes on its fully honorific sense of being worth remembrance. As images they are truly memorable and not merely recollectable: they stay with us in primary and secondary memory, and staying with us as they do they change us—*they become us*. *Rules of the Game* lives on in us as part of ourselves, selves made lastingly different by its ongoing ingredient within.

Such staying with and staying on—such staying power—is a *retention* in the richest sense; and retention is the distinctive work of memory. Art, memorable art, *gives us to keep;* we play art for keeps and keeping it (in memory—where else?) we are given to ourselves differently.[2]

Stan Brakhage has written that "to see is to retain—to behold," that "one can never go back, not even in imagination," and that "memories may sustain [a] person in [a] particular realm the rest of his life."[3] These statements, seemingly disparate, closely parallel what I have just been trying to say. Seeing in art, seeing of art—beholding—is retentive, not merely immediate and impressional: not just "retinal" in Duchamp's term. One cannot go back to the pristine moment of a first encounter—except in memory; and even then there is a strict limit not trespassable, not even in imagination: as Husserl says, "I can re-live [*nachleben*] the present [in secondary memory], but it can never be given again."[4] And yet what *is* retained in the prism of memory can sustain us for the rest of our lives: "rest," after all, means remainder, the remaining part; and it is precisely the task of memory to take care of what remains over in human experience—to preserve it as sustaining some sense of continuity in that experience.

II

We first meet up with works of art—even in an extreme instance like conceptual art—as perceived presentations. The image, to begin with, is always a perceptual image, where "image" means nothing subjective or ideational. It is, in Stan Brakhage's term, what we "behold," that is to say, what is

held together as one more or less coherent whole within our perceptual field thus presenting itself as *one* work, even if its unity is itself made up of a disconcerting multiplicity (of colors or shapes, narrative voices or points of view);

and held together by me, the viewer, who as a witness of the work is obliged to perform various unifications: synesthetic, temporal, cognitive; without these syntheses of the perceptual manifold, I could not even speak of a manifold but would be confronted by utter chaos or disarray—which is, at the limit (and precisely our human limit), *unexperiencable*.

Now, these two moments of the beholding of the work, one proper to the work and the other to the human subject before the work, are moments of a memorial structure which I shall call (after Husserl) "retaining-in-grasp."[5] Retaining-in-grasp is a phase of remembering which is to be located *between* primary memory (which is responsible for the distension of the present instant of perception into a drawn-out 'now' with fading fringes) and secondary memory (the sloe-eyed look into a past no longer directly reverberating in my present). Such retaining is of special significance in the experience of art, for it establishes at once the horizon and identity of the work qua presented image (as just *this* self-contained work) and the unit in terms of which subsequent recollective remembering will most naturally take place: "I remember seeing *Tess* the other night"—where what is retained-in-grasp is this very film as a single durational unit. Notice that this retaining does not require a detailed secondary memory of the film itself. All that counts, and what we signify by using the film's title '*Tess*' as a memorial marker, is that the remembered film is held together as one *rememberatum* in what Brakhage calls my "optical mind."[6]

Thus retained-in-grasp, the work can stand on its own as a single self-identical thing. Contributing further to this cohesion and ingathering of the work is the fact that it functions in aesthetic experience as a *presentation, not as a representation*. "Presentation" differs from "representation" by virtue of not having as its primary feature an indexical or iconic sign-relation to what it signifies. To represent something is to offer a second something that has the self-effacing function of directing the mind or the senses back to the first something, with which it is connected in various particular ways. In Husserl's terminology, a representation is prototypically an "indicative sign" (*Anzeichen*), a sign which, itself an existent thing, points to the presumed existence of another thing. In Jung's language, it is simply a "sign," since every sign relates one known term to another known term.

What then is a presentation if it is neither an indication nor a sign *simpliciter*? Is it an "expressive sign" (in the only alternative Husserl offers us) or a "symbol" (in Jung's alternative)? An expressive sign bears its meaning within itself: rather than being self-eclipsing in the manner of a pointing finger (which points precisely away from itself), it is self-sustaining. A word is, for Husserl, the paradigm of an expressive sign, and above all a word pronounced silently to oneself such that its meaning is compresent with its inward articulation. But such merging of meaning and saying in "solitary mental life"[7] cannot serve as a model for what happens in the experience of art where the presentation is public by its very nature: it is an "event" available to all. Unlike the fully expressive (because silently intoned) word, the art work stands before us as an initially mute presence; it is perceived, beheld, not articulated or spoken by us; we are beholden to it, not it to us.

Is the work qua presentation a symbol then—as such diverse bedfellows as Jung and Gadamer, Cassirer and Fredericksen have held? Much depends on what is meant by "symbol." For Jung, a symbol refers us to the unknown:

> The concept of a symbol should in my view be strictly distinguished from that of a sign. . . . A symbol always presupposes that the chosen expression is the best possible description or formulation of a relatively unknown fact, which is nonetheless known to exist or is postulated as existing.[8]

For Gadamer, in contrast, a symbol makes manifest what is already there and known to be there:

> A symbol manifests as present something that really is present . . . it makes something immediately present.[9]

This is not to say that the symbol is the thing itself; it is a "delegate" or "representative" (*Stellvertreter*) for what it symbolizes and as such cannot add on any extra significance of its own: it has a borrowed being.

Another way of putting Gadamer's point is to say with semiologists that a symbol, unlike a sign, is "motivated"; that is, its relation to what is symbolized is based on causality, contiguity, similarity, or delegation. Each of these latter relations motivates, gives a *raison d'être* for a particular symbol—even though in every case the relationship between symbol and symbolized will be "non-necessary" (for a symbol and what it symbolizes might *not* have become linked at all). Despite this independence of terms in the symbolic relation, there must be in addition a "more or less stable association between two units or the same level"[10]—thus a certain homogeneity, whether between two signifiers or between two signifieds. In Ducrot and Todorov's standard example, "flame" can symbolize "love" because the meanings of the two terms overlap in the common semantic core of "something warm."[11]

Notice how the plot has now thickened: granting that a work of art is no mere representation in the manner of an indicative sign and also not a composite of expressive signs, it might seem by default to be (a) a *presentation* (*Darstellung*, with all that this German word connotes of being an exhibition, of being-on-stage) which is (b) *symbolic* in status. But symbolism, strangely, takes us either into the unknown with Jung or into the intricacies of a ramified semiological analysis. Since the unknown is unknown, let us stay with semiological analysis for the moment, noticing how it applies in the case of film:

—film is *motivated* by virtue of its essential causal connection with the circumstances of its origin—which is to say, its actual production: it can also be said to resemble this production (a point to which I shall return shortly) and to be its manifestation in the public world of viewing;

—it is *non-necessarily* related to these same circumstances, since it might have been produced differently: for instance, sham objects can be used as effectively as the genuine article in achieving the same visual effect;

—it displays a *unity of homogeneity*, often at both levels of significance: at the level of the medium (the signifier), above all insofar as a particular quality of the filmic image (especially its atmospheric cast: think of the night scenes in *Rules of the Game*) can convey and match the quality of the depicted scene; and at the level of the meaning or the signified, as in the round-dance at the end of *8½*, whose closure signifies, minimally, the completion of the film and Fellini's career up to that point, while the child within the circle symbolizes what is to come by a mimesis of meaning (here "the new," "the future").

III

Even if you are disposed to accept this analysis—which makes film qua presentation into a straightforwardly symbolic medium—I doubt that you will find it adequate to your actual experience of film. It does demonstrate (in Umberto Eco's words) how "a work of art performs a semiotic redemption of its basic matter"[12] and how art works involve "aesthetic overcoding"[13] since every feature and subfeature yield with astonishing rapidity to the advancing imperialism of semiotic examination. As Eco concludes:

> a work of art has the same structural characteristics as does a *langue.*
> So that it cannot be mere "presence"; *there must be an underlying system
> of mutual correlations, and thus a semiotic design which cunningly gives
> the impression of non-semiosis.*[14]

But more than cunning or subtlety of structure is at stake here. The very persuasiveness of semiotic analysis in the hands of Eco or Metz, Barthes or Lotman leads us to turn around Eliot's dictum when it comes to an art like film—not "we had the experience but missed the meaning," but we have the meaning all right, yet are somehow missing the experience.[15]

This experience is of an *event* of presentation—not just of an *object* of presentation, which would lend itself to semiotic dissolution with less sense of loss, of unacknowledged residue. In fact, the residue unrendered and unredeemed in semiology is of three fundamental kinds:

—the eventfulness of the work itself
—its imagefulness
—its beingfulness.

I shall consider these features in reverse order, keeping my focus almost exclusively on film. In this rather roundabout way, I hope to come closer, in the end, to what Jung may have meant by the symbolic—and thus to what Fredericksen, following Jung, calls "the symbolic cinema."[16] At the same time, we shall begin to understand how film and memory intersect, that is, how filmic images can be so uniquely memorable.

(a) *Beingfulness.* By this admittedly awkward term I refer to a so far neglected characteristic of works of art, one which is especially striking in the case of film. This is a *double transformation* that occurs in almost all experienced art works: first, a transmutation of what Eco has just called its "basic matter," its specifically material mode of presentation, whether these be actual brushstrokes on a canvas, printed words on a page, or filmic images on a beaded silver screen. What is remarkable here is that these material elements, which must (as I stressed earlier) begin by being perceived, are in the end more-than-perceived (though not other-than-perceived). They become factors in a configuration which is that of the art work as a whole and which is properly what is retained-in-grasp. The transfiguration here in question is much the same as that which Ingarden calls the movement from the "work of art" to the "aesthetic object" and Heidegger the transition from "earth" to "world." It is a matter of matter—of the elemental, the *prima materia* of a given work—on its way to becoming what we finally contemplate, get wrapped up in, and criticize in the experience of art: the work's world, which is our world too as its engrossed viewers (think of entering the dramatic-nostalgic world of *Citizen Kane* and you will know what I mean).[17]

A second transformation at work in the work is most prominent in the literary and particularly the pictorial arts. I refer to the way in which not the actual materiality of the medium but the entities and events of an original scene or occasion are taken up and changed, often radically and even to the point of unrecognizability (which does not occur in the first kind of transformation). The subject who sits for a Francis Bacon portrait finds himself transmogrified into an object of horror, a leering death's head. The actors on a given set discover that their casual and flippant movements have become, in the finished film, the movements of characters *in the film*—beings no longer themselves or rather themselves as more-than-themselves.

The "more" at stake in both sorts of transformation is an *ontological* more. Thanks to such transfigurations, we cannot be said to *know* more; but, nonetheless, more has been made present, more *is*, than was previously the case. It is thus a question of what Gadamer has christened an "augmentation of being" (*Zuwachs an Sein*):

> That a [work] has its own reality means . . . that the original [object or scene] comes to be presented in the presentation [*Darstellung*]. . . . But if it presents itself in this way, this is no longer a merely casual event but belongs to its very own being. Every such presentation is an ontological event [*ein Seinsvorgang*] and brings about the level of being to which what is [thereby] presented belongs. Through being presented, it experiences, as it were, an *augmentation of being*.[18]

It is a matter of *becoming more*, which is something that a semiology of film has difficulty accounting for (except in a reductionist manner as a 'change of codes')[19] and yet which the humblest moviegoer experiences without fail. *Of course*, he or she would say, the film as viewed rises above its own origins, emanates beyond them in an outstreaming which is essentially (and not just accidentally) more than the elements—perceptual or scenic, historical or occasional—of which it is composed. This is one way, at least, in which the known leads into the unknown—here the unknown of increased being (for just *how much* increase is not known or measurable as such).

(b) *Imagefulness*. But what exactly ends up with more being? The presentation, surely; yet the presentation, as we saw some time ago, comes to us in the form of an image; or as Gadamer puts it lucidly:

> That the presentation is an image [*Bild*]—and not the original [*Urbild*] itself—does not mean anything negative, any mere diminution of being, but rather an autonomous reality. So the relation of the image to the original is basically quite different from what it would be in the case of a copy [*Abbild*]. *It is no longer a one-sided relationship.*[20]

The work as image, then, possesses an "autonomous reality" (*eine autonome Wirklichkeit*), and its relation to its original is not copylike: it is not the pale reflection of this original considered as some greater reality. It was just this "one-sided" Platonic view of the image as a lesser reality with which I began this essay. Now we must understand why this view must be rejected in the case of film and what other notion of the image should take its place.

Brakhage proclaims discerningly that "nowhere in its mechanical process does the camera hold either mirror or candle to nature."[21] But wait! Surely there *is* a sense in which some candlework and mirrorwork is being done after all: the *camera* is never entirely *obscura*. It does have, or is, an eye, however much it may astigmatize the world before it. It records what it sees even if it records aslant, in motion, belensed, handheld, and in accordance with elaborate preplanning. The camera is certainly directed by a mind but is itself mindless insofar as it simply takes in what is there to be taken in. Does it not then give us—on film and on the screen—something like a mirror image of what is (was) in fact there?

No, it does not; but just *why not* needs to be stated with some care. For one thing, a mirror image is more than a copy, whose entire being consists in its resemblance to an original.[22] A copy is always only a mere means: the photograph on a driver's license or passport exists strictly for the sake of identification, hence our characteristic refusal to consider it as an adequate image of *ourselves*. When we look into a mirror, however, we are confronted with an image which we can hardly refuse, however much we might wish to. A mirror image is an exact, an unvarnished, likeness; this is why it is so telling. Mirroring is thus the paradigm form of what Plato calls *eikastikē*, "likeness-making." Its peculiar power,[23] both in early life (as in Lacan's "mirror stage," basic to the formation of the human ego) and later on (when it so painfully details our physical decline), is explained by the fact that we know that it gives back to us in image-form what is truly before it:[24] *in the mirror image we behold what the mirror beholds and are perforce its captive.*[25]

The mirror experience is, then, a special kind of thralldom, a species of picture magic. Movies captivate and enthrall us too; and they are certainly magical, as Méliès first fully suspected. But movies do not convey mirror images to us; or, rather, when they do (as in the sequence in *L'Age d'Or* when clouds fill the empty mirror on a woman's dressing table), we instantly recognize the difference between filmic and mirroring imagery. This difference cannot be reduced to the mechanical fact that mirror images are "mere appearances"[26] which occur only on the surface of mirrors and in the presence of a properly situated viewer, whereas filmic images exist both on film and on screens—and can exist in both places without any viewers whatsoever. The difference is more deep-going than this; and it can be encapsulated by saying that if mirroring is a matter of *eikastikē*, moviemaking is an activity of *phantastikē*—of making semblances.[27]

A semblance is no longer in thrall to that of which it is a semblance. It *may* resemble its original, though even here it enjoys a freedom to alter proportions and dimensions that is denied to mirror images, which can change merely the right-to-left alignment (and sometimes also the clarity, color, or texture) of what they present. As Plato says, "artists, leaving the truth to take care of itself, do in fact put into the images they make, not the real proportions [as would be required of an *eikon*, an exact replica] but those that will appear beautiful" (*Sophist* 236a). But if truth can truly be left to take care of itself, then resemblance itself is no longer needed; we can veer in good conscience even into dis-semblance. And this is just what many movies do fortuitously and what experimental films do systematically. In what does such dis-sembling consist?

It consists, first of all, in breaking the one-way hold which, in mirror images, things have over their own reflections. The compulsion to convey what is there—immediately and simply there before us—is replaced by a two-way process in which the dis-sembling film image affects its own origin, whether by instituting it expressly *as* origin[28] or by challenging it, flying in the face of it. The process is dialectical, reciprocal, transformational. Rather than being simply identifiable as an image of x or y (as is necessarily the case with mirror images, the identity of whose contents *must* reflect that of their originals), it becomes a cinematic image whose primary identity is not the identity of anything other than itself. It has become, in short, a presentation: something that presents itself *as itself*.

For this to happen, a second difference between mirroring representation and filmic presentation has to have occurred. This is the intervention of the film-maker in the bivalent circuit of image and original. Dis-sembling includes tampering with what in nature—and precisely Nature viewed as a single great Mirror—would be infinite circulation of the same: the same thing, the same image. The mark of the maker is at once highly personal (no one else could make just *this* film) and highly stylized (every film belongs ultimately to some genre, albeit a genre it alone instantiates). This mark makes the film image more than it would be, could be, as a purely reflective process—i.e., as something dumbly documentary.

Now in both of these decisive differences between film-imaging and mirror-imaging we observe at work an *aggrandizement of the image*: an augmentation of imagefulness parallel to that increase in beingfulness discussed just above. The filmic image is more than an *eikon* of its original; it is an authentic *phantasma,* possessing the rights and unique properties of a free fantasy unbeholden to its own origins. Taken together, the totality of cinematic images in a given film make up a *phantasmal field,* closely akin to what Merleau-Ponty called the "phenomenal field."[29] Just as the latter presents traits of Gestalt contexture which cannot be reduced to sensory constituents taken additively, so the dissembling phantasmal field of a film exhibits features irreducible to the sum of single shots from which the film is nonetheless built up. The vision in this "art of vision" is in this respect visionary, allowing us (indeed inciting us) to see more than we see— which is what we cannot do in the mundane viewing of mirror images.[30] The *phantastikē* of filmmaking is indeed phantastic; it is also phenomenal, for it is on the phenomenal surface of the perceived screen that the phantasmatic (and sometimes phantasmagoric) film image comes into its own. It realizes there its full being as pure presentation; it has become maximally imageful.

(c) *Eventfulness.* But a film is more than full of images; it is full of moving images: it is a moving picture show. Movement means—movement makes—events.[31] A film, thanks to its movingness, is an event from beginning to end. From the beginning: shooting a film is itself an event and a quite complex event at that, since it is in fact a congeries of coordinated events: acting, directing, filming per se—not to mention concurrent mental events such as thinking, imagining, remembering. To the end: through intermediate stages of editing to the final event which is the presented film itself. It is this latter—the film's being seen on the screen—which is the most fateful, the most eventful. How so? What is happening in this happening?

Semiology fails us almost entirely at this point. What it means by *mise en scène* and "narrativity" does not begin to fathom the truth of the simple statements that a film is an "event presentation" or that it is "an ontological event."[32] A film is an event in which images come to *presentation,* in which they come to *be.* But just how is not yet clear.

Movement is the main key. A stilled movie—such as has been attempted by Warhol and others—is still a movie; it still moves. If the images do not move among themselves, the one image (say, of one room or of one building) which is presented itself moves—moves through time, as is signified by the seeming changes (however subtle) in its iridescent surface. Time, said Aristotle, neither is movement nor can exist without it; it is the enumeratable aspect of movement considered with respect to the forward and afterward aspects of the now in which it is perceived.[33] There is no now which is not in time and which is not therefore measurable by movement of some sort—if not of a physical object, then of our own minds as we think in the dark.[34] Film is an experience in the dark too, and if we are presented with a single stillborn image in this well-framed obscurity our minds will wander (and wonder!): they will move in it and around it, creating a cinematic event with two epicenters, one static and the other dynamic.[35] In the more usual case, the epicenter located in the subject will be obscured because his or her mind will be caught up, and thus measured, by kinematic action on the screen. Whatever the units of this action (to determine them is precisely a task for the semiotician), it constitutes an event for the viewer—a happening which we describe starkly in English as "seeing a movie."

This is a peculiar event indeed. First, it is phantasmatic in status: nothing is really happening, that is, nothing at the level of the actions as *presented* in the train of filmic images. Though certainly presupposing the perception of particular forms and shapes, the imaged movement cannot be reduced to these; it is, once again, phenomenal in nature, exceeding the sensed particularities on which it is based. Also peculiar is the schematic character of this action, which seems to be offered in a curiously profiled form and which does not require an explicit beginning point or terminus: in film we are always *in medias res* with respect to movement, always swept up in it (even when we feel disaffected or disgusted by it). Yet this *res,* this thing, is no thing at all—nothing akin to the perceived *kinēsis* of discrete substances, being closer in fact to revery, a state of daydreaming or imagining.

If these remarks begin to circumscribe the cinematic event, they have not yet done justice to what is truly *eventful* in film, what is more than just a collection of events. This eventfulness arises in two forms, each of which can be regarded as an aspect of film's symbolic nature: communalization and visibilization.

(i) *Communalization.* Gadamer speaks of the way in which an image "shares in the being" of what it presents to us—is continuous with its own content.[36] We can extend this notion to include sharing between:

(1) the work and its own original: i.e., between an image and its original, from which it is not cut off even if it does not serve merely to mirror it;

(2) the work and its individual viewers: there is a sharing or a drawing together insofar as viewers have the sense of merging with the film presentation, of becoming part of its very movement;

(3) members of the viewing audience with one another: here a special filmic fellow feeling is notably (even if not always equally explicitly) present, especially on those rare occasions on which we can speak of a conjoint commotion, a being moved together, an event of co-catharsis in which each emerges ecstatically out of egoic limitations; it is at this moment that a sense of community precipitates out of the general movement of communalization. The memory of such a moment will be, moreover, an act of commemoration.[37]

(ii) *Visibilization.* Film, bringing events to full visibility, makes them more than merely watched occurrences. Here the symbolic movement is the opposite of that designated by Jung; it is from the unknown to the known—or at least to the visible. But this movement in reverse is no less difficult to comprehend, involving as it does a "mysterious radiation of being"[38] from the originals onto their images. There is, as it were, an increase in luminousness (not to be confused with natural luminosity!) as we move from *Urbild* to *Bild,* from what is presented to the presentation itself. Think of the way in which scenes of a film like *L'Avventura* shine with a light seemingly of their own provenance rather than being borrowed from some external source. Such inward illumination of images is unique to film; it is the basis of its most profound eventfulness. Here, above all, "the image is an ontological event, [for] in it being becomes meaningfully visible."[39] The event of eventfulness, its advent, is the becoming visible of the image: a principle which applies more completely and more strikingly to film than to any other art. Films help incipiently imageful events to become more fully luminous—to become maximally eventful to the viewing eye and thus finally to exist on their own terms, to *be.*

IV

So far, then, we have seen being, image, and event come together in the work of art, the film work considered as a presentation to the senses and to the mind. In each case an augmentation or enhancement takes place, whether this be in the form of an "increase of being" through a quasi-emanational overflow, a transition from sheer likeness to self-sustaining dis-semblance, or a movement from events as bare occurrences in motion to communalized and visibilized presentations. All three dimensions of the work contribute powerfully to its symbolic status, beyond its semiological features of non-necessary motivation and homogeneity of signifying and signified units. Just as it is more than a copy and more even than a mirror image, it is more than a sign; and in all three respects it is more than a representation. This "more," which has become something of a leitmotif, is what I have tried to capture in speaking of a characteristic "fullness" in each of the dimensions thus singled out. There is something especially plenitudinous about the film work and its experience—particularly in contrast with, say, literature, whose many "spots of indeterminacy" (in Ingarden's expression) invite analysis that, like a structuralist approach, thrives upon absences and differences rather than upon presences and fullnesses, terms more appropriate to the world of film, which gives itself to us as complete, as fulfilling and fulfilled, as somehow always *just enough* and satisfying as such.

Yet precisely if this is so, a last problem looms large. This is that memory, my other main concern in this essay, seems to have more to do with absence than with presence. Consider that it always, directly or indirectly, deals with *past* time, time that has elapsed from the full presence of the present, and with events which have already occurred—which are not occurring in the now of perceived motion.[40] Remembering represents, of course, the attempt to recover this past and these events: to cut short the losses, possibly even to redeem them. But this is a battle which, even in the best of circumstances, is largely lost and is, more generally, foredoomed to failure, since Time's winged chariot presses ever onward. The losses cannot be cut short; indeed, they increase alarmingly over time, *with* time and *in* time. Absences accumulate; presences vanish.

How then are we going to reconnect remembering, obsessed as it must be with absence and loss (that is, with a decided diminution in being), with images of a sort that promote presence and gain (with an enlargement in being)?

V

Let us start with the basic fact that movies *are* memorable—not always, of course (nothing is *always* memorable) but nonetheless notably and sometimes hauntingly and persistently so. That this memorability is fragmentary and imperfect should not surprise us, for we rarely remember the entirety of any experience. What is more striking is the timing through which our movie memories typically arise: either just after viewing a film and through the next day or so (here they act as a quasi-narcotic "night residue") or in a long-term but intermittent fashion. In this latter case, they may return unbidden at the most unexpected moments, suddenly springing forth in the manner of Proustian involuntary memories; or they may come back in a more subtle form as vaguely felt presences with much of the detail omitted (think of the many times when you cannot recall the proper names even of leading characters); or they may simply remain in the margins of our awareness as subliminal guests who together constitute a kind of latent movie memory bank. In all three ways, our remembering of movies takes on a strange life—or, better, a species of half-life—all its own. Although it would be too much to claim that such remembering is altogether different in kind from other sorts of remembering, there is a sense in which movies can be said to be especially memorable phenomena, i.e., to lend themselves not just to ordinary rememoration or secondary memory but to that more emphatic and meaningful re-experiencing which we term "being memorable." How is this so? What about film gives rise to this heightened memorability?

There are at least two *preliminary* conditions of the particular memorability of filmic images.

(i) The first is the *isolation of the screen* from its surroundings. This is a decontextualization which permits the screen to stand out from its immediate environs: to become an entity in its own right, to be focused on for its own sake, and thus remembered as a thing formed in itself and by itself. This self-framed standing-out is a negative condition insofar as it aids in eliminating distraction—hence its natural analogy to the aim of the phenomenological reduction, which is to put into suspension the distracting beliefs of the natural attitude.[41] As these beliefs need to be set aside for the time being in order to achieve eidetic insight, so our neighboring spectator's spontaneous remarks and candy paper rattling—not to mention the details of the internal architecture of the theater—need to be held in abeyance so that our relatively undistracted attention can turn to the film presentation. The closer this latter is to a sheer presentation, the more likely it will be recalled intact, as just this luminous presence emerging out of the dimness—much as many non-filmic memories also seem to arise from an aura of the indefinite: out of 'nowhere' as we are often tempted to say in cases of suddenly re-illuminated regions of our past. But this factor of isolation, helpful as it may be, is by no means a sufficient (and probably not even a necessary) condition of remembering. It is not clear, for example, that de-contextualization is always beneficial in recollection; in fact, context (what James called "contiguous associates")[42] may itself provide one of the most valuable cues or inroads to a given memory, especially one for which we need to do some mental searching. I might even be *better* able to recall a given film if I can recall just where—in what precise surroundings—I viewed it.

(ii) A second preliminary condition may be termed *surprise* or the *unexpected*. Perhaps the main reason why we do not remember boring movies well is that they fail to provide the unforeseen, the irregularities which offer points of attachment for subsequent remembering. This can be seen most clearly in the case of narrative structure. Although this structure may act as a potent vehicle for remembering by providing an endoskeleton or internal context within which to locate particular to-be-remembered actions, it may also serve to deaden recollection when it is present in some merely formulaic and all too easily anticipatable form. Such a form holds no surprises for us: there is a predictable unfolding of events but no appearance of what Kierkegaard called the "sudden,"[43] whether the sudden occurs as the shocking, the frightening, the deeply moving, the rapid about-face, or whatever. Not only are these particular moments in narrative sequence eminently rememberable, but they facilitate the remembering of other parts of the same sequence as well.

Let me turn now to what is a more decisive condition of the vivid remembering of movies. This is *point of view*. In seeing a film, we find ourselves spontaneously assuming the point of view offered by the camera;

we make this point of view our own, as if what were being experienced from its perspective were our own experience in the first person: as Pudovkin said, "the lens of the camera is the eye of the spectator."[44] And indeed the experience presented in the film does become the primary content of our experience; a "fusion of horizons"[45] occurs which may never be quite complete (to be complete would be to enter a state of hallucinatory immersion) but which is sufficient to give us the sense of entering another world. Not only are we privy to this world, but in having a particular point of view on it we seem placed securely in some determinate relation to it and to be on intimate terms with it—just as we would be were we actually to enter the presented world in question: there is no human experience without some sense of the emplacement, the "stand," of the subject whose experience it is. What the film presentation offers to us is thus, quite literally, a "stand-in" point of view, i.e., a position which by projective identification[46] we can take to be our own. (This is so even when, in a given film, the initial point of view is anonymous or unidentified; or when there is a rapid oscillation of points of view or a sudden switching between "subjective" and "objective" points of view.)

I want to contend that this point-of-view phenomenon acts as a distinctive *aide-mémoire*, for it reenacts and reinforces two basic features of all usual recollection.

(a) In ordinary remembering there is also a fusion of horizons at work—a strictly temporal fusion between the explicit or implicit limits of my present experience as the 'now' and the felt limits of the past experience being remembered (e.g., "last Friday" or "my last year at college"). If I am to remember at all, the internal horizon of the now must be receptive to the external horizon of the then: must admit it into its presence, must allow overlap, however partial. In film experience the fusion is in fact twofold. It is spatial insofar as I am letting the perceptual scene in which I am situated (the darkened theater) include within its horizon the very different horizon of presented filmic space. But it is also temporal as I am conscious of the difference between the actual now of the viewing and the now being viewed: between ongoing and filmic time, narrating-time and story-time, *Erzählzeit* and *erzählte Zeit*.[47] Both forms of horizonal fusion, especially the latter, parallel what happens all the time in memory. It is not surprising, then, that they aid our very remembering of films themselves, which can be seen in this regard as para-memorial in structure.

(b) But fusion of horizons, whether in garden-variety remembrance or in filmic experience, is never realized in a perspectival void. In both cases, the fusion is effected from some particular point of view. In remembering, I, the rememberer himself or herself, am always a privileged witness of (or participant in) what I am recalling to mind: I don't remember my fortieth birthday *simpliciter*, as a freefloating event suspended in an egoless abyss; I remember how this birthday was *for me*. Or, if I am expressly recalling how others experienced the same event, I am recollecting how it was for them—but still also for me, that is, from my point of view. There is no escaping this for-myselfness of remembering, whatever my role may have been in a given remembered event. The exact analogue in film would be a film like *The Lady and the Lake* in which the protagonist actually carried a camera strapped to his chest at all times.[48] But this is not required; there may even be a splitting of several simultaneous points of view (as when the sound track offers a different perspective from the camera); what matters is that some point of view be proffered—as it always is, however complexly or subtly. To this extent, and in this way, another significant para-memorial structure is present in film, thereby further reinforcing its recollectability.

VI

Isolation, surprise, and above all point of view contribute importantly, albeit quite variously and often unpredictably, to the better remembering of films. But even when taken together, they still do not explain fully the special memorability of cinematic experience. We need to look elsewhere, finally, to understand the latter more adequately. Yet we need not look very far: it is precisely in what I have called imagefulness that an explanation suggests itself. Preoccupied as we are with making up for absence and loss in human experience, our remembering may be said to possess a veritable hunger for content. It has an acutely sensed need to fill up the void which time's evanescing inevitably leaves in its wake: a need which may come to conscious awareness as nostalgia. Just as in nostalgia we seize upon internal or external images of lost or missed objects as welcome (even if painful) presences, so in remembering generally images are welcomed as reassuring reminders or revivals of the past—a past which they presentify in condensed format. And in both cases the more full-bodied these images are, the better!

It is hardly unexpected, accordingly, that filmic images—which we have seen to be much more than pale eikonic replicas of their originals—are embraced warmly by an image-hungry memory, which is rarely satiated by ordinary memory images. The same reception awaits other robust images such as those stemming from dreams, hallucination, active imagination (in the Jungian sense), visions, and any extraordinary perceptual experience. The transition from initially presented, pre-memorial image to memory image proper is facilitated in each case by the intensity of the imaged presentation—by its power to arrest, grip, startle, or strike our attentional consciousness. Contrast this situation of image-seizure with that obtaining in the case of mirror images or, indeed, most memory images themselves. When did you last experience *a memorable mirror image*? My suspicion, in keeping with the above analysis, is that a mirror image is too beholden to its own origin, is too much a one-way affair, to be memorable in its own right. The non-memorability of most memory images themselves has a similar basis. I might well remember vividly images of the palace in *Last Year at Marienbad*, and I might also easily recollect an actual visit to this same palace (and the two experiences, moreover, would probably strengthen each other), but I doubt that memory images of either experience would be reliably and recurrently impressive. Why is this? Most likely because we tend to regard memory images as a *via media* into the past, a way back to something other than themselves, thereby demoting them to the status of mere mediators, pale purveyors of the remembered. They seem to be transitive, rather than intransitive, objects, and thus we tend to rush over them, often leaving them in schematic form—and just as often forgetting them altogether, oblivion thereby becoming their all too common fate.

A skeptic might respond at this point that a film presentation is also only a matter of mediation in the interest of taking us beyond—beyond the screen into the unreal, as Sartre and the surrealists would insist. We need not go to the opposite extreme of Krakauerian realism (for which film is the redemption of physical reality)[49] to realize, however, that the robustness of film, the foundation of its memorability, presupposes that an intransitive filmic world of dynamized space and spatialized time[50] comes to be constituted on the very surface of the screen itself: nested within it, as it were. My animadversions earlier against the reduction of the filmic image to an indicative sign, a likeness, even a symbol in any narrow sense, amount to the same claim—as does, of course, the general thesis that a film is presentational rather than representational. Being presentational, film is more than mediational. It presents its own immediate world,[51] a world robust enough to be an adequate basis for memorability.

Memorability is compatible with incomplete, and even failed, rememorability. I need not recall the details of film—details of plotting and naming, much less of cutting and framing—for it to be fully memorable. I must just remember some of its images, not even necessarily the most moving ones: images of single shots will suffice, so long as they move me to remember them. The robustness, in other words, resides *in the images that compose a film's world*. They, and they alone, possess that "autonomous reality" which ensures that they are more than beholden and derivative; they are experienced as having a being-for-themselves which aids in remembering them for themselves; they are not place-holders for something else more worthy of remembrance, whatever world-historical importance might attach to their content outside the context of film-viewing itself. It is due precisely to their autonomy that the unique imprint of the film-maker can become visible—and make itself memorable, such that we cannot dissociate from the memory of a given filmic image the indelible mark of, say, Resnais. Personal style per se is not, however, a prerequisite of the memorability of filmic images, which may remain memorable on their own account and without reference to their maker.

VII

It is strange indeed that something as unabashedly phantasmatic and frankly dissembling as "mere" film images could be so memorable and even be in several important respects a paradigm of the memorable in human experience. If they are such, it is due largely to their having the right robustness. "Robustness" itself, as should be evident by now, is only another way of speaking about what I have called generically "imagefulness": the power of the image in art, particularly in film art, to exceed and enhance its own origin. It is also therefore a way of speaking about "beingfulness," the increase in being which art works manage to effect by their very transformational presence; and, by the same token, a matter of "eventfulness" too, of happenings which are more than mere occurrings, of a communalization that is genuinely commemorative and of a visibilization that represents an apogee of the rememorative.

Film makes a special virtue, a special gift and point, of these three forms of closely related "fullness"; it supplies a plenitudinous presence in its luminous showings. Small wonder then that remembering seizes upon all this plenitude, this plenty-enoughness, and finds it especially memorable: all this nourishing abundance in the midst of all the dearth of our normally unsaturated memorial lives! Film is a maximalizing medium which is in the end no medium at all but its own object. Or better: its own subject (in the sense in which Dufrenne argues that the aesthetic object is a quasi-subject).[52] Or better yet: *its own image.* This image—film not just as composed of multifarious image-bits, but *film-as-image*, super-image of itself—can be considered as itself an analogue of human memory. We have seen how it is so in the particular case of point of view, with its fusion of horizons. But let me suggest in closing how film *as a whole* can be regarded as para-memorial in nature—as a quasi-bionic memory machine.

Consider how film presents to the viewer events which, in relation to the time of viewing itself, have already taken place. It is their witness, their objective memory. It conveys past presences to us in the present, as if they were happening in this present and as if we were immediately present to them—but *when* exactly is this objective memory occurring? Certainly not then (at the time of filming) but not simply now either: for the 'now' of viewing, being itself a complex fusion of past and present, is no longer the simple instantaneous now of unalloyed perception.[53] In watching film, we are in a strange no-man's land in which past and present are not clearly distinguished—opening up a space in which we can quasi-remember. It is very much *as if we were remembering* what is being presented to us in images: as if it were familiar enough to be genuinely recognized by us. Yet we know very well (unless the images in fact bear on particular things we have experienced before) that we are not *really* recognizing. The familiarity is a pseudo-familiarity only, *an as-if of an as-if*—not the real article. The same deconstruction applies to our sense of being there, *in* the scene presented: it is a quasi-being-there, thanks to our intimate insertion therein by the camera eye, which ushers us into a scene as if we were present in person (just as we feel present in person in our own memories). Yet we are quite aware that we are not in fact there—any more than we are still present in the scene (the spatio-temporally specified scene) of our ordinary memories either; in both cases, it is a matter of a presence *manqué:* of our presence as an absence, an amalgam of the two main modes of self-being.

Now it is this curious amalgam which embodies our experience of *ourselves* in film as in remembering generally. It represents the soft center, a fold or hollow, in the midst of what is otherwise a plenum of images. It is the invisible in the heart of the visible, the blind spot in the camera-*cum*-mind's eye. But it is nonetheless ourselves, our freely wandering selves astray in a collection of cinematically memorial images which, without our vanishing presence, would have no witness. This filmscape, unlike the perceptual landscape, is radically finite, coming to an end at the edge of the screen as at the edge of our remembered lives. With finitude, however, comes freedom: just as we are free to look away from the screen and close out the filmic world, so we can look away from our past and "actively forget" it; whereas there is no final overlooking of the perceptual world, which does not come to any finite end.

1. Samuel Beckett, *Imagination Dead Imagine* (London: Calder and Boyars, 1965), p. 7.

2. On the keeping/gathering aspects of memory, see Martin Heidegger, *What Is Called Thinking?* trans. J. Glenn Gray (New York: Harper & Row, 1968), pp. 139 ff., 150 ff.

3. Stan Brakhage, *Metaphors on Vision,* ed. P. Adams Sitney (New York: Film Culture, Inc., 1963), pp. 1 and 20.

4. Edmund Husserl, *The Phenomenology of Internal Time-Consciousness,* trans. J. S. Churchill (Bloomington: Indiana University Press, 1964), p. 66.

5. Husserl's discussion of this term occurs at *Experience and Judgment,* trans. J. S. Churchill and K. Ameriks (Evanston: Northwestern University Press, 1973), sec. 87c. I have extended Husserl's notion in my "Perceiving and Remembering," in this volume.

6. Brakhage, *Metaphors on Vision,* p. 1.

7. Edmund Husserl, *Logical Investigations,* trans. J. N. Findlay (New York: Humanities Press, 1970), I, p. 279 (sec. 8). Cf. sec. 2, "The Essence of Indication," for Husserl's view of indicative signs.

8. C. G. Jung, *Psychological Types* (Princeton: Princeton University Press, 1971), pp. 473 ff.; his italics. Jung adds that "an expression that stands for a known thing remains a mere sign."

9. H. G. Gadamer, *Truth and Method* (New York: Seabury Press, 1975), p. 136.

10. O. Ducrot and T. Todorov, *Dictionnaire encyclopédique des sciences du langage* (Paris: Seuil, 1972), p. 134.

11. Ibid.

12. Umberto Eco, *A Theory of Semiotics* (Bloomington: Indiana University Press, 1976), p. 268. Eco adds: "thus succeeding in a task that the Plotinian God never managed to accomplish, in spite of his emanational power."

13. On aesthetic overcoding as involving a "surplus of content" and a "surplus of expression" (in Louis Hjelmslev's sense), see ibid., pp. 269 ff.

14. Eco, *A Theory of Semiotics*, p. 271; my italics.

15. Admittedly less so in the case of literature, where semiotic success seems less objectionable—due no doubt to the dominating role of verbal language.

16. Cf. Don Fredericksen, "Jung/Sign/Symbol/Film" in *Quarterly Review of Film Studies* (Spring 1979): 167–92. I wish to thank Fredericksen for his encouragement and support of the present project, which was first given as an invited lecture at Cornell University on 25 April 1980.

17. On the foregoing, see Martin Heidegger, "The Origin of the Work of Art," in A. Hofstadter and R. Kuhns, eds., *Philosophies of Art and Beauty* (New York: Random House, 1964), pp. 649–741; R. Ingarden, *The Literary Work of Art*, trans. G. Grabowicz (Evanston: Northwestern University Press, 1973), chap. 1–3; Mikel Dufrenne, *The Phenomenology of Aesthetic Experience*, trans. E. S. Casey et al. (Evanston: Northwestern University Press, 1973), chap. 5.

18. Gadamer, *Truth and Method*, p. 124; his italics. Cf. also pp. 125, 134–35. I have had to modify this translation here and below, to accord better with the German.

19. On change of codes, see Eco, *A Theory of Semiotics*, pp. 273–75.

20. Gadamer, *Truth and Method*, p. 124; his italics.

21. Brakhage, *Metaphors on Vision*, p. 4.

22. On this point, see Gadamer, *Truth and Method*, p. 122: "it is of the nature of the copy that it has no other task but to resemble the original." As will be evident, I am indebted to Gadamer for much of what follows below.

23. As Gadamer remarks, '*bilidi*,' the Old High German word for 'image,' meant power (*Macht*). Cf. ibid., p. 514, n. 56.

24. "In a mirror image there appears the thing itself in image-form, so that I have it itself in the mirror image" (ibid., p. 122).

25. Another way of putting this is to say that the image and thing imaged here realize an indissoluble union such that they cannot be pried apart from each other. Cf. ibid., p. 123.

26. A mirror image, says Gadamer, "is nothing beyond its mere appearance . . . for it has no being-for-itself. It reflects back an image, making what it reflects visible to someone only for as long as he looks in it and sees his own reflection or whatever else is reflected in it" (ibid., p. 122).

27. For Plato's distinction between these two kinds of image-making, see *Sophist* 235d–236c.

28. As Gadamer stresses: "strictly speaking, it is only through the image that the original (*Urbild*) becomes the original image (*Ur-bild*); that is, it is the image that makes what is presented imagelike (*bildhaft*)" (*Truth and Method*, p. 125).

29. Cf. Maurice Merleau-Ponty, *The Phenomenology of Perception*, trans. C. Smith (New York: Humanities Press, 1962), Introduction, chap. 4.

30. Cf. P. Adams Sitney, *Visionary Film: The American Avant-Garde 1943–1978* (Oxford: Oxford University Press, 1979), passim.

31. See Brakhage's discussion of "Move Meant" in *Metaphors on Vision*, pp. 10 ff.

32. See Gadamer, *Truth and Method*, pp. 134 and 124 respectively. On narrativity in film, see Seymour Chatman, *Story and Discourse: Narrative Structure in Fiction and Film* (Ithaca: Cornell University Press, 1978), passim.

33. Aristotle, *Physics* IV, chap. 10–13.

34. Cf. ibid., 219a 1–9 for an analysis of the importance of self-perceived movement of one's thought when in darkness.

35. Donald P. Kuspit has explored this aspect of viewing a "pure" art work in his essay "The Unhappy Consciousness of Modernism," *Artform* (January, 1981): 53–57.

36. The being of an image is "not absolutely different from what it presents, but shares in the being of the latter. . . . The difference between an image and a sign has an ontological basis. The image does not disappear behind its pointing function but, in its own being, shares in what it presents" (Gadamer, *Truth and Method,* p. 135; cf. also p. 123).

37. One of the original meanings of "symbol" was that of the *tessera hospitalis,* whereby possession of suitably fitting parts of a shattered clay plate or other object meant membership in a given community.

38. "Even an individual portrait, if it is a work of art, shares in the mysterious radiation of being that flows from the ontological level of that which is presented (Gadamer, *Truth and Method,* p. 132).

39. Ibid., p. 127. Cf. also p. 126: "art as a whole and in a universal sense brings an increase in 'pictorialness' (*Bildhaftigkeit*) to being."

40. Memory sometimes treats time which *will have occurred,* as in my remembering an appointment tomorrow. But in this case I am treating the future under the aspect of the past: the future as if it has already become past.

41. On phenomenological reduction, see Edmund Husserl, *Ideas,* trans. W. R. B. Gibson (New York: Collier, 1975), sec. 31 and 32.

42. Cf. William James, *The Principles of Psychology* (New York: Dover, 1950), I, pp. 655 f.

43. Cf. Sören Kierkegaard, *The Concept of Dread,* trans. W. Lowrie (Princeton: Princeton University Press, 1957), pp. 78 f., 116 f.

44. V.I. Pudovkin, "The Plastic Material," in *Film: A Montage of Theories,* ed. R. D. MacCann (New York: Dutton, 1966), p. 31.

45. "*Horizontsverschmelzung*" in Gadamer's term. See *Truth and Method,* p. 273 f.

46. This term comes from Melanie Klein, who uses it for very different purposes.

47. For a discussion of these latter terms, see Chatman, *Story and Discourse,* pp. 62 ff.

48. See Chatman's analysis of this film in ibid., p. 160.

49. See Siegfried Krakauer, *Theory of Film* (Oxford: Oxford University Press, 1965), p. 300.

50. These are the terms of Erwin Panofsky's classic analysis in his "Style and Medium in the Motion Pictures," reprinted in O. Talbot, ed., *Film: An Anthology* (Berkeley: University of California Press, 1966), pp. 18 ff.

51. "The immediacy of what a film shows us consequently surpasses anything in other arts" (R. Stephenson and J. R. Debrix, *The Cinema as Art* [Harmondsworth: Penguin, 1967], p. 101).

52. Cf. Dufrenne, *Phenomenology of Aesthetic Experience,* pp. 146, 190, 196, 227, 382.

53. Thus it is misleading to say merely that "when we watch a film, it is just something that is happening—*now*" (*The Cinema as Art,* p. 101; italics in text).

The Memorability of Inhabited Space

*I can only say, there we have been: but I cannot
say where. And I cannot say, how long, for that
is to place it in time.*

—T. S. ELIOT
"Burnt Norton"

MEMORY OF PLACE is a conspicuously neglected area in the investigation of remembering. With the notable exception of the method of *loci* as a mnemonic device,[1] the recollection of place has been systematically subordinated to the remembrance of things past: Mnemosyne has been subjected to the order of Chronos, place being subsumed under time in a characteristically Western way of stressing the successive and teleological over the simultaneous and the spatial. Dia-chrony and syn-chrony are both considered dimensions of the chronological, despite Aristotle's early warning that time is supervenient on motion, which is in turn dependent on place.[2]

Place is paramount in human experience; it is the very basis of landscape taken in the generic sense of all that underlies geographic orientation and representation: the *Ort* is essential to the *Ortschaft*.[3] "Ortschaft" means 'place of habitation,' and it is remarkable how often memory of place is of *inhabited* place—for reasons I shall suggest in this chapter. But it is also remarkable how often memories themselves are of being in a place, inhabited or not; this is especially true of childhood memories, but it remains a main tendency in adult memories as well. How often do you remember *a time?* Though we attribute time to most of our memories (except precisely for many childhood memories), we do not tend to remember them *as* a time, as placed in time and dated there. Date is more like a locatory signal or index; it is intrinsic to the memory only as a sort of shorthand expression of it: 'last summer,' 'my seventeenth birthday.' But *what* we remember is rarely the identifying or locating time as such; it is our having been in a certain place at that time. In its broadest extension, "place" means circumstance or situation; in its stricter use, it means a particular spot in space, an *Ort* or *topos*. We remember places of many sorts, then, not one kind only; but among these, and among the most memorable, are inhabited places, *Ortschaften*. What is it about such places that makes them especially memorable and that belies any effort to reduce their remembering to strictly temporal terms? To explore this question is to begin to understand the primordiality of memory of place itself.

I

Let us begin with a very particular memory of inhabited place—the memory of falling asleep in a bedroom. This will serve as something of a paradigm for the manner in which the lived body functions centrally in memories of those inhabited places called "rooms." Such remembering might seem paradoxical as a paradigm insofar as the moment of falling asleep is often one in which memories—especially of the day's events—are placed into an abeyance from which they may return only in an oneiric guise. Nevertheless, it is also a moment which is quite conducive to remembering—of other places at more remote times. And it has its own distinctive memorability, which is built upon three constitutive factors: level, kinesthesia, and attuned space. Each of these, as we shall see, is an aspect of the quite fundamental role of the lived body in memory of place, a role which is primarily one of orientation.

1. *Level.* This is exceedingly basic in all memory of place: we remember each place as having its own level. It is normally so stable and expectable that we are not aware of it at all; only in dizziness or in experimental situations such as those devised by Stratton[4] and Wertheimer[5] do we become conscious of it because of the demands made by suddenly changing levels. The sense of level is not something imposed by any particular room in which I find myself; it is only *suggested* by it insofar as the room presents itself as a "possible habitat" which calls for virtual as well as actual movements on my part.[6] In the present case, it is the blatant horizontality of the support on which I remember myself lying, accentuated by the parallel horizontals of floor and ceiling, that induces a fundamental horizontal ground level for the situation.[7] But only if my body joins in and affirms this suggestion by taking up a more or less prone position does the level of the recollected bedroom about me congeal and stabilize.[8] Here is a factor which contributes powerfully to orientation in place and therefore to memory of being in a particular location.[9]

2. *Kinesthesia.* Movement is the major way in which the human subject explores and comes to know circumambient space.[10] The body of this subject can itself be considered as "the place of passage between movements received and movements thrown back."[11] Received and

thrown back from where?—precisely from place conceived as "possible habitat." Or, to be more precise: bodily motions, real and virtual, create a strictly local place (the "place of passage") which acts as the immediate site in the surrounding space of the place-at-large within which the lived body finds itself. The limits of the place-at-large are in fact determined by the orbit of possible movements of the subject—an orbit concretely traced out by the kinesthesias of this subject's body.[12] In the case at hand, these would include such sensed movings as turning over, stretching one's arms and legs in various directions, rotating one's head, shifting weight, etc.—as well as innumerable imagined or virtual variations upon these. The non-executed but intended movements are especially important in the instance of falling asleep, for they indicate what one might do in the situation but need not actually effect ('I could walk over and touch that wall by just taking a few steps in that direction'). Even though imagined only, such a quasi-movement is accompanied by its own quasi-kinesthetic sense, and, more importantly, it serves to give specificity to the surrounding space, the room, in which one finds oneself.

3. *Attuned Space.* This can be considered the consolidated achievement of a sense of spatial level and of the kinesthetic movements that become possible in a leveled space. But it does not represent the attainment of an objectively determined geographic space or an isotropic or "indifferent" space.[13] Both of these latter, closely connected, forms of space involve an essential detachment or disengagement of the embodied subject from his or her place-at-large, sometimes to the point of alienation from it. Lived space becomes spatial*ized* rather than spatial*izing*,[14] something to be beheld, not to be acted in or on. Yet there is no position outside space—space, as Plato reminds us in the *Timaeus*, is a matter of Necessity and is coeval with the Forms themselves—just as there is no space without a place, no Erewhon. Nowhere is this more evident than in the case we are examining. In falling asleep there is certainly disengagement too, something akin to phenomenological bracketing. But rather than achieving a neutral, empty, or planar spatiality (in effect, an a-spatiality), a quite positive spatiality is experienced: an *attuned* spatiality in which the subject resonates with his or her nocturnal habitat, finding not so much solace as sustenance there, a momentary *modus dormandi*. The attunement to place need not be active and outgoing or require particular expressions of empathy or sympathy (as it so often does in attuned social space, shared explicitly with others). Precisely in the case of falling asleep, the attunement to ambient space is quiescent, a product of a passive synthesis of experience. And yet it is felt as such, has its own distinct pleasure, and is a genuine mode of sensing in relation to a particular placescape. Its absence is no doubt even more acutely felt, as when we feel distinctly "out of tune" with our environs in falling asleep—not quite at-home in our own house. Attunement in space is

thus basic to our sense of familiarity-with-place, being a manifestation of such familiarity.

II

Having isolated the factors of level, kinesthesia, and attunement as important constituents of the memory of the inhabited space of bedrooms, let us look at an exemplary description of one such memory, that of Marcel Proust at the very beginning of *À la recherche du temps perdu:*

> . . . for me it was enough if, in my own bed, my sleep was so heavy as completely to relax my consciousness; for then I lost all sense of the place in which I had gone to sleep, and when I awoke at midnight, not knowing where I was, I could not be sure at first who I was; I had only the most rudimentary sense of existence, such as may lurk and flicker in the depths of an animal's consciousness; I was more destitute of human qualities than the cave-dweller; but then the memory, not yet of the place in which I was, but of various other places where I had lived, and might now very possibly be, would come like a rope let down from heaven to draw me up out of the abyss of not-being, from which I would never have escaped by myself. . . . For it always happened that when I awoke like this, and my mind struggled in an unsuccessful attempt to discover where I was, everything would be moving round me through the darkness: things, places, years. My body, still too heavy with sleep to move, would make an effort to construe the form which its tiredness took as an orientation of its various members, so as to induce from that where the wall lay and the furniture stood, to piece together and to give a name to the house in which it must be living. Its memory, the composite memory of its ribs, knees, and shoulder-blades, offered it a whole series of rooms in which it had at one time or another slept; while the unseen walls kept changing, adapting themselves to the shape of each successive room that it remembered, whirling madly through the darkness. And even before my brain, lingering in consideration of when things had happened and of what they had looked like, had collected sufficient impressions to enable it to identify the room, it, my body, would recall from each room in succession what the bed was like, where the doors were, how daylight came in at the windows, whether there was a passage outside, what I had had in my mind when I went to sleep, and had found there when I awoke.[15]

The sequence in this passage from the "Overture" to *Swann's Way* is itself most revealing: from an initial state of deep sleep in which all sense of place or person has been lost ("not knowing where I was . . . [or] who I was") to a transitional period in which possible spatial and temporal moorings ("things, places, years") whirl about in the darkness as so many tempting perches for the awakening consciousness,[16] and from thence decisively to particular places—the various places in which the same sleeper's body has awakened on previous occasions in his life. In this last step, which occupies the next several pages of the text, time is left out of account, while "things" are assimilated to places.[17] The transition to place is effected, and sustained, by reference to orientation realized by the body in the form of its specific postures in falling asleep and thus its actual and virtual movements. The "orientation of its various members" answers precisely to the various bedrooms in which the insomniacal narrator had tried to fall asleep on earlier occasions in his life. Each of these represents a remembered habitat in which particular bodily actions were appropriate. These actions are projected by the narrator into the dark of the so-far unidentified room in which he is at present lying—whose name he is trying in vain to specify and whose space is therefore not yet "attuned" in the sense discussed just above: not yet familiar enough to have its own place-name.[18] At the same time, level is being established by means of inducing from the body's orientation "where the wall lay and the furniture stood": "lay" (as in "lay of the land") and "stood" (as in "stood upright") refer respectively to the horizontal and vertical axes by which the level of a room is typically discerned.

Just here, however, Proust introduces a notion we have not considered thus far. The lived body, in addition to being the *fil conducteur* for memory of place, generally has its *own* memory of place as part of its very constitution: "*its* memory, the composite memory of its ribs, knees, and shoulder-blades offered it a whole series of rooms in which it had at one time or another slept." Such memory is special—so much so that it cannot even be considered a species of what Bergson would call "habit memory." For it need not have been formed by *repeated* experiences of the same place, much as such experiences often do contribute to the consolidation of such a corporealized memory.[19] The lived body, beyond being a centerplace or zero-point in memory of place, and beyond even being the basis for orientation in remembered rooms in terms of level and kinesthesia, possesses its own memory of place, internal to it alone, in-corporated into its being as singular fund or source.[20] This body memory is, in short, a *resource* which underlies the memorial powers of what Proust here calls the "brain," whose work consists precisely in dating (determining "when things had happened"), specifying visual appearances as such ("what they had looked like"), naming-and-identifying (collecting "sufficient impressions to enable it to identify the room"). In contrast with these activities, which belong to time, to geographic or indifferent space,[21] or to language, the ambience of body memory proper is found wholly in the pre-objective (i.e., pre-world-time and pre-world-space) and pre-linguistic landscape that is disclosed by the body's own gestures and movements.

We are indebted to Proust for another insight as well, one which draws together several strands in the previous analysis. Immediately following the above passage, the narrator ("Marcel") revisits in memory "rooms in winter," followed by "rooms in summer," a "Louis XVI room," and finally a room which was difficult to become accustomed to because of a strange vanishing ceiling, ever odorous wildflowers, harshly violet curtains, a clattering clock, and a "pitiless" mirror. Marcel recalls both his chagrin at trying to fall asleep in these difficult surroundings and his gradual triumph in transforming them into something somewhat more soothingly soporific:

> [At last] custom had changed the colour of the curtains, made the clock keep quiet, brought an expression of pity to the cruel, slanting face of the glass, disguised or even completely dispelled the scent of flowering grasses, and distinctly reduced the apparent loftiness of the ceiling. Custom! That skillful but unhurrying manager who begins by torturing the mind for weeks on end with her provisional arrangements; whom the mind, for all that, is fortunate in discovering, for *without the help of custom it would never contrive, by its own efforts, to make any room seem habitable.*[22]

This is in effect a description of what Merleau-Ponty would call the *customary* body, which acts to make the unfamiliar familiar, the not-at-home at-home.[23] Such truly domesticating work both draws on body memory and, in such demanding circumstances, goes beyond it by an act of habituation to these circumstances. "Custom," as here conceived, falls between the self-assured dating-noting-verifying powers of an analytic or reconstructive memory of place and the equally self-assured but fully sedimented powers of bodily memory of place. It is this middle-range customary memory which is responsible for the achievement of what I have called "attuned space," that is, the space of familiarity and intimacy, the space within which the Lares of home and habitation have been indwelling hosts.[24] For it is precisely the habituation effected by the customary body that brings about an abiding sense of habitation—that makes out of a succession of possible habitats (e.g., of just the sort which Marcel revisits in his waking dream of memory) an actual habitat, a place in which one is finally anchored, a room one can genuinely call one's own. It is just such gradually achieved attunement, this actualization of in-habitation, this placing of place, rooming of room, which is documented in the sentence that follows the passage on custom just cited:

> Certainly I was now well awake; my body had turned about for the last time and the good angel of certainty had made all the surrounding objects stand still, had set me down under my bed clothes in my bedroom, and had fixed, approximately in their right places in the uncertain light, my chest of drawers, my writing-table, my fireplace, the window overlooking the street, and both the doors.[25]

The end of trying to fall asleep coincides with the end of the bodily movements that invoke other places, other rooms; and the resulting lucidity, born of the customary body, brings with it the certainty of definite position for the various objects surrounding oneself. These "things" are now named and identified since they are "in their right places," their places within the place provided by the bedroom itself. Lest we think, however, that we have attained to an indifferent space in which there are *only* punctate positions (e.g., as in a Cartesian co-ordinate system), Proust withholds from us the proper name of this bedroom itself: we presume that it is the bedroom, the presently occupied bedroom, of the narrator himself, but its own place, its location, is not nominalized. Moreover, instead of remaining satisfied with the achievement of his customary body, the narrator lapses into still further remembering:

> . . . for memory was now set in motion; as a rule I did not attempt to go to sleep again at once, but used to spend the greater part of the night recalling our life in the old days at Combray with my great-aunt, at Balbec, Paris, Doncières, Venice, and the rest; remembering again all the places and people that I had known, what I had actually seen of them, and what others had told me.[26]

III

It is significant that Proust, in the last-cited passage, moves from names of rooms (and specifically bedrooms) to names of entire cities (Balbec, Paris, Venice). Before we, too, expand the scope of memory of place, we need to reflect on the propensity of the room to act as a basic module of such memory. Proust does not begin *Remembrance of Things Past* with memories of rooms as a matter of mere coincidence. Nor should we be surprised that Merleau-Ponty opens Part Two ("The World as Perceived") of his *Phenomenology of Perception* with an analysis of being in a room in his apartment in Paris:

> Our body is in the world as the heart is in the organism: it keeps the visible spectacle constantly alive, it breathes life into it and sustains it inwardly, and with it forms a system. When I walk round my flat, the various aspects in which it presents itself to me could not possibly appear as views of one and the same thing if I did not know that each of them represents the flat seen from one spot or another, and if I were unaware of my own movements, and of my body as retaining its identity through the stages of these movements.[27]

But rooms are not of such unusual memorial importance just because we can take up successive positions, actual or virtual, in them and so regard them as single rooms seen from various possible positions. And it will not suffice to claim that their stability and ever-the-sameness are crucial to our own personal identity (so they are, but so are many other constancies in our environment, including our own mirror-image); or that in their return-to-ability day after day or night after night they supply security (once again, they certainly do, just not uniquely); or that, still less plausibly, they provide shelter (so does a hut, a lean-to, or a tent). We must consider, rather, that rooms are the smallest significant units of inhabited enclosure; and it is as such that they serve as natural, if not necessary, modules of memory of place.

Enclosure is the key term here. To be enclosed in a room is not just to be covered over or around by it but to be contained in such a way as to preserve a special sense of being inside and yet possibly outside. The room as enclosure includes its own egress, its own way out. Having an entrance or exit, and thus an inside and outside, can be considered, much like the notion of level,[28] a matter of directionality and thus a function of the lived body:

> . . . if the words "enclose" and "between" have a meaning for us, it is because they derive it from our experience as embodied subjects. In space *itself* independently of the presence of a psycho-physical subject, there is no direction, no inside and no outside. A space is "enclosed" between the walls of our room.[29]

The inside/out of the body—experienced not only by means of bodily apertures but also by special sensations of coenesthesia and visceral kinesthesias—finds its analogue or correlate[39] in our sense of a room's inside/outside bipolarity. Such mutual fit or suitability between body schema and room structure is not only comforting or reassuring; it contributes constructively to memory of place—and favors a pre-eminence of rooms in such memory—by underscoring the extraordinary in-timacy with which rooms can be experienced in perception and memory alike. More enclosing than an ancient aedicula—which had no walls, only columns and a roof[31]—but less stifling than a prison cell (with its door locked from the outside), a room in a house, and pre-eminently a bedroom, provides a most auspicious aegis for intimate living.

But a room, however appositely appointed, situated, or structured it may be for the sake of remembering, almost always gives onto other rooms, usually via connecting corridors. The "out" or its inside/out directionality is typically out onto still more rooms, each with its own special character,[32] and ultimately onto an entire building or house, the superstructure which holds all these intra-structures together under one roof (often through a network of floors, stairways, chimneys, etc.). But the house, as the next largest unit in the memory of inhabited place, is more than a mere collection of rooms. It is, or contains, a spatial world of its own—as we realize whenever we speak of "haunted houses" or "my childhood home" (at least where "home" is equatable with a house).[33] Its multiplicity of rooms reflects the multiplicity of needs and interests of the people who live there, most frequently in the form of families.[34] A house contains therefore not just hosts of individuals' memories but collective memories as well, memories belonging to its co-occupants.

It might be thought that in rising to the level of the house, we have left the lived body behind as a factor in memory of place. Far from it! Not only is this body centrally at play in traversing a house—in going from room to room in it—and not only does it have its own more massive inside and outside, but the house itself can be understood as a para-body: a gigantized quasi-living body, with windows for eyes, front door for mouth, its own backside, etc. As Kent Bloomer and Charles Moore have said discerningly:

> The single-family house [is] free-standing like ourselves, with a face and a back, a hearth (like a heart) and a chimney, an attic full of recollections of *up*, and a basement harboring implications of *down*. In children's drawings of houses . . . there is generally a door like a mouth, windows like eyes, and a roof like a forehead, with symmetrical enhancements in front. In real houses, however modest, details of craftsmanship and signs and artifacts are developed at critical places to tell a story about the interior of the house, just as the expressions of the human face speak of inner feelings.[35]

Even if in the case of a given house there is no detectable literal resemblance between a house and a human body or face, the house remains a massive body for the people who live there, "a single-body metaphor for several persons."[36] The basis for our experience of our domicile as a quasi-collective body is two-fold.

(a) *Parallelism of Role.* Just as the individual's lived body can be considered the primary *organ* of habitation in general—of his or her being-in-the-world as such—so the house is the main *place* of human inhabitation. Each is in the world "as the heart is in the organism," that is, by manifold ties of sensory, imaginal, and memorial integumentation. At the same time, each can be considered a microcosm of a larger world without: one's own body is as much a mini-world constituted of sensations, imaginings, and rememberings (all of which reflect, however diversely, a macro-world of one's experience)[37] as a house is a world within a larger world (whether this latter be its neighborhood, city, or surrounding countryside). A house is "a semblance of the world you know"[38] and, though "its site is only a tiny piece of the real world, yet this place is made to seem like an entire world."[39] Much as the lived body is a world *in nuce,* so the house can be seen as a world in miniature, a world that contains and is defined by the movements of the lived bodies who inhabit it.[40]

(b) *Place for Collecting and Holding Memories.* We have seen how the lived body, through its familiarizing actions and knowledge, literally embodies a customary memory which is continually ingredient in human experience.[41] In this regard, the body can be seen as an active repository for a lifetime of acquired habitudes, of oriented rememberings-how—a center-place for them. So too a house gathers memories over a lifetime; it is a natural, perhaps the most natural, receptacle for memories, especially for long-term recollective memories.[42] This is accomplished in various ways: (i) the house itself, its very structure or location, may represent, or actively induce, a recollection of another house: either by a given pattern or style of building (Gothic, Colonial, etc.) or by a particular reference to a specific building;[43] (ii) regions of the house, especially certain rooms and recesses between them, will act as the particular *topoi* of memories; (iii) a special part of the house, perhaps most typically the hearth in Western homes, will act as a literal centerplace for memories, as is often signaled by the display of an heirloom at this precise point, i.e., an object which itself embodies family memories;[44] (iv) any collection of artifacts (of books, maps, matchbook covers, etc.), whether familial in origin or not, introduces a memorial component into the house;[45] (v) gardens, yard, and other elemental outworks can be considered "microcosms of earth, air, fire, and water which renew our recollections of a world inhabited over time, of primal beginnings not yet forgotten";[46] (vi) a house inhabited over a long period will leave profound traces in our bodily, habitual memory: "over and beyond our memories, the house we were born in is physically inscribed in us. It is a group of organic habits [which we still possess]."[47] If we reflect that memory itself can be considered the most potent in-gathering force of the psyche, then houses, as in-gathering in their very structure and function, will be powerfully privileged repositories of memories in these (and doubtless still other) ways. If houses are indeed "special places within places,"[48] this is because they, and the rooms of which they are composed, are such markedly propitious places for remembering to take place spontaneously and in an unforced way. Houses build "the body of memory"[49] as surely as lived bodies themselves do.

We should notice as well that a house, like the body itself, is a "general medium"[50] for memory. Not only do both "gear us to the world"[51] and "anchor"[52] us there, but each is a *tertium quid* in its own right: the lived body mediates, makes interaction possible, between the subject and the perceived world (which includes other perceiving subjects), while the house is midway between the room (which you reach as you build *in*) and the neighborhood and the city (attained as you build *out*). Both, in short, are indispensable middle terms in human experience.

IV

Both also, being in this middle way, involve *boundaries,* and it is to the notion of boundary and its role in the memorability of built places that I want to advert in the remainder of this chapter. In doing so I shall necessarily be invoking Hermes, god of boundaries as marked out by stones:

> In origin, the god Hermes is supposed to have been nothing more than
> a protector, and the stone pillars and heaps of stone in front of farm houses
> and along roads point to his presence.[53]

Hermes is a god of borderlines in many ways other than the strictly
geographical. He is a perpetual wanderer: "always on the road between
here and yonder."[54] He has no locale of his own, and his most characteristic
role is accordingly as a *truchement* or go-between of the gods.

> Hermes permeates the whole world because of his possibility of making
> connections, his commerce with, and constellation of, the other Gods
> from his borderline. He is the connection-maker and he is the Messenger
> of the Gods.[55]

Hermes is also a boundary figure in his ability both to guide and to lead
astray, to be wise yet cunning, to be a thief and trickster, to represent "the
weirdness of twilight"[56] and the sudden invasion of darkness into the day.[57]
Hermes may be present, like Charon, at the Acheron, the river of woe that
is itself the borderline between the underworld and the world of the living;[58] and he can be considered the appropriate archetypal basis for
hermaphroditism—indeed, for borderline conditions of all psychosexual
as well as psychopathological sorts.[59]

   If Hermes is the god who at once oversees and oversteps—by sheer
guile—all boundary situations (whose existential importance has been
underlined by Jaspers in his analysis of *Grenzsituationen*),[60] there are less
majestic and mercurial gods who concern themselves specifically with the
boundaries involved in human dwelling. Terminus, for example, was a
Roman god who presided over the fixing of boundaries and frontiers of
inhabited places. Marker stones or *termini* were erected at the borders of
estates, and annual Terminalia festivals were held each February.[61] Closely
related to Terminus[62] were the equally Latin deities, the Lares, who had
both a public and a private cult. The latter was found in the form of the
Lar, a household god who protected a given family in their home by being
the 'owl' of the ancestors who watched over their descendants. The more
public Lares were situated not in homes but at crossroads or where two
fields adjoined.[63] In the case of the Lares, then, we observe an explicit combining of home and boundary, of habitation and borderline, of something
Hermetic and Terminal yet also having a foothold in the home.

   A brief "topo-analysis"[64] of boundaries as they bear on human habitation is here in order. Any bounded space within which such habitation
occurs I shall call a location or (as termed earlier) place-at-large. It is over

this sense of place that the *genius loci* is guardian, even though strictly speaking *every* place had its Genius for the Romans.[65] The borderlines of any such location are established in a number of ways—by hedgerow or wall, road or path, palpable markerstone or imaginary surveyor's line. Although some of these demarcations of outermost limits can serve to close off definitively—to keep the inside inside and the outside firmly outside (as occurs dramatically in ancient Egyptian pylons[66] or in walled cities and citadels)—it is of interest that the first organized effort to institute boundary stones, that of the Mesopotamian *kudurru* circa 1500 B.C., may have involved keeping the stones (carved boulders in the form of steles) in temples and *not* on the perimeters of the property whose exact extent and rights they specified:[67] here the determination of the outside was placed inside, suggesting that literal delineations of borderlines is not what is most crucial and allowing for that free interinvolvement of inside and outside which we shall see at work elsewhere in the structure of inhabited places.

Within the location or place-at-large—which can be as capacious as city-limits or as confined as a quarter-acre property lot—is found the locus, that is, the particular space in which an actual dwelling is located. It coincides, in the dimension of the horizontal plane, with the foundations of the dwelling, however humble these may be (it has been conjectured that the first 'houses' were little more than round or oval troughs scraped in the ground, the ancestors of our basements).[68] In the vertical plane, the locus is constituted by a shaft of space whose upper limit is only ill-contained by the roof of the dwelling. It is the dwelling or house proper which occupies this site, and it, as we know, is composed of rooms, connecting spaces, and sometimes several levels—all of which therefore count as places-within-place.

There are, accordingly, three main types of boundary in relation to human habitation:[69] that which defines the location or place-at-large (the 'external' space, the outer boundary, the 'property line'), the locus or place of the dwelling itself, and the places-within-places which subdivide the dwelling and make it into a complex of 'internal' spaces.

Each of these kinds of boundary has its own distinctive mode of being remembered, and it would be too considerable a task to treat them here even summarily. Instead, I shall limit myself to two basic strands in the fabric of boundaries as they delimit place: to the dialectic of inside and outside which has already been initiated and to another factor to be designated as "horizoning." Each of these factors contributes, not just to the memory of place generally, but more particularly to the intrinsic *memorability* of places—those very places which we revealingly call "special places." For a special place is *eo ipso* a memorable place—a place not just worthy of being remembered but one we find ourselves remembering repeatedly, involuntarily, and with pronounced care, concern, or passion.

A. *Horizoning.* By this term I mean a particular aspect or effect of boundary which contributes significantly to the memory of place. Horizoning is constituted by the boundary's extremities, its beginning and end, as well as by its enclosing arc. Everyday instances are so commonplace as hardly to be noticed, e.g., in the form of front and back entrances to houses or compounds. Such entrances (which we shall analyze further below) are often festooned or otherwise ornamented to mark their importance as the beginning or ending of a journey, a meeting, a visit. Frequently, the initial moment is most stressed, as in Bernini's forecourt for St. Peter's or in the series of gateways to the Imperial Palace in the Forbidden City in Beijing.[70] In both cases the emphasis falls on the adequate preparation of the pilgrim for an uplifting experience within. In other instances, equal stress is placed on the moment of exiting, as at the Place Vendôme in Paris, where the circulation of traffic is a concern. Wherever the accent falls, the psychologic at work is evident: entrances and exits provide opportune points for greeting and parting—as well as for challenge, confrontation, or inspiration. Thus they are fraught with emotionality by their very positioning as strategic border-points in human habitation. And where emotion— which is to say, "heart"—is at stake, there remembering will be active: the link between *Gemüt* (heart or disposition) and memory (*Gedächtnis*) is profound.[71]

Beyond marking the heart-significant *topoi* of meaningful human interchange, the end-points of place-horizons may serve to commemorate the very act of building or dwelling itself. They signify to their viewers or participants that *here* human habitation—or at least human habitation of a special sort—began, and *there* it ends. In this way they demarcate a boundary as boundary *for*, or *of*, human habitation. But the full effect of horizoning involves the active role of the embracing arc between the end-points. This can occur in at least two ways.

(i) *External Horizon*.[72] The Greek word for boundary is *horismos*, also translatable as "horizon." Horizons, whether internal or external, open as well as limit; in their arc-like quality, they are also, like the human body itself, enclosing in nature.[73] A boundary qua horizon is, then, "not that at which something stops, but, as the Greeks recognized, the boundary is that from which something *begins its presencing*."[74]

An apt instance of specifically external horizoning is provided by John Ruskin in a description of a walk he once took in a pine forest in the Jura Mountains.

> It is a spot which has all the solemnity, with none of the savageness, of the Alps; where there is a sense of a great power beginning to be manifested in the earth, and of a deep and majestic concord in the rise of the long low lines of piny hills; the first utterance of those mighty mountain symphonies, soon to be more loudly lifted and wildly broken along the battlements of the Alps. But their strength is as yet restrained; and the far-reaching ridges of pastoral mountain succeed each other, like the long and sighing swell which moves over quiet waters from some far off stormy

sea. And there is a deep tenderness pervading that vast monotony. . . . It would be difficult to conceive a scene less dependent upon any other interest than that of its own secluded and serious beauty; but the writer well remembers the sudden blankness and chill which were cast upon it when he endeavoured, in order more strictly to arrive at the sources of its impressiveness, to imagine it, for a moment, [as] a scene in some aboriginal forest of the New Continent. The flowers in an instant lost their light, the river its music; the hills became oppressively desolate; a heaviness in the boughs of the darkened forest showed how much of their former power had been dependent upon a life which was not theirs, how much of the glory of the imperishable, or continually renewed, creation is reflected from things more precious in their memories than it, in its renewing. Those ever springing flowers, and ever flowing streams had been dyed by the deep colours of human endurance, valour, and virtue: and the crests of the sable hills that rose against the evening sky received a deeper worship, because their far shadows fell eastward over the iron wall of Joux, and the four-square keep of Granson.[75]

Here is a striking instance in which human habitation—operative at, and *as*, the boundary of a landscape—makes that very landscape, idyllic as it is in itself (I have omitted passages which sketch still more vividly its natural beauty), so remarkably memorable for Ruskin. The "iron wall of Joux" and the "four-square keep of Granson" serve as horizons for the scene, allowing it to presence (or rather to re-presence, since Ruskin is remembering the scene as he writes about it). They are in fact external horizons for what is being remembered, exercising their memorializing effect from a position of the outermost *peras* or border. As such, they de-limit from without, enclosing the scene remembered much as a frame might if the scene were to have been painted.

(ii) *Internal Horizon*. But the memorable effects of enclosing lived space can also occur in another way. An effective instance of this occurs in the basic layout of the seaport town of Stonington, Connecticut.[76]

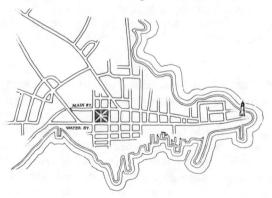

Here it is evident that the two main interior streets (quite appropriately called "Main" and "Water") furnish a double horizontal axis for the entire peninsular town, which stretches between the "Green" or park at its northern end and a lighthouse on its southern end. When one considers as well the charming eighteenth- and nineteenth-century buildings, the result is a most memorable place: for many, "it is remembered with fondness as a very special Place."[77] But just why is it so remembered? Certainly not only because of its buildings or its seaside location—both of which are to be found in abundance in other towns along the Connecticut coastline. Nor is it due primarily to two factors recently singled out in an insightful analysis of the town: its isolatedness and its various forms of uniqueness.[78] Much more crucial in my view is the role of Water and Main Streets in one's experience of the town as one walks through it or lives in it. These are genuine arteries of the city politic; on them life of the *polis*, commercial as well as residential, depends. For on them (or situated just off them) are found all the buildings and parcels of land that make up the landscape space of the village as a whole—its location as such. In particular, *from* these streets one can glimpse almost all the remaining parts of the town as well as the seascape beyond.[79] Thus, a critically determinative inner boundary (reinforced by its very doubleness)[80] gives access to outer boundaries found in the shoreline per se. The situation is the reverse of that described by Ruskin, for whom a landscape acquired memorability only by being bounded by the external horizon of human habitation—whereas now axially structuring lines of such habitation provide an internal horizon for the seascape beyond. In both cases, however, boundaries are genuinely disclosive or opening-up in character and make what Heidegger calls "presencing" (*Anwesen*) possible—a presencing which is at once spatial and temporal.[81] Boundaries, often themselves memorable (and made deliberately still more memorable by decoration or other forms of emphasis), make the places for which they serve as internal or external horizons memorable as well.[82]

B. *The Dialectic of Inside and Outside.* (i) At the level of location or place-at-large, boundaries can be opening or closing in character—opening out to embrace a still larger place (such as an entire countryside[83] or city) or closing in so as to close out contiguous places. The difference is that between an open lawn such as that which originally ran without interruption from Jefferson's University of Virginia buildings to the river below and the entirely walled-in yards of many houses of Mexican or Spanish origin. A mean between the two is often achieved by the use of marker objects such as bushes, trees, picket fences, or driveways. In these latter cases, an interchange between inside and outside is allowed and even encouraged: "good fences make good neighbors" precisely by permitting communication while preserving difference of domain. Indeed, the very concept of neighborhood (as of 'block,' 'street,' 'section,' 'town,' or 'ghetto') calls for boundaries between places-at-large which facilitate or prohibit the free exchange of those who find themselves inside or outside these boundaries.

Even when the place-at-large is as awe-inspiring and monumental as was Darius's sacred shrine at Persepolis, the Grand Stairway and Gate of All Nations through which one entered the vast compound were (unlike Hatshepsut's Pylon entrances in Egypt) mixtures of the inviting and the forbidding. The double Stairway, not overwhelming in its width of twenty-two feet, diverged outward in two directions and returned on itself toward the top—as if both to prepare for and to ease the moment of arrival, which was soon succeeded by the majestic Gate.[84] The latter was guarded by high walls whose bases contained colossal winged bulls facing those who were entering: the human faces of these bulls, however, lent an anthropomorphic touch to this outer boundary. Moreover, as a "Gate of *All Nations*," it generated an expectation that people of all sorts might be admitted into the spiritual domain within—as some ten thousand people did on various occasions—where the splendors of the Apadana of Xerxes, the Hall of a Hundred Columns, and the Palace of Darius himself awaited them. Here, in massive scale, the official outside for the inside allowed for a gradual and staged penetration of an inside which had its own complex insides.[85]

(ii) At the level of locus—when this is meaningfully distinguishable from place-at-large[86]—we often find, in miniaturized form, a similar drama at the doorways of houses: stairs upward or a stoop, perhaps a porch (which surrounds and protects the "front door," permitting people to linger near it), pediments over the door, and other ornaments around it (or on the door itself or its latch). We ought not to be surprised at all this liminology. Much as at Persepolis, others, sometimes strangers, are being admitted to a sanctum within through just this delicate point of transition between the inside and the outside. It is a break in the inner boundary which announces itself as such—which proclaims that it can be open or closed, or simply ajar.[87] Small wonder, then, that people cluster and congregate at front doors in moments of greeting (when the movement is from without in) and especially of parting (when the more difficult move back out is being made). It is a place of testing (as when we are confronted by a salesman seeking entry) or of savoring (e.g., of the evening just spent together within), of reticence (as when we are left speechless by the wholly unexpected arrival of a friend) or of recounting (when time allows for reminiscing about other places shared together). It is a poignant boundary-place where inside and outside, time and space meet and commingle, favoring spontaneous recol-lection—as must have been the case, in much grander scale, at Persepolis some twenty-five hundred years ago. All doorways, inner as well as outer (though especially the latter),[88] encourage us to pause and ponder, since they are at once beginning- and end-points of human habitation. Nowhere is the ambiguity of human existence in its spatial dimension—in its chiasmatic structure of inside and outside[89]—manifested more tellingly than at such liminal points:

How concrete everything becomes in the world of the spirit when an object, a mere door, can give images of hesitation, temptation, desire, security, welcome, and respect. If one were to give an account of all the doors one has closed and opened, of all the doors one would like to re-open, one would have to tell the story of one's entire life.[90]

The other critical components of the immediate boundary of the inhabited locus—occupied paradigmatically by the house—are walls, windows, and roofs. Walls and roofs are mainly enclosing for good practical reasons, though even here meaningful (if not strictly reciprocal) interchanges between inside and outside take place. Unless they are deliberately deceptive, both reveal much about the shape of a house's interior space and about its horizontal–vertical axiality. Roofs not only cap or clamp down, they point up and out whether by arches or gables; and they literally let the interior out through chimneys, and the exterior in through skylights. Walls jut *out* as well as close *in*—as is most evident in built-out bays and acute corners of houses—and may even be largely composed (as in Japanese domestic architecture) of screens. Frank Lloyd Wright has said in this connection:

My sense of "wall" was no longer the side of a box. It was enclosure of space affording protection against storm or heat only when needed. But it was also *to bring the outside world into the house and let the inside of the house go outside.* In this sense I was working away at the wall as a wall and bringing it towards the function of a screen, a means of opening up space which . . . would finally permit the free use of the whole space [of the house] without affecting the soundness of the structure.[91]

Windows, of course, literally "bring the outside world into the house and let the inside of the house go outside"—as Wright himself was well aware.[92] Curiously, the full significance of windows in this role was not realized until the Renaissance; they were notably absent from monumental Mesopotamian and Egyptian architecture.[93] Yet windows are in fact, as Giedion drily remarks, the "simplest means of communication between interior and exterior."[94] They let light and air and views into a house, and they transmit versions of these same things back outside. The traffic is two-way to such an extreme extent that (at least in the case of open-air windows and transparent glass) the outside seems literally to invade the inside and the inside to 'fly out the window.' Hence an explicable tendency on our part toward paranoid shade-pulling, which an artist of interior domesticity like Edward Hopper countermands by painting scenes seen through windows apparently without any glass whatsoever. The effect of such window-transparency is startling, yet only heightens what is already the case normally. Either (as in Hopper's *Room in New York* [1929]), we have the sense not merely of looking into a living room in which are positioned a married couple indifferent to each other's presence but also of being actively ushered into that very interior and being beside the couple; or (as in *New York Office* [1962]) someone depicted in an enormous street-level window seems not just to be seen there limpidly but somehow to be stepping out into the street itself. Hopper carries windowing as boundary-piercing to its limit, a limit at which the outside can just as easily transpose itself into the inside as the converse. As at doorways, but perhaps even more acutely here, memories are given a natural habitat, a point of attachment where they can abide indefinitely. It is above all at these two boundary points of the inhabited site that "memories are motionless, and the more securely they are fixed in space, the sounder they are."[95] It is difficult to imagine anything more manifestly motionless than human figures in a Hopper painting as they are seen through a window or at a doorway,[96] just as it is difficult (in modern representational art at least) to conceive of anything more memorable.

(iii) As we move into the last level—into the place of habitation itself, the house—we reach a kind of climax with regard to the issue of boundaries: like the felt inside of one's body, it is an inside of the inside and as such is the space of intimacy itself. What Wright calls "interior spaciousness"[97] is closely affiliated with what Bachelard calls "the being of within."[98] Bachelard is insistent on the non-confined space within a house; especially since this space is subject to daydream and revery (and is not only a scene of practical action), it can realize an "intimate immensity" in which there is a merging of space inside-the-house and space outside-the-house:

> . . . it is through their [respective] "immensity" that these two kinds of space—the space of intimacy and world space—blend. When human solitude deepens, then the two immensities touch and become identical.[99]

There is an essential expansiveness of the house—even as it contracts into enclosed spaces. If it is tempting to liken a house to a body or to a nest, shell, cell, or chrysalis, it is important to recognize that houses (like all works of architecture in this respect) are "means of extending inner order outwards."[100] How is this so? In answering this, we shall once more find a dialectics of the inside and outside at work—now in the very heart of human habitation.

I shall limit myself here to a discussion of just those features that favor memorability—that make houses as lived from within "one of the greatest powers of integration for the thoughts, memories, and dreams of mankind."[101] These features will be grouped under the two headings of directionality and roominess.

(a) *Directionality* inside houses has to do with movement actually allowed or at least suggested—and thus with enframing and facilitating de facto or virtual bodily motions. These motions are essentially tri-directional:

—*across*. Horizontal or transverse movements across or athwart rooms, halls, open living areas. It was just such movement that Wright (in his Prairie houses) and Mies van der Rohe (e.g., in his unrealized brick country house of 1923)[102] attempted to foster and free; here we have the sense of moving *through* a house—which may itself be a memorable event (e.g., when we are given a guided tour through a French château).

—*up/down*. This is the dimension of directionality missing in many apartments and ranch-style homes, much to the dismay of architecture theorists.[103] When "home has become horizontality,"[104] it is even questionable whether it can be regarded as a home any longer—at least as a fully memorable home, an "oneiric house"[105] in Bachelard's term. Two stories seem to constitute a psychical minimum, in addition to attic and basement, which often have their own diverse memorabilities by serving as top and bottom of the vertical axis of a house. We only remember going *up* into the attic and *down* into the basement as Bachelard observes;[106] but the body is engaged here less through motion per se than by its own upright posture, its "verticality"[107] as magnified in the house's own way of standing and staying up.

—*around/within*. This last directional feature includes what has been discussed above under the heading of "centerplace" (e.g., the hearth). It is what Bachelard calls the "concentric being" of a house, its "center of magnetic force";[108] but it is crucial to realize that this center need not be literal or one-of-a-kind. Not only may the interior of a house be polycentered for purposes of memory (as well as of domestic function), but some of the most likely such centers are not "central" in any obvious spatial sense. They may be refuges, redoubts, nooks—whatever serves as a "center of solitude,"[109] since it is often times of being alone with oneself in some cozy corner of the house that furnish the most memorable moments. It is just there that we are apt to enter the bemused or daydreaming state whose concomitant sense of well-being may be so memorable, especially in childhood.[110] We need to move around within a house—circulate in it—in order to find such special spots; we have to move *in* and *out* of rooms in our search for such a "zone of psychic protection":[111] here the dialectic of inside and outside is played out within the aegis of the house.

(b) *Roominess* refers to the disposition or layout of rooms within a house and to their own internal structure. Once more, several factors contribute to the overall boundary structure of inside/out. These may be memorable separately or in their conjoint action; but in every case it is a matter of "the essential qualities which give rooms a memorable sense of being special places to inhabit."[112] Among these qualities are the following:

—*internal shape*. What matters here is not the strict geometrical shape ("inhabited space," says Bachelard, "transcends geometrical space"[113]) but the lived sense of shape: how the floor, walls, and ceiling fit together into a total felt *Gestalt*, a Gestalt which we tend to name with such general adjectives as "spacious," "continuing," "squat," or "narrow," as well as such quasi-geometrical terms as "cube-like," "oval," or "rectangular." All of these shapes are matters of boundaries in a double sense—of the boundaries presented by the inner surfaces of the room itself and of those of our own body, either as it actually touches these surfaces or as it imaginatively projects itself into them (as in the Proustian narrator's projection into the domed ceiling of one of his childhood bedrooms).[114] The very role of the virtual body in the determination of felt shape makes it unlikely that there is any set number of perfectly proportioned rooms (Palladio thought there were seven such);[115] thanks to this role of the body, and to an active imagination as well, the shape of almost any room is expandable or contractible to suit our fancy or needs at the time.[116]

—*light/texture*. Light, being diffuse, may not itself be a boundary; but it is, along with internal shape, one of the most determinative factors in the constitution of boundaries in rooms; and its source, whether natural or artificial, is equally important in creating a sense of insideness versus outsideness. Where light falls, moreover, is definitive for the felt surface or texture: "what we mostly remember [in rooms] is not the light source itself, but the surfaces onto which the light falls: the polished floor, the casements, the wall."[117] Light both *has* direction (i.e., in its beaming and shining) and *gives* direction (i.e., in directing our gaze onto various objects in, or parts of, the room). Finally, light in rooms has varying quality—or value, intensity, even color—which affects our experiences of these rooms dramatically (and therefore our memories of them as well).[118]

—*focus/outlook*. Almost every inhabited room has yet another axis than that of simple three-dimensionality. This is an axis often determined as much by our personal or collective interests or purposes in being there as by the room's own structure. But it is powerfully effective in drawing out our attention in two disparate vectors. On the one hand, every room (even the barest prisoner's cell) has some focal point or several of them. This can be provided by a particular piece of furniture, e.g., the dining table in dining rooms, the television set in family rooms; by a set of objects such as a group of paintings or books; or by an inbuilt architectural feature, e.g., the fireplace in many living rooms or the ornamental niche or *tokonoma* in Japanese houses. When the focus is multiple, movement of the eye or body is more actively called for (as in Charles Moore's Stern house of 1970);[119] but however dynamic such movement may be, its primary orientation is *within* a room (or, as in the Stern house, within a long gallery): it is a matter, once more, of "concentric being." Outlook, on the other hand, takes our look or bodily movement *outside* the room, whether this is done by eaves, windows, doors, screens, or even heating fixtures (the clanking of a radiator tends to draw us down into its source in the furnace). The "picture window" is doubtless the epitome of the outlook, for it frames the outdoors from indoors, practically forcing our view outward (no wonder that the picture is often made less compelling by the strategic addition of curtains, ready to be drawn at any moment!); it is to be contrasted with the much more subtle 'inlooks' afforded by interior gardens in Japanese homes[120] and by discreetly placed bay windows in many Western homes.

In sum, roominess consists in being "fixed in space by [internal shape] . . . animated by light [and texture], organized by focus, and then liberated by outlook."[121] As in the case of directionality, it embodies an active dialectical relationship of inside and outside.

V

At all three of the main levels of inhabited place—location or place-at-large, locus, and place-within-place—we have found a dynamic dialectic of inside and outside, an interchange between what is *en deçà* and what is *au delà* of a given boundary. Whether at the micro-level of the room or at the macro-level of an entire settlement, there is a constant crossing-over of light, persons, looks, and movements as that which is inside traverses the outside and vice versa. Nor is such reciprocal traversal limited—as my analysis might imply—to transitions within a single level or between two contiguous levels. It can go from the most intimate interior nook to the most expansive public space, and often does so in one continuous leap. Such a leap is described by Robert Duncan in his "Tribal Memories":

> . . . the poet's voice speaks from no
>   crevice in the ground between
>   mid-earth and underworld
> breathing fumes of what is deadly to know,
>   news larvae in tombs
>   and twists of time do feed upon,
>
>   but from the hearth stone, the lamp light,
>   the heart of the matter where the
>
>   house is held

> yet here, the warning light at the edge of the town!
> the City will go out in time, will go out
> into time, hiding even its embers.[122]

From the hearth to the edge of the town is a considerable distance, not just in geographic space but in landscape terms as well; it is a removal from a paradigm of place-within-place (the hearth, as we have seen, is the centermost central place) to the very limit of a place-at-large: the 'city-limit.' And yet, thanks to the dialectic of lived space, such an objective distancing is, both for the poet and for the inhabitants (the "tribes")[123] of the city he writes about, an experience of de-distancing, a "nearing nearness" as Heidegger calls it.[124] Such *nähernde Nähe* is achievable in human inhabited space by the interplay of inside and outside in the various ways which have been sketched out in the preceding pages.

This interplay is itself an instance of a still more encompassing dialectic which would ultimately include space and time themselves—no longer pitted against each other in a *Gigantomachia* but realizing a mutual mirrorplay or round-dance.[125] This is what happens in Duncan's poem, where the spatial move from hearth to edge of town is immediately succeeded by complementary actions of the City's going out in time and going into time as well.

There are many more names for this most embracing dialectic, which Heidegger might call "*Ereignis*" and Derrida "*Différance*." My own preference lies with Merleau-Ponty's notion of "intertwining" (*entrelacs*), for it is remarkably descriptive of the experience of inhabited space and in particular of the interplay between inside and outside. Briefly stated: intertwining is the accomplishment of "an intercorporeal being, a presumptive domain of the visible and the tangible, which extends further than the things I touch and see at present."[126] Not only are the visible and the tangible experienced in intertwining in a more than literally seen and touched way—as they are in architecture, where the virtual body makes just such an extension possible—but they are themselves intertwined, and thus become reciprocal or "reversible" in relation to each other (much as space *and* time become space-time for Heidegger and Einstein):[127]

> There is a circle of the touched and the touching, the touched takes hold of the touching; there is a circle of the visible and the seeing, the seeing is not without visible existence; *there is even an inscription of the touching in the visible, of the seeing in the tangible—and the converse.* . . .[128]

Merleau-Ponty calls this reversibility of touching and seeing—as of any such intimately fused terms—"chiasm," a simultaneous holding and being-held of juxtaposed things.[129] Chiasm is the very action, the critical moment, of interlacing: "the heart of the matter where the house is held." Houses, and other places of inhabitation, display precisely the chiasmatic-interlacing property of being or having holds on us (hence the root *habere,* to have, of 'in-habit') while we hold them—hold onto them by seeing and touching them throughout, and hold them together by living in them and thereby constituting them as units of habitation. In human habitation, the hold is indeed held: held fast within and without the habitual body and its habitat. The chiasmatic axis of inhabitation, then, is just that of inside and outside regarded as boundaries of human dwelling (*habitare* is 'to dwell'). These boundaries bind by an intrinsically memorable holding action. They hold the held together not only in dwelled-in space exterior to the body of the inhabitant but in the felt space within that body as well. This body, beyond being a body of customary and virtual action, is a body with its own experienced insideness—as is seen most readily in the way in which we can touch ourselves touching.[130] It can be argued, moreover, that the haptic sense is the most fundamental sensory system in the experience of architecture—even more crucial than sight.[131] If so, then the inside-outside relation can be seen to have a specifically bodily basis in the chiasmatic relation of touch/touching—which is to say, in all fully palpating sensory experience:

> The very pulp of the sensible, what is indefinable in it, is nothing other than the union in it of the "inside" with the "outside", the contact in thickness of self with self. . . .[132]

What this means most concretely is that in my own bodily self-experience of touch I realize that I am at once an inside (a *touched* who is doing the touching) and an outside (who touches some material surface, whether it be that of a chair, a wall, or my own flesh). This intertwining of inside/outsideness is not self-contained but "dehiscent";[133] and it corresponds to a like dehiscence in the horizoned/horizoning world about me, which has its inside and outside, especially in the form of human habitations constructed in accordance with a double dialectic of the out and the in, the in and the out. In fact, we have to do with a complex chiasmatic situation in which two reversible inside/outs—bodily and built respectively—intertwine:

> chiasm [of] my body—the things, realized by the doubling up of my body into inside and outside [paradigmatically through touch]—and the doubling up of the things (their inside and their outside).

> It is because there are these 2 doublings-up that are possible: the insertion of the world between the two leaves of my body [and] the insertion of my body between the 2 leaves of each thing and of the world [which would include, par excellence, habitations in the world]. . . .

> Start from this: there is not identity, nor non-identity, or non-coincidence, there is inside and outside turning about one another.[134]

We may not get all the way to the structure of Being—which is where Merleau-Ponty, as much as Heidegger, wishes to take us[135]—but a doubly chiasmatic movement of inside and outside will certainly take us into inhabited being. Houses and other habitations are held within-without and without-within, and the more closely they are thus interlaced the more memorable they will be. If architecture is indeed "the making of places,"[136] its true accomplishment, its very perfection, lies in the making of memorable places—whether these be locations, loci, or places-within-places. And places are made memorable mainly by their Laresian virtues as boundaries: by providing the horizons of a given scene (seen or traversed) or, more completely, by furnishing the double borderlining of bodily and built inside-outsideness, their intimate interleaving.

John Ruskin wrote in *The Seven Lamps of Architecture* (one lamp of which is precisely "Memory"): "Architecture is to be regarded by us with the most serious thought. We may live without her, and worship without her, but we cannot remember without her."[137] Ruskin was right—perhaps righter than he realized. The richest remembering is remembering of place, and the places most ready to be remembered—*made* to be remembered if well-made at all—are the dwellings, the inworks and outworks in terms of whose horizons we live our inside-out, outside-in lives. Remembering thus at the boundaries of built places, we remember ourselves in place: we attain an abiding implacement of body and soul.

1.   Cf. Frances Yates, *The Art of Memory* (London: Routledge and Kegan Paul, 1966), esp. chap. 1–3.

2.   See Aristotle, *Physics* IV, chap. 1–5.

3.   On landscape versus geography, see Erwin Straus, *The Primary World of Senses*, trans. J. Needleman (Glencoe, Ill.: Free Press, 1963), pp. 318–23. *Ort* means 'place,' 'location.'

4.   Stratton's classic 'inverted room' experiments are discussed by Maurice Merleau-Ponty in *Phenomenology of Perception,* trans. C. Smith (New York: Humanities Press, 1962), pp. 244–48.

5.   Wertheimer's experiments, in which subjects perceive a room through a mirror slanted at forty-five degrees from the vertical, are analyzed at ibid., pp. 248–51.

6.   "What counts for the orientation of the spectacle is not my body as it in fact is, as a thing in objective space, but as a system of possible actions, a virtual body with its phenomenal 'place' defined by its task and situation. . . . As soon as Wertheimer's subject takes his place in the experimental situation prepared for him, the area of his possible actions . . . outlines in front of him, even if he has his eyes shut, a possible habitat" (ibid., p. 250). So too with the bedroom spectacle we have been examining.

7.   Perhaps this is why waterbeds can be at once so disconcerting and intriguing.

8.   As Merleau-Ponty says, spatial level "makes its appearance where my motor intentions and my perceptual field join forces, when my actual body is at one with the virtual body required by the spectacle [and] with the setting which my body throws round it" (*Phenomenology of Perception,* p. 250). Establishing spatial level is thus one basic way in which my body becomes "geared to the world" (ibid.).

9.   It is noteworthy that Merleau-Ponty vacillates as to which is more basic—spatial level or orientation: at first, the body's orientation is said to be received from "the general

level of experience" (*Phenomenology of Perception*, p. 249); then, however, the body is said to "play an essential part in the establishment of a level" (ibid.). Perhaps we should say that they are coeval and co-constitutive factors in lived space.

10.   "Our bodily experience of movement is not a particular case of knowledge; it provides us with a way of access to the world and the object, with a 'praktagnosia' " (ibid., p. 140).

11.   Henri Bergson, *Matter and Memory,* trans. W. S. Palmer (New York: Doubleday, 1959), p. 145. Bergson underlines "place of passage."

12.   It is of interest that Husserl makes kinesthesis an essential element of his doctrine of the human psyche—in criticism, for instance, of Kant's antiseptic notion of mind. Cf. *The Crisis of the European Sciences,* trans. D. Carr (Evanston: Northwestern University Press, 1970), pp. 103–14.

13.   "Indifferent space" (in contrast with "sympathetic space") is discussed by Erwin Straus in *The Primary World of Senses,* pp. 387–90.

14.   For this distinction, see Merleau-Ponty, *Phenomenology of Perception,* p. 244.

15.   Marcel Proust, *Swann's Way,* trans. C. K. Scott Moncrieff (New York: Random House, 1970), pp. 5–7.

16.   Thus Proust describes himself awakening as being "in a state of darkness, pleasant and restful enough for the eyes, and even more, perhaps for my mind, to which it appeared incomprehensible, without a cause, a matter dark indeed" (ibid., p. 3).

17.   Only just before Proust has indicated why time is an inappropriate parameter for this situation: "when a man is asleep, he has in a circle around him the chain of the hours, the sequence of the years, the order of the heavenly host. Instinctively, when he awakes, he looks to these, and in an instant reads off his own position on the earth's surface and the amount of time that has elapsed during his slumbers; *but this ordered procession is apt to grow confused,* and to break its ranks" (*Swann's Way,* p. 4; my italics). Time, in other words, is not sufficiently stable to orient oneself in the disoriented situation of awakening; its structural units (hours, years), even when in orderly progression, cannot contain or withstand the confusion. Place alone, as the passage we are examining above intimates, is capable of realizing this containing role in an effective way.

18.   On the significance of place-names, see Proust's own treatment under the title "Place-Names: The Place," in *Within a Budding Grove,* trans. C. K. S. Moncrieff (New York: Random House, 1970), pp. 158 ff.

19.   Proust explicitly envisages the formation of a quasi-permanent body memory based on a single experience: "the path that [a lonely traveler] followed [was] fixed forever in his memory by the general excitement *due to being in a strange place,* to doing unusual things, to the last words of conversation. . ." (*Within a Budding Grove,* p. 3; my italics).

20.   For further on bodily memory see ibid., pp. 289–91.

21.   For it is in indifferent, objectified space that the queer "look" of perceived things belongs. On this point, see Straus's discussion of vision as an essentially distancing and distanced sense in *Primary World of Senses,* pp. 367–86.

22.   Proust, *Swann's Way,* p. 7; my italics.

23.   Cf. Merleau-Ponty, *Phenomenology of Perception,* p. 82.

24.   "For a knowledge of intimacy, localization in the spaces of our remembered intimacy is more urgent than determination of dates" (Gaston Bachelard, *The Poetics of Space,* trans. M. Jolas [New York: Orion Press, 1964], p. 9).

25.   Proust, *Swann's Way,* p. 7.

26.   Ibid.

27.   Merleau-Ponty, *Phenomenology of Perception,* p. 203. Even if I attempt to take a "mental bird's eye view" of my apartment, "the mediation of bodily experience" (ibid.) remains essential.

28.   Level can be considered the basis for distinctions of top and bottom, right and left, and even depth and size—but, significantly, not for inside and outside. Cf. Merleau-Ponty, *Phenomenology of Perception,* p. 266. It is also noteworthy that the differentiation between inside and outside does not require the body as a *center* of action or orientation, unlike the

other distinctions just mentioned, each of which calls for the body as a central term *between* the terms distinguished.

29.   Merleau-Ponty, *Phenomenology of Perception*, p. 204.

30.   Merleau-Ponty speaks of a *réplique* in this connection: ibid., p. 205.

31.   For a discussion of aediculae, see John Summerson, *Heavenly Mansions* (New York: Norton, 1963), chap. 1. The aediculae continues to be utilized in contemporary architecture, e.g., in the work of Charles Moore. See Charles Moore, Gerald Allen, and Donlyn Lyndon, *The Place of Houses* (New York: Holt, Rinehart & Winston, 1974), pp. 50–55 (the Jobson house) and pp. 60–62 (Moore's own Orinda house).

32.   This character has been analyzed by Bachelard in *The Poetics of Space,* esp. chap. 1–2; and by Kent Bloomer and Charles Moore, *Body, Memory, and Architecture* (New Haven: Yale University Press, 1977), pp. 2–5, 46–49. As will become evident, I am deeply indebted to both of these seminal works.

33.   ". . . our house is our corner of the world. As has often been said, it is our first universe, a real cosmos in every sense of the word" (*The Poetics of Space*, p. 4).

34.   This is no doubt why early childhood memories are so often placed in houses— especially when one looks back to an entire epoch: the enlarged temporal matrix is matched by the enlarged spatial *situs.*

35.   Bloomer and Moore, *Body, Memory, and Architecture,* pp. 1–2; their italics. Compare the following lines from R. M. Rilke: "House, patch of meadow, oh evening light / Suddenly you acquire an almost human face / You are very near us, embracing and embraced" (cited by Bachelard in *The Poetics of Space*, p. 8).

36.   Bloomer and Moore, *Body, Memory, and Architecture*, p. 51. Cf. also pp. 46–49.

37.   This is why Bergson considers the body as a certain collection of images within the world viewed as a vast collection of images. See *Matter and Memory*, chap. 1.

38.   Moore, Allen, and Lyndon, *The Place of Houses*, p. vii.

39.   Ibid., p. 49.

40.   On miniaturization, see ibid., pp. 66–67, 125, 143–44; and for a more general treatment, cf. Bachelard, *The Poetics of Space*, chap. 7–8.

41.   This is so even when ordinary recollective memory is defective or lacking: 'H.M.,' the much-analyzed epileptic with severe memory loss, could still find his way around his home and neighborhood even though his powers of acquiring new memories were virtually nonexistent: much as we can find our way about our houses when sleepwalking. (On H.M., see B. Milner, "Memory and the Medial Temporal Regions of the Brain," in K. H. Pribram and D. E. Broadbent, eds., *Biology of Memory* [New York: Academic Press, 1970], pp. 29–50.)

42.   Bachelard relates this role of the house precisely to its enclosing character: "something closed must retain our memories, while leaving them their original value as images" (*The Poetics of Space*, p. 6).

43.   Henry Mercer's 'Fonthill' (in Doylestown, Pennsylvania) "drew specifically upon [Mercer's] recollections of shapes and details in other buildings which he had admired during his travels. . . . For Mercer himself each reference was quite specific, recalling for instance a particular afternoon in Salonika" (Moore et al., *The Place of Houses*, p. 132).

44.   On the significance of such heirlooms as virtual "icons," see Bloomer and Moore, *Body, Memory, and Architecture*, p. 51.

45.   Concerning this point, see Moore et al., *The Place of Houses*, pp. 61, 64.

46.   Bloomer and Moore, *Body, Memory, and Architecture*, p. 51. Notice that in this case a Bachelardian "material imagination" plays a memorializing role.

47.   Bachelard, *The Poetics of Space*, p. 14.

48.   Moore et al., *The Place of Houses*, p. 50. Thus the room would be a place within a place within a place!

49.   Bloomer and Moore, *Body, Memory, and Architecture*, p. 51.

50.   This term is applied to the lived body by Merleau-Ponty in *Phenomenology of Perception*, p. 98.

51. The body provides "that gearing of the subject to his world which is the origin of space" (ibid., p. 251).

52. On the body as anchoring, see ibid., pp. 144, 249.

53. Walter F. Otto, *Dionysus: Myth and Cult,* trans. R. B. Palmer (Bloomington: Indiana University Press, 1973; rept., Dallas: Spring Publications, Inc., 1981), p. 9.

54. Walter F. Otto, *The Homeric Gods,* trans. Moses Hadas (Thames and Hudson: London, n.d.), p. 117.

55. Rafael López-Pedraza, *Hermes and His Children* (Spring Publications, 1977), p. 8.

56. Otto, *Dionysus,* p. 9.

57. "The marvelous and mysterious [quality] which is peculiar to night may also appear by day as a sudden darkening or an enigmatic smile. This mystery of night seen by day, this magic darkness in the bright sunlight, is the realm of Hermes, whom, in later ages, magic with good reason revered as its master" (Otto, *The Homeric Gods,* pp. 117–18).

58. On this point, see Carl Kerényi, *The Religion of the Greeks and the Romans* (New York: Dutton, 1962), p. 266.

59. This last theme is developed discerningly by López-Pedraza in his *Hermes and His Children,* passim.

60. See Karl Jaspers, *Philosophy,* trans. E. B. Ashton (Chicago: University of Chicago Press, 1970), II, pp. 177–222.

61. In these festivals, holes were first prepared with the blood of sacrificial animals, honey, wine, incense, and products of the fields and then filled with a stone covered with oil and strewn with flowers and ribbons. Anyone who would pull up this stone after its dedications became cursed and subject to the threat of death.

62. On Terminus himself, see H. S. Robinson and K. Wilson, *Myths and Legends of All Nations* (New York: Garden City Publishing Co., 1950), p. 137.

63. See *Larousse Encyclopedia of Mythology* (New York: Prometheus, 1950), p. 226. The affiliated penates protected the welfare and property of the family and especially of the state (hence the phrase '*penates populi romani*').

64. The term is Bachelard's in *The Poetics of Space,* pp. xxxii, 8, 10.

65. "The Genius was the anonymous deity who protected all groups of people and the places of their group activities. The number of genii was unlimited. . . . Every corporation had its Genius, as well as every house, gate, street, and so on" (*Larousse Encyclopedia,* p. 226).

66. As in the case of Pylon VIII of Hatshepsut's Ramessides temple: see Siegfried Giedion, *The Eternal Present: The Beginnings of Architecture* (New York: Pantheon, 1964), pp. 376–77, where it is claimed that the common people were never admitted beyond the narrow entrance gate of this imposing pylon that marks the temple's outer boundary.

67. See ibid., pp. 20, 125–8, 234, esp. p. 126: "these *kudurru* are in the shape of the boulders that lie scattered over the highlands of Kurdistan whence the Kassites had come. They are often considered boundary stones which guaranteed property rights. Contenau, however, states that 'they are the authentic deeds, documents, which were never placed in the fields . . . but in the temples in the custody of the gods'. "

68. Cf. ibid., pp. 178 ff., esp. p. 179; it is highly probable that "the starting point for the house was provided by the form of its dwelling area rather than the shape of its roof."

69. By saying "human habitation" I leave open the question of whether the activities realized therein are domestic (matters of "living") or work-oriented. Nevertheless, my entire analysis has tended to make the house qua home a privileged place of habitation.

70. These two examples are analyzed along somewhat different lines in Bloomer and Moore, *Body, Memory, and Architecture,* pp. 92 and 77–78 respectively.

71. " 'Memory' initially did not at all mean the power to recall. The word designated the whole disposition (*Gemüt*) in the sense of a steadfast intimate concentration upon the things that essentially speak to us in every thoughtful meditation" (Martin Heidegger, *What Is Called Thinking?,* trans. J. Glenn Gray [New York: Harper & Row, 1968], p. 140). Cf. also ibid., pp. 139, 141, 144, 148, 150.

72.   For the distinction between internal and external horizons, see Edmund Husserl, *Experience and Judgment,* trans. K. Ameriks and J. Churchill (Evanston: Northwestern University Press, 1973), pp. 149 ff.

73.   On the body as enclosure, see Maurice Merleau-Ponty, *The Visible and the Invisible,* trans. A. Lingus (Evanston: Northwestern University Press, 1968), pp. 263 and 271. The latter passage explicitly links the horizontality of the perceived world to the body as enclosure.

74.   Martin Heidegger, "Building Dwelling Thinking" in his *Poetry, Language, and Thought,* trans. A. Hofstadter (New York: Harper & Row, 1971), p. 154; his italics.

75.   John Ruskin, *The Seven Lamps of Architecture* (London: Dent, 1956), pp. 180–81.

76.   I adapt the layout below from *Body, Memory, and Architecture,* p. 111. Bloomer and Moore discuss Stonington movingly at ibid., pp. 111–14.

77.   Ibid., p. 111.

78.   Cf. ibid.: "the sense of isolation from the rest of the world, both in time and geographic place, is vital to the memorability of this village"; and p. 114: "[Stonington] has only one center or heart, one main commercial street, one point, one lighthouse. This property of things being unique confers special importance on very modest places."

79.   As Bloomer and Moore themselves say, from Main Street alone "one can experience virtually all the edges of the town. . . . The peninsula crests on a line approximately defined by the Main Street / Water Street circuit so that all streets slide down toward the water, affording easy views and comfortable movement to the shore" (*Body, Memory, and Architecture,* p. 112).

80.   The significance of doubling in relation to inside /outside phenomena will be explored below. Bloomer and Moore point to "the sense of inside versus outside that pervades movement through the town" (*Body, Memory, and Architecture,* p. 113).

81.   This role of *Anwesen* is developed in Heidegger's "Time and Being," in *On Time and Being,* trans. J. Stambaugh (New York: Harper & Row, 1972), pp. 14 ff.

82.   The example of Stonington brings with it yet another dimension of memorability: what can be called the 'alpha-omega effect.' This was already implicit in the introductory remarks above concerning the special significance of end-points in horizoning. However, the beginning and end of a given place often possess an inherent memorability which is independent of the emotional value they absorb from connotations of arriving and departing. This memorability arises from the sheer fact of two extremities of a given horizonal arc— e.g., the Green and the lighthouse at Stonington—being in an initial and terminal position with respect to traversing the arc in a particular direction. Following such a traversal, one will often remember vividly both the beginning and the ending of the sojourn, while many intermediate points will be remembered only dimly. Such a result is importantly parallel to what are termed "primacy" and "recency" effects in serial list recollection experiments undertaken by cognitive psychologists. For any given list of items—words, colors, sounds, etc.— and at whatever rate these items are presented, there is a pronounced tendency on "free recall" (i.e., on being asked to recall what has just been presented, not necessarily in order) to remember the last-exhibited items best ("recency"), followed closely by those first-exhibited ("primacy"), whereas those in between are least well recalled. For a discussion of these temporal analogues to the alpha-omega effect in space, see Robert G. Crowder, *Principles of Learning and Memory* (Hillsdale, N.J.: Erlbaum, 1976), pp. 136, 140–41, 146–50, 453 ff.

83.   The most dramatic and carefully conceived cases of this occur in certain Greek temples (e.g., Delphi, Paestum, the Acropolis) as Vincent Scully has demonstrated convincingly in *The Earth, the Temple, and the Gods* (Praeger: New York, 1969). According to Scully, such temples "created an exterior environment . . . that was wider, freer, and more complete than other architectures have encompassed" (p. 1). This "exterior environment" included hills, mountains, and there was also a special site within which the temple was set: the "holy place," which, "before the temple was built upon it, embodied the whole of the deity as a recognized natural force" (ibid.).

84.   For a remarkably similar but still more monumental divergent-*cum*-convergent ceremonial stairway, see Bramante's stairway to the Cortile del Belvedere (Rome, 1537–41)

as discussed by Siegfried Giedion in *Space, Time, and Architecture* (Cambridge: Harvard University Press, 1954), pp. 64 ff.

85. Ziggurats also encouraged gradual approaches, but in their case there was no meaningful inside. Buddhist stupas, like Persepolis, but on a much more concentric pattern (e.g., as at Borobodur), combine both features. On Persepolis, see A. U. Pope, *Persian Architecture* (New York: Brazilier, 1965), pp. 23–43.

86. Cases where it is not include many medieval fortresses, dwellings in crowded European towns, and modern apartment buildings.

87. Bachelard regards the "just barely ajar" position as the most suitable for revery: see *The Poetics of Space*, p. 222.

88. "Front doors and their surroundings are important landmarks for visitors. The lavish attention that has been spent on entry places in all forms of architecture attests to the importance of the territorial distinction between inside and out. The point of transition between the two has persistently been used as a spot where information is conveyed about the building and its purpose" (Moore et al., *The Place of Houses*, pp. 214–15).

89. For Merleau-Ponty's understanding of chiasm as "reversibility" of juxtaposed terms (e.g., inside / outside), see *The Visible and the Invisible*, p. 266.

90. Bachelard, *The Poetics of Space*, p. 224.

91. Frank Lloyd Wright, *The Natural House* (New York: Horizon Press, 1954), p. 38; my italics.

92. Ibid. Windows in Wright's houses "would sometimes be wrapped around the building corners as [an] inside emphasis of plasticity and to increase the sense of interior space. I fought for outswinging windows . . . [which] have free openings outward" (ibid., p. 40).

93. Cf. Giedion, *Space, Time, and Architecture*, pp. 50–58.

94. Giedion, *The Eternal Present*, p. 523. The hollowed-out, interior space of which windows are the natural expression is itself a relative latecomer in architecture whose first complete realization occurred in Hadrian's Pantheon at the beginning of the second century A.D., inaugurating what Giedion calls "the second architectural space conception" (pp. 523–25).

95. Bachelard, *The Poetics of Space*, p. 9.

96. Two striking examples of this latter situation are to be found in Hopper's "High Noon" (1949) and "Carolina Morning" (1955).

97. Wright, *The Natural House*, p. 40.

98. Bachelard, *The Poetics of Space*, p. 7: "within the being, in the being of within, an enveloping warmth welcomes being."

99. Ibid., p. 203. Cf. all of chap. 8, "Intimate Immensity."

100. Bloomer and Moore, *Body, Memory, and Architecture*, p. 77. See also pp. 94 and 100.

101. Bachelard, *The Poetics of Space*, p. 6. Cf. also p. 8: "thanks to the house, a great many of our memories are housed."

102. For a discussion of this project, see Moore et al., *The Place of Houses*, pp. 79–81. On pp. 77–78 of ibid. there is a treatment of Wright's 1902 Willitts House from this point of view.

103. Among them Bloomer and Moore at *Body, Memory, and Architecture*, pp. 105 ff. and Bachelard in *The Poetics of Space*, pp. 26–29 (regretting his own apartment at the Place Maubert: "in Paris there are no houses, and the inhabitants of the big city lived in superimposed boxes" [p. 26]). Apartments and houses are, however, both forms of what I call "dwelling."

104. Bachelard, *The Poetics of Space*, p. 27.

105. Ibid., p. 25 et seq.

106. Ibid., pp. 25–26. While attics typically are storehouses of dusty family memorabilia, basements provide "the intimate space of underground manoeuvers" (ibid., p. 22).

107. For the general, even ontological significance of verticality, see Merleau-Ponty, *The Visible and the Invisible*, pp. 235, 271–72.

108. Bachelard, *The Poetics of Space*, pp. 29 ff. Cf. also Stephanie A. Demetrakopoulos, "Hestia, Goddess of the Hearth," *Spring 1979*: 55–75.

109. Bachelard, *The Poetics of Space*, p. 32.

110. On this last theme—that it is the daydreaming as re-daydreaming in memory, not the explicit recollection of events taking place in houses, which is critical in memories of early childhood—see ibid., pp. 6, 8, 10, 14–16, 26, etc.

111. Ibid., p. 31.

112. Moore et al., *The Place of Houses*, p. 82. I am especially indebted to this book for the following analysis, even though I cannot agree with the authors' general definition of rooms as *"unspecific spaces*, empty stages for human action, where we perform the rituals and improvisations of living" (ibid.; their italics).

113. Bachelard, *The Poetics of Space*, p. 47. Cf. also pp. 48, 51, 61, and my earlier remarks on geographic versus landscape space.

114. "The vertical dimensions of rooms, since they are relatively free from 'functional' imperatives, are able to carry more than their share of emotional content" (*The Place of Houses*, p. 91). Cf. Proust, *Swann's Way*, p. 7.

115. Cf. Moore et al., *The Place of Houses*, pp. 85–87.

116. Bachelard cites René Char's line in which the poet is in "a room that grew buoyant and, little by little, expanded into the vast stretches of travel" (*The Poetics of Space*, p. 54). This is itself only an instance of Bachelard's general rule that "the house, even when reproduced from the outside, bespeaks intimacy" (p. 72).

117. Moore et al., *The Place of Houses*, p. 96.

118. "The qualities of light—soft, sharp, pellucid, or crystalline—stay vividly in our minds" (ibid., p. 97). Proust remarks that "difference of lighting modifies no less the orientation of a place, constructs no less before our eyes new goals which it inspires in us the yearning to attain, than would a distance in space actually traversed in the course of a long journey" (*Within a Budding Grove*, p. 183).

119. For a discussion of the Stern house, see Moore et al., *The Place of Houses*, pp. 99–102.

120. An example of this latter is given in Plate 45 of ibid., p. 103. For the authors' own analysis of picture windows as forms of self-exposure, see ibid., p. 107.

121. Moore et al., *The Place of Houses*, p. 82.

122. Robert Duncan, *Bending the Bow* (New York: New Directions, 1968), pp. 9–10.

123. Duncan's poem begins with these lines: "And to Her-Without-Bounds I send,/wherever she wanders, by what/campfire at evening/among tribes setting each the City where/we Her people are/at end of a day's reaches. . . ." "Her" refers to Attis, Mother of the Gods, but also to Mnemosyne, "the Mother with the whispering feathered wings" (ibid., p. 10).

124. For Heidegger's account of de-distancing (*ent-fernen*), see *Being and Time*, trans. F. Macquarrie and E. Robinson (New York: Harper & Row, 1962), sec. 70. On "the nearing of the near," see "Time and Being," pp. 15 ff.

125. On this last theme, see Heidegger, "Time and Being," pp. 14–17; and *Poetry, Language, Thought*, pp. 174 ff.

126. Merleau-Ponty, *The Visible and the Invisible*, p. 143.

127. Heidegger prefers to speak of "time-space" (*Zeitraum*): cf. "Time and Being," pp. 14 ff.

128. Merleau-Ponty, *The Visible and the Invisible*, p. 143; my italics.

129. "The idea of *chiasm*, that is: every relation with being is *simultaneously* a taking and a being taken, the hold is held, it is inscribed in the same being that it takes hold of" (ibid., p. 266; his italics). Compare Heidegger: "what keeps us in our essential nature holds us only so long, however, as we for our part keep holding on to what holds us. And we keep holding on to it by not letting it out of our memory" (*What Is Called Thinking?*, p. 3; cf. also p. 151).

130. Merleau-Ponty stresses this in *The Visible and the Invisible*, e.g., pp. 140 ff., and esp. p. 255: "to touch is to touch oneself. . . . The touching oneself and the touching have to be understood as each the reverse of the other." Thus touch presents us with a bodily paradigm of chiasm.

131.   This is the position of Bloomer and Moore in *Body, Memory, and Architecture,* chap. 4–5.

132.   *The Visible and the Invisible,* p. 268. Elsewhere in this book, Merleau-Ponty calls this "pulp of the sensible" *"flesh,"* as when he writes: "the flesh = the fact that the visible that I am is seer (look) or, what amounts to the same thing, has an *inside,* plus the fact that the exterior visible is also *seen,* i.e., has a prolongation, in the enclosure of my body, which is part of its being" (p. 271; his italics). But there is also a "flesh of the world" composed of its internal and external horizons: cf. pp. 267, 271.

133.   On dehiscence, see ibid., p. 265 inter alia.

134.   Ibid., p. 264.

135.   "This is not anthropologism: by studying the two leaves [of each body and of the world] we ought to find the structure of being" (ibid., p. 264).

136.   Bloomer and Moore, *Body, Memory, and Architecture,* p. 105.

137.   Ruskin, *The Seven Lamps of Architecture,* p. 182.

SOUL IN TIME AND PLACE

Time out of Mind

*Philosophical thinking is . . . far less a discovery
than a recognition, a remembering, a return, and
a homecoming to a remote, primordial, and inclusive household of the soul.*
　　　　　　　　　—FRIEDRICH NIETZSCHE
　　　　　　　　　Beyond Good and Evil

I

AS IF ANTICIPATING Jungian typologies, Western philosophers have
often espoused a fourfold classification of mental activities or faculties.
Although the exact constitution of this *quadrivium* of mind differs from
philosopher to philosopher, there is a marked tendency from Aristotle onward to focus on four crucial members: thought (in its various guises as
intellect, reason, understanding, etc.); perception (sensation, sensory experience of various kinds); imagination (entertaining mental images,
projecting the possible); and memory (retention, recollection, recall). Why
these four? Beyond their sweepingly synoptic character when taken together,
the four activities in question have the economic advantage of forming two
pairs of terms in each of which there is a compensatory or reciprocal relationship. Thus *thought* and *perception* fall together insofar as what perception gives (i.e., concrete sensory "data") thought lacks, and what thought
supplies (i.e., categories, concepts) perception does not possess: "thoughts
without [sensory] contents are empty, intuitions without concepts are blind"
(Kant, *Critique of Pure Reason*, B 76). Similarly, *imagination* and *memory*
belong together by virtue of the fact that memory looks backward toward
what has been, while imagination looks forward toward what might be.
Such retrospection and prospection complement each other by their very
disparateness of directionality.

Philosophers have stressed the importance of the first pair of terms in the context of strictly epistemological questions (the paradigmatic case is that of Kant), whereas the second dyad is singled out in the pursuit of pure description or phenomenology (the paradigm here is Husserl). But we may bring the two pairs together by considering them as forming perpendicular axes in the following fashion:

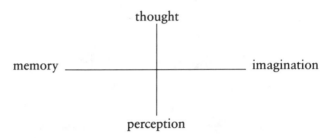

What this simple schema brings to awareness—an awareness which is no less certain for being almost wholly intuitive—is the way in which the two pairs of acts in question relate to the dual dimensionality of *temporality* or time-as-experienced by human beings. (i) First, the vertical axis un-equivocally signifies the *synchronic* dimension of temporality—especially as this is exemplified by the instant or by eternity, neither of which develops or endures in time.[1] Now, perception tends to take place instantaneously: it apprehends what is *now* present to the senses and is often confined (by the logic of "local partitioning") to this now-point as a "restrictive focal setting."[2] Thought, in contrast yet equally synchronically, ranges over *all* time, time-as-a-whole, and aims at what is *forever* true: its objects are "omnitemporal" in Husserl's term, "eternal" in Plato's. But it is Plato who also tells us that time itself is to be conceived as "the *moving image* of eternity" (*Timaeus* 37d). (ii) Second, the horizontal axis of memory and imagination is the axis of *diachronic* development. On this axis, move-ment proceeds by images—remembered images retrieving the ever receding antipode of the past, imagined images (or, better, imagin*ing* images) leading forward into the future. Beyond this past–future bipolarity, there is a fur-ther meaning of the horizontal line: it symbolizes a *fall* into time from the aether of pure thought. The lateral axis is the fallen axis; it is diachronically diffuse; here objects or events falter, linger, and languish.[3]

The foregoing axial opposition may also be thought in archetypal terms: the erect Apollonic-heroic vertical axis always resisting collapse into the Dionysian dispersion of the horizontal.[4] The temporal dis-tension of the horizontal sweep of time reflects the dismemberment of Dionysus. And, just as Dionysus is re-membered annually, so the time-line becomes a ring, an *anulus*, when we recollect a past event which, unrecalled, sinks into shapelessness. A second ring is formed by the anticipation of the future in imagination: imagining projects the future as pure possibility. It is in this double circularization of temporality that the linearity of the horizon tal axis (the "time-line")[5] is overcome and that Dionysus's recumbency is transformed into the creative cycles of *Rausch*.[6]

II

It is a signal fact, worthy of much wonder, that Western philosophers have (a) assimilated imagining and remembering to each other and even considered them to be the *same* act;[7] and (b) consistently demoted the importance of these two acts, considering each to be inferior or secondary to thought and perception. The latter are typically regarded as *origins* or *sources* of experience and knowledge in contrast with the derivative, non-original character of imagining and remembering. It is not surprising, then, that imagination and memory seem to belong so naturally to a fallen horizontal order of time in which their demoted status is made manifest. Precisely as retrospective and prospective respectively, remembering and imagining exist and exfoliate wholly *within* time, wherein as children of Chronos they are devoured at birth by their own progenitor.

In philosophers' eyes, to be thus subject to the ravages of time is to be of lesser value than to be above, beyond, or even beneath time: time's winged chariot is a chariot of devastation and dis-grace. At the same time, to be a creature of time is to be difficult to distinguish from *other* fallen temporal acts and entities; *diakrisis* is rendered problematic by diachrony, whose distendedness creates a continuum of poorly differentiated *temporalia*. The result is that temporally bound acts such as imagining and remembering, situated as they are on this kind of continuum, are quickly assimilated to each other; their differences are reduced to differences of degree or nuance only:

> This *decaying sense*, when wee would express the thing it self, (I mean *fancy* it selfe), wee call *Imagination*. . . . But when wee would express the *decay* and signifie that the Sense is fading, old, and past, it is called *Memory*.[8]

Although memory concerns what is fading and old, even imagination is in Hobbes's view a form of decay, of decomposition; both are conceived as mere remnants, *revenants*, of sensation, the only undecayed form of human experience. Sensation itself exists in a pristine, privileged state precisely because it takes place *in the instant:* there is *no time for decay* in a present moment that is by definition ever fresh and new. Here the winged chariot appears and disappears so rapidly that it cannot even begin to be late, out of date, or deteriorated. Chronos does not have time to devour his own children, for they have not yet even been brought forth from his own engendering.

Yet we must ask: Is this to do justice to imagining and remembering?

Do they simply sit aslant consciousness as limp, lateral acts? Are they of wholly horizontal significance? Are they to be merged with each other—and then sacrificed to the maw of thought or perception? Certainly not. This is not the place to rehearse arguments for the eidetic distinctness of the two acts or for their non-derivativeness from perception.[9] Nor is it the occasion to argue for the autonomy of imagination—for its unique freedom of mind, which has no parallel in other mental activities.[10] Instead, I shall restrict myself to two points, each unacceptable to mainstream Western thinking: the conjointly crucial (the literally "diacritical") role of the two acts in the constitution of time-consciousness, and the deeper significance of these acts insofar as they exceed the confines of the everyday awareness of time.

III

Imagining and remembering undeniably have to do with, even if not *only* with, time. Indeed, they are co-essential to the human experience of temporality—which is to say, equally and simultaneously essential. This can be seen most readily if we adopt the model of time-consciousness proposed by Husserl in his *Phenomenology of Internal Time-Consciousness*. On this model, time-consciousness consists of five phases: the now-point or the present per se, the "retention" of the immediate past, the recollection or "secondary remembrance" of the more remote past, the "protention" of the immediate future, and the "anticipation" of the more remote future. Husserl credits memory (as retentive and recollective) with the constitution of our experience of the past. Yet he fails to specify that it is by *imagining* that our protending and anticipating of the future take place. Of all mental acts, imagining alone is capable of projecting the future as a region of incompletion and pure possibility. Where memory concerns itself with events as already complete and thus as having what Husserl calls "the unity of the remembered,"[11] imagination moves us into the indefiniteness of the *not yet*, of what *might be*. The closed, chthonian character of the one contrasts with the open-ended, aethereal nature of the other. Schematically represented:

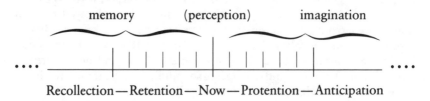

It is evident that, in terms of this emended model, imagining and remembering are co-constitutive of time-consciousness. This is all the more the case if it is true, as Derrida has recently argued,[12] that there is no such thing as the unalloyed *perception* of the present: if so, our fundamental consciousness of time is wholly the work of imagination and memory.

Yet the symmetry of the model is misleading. The following asymmetrical aspects of the experience of time must be acknowledged. (i) Imagination is often involved in our awareness of the past. As screen memories and déjà vu experiences most clearly illustrate, the past is as much constructed as it is reconstructed, and imagination is the source of the constructive element that appears in the form of hypotheses, fantasies, and variations on what actually happened. (Such, incidentally, was the significance of Freud's abandonment of the seduction theory of hysteria of 1897: genuine memories could not be distinguished from imaginings masquerading as memories.) (ii) While remembering always concerns itself with the past (or with what purports to belong to the past), imagining knows no comparable constriction in regard to the future. We can actively imagine the past (i.e., what the past was like) or the present (i.e., what is taking place *somewhere else* in the present). Indeed, we can imagine things that have no relationship at all with the past, present, or future regarded as three distinct phases of "lower time." *When* is the golden mountain I construct in imagination? At no designatable time: purely fictitious imagined objects are atemporal. And when imagining is extended in creative visualizing, what is experienced may present itself neither as temporal nor as atemporal but as belonging to time of another order, e.g., to what Tarthang Tulku calls "Great Time."[13] (iii) Just as imagining exceeds the confines of the anticipatable future, so remembering overruns the boundaries of the delimited past as described by Husserl. Memory extends not only to the immediate past (still "reverberating" in retentional consciousness) and to the past recaptured in recollection (that is, the consolidated personal past which I revive in recall), but to another form of the past as well: the *immemorial* past that stretches beyond anything I have previously experienced in my personal past.[14] "Im-memorial" signifies what is not to be remembered in any usual way, that is, by retentive or recollective modes of rememoration. It is a matter of *anamnēsis* or "reminiscence" in Plato's sense of the word: calling back to mind what was never before encountered as such in conscious experience. Here it is more than a question of acknowledging that imagination has more to do with Hades, and memory with Zeus, than on Husserl's antiseptic, Saturnine model. The whole model, and thus imagining and remembering as well, is subtended by an immemorial Chaos preceding ordered time.

IV

Time binds. Time, as it is consciously comprehended and experienced, keeps us confined to the personal past and future. These latter are knit together into a tight unity—a unity as tight as that of our defensively structured ego itself. Even as "life-history," time is a binding force, and it is understandable that human temporality is so often viewed as a form of fallenness (and even as fallenness itself: Heidegger links *Verfallensein* and *Zeitlichkeit*).[15] Likewise, the kind of history that recounts the collective experience of the past, seeing in it a mere sequence of events, is situated on still another horizontal time-line traversing lower or ordinary time. But beyond the personal and collective past is a past which is expansive rather than contractive. Such a past is a timeless time, inchoate and antedating history or personal experience. It is a special case of Great Time. It is also mythic in status, and its temporality is that of *in illo tempore:* in *that* time, a time before measurable, Chronic time. Such a time never was actual and is hence not remembered *as* actual. This means that it is not remembered at all in the usual sense. Rather, the mythic past is re-collected in an act of reminiscence whose content is impersonal or prepersonal: non-egological.[16] Re-*collected* from what?

Not from perception, thought, or personal memory, but from the *imagining* of archetypal presences. An archetypally enlivened imagination creates *imagines agentes* that move the soul. These active images are not projections of the future, nor even moving images of eternity. They are beyond *mimēsis* just as they are beyond quantified time. Even if experienced *in* time, archetypally active images are themselves transtemporal: outside the self-enclosing limits of ordinary time. As such they remain objects of imagination, which is uniquely capable of leading us beyond determinate temporality. Yet when imagining becomes archetypal in its activity, it also has to do with presences that revive in consciousness by means of *anamnēsis*. Although originally presented and structured in acts of imagining, these presences are re-experienced as re-collected *memoria*—as if they had already occurred or been experienced before. Which they have: *in imagination*. All significant human experiences are re-experiences.[17] This is the core of truth in Plato's theory that the objects of reminiscence have been encountered before, not in this life but in a form of pre-existence which the soul alone has experienced. Soul, being immortal, *has been* in contact with what is immemorial, with what is truly archaic. But this archaic residuum is archetypal before it is eidetic: having first arisen before the fall into personal or historical time, it is chaotic and achronic before being made manifest in cosmic-eidetic patterns of the sort which Plato and post-Platonists seek.

We are left, then, with a strange supermyth or myth of myths. The soul is driven to construct the myth of pre-existence or pre-experience in order to account for its sense of familiarity with archetypal presences that appear in and through the active images sustaining myths proper, the tales of the gods that are recounted and written down. But the arche-presences themselves are the specific concern of an archetypal imagination which envisions entities and events pre-existing finite, sublunar time. There is a profound circularity of the divine, of the gods. Our own delimited imagining, taking place in the present, rekindles divine presences which are felt to have been *toujours déjà là* and re-memorable as such. And they *have* always already been there, since an archetypally alive imagination has *never not been active* in putting them there. *This* imagination, which is the indefatigable demiurge of soul and which belongs to no one person (and perhaps to no *person* at all), undergirds our everyday imagining as surely as our more paltry powers of memory are underpinned by the anamnesic rememoration of which we are on occasion capable.[18]

The circularity in question is also, and ultimately, a circularity of imagination and memory themselves. The continuity of the archaic and the archetype, of pre-temporality and a-temporality, and of lower time and Great Time represents a species of collaboration between imagining and remembering which Western philosophy has been loathe to recognize. Small wonder. For such an extraordinary collaboration of the two powers departs radically from the schema of horizontal and vertical axes discussed at the beginning of this chapter. A truly re-collective memory and an archetypally active imagination join forces in a manner that cannot be charted or contained by diachronic–synchronic perpendicularity. They combine in the conjoint work of soul-making, an *opus* that cannot be captured adequately by contrasting images of height and fallenness. In soul-making, time is not the time of the person or even of the world but a time outside both, an acosmic time not representable by any axis or time-line. It is a time out of mind, a time of soul, a Great Time made accessible by the complementary activity of imagining and remembering in their most profoundly circular co-agency. Yet it is a time not known or knowable as such:

Great Time is the self. But the self cannot fathom Time.[19]

1. For we must distinguish the *everlasting,* i.e., indefinitely protracted duration, from the *eternal,* which is a sheerly static *nunc stans.* This distinction is already made by Plato at *Timaeus* 37–38.

2. On focal setting and partitioning, see Tarthang Tulku, *Time, Space, and Knowledge* (Emeryville, CA.: Dharma, 1977), pp. 85, 125. (Hereafter designated as *TSK.*)

3. This is so even if the projection of the vertical axis onto the horizontal axis constitutes the essence of poetic language, as in Jakobson's conception. Cf. Roman Jakobson, "Linguistics and Poetics," in R. and F. De George, eds., *The Structuralists* (Anchor, 1972), pp. 95–97. On the "endless diffusion" of lower time on the lateral axis, see Tulku, *TSK*, pp. 137 f., 171. On the horizontal character of lower time (i.e., "ordinary time"), see Tulku, *TSK*, pp. 145, 168–69.

4. An equally valid basis for contrast is suggested in Charles E. Scott's seminal discussion of archetypal differences between Zeus and Hades, aether and darkness, in his essay "Freedom with Darkness and Light: A Study of a Myth," *Studies in Non-Deterministic Psychology* (1980).

5. "Duration is but as it were the length of one straight line, extended *in infinitum*"

(John Locke, *Essay on Human Understanding*, Book II, chap. 15, 11). For Tulku's discussion and critique of linear temporality, see *TSK*, pp. 121–27, 136–41, 181.

6. Martin Heidegger finds Nietzsche's conception of *Rausch*, "ecstatic intoxication," to be central to the latter's conception of art and of Dionysus: cf. "Der Rausch als ästhetischer Zustand" in Heidegger's *Nietzsche* (Pfullingen: Neske, 1961), I, pp. 112 ff. In the light of what has just been said above, compare Heidegger's notion of the "round dance" (*der Ringen*) of the fourfold figures (*das Geviert*)—wherein man and earth seem to arrange themselves on a horizontal axis and sky and gods on a vertical one. Cf. Martin Heidegger, "Das Ding," in *Vorträge und Aufsätze* (Pfullingen: Neske, 1954).

7. See Thomas Hobbes, *Leviathan,* ed. C. B. MacPherson (Penguin, 1968), p. 89: "*Imagination* and *Memory* are but one thing" (his italics).

8. Ibid.

9. On the originary, non-secondary character of imagination and memory, see Tulku, *TSK*, passim. Cf. also my "Imagining and Remembering," in this volume.

10. Cf. my *Imagining: A Phenomenological Study* (Bloomington: Indiana University Press, 1976), esp. chap. 8 and 9.

11. Edmund Husserl, *The Phenomenology of Internal Time-Consciousness,* trans. James Churchill (Bloomington: Indiana University Press, 1964), p. 75.

12. Jacques Derrida, *Speech and Phenomena,* trans. David Allison (Evanston: Northwestern University Press, 1973), passim.

13. See Tulku, *TSK*, chap. 7, 8, 9, esp. p. 156: "if we see 'things' as 'space' and 'time,' *we can move and open through these dimensions to expose infinite fields of possibilities* within what seemed a finite encounter" (his italics). It is evident that such fields of possibility are made available through active imagining, which has the purely possible as its proper object. (On this last point, see Casey, *Imagining*, chap. 5: "Indeterminacy and Pure Possibility.")

14. For exercises in which remembering is allowed to assume this transpersonal role, see Tulku, *TSK*, pp. 174–81 (esp. Exercises 18, 19, 20).

15. " 'Spirit' does not fall *into* time; but factical existence 'falls' as falling *from* [*verfallende aus*] primordial, authentic temporality" (Martin Heidegger, *Being and Time*, trans. J. Macquarrie and E. Robinson [New York: Harper & Row, 1962], p. 486; his italics). Cf. Tulku's strikingly similar notion of the self as already fallen into lower time: *TSK*, p. 166.

16. " 'Lower time' amounts to an attempted taming and appropriation of Great Time for egoistic purposes" (Tulku, *TSK*, p. 137).

17. "The finding of an object is in fact a refinding of it" (Sigmund Freud, *Standard Edition of the Complete Psychological Works*, 24 vols. [London: Hogarth Press, 1953–74], 7: 222). Compare with this strangely Platonic statement Tulku's view that the self is "a patterning or embodying tendency of 'time', and *as such*, bears 'knowingness' throughout the full extent of its formation" (Tulku, *TSK*, p. 166; his italics).

18. For further thoughts on such an imagination, see my two essays "Toward an Archetypal Imagination" and "Time in the Soul" in this volume.

19. Tulku, *TSK*, p. 170.

Time in the Soul

Time is nothing else than an extendedness . . . of
the soul itself.

—St. Augustine

I

CHRONOS OR KRONOS devoured his children in an effort to curtail their lives, and the gnawing tooth of time has been keenly lamented by poets ever since:

> —O Grief! O Grief! Time eats away our lives,
> And the dark Enemy that gnaws the heart
> Drains the blood from us on which he thrives![1]

Dark enemy or not, time, that most pervasive and yet most vanishing dimension of our lives, must be reckoned with by each of us. One way to do so is to reflect on it philosophically and psychologically so that something of its Logos, of its innermost being, may emerge with increased distinctness. In what follows, the differing luminosities of philosophy and psychology—of which Jung said that neither "can do without the other, the one always furnishing the implicit, and frequently even the unconscious, primary assumptions of the other"[2]—will be brought to bear on the vexatious problem of time.

That time has tantalized and tormented philosophers is evident in St. Augustine's celebrated question: "If no one asks me, I know what time is; but if someone does ask, I cannot say."[3] This question—whose paradoxical character is closely akin to the paradox of knowledge posed in Plato's *Meno* and which has much the same resolution: we both know (tacitly) and do not know (explicitly) what it is—has its own history of revealing repetitions by philosophers who have concerned themselves with time,

Husserl and Waismann being among the most recent cases in point.[4] In our raising and repeating the question of time in this particular form, its mystery is at once acknowledged and denied. Moreover, the philosophical quandary of claiming both to know and not to know what time is also bespeaks a psychological ambivalence of simultaneously loving and hating the same phenomenon: we do in fact cherish time as well as curse it. What else *can* we do as children of time, especially of an infanticidal but all-embracing Chronic time which at once cuts short so much in human existence yet also makes it all possible?

The quandary and the ambivalence alike are rooted in a fundamental fact about time: namely, its being both nowhere and everywhere. Time as a totality is ubiquitous while its central unit, the 'now,' slips through our experiential and conceptual fingers. Heraclitus first glimpsed this when he said that "everything flows" (*panta rhei*),[5] itself a marvelously condensed expression of the problem at hand: "everything" (i.e., the universe at large, the cosmos as the ultimate matrix of time) "flows" (i.e., flows through the needle's eye of the now, which, precisely as an opening, is empty). Aristotle proclaimed that, although "time is present equally everywhere and with all things,"[6] it also "does not exist at all or barely, and in an obscure way,"[7] that is, when it is regarded from the perspective of the now. For the now is either already elapsed or is yet to come—is never itself steadily the still point of the turning center.[8] Or in two words again, *tempus fugit:* it not only flows but flees, and flees flowing from a vanishing centerpoint which lacks the requisite viscosity to hold it. And this "it"? It is just that universal factor which, being indifferently everywhere, has been spread so thin that it might as well be nowhere at all; indeed, this may be what the cipher of the now, its very emptiness, implicitly signifies.[9]

It is precisely the human experience of time—*being in time*—that is so conspicuously overlooked in cosmological conceptions such as Aristotle's. Despite its pressingly impingent character in daily demands, such being in time is the true fugitive,[10] evading our efforts to pin it down—to see the point in it, to make it into a point. If it is true, as Derrida remarks, that "it is always too late to pose the question of time, since it [time] has already occurred,"[11] how are we to catch up with, much less talk intelligibly about, this elusive phenomenon, as fleetfooted as Hermes? It is not sufficient to remark merely, as does Aristotle, that "to be in time" is "to exist when time exists."[12] This begs the question—or, rather, evades it just one more time. The question is: How does time exist *for us*? What is *our* experience of it? What is it to *be-in-time*? And, as a corollary question, does being in it imply that we can somehow be *out* of it?

"In," as Heidegger reminds us, is etymologically linked to the archaic German verb *innan*, "to dwell," so that a basic sense of being *in* time is dwelling in it, being at home there, *chez soi*.[13] As a dwelling-place, time is what is close and familiar; it draws near what is in its ambit; it is even "the nearing of nearness."[14] But the nearness has a farness built into it;

the more deeply into time we enter—the farther in we go—the more the prospect of transcending time itself beckons. Thus the very nearing effected by time's in-timate *Inheit* invites the surpassing of its same intimacy, e.g., by being not altogether present within the living present itself: "we bracket everything temporally outside the living present, then find it all again inside the present, since even the past and the future take place there."[15] Indeed, we effect such two-timing all the time. It is, above all, part and parcel of being in time to be partly out of cosmic, physical time as well as that "world-time"[16] which we are already inexorably in together as public beings. We achieve such partial transcendence whenever we gain access to diverse temporalities of which human beings are uniquely capable: the time of art and philosophy, the time of ecstasy and exhaustion, the time of the intensification of spirit. Beyond these departures into the outer reaches of the temporal, there are still more radical possibilities of transcending time, getting out of it in its cosmic or mundane form. These are provided primarily by acts of imagining, which offer ways in and through time to go beyond it.

II

Contrary to what one might suppose, imagination is very much part of our being in time—in fact, intrinsic to it. Despite its apparently aimless vagabondage, like the planets as depicted in the *Timaeus*,[17] imagining "wanders"; but it wanders with a certain purpose. The task, then, is to track the regularities of imagining's movements while not denying the significance of the irregularities manifest in its course as errant cause of the psyche.

Consider, first of all, that portion of being in time which we conventionally label "the future." Any close look at futurity-as-experienced shows it to have two basic forms: that which is about to be (the "protended" as Husserl calls it) and that which may eventually be (the "expected").[18] Now neither of these *Grundformen* of the future could be experienced by us unless imaginative activity were somehow at work. In the one case, a primary imagining (as I prefer to call it) adumbrates the edge of the oncoming. This primary imagining is doing so *right now* as you anticipate the successively presented works of this unfolding sentence itself. In the other, a secondary imagining actively projects a future event—as when we try to imagine in some detail what will be happening to us this coming February. This is not merely a matter of prediction or of probability; it is a matter of imagining what *might* become the case, whatever its actual likelihood.

Such active imagining is the essential way in which we get at any future that does not flow immediately from the present. Indeed, we must ask: How *else* is it accessible to us?[19] What is most remarkable here is that this projection of the future is itself only one concretion of a vaster function of imagining: the projection of the purely possible. Precisely as projective of what is purely possible, imagining also enriches our conception or sense of the past and the present as well as the future. We can, and frequently do, imagine what *might have been*, even if we know very well that it was not so. Thus T. S. Eliot misleads us when he says that "What might have been is an abstraction/Remaining a perpetual possibility/Only in a world of speculation."[20] In a world of imagination, a greener world than that of arid speculation, the might-have-been is entertained as a pure, even if not always as a perpetual, possibility. Similarly, the present itself—"what might have been and what has been point to one end, which is always present,"[21] comments Eliot—is leavened and livened by this projection of the possible, as when we imagine in the present what is going on somewhere else simultaneously in the same present. The present, far from being the mere minion of perception as is so often assumed by philosophers and psychologists alike, is co-constituted by imagination in its possibilizing role.

Here we have to ask: Why is possibility of such critical importance for human beings in time? Is not time precisely that which de-cides what is to be and not to be—severing, like Atropos, the string of fate just at the point where the actual is discernibly different from the possible? To enter time, to be in time at all, does not something have to be *actual*? Is this not what it means to say that something *is* in time: to be there as fully actualized? This tiny "is" is at once the clue and the culprit of the situation. Its very compactness epitomizes the constrictiveness of any philosophical theory of time as actual only—and of those corresponding forms of psychotherapy that operate under the rubrics of "reality therapy," "adaptation to the real," and the like. For the "is" has covertly controlled much of Western thinking about time, just as it has dominated Being itself. As Heidegger observes:

> The limitation of the meaning of "Being" [when confined to the "is" form alone] remains within the sphere of actuality and presence, of permanence and duration, of abiding and occurrence. . . . The definite and particular verb form "is", the third person singular of the present indicative, has here a pre-eminent rank.[22]

When Heidegger adds the following comment to this somewhat sweeping indictment, we begin to grasp the profound consequences for psychotherapy as well as for time:

> We understand "Being" not in regard to the "thou art", "you are", "I am", or "they would be", though all of these, just as much as "is", represent verbal inflections of [the infinitive] "to be".[23]

Just as many persons are always actively at work in therapy even if just two legal entities confront each other there—as well as some extra-personal beings (the 'they' of 'they would be' [*sie wären*] is not the merely impersonal *das man*, 'the one', but in archetypally oriented therapy would include the gods)—so too there are many modes of being involved in temporal process. In fact, to press the point, we might consider with Plato that the 'is' is if anything a *non*-temporal form, referring in all strictness to eternity:

> We say that [eternal being] was and is and shall be; but "is" alone really belongs to such being and describes it truly; "was" and "shall be" are properly used of becoming which proceeds in time, for they are motions. . . . [they] have come into being as forms of time, which images eternity and revolves according to number.[24]

But 'was' and 'shall be' are not the only forms or 'parts'[25] of time. The 'would be' just mentioned, the 'might be' and 'might have been' discussed earlier, the 'could be' and 'could have been' (in reference to capacity), the 'will have been' (the future perfect tense, which manages to merge past and future into a single temporal mass)[26]—not to mention the negations of these ('might not have been', 'could not be', 'would not be', 'will not have been')—all of these are not just valid grammatical forms but *forms of time*. Further, *each involves possibility*, whether as conditionality (the 'would'), potentiality (the 'could'), or as a special mode of futurity (the 'will have been'); accordingly, *each involves imagination*, the sole projector of the possible in human experience and its true proprietor. Only in and by imagining do we enter into such variants of the actual or the eternal as these verbal forms specify, thereby realizing a genuine *alchimie du verbe*: an alchemy of the word bound up with, and helping to delineate, that psychical alchemy to which Jung first drew our attention. We range freely over time in tenses—there is now an entire tense-logic that studies the formal structures of such ranging[27]—just as we range freely among possibilities in imagining.

At this point you might well be wondering: Is there anything but a purely formal link among these three salient factors—imagination, temporality, and possibility? What is the secret motor that ties them together intrinsically and not just externally by contingent congruence? A hint as to the answer—at least to half of it—is buried in the statement that was just cited from Plato's *Timaeus:* " 'was' and 'shall be' are properly used of becoming which proceeds in time, *for they are motions*. . . ." Time as such is defined by Plato as "a *moving* image of eternity."[28] Motion itself is the secret motor. How is this so?

Motion and movement are forms of change—the Greeks used the same word, *kinesis*, to refer to all three[29]—and change is a matter of becoming. Becoming in turn can be a process of transition from the possible to the actual (as when one finally *becomes* an adult, that which was always only possible as a child) or from the actual to the possible (as when possibilities of *further* growth emerge from the attainment of adulthood itself). In either case, a span of temporal duration is inherently involved. Moreover, and conversely, we do not experience time's passing apart from change or becoming of some sort. Try apprehending any lapse of time whatsoever without *kinēsis* of some kind, and I'll wager that you will fail. Even Eliot's still point is still a *turning* one.[30] This is no doubt the basis of the adage that "you cannot catch time by the tail." Since time is indissociable from change, you won't catch time without change: changelessness is a predicate precisely of eternity, "that which *is* forever in the same state *immovably.*"[31] In the sublunar realm, the realm in which human beings find themselves, "you cannot step twice into the same river, for other waters are continually flowing on."[32] Such flowing is a moving and is integral to being in time. Commenting on all this, Aristotle says soberly that "time is neither movement nor independent of movement."[33] If it is not to be reduced to movement alone, it still cannot exist without it.

The movement in question can be of many sorts: externally perceived physical movement (notice how the merest gesture of the hand traces out a trajectory not just in space but in time and has its determinately observable beginning and end even if we have not clocked it in seconds); the movement of this essay itself (whose sequence of ideas and themes, moving slow or fast for you, will be closely correlated with your sense of how rapidly time is passing as you read it); the movement of your body as a whole, which, even if not viewed externally by yourself, will have *its* time in accordance with *its* changes; and the movement of your mind in thinking with me (or against me!), in remembering what was just said, and in imagining what could or should have been said differently.

In imagining: here is the most moving thing of all. *Images move:* this is their very being. They move us and move themselves; and in them much else moves besides. But sticking with the image as it presents itself to us in experience and aside from its teeming content, we cannot help being struck by its very inconstancy, its ephemerality, its tendency to decompose before our very eyes: thus Hobbes spoke of its "Celerity."[34] Images have a way of moving on—on into other images, constituting thereby an indigenous flow and life. Their turning is a turnover into one another. This is true not only of actively entertained images but of passively undergone ones as well; indeed, these latter, by their very contrast with our own mute stance, may seem to move still more, to be more moving in the end. Images *ruminated* often move most tellingly; and even if we cannot tell the exact world-time they take, we can with more certainty tell that *time has been taken* than when we are suddenly shocked by an instantaneous image (which seems to puncture or punctuate time rather than to take it). It is therefore evident that our preoccupation with images is strictly correlated with the experienced duration of these same images; and their movements determine in turn the experience of our own being in time when we contemplate them.

Small wonder then that Plato called time a "moving image," that species of *eikon* which, like a statue fashioned by Daedalus, is not only movable but seems to move on its own initiative. Nor is it surprising that he excluded time from the realm of Necessity, the proper province of space. Time is a matter of actuality and possibility, the other two great modalizations of Being: this is because time always involves movement, which combines the actual and the possible in that process which we label "becoming" or "duration." And where images are concerned, the possible is predominant, since imagining *is* possibilizing.[35] (The underlining of the "is" in the last sentence points to the paradox of speaking about an incessantly self-proliferating process such as imagining in the language of the indicative, the singular, and the third person. As an icon, a "likeness," an image is in any case always a *two*-way matter: either an image *of* [as in pictographic theories of the image][36] or an image *for* [for the imaginer, to whom images speak]. In this regard a more appropriate grammatical form for images is the second person, conditional, plural: 'you would be.' Jung said: "the soul cannot exist without its other side, which is always found in a 'you.' "[37] Images are what you would be—and not only, as in Heidegger's phrasing, what 'they would be.' Or, rather, they are what you would be by being what *they* would be: you *as* they, they *as* you.)

But beyond movement, there is—*soul*, the other secret motor that links together time, imagination, and possibility. Soul for the Greeks is particularly the source of all animate movement; and it is this source by being capable of *moving itself*. Soul is a self-moved mover[38] and as such "the source of motion"[39] in other things. Its own movement, being perfect in kind, is circular; thus Plato speaks of the soul as "revolving within its own limit"[40] and as composed of circles or rings of the Same and Different.[41] Despite the common bond provided by circular movement, we might well wonder, however, how time and soul are related to each other. Is not the soul precisely that which for Plato and for Greek logocentrism generally leaps *over* time by manifesting an affinity with eternity, above all in its innate knowledge of the eternal Forms?

Heraclitus warns us, though, that "soul is the vaporization out of which everything else is derived; moreover, it is the least corporeal of things and is in ceaseless flux, for the moving world can only be known by what is in motion."[42] Even if soul links up with Logos, even if it knows Forms, it is itself embroiled in the same flux and motion as is everything else existent. For this reason its own changes are perfectly legitimate indices of time; in fact, without these soul-changes, time would seem to stand still: which is to say, it would cease to be time as we experience it. This is not only because soul is necessary to the measurement of time, as Aristotle suggests:

> Whether if soul did not exist time would exist or not, is a question that may fairly be asked; for if there cannot be someone to count, there cannot be anything that can be counted, so that evidently there cannot be

number. . . . [Thus] if nothing but soul, or in soul reason, is qualified to count, there would not be time unless there were soul.[43]

More to the point is Aristotle's own earlier remark that explicitly connects time, soul, and movement with one another:

> If, then, the non-realization of the existence of time happens to us when we do not distinguish any change, but *the soul seems to stay in one indivisible state*, and when we perceive and distinguish we say time has elapsed, evidently time is not independent of movement and change.[44]

Now the soul does not stay in "one indivisible state"; it moves, moving itself—even in the dark, where in the absence of externally perceived movement we at least apprehend the movement of our soul by itself, e.g., in imagining and thinking.[45] But it would be too extreme to say, as does Derrida, that "time is the form of what can occur only *en tē psychē*."[46] Time is certainly also the form of many *non*-psychical movements, e.g., of chemical elements reacting in a solution. Yet psychical movement may nonetheless be considered the acid test, and even the ultimate sine qua non, of time's experienced presence, since what appears in time externally to soul will also, and at the same time, appear *in time in soul;* and in the absence of the former we have only the latter to fall back on, as Kant stresses in his conception of time as the pure form of "inner sense":

> Time is the formal *a priori* condition of all appearances whatsoever . . . since all representations, whether they have for their objects outer things or not, belong, in themselves, as determinations of the mind, to our inner state; and since this inner state stands under the formal condition of inner intuition, and so belongs to time, time is an *a priori* condition of all appearance whatsoever. It is the immediate condition of inner appearances (of our souls), and thereby the mediate condition of outer appearances.[47]

"Of our souls?" Kant, despite his eventual denial (in "The Paralogisms of Pure Reason") of knowledge of the soul, nevertheless allows (parenthetical) reference to it to stand in the context of his most explicit discussion of time in the *Critique of Pure Reason*. When one considers further that he links time with motion in the Transcendental Aesthetic of the *Critique* and with imagination in the chapter on "The Schematism of the Pure Concepts of Understanding,"[48] one realizes how remarkably continuous is the Western philosophical tradition of relating time and soul through movement. This continuity is maintained both in Hegel's conception of time as "pure being-within-self as sheer coming-out-of-self"[49] and in Heidegger's effort to root temporality in Dasein (human existence). As Heidegger himself avers:

Although, proximally and for the most part, the ordinary experience of time is one that knows only "world-time", it always gives a *distinctive* relationship to "soul" and "spirit", even if this is still a far cry from a philosophical inquiry oriented explicitly and primarily towards the "subject".[50]

III

More than continuity is at stake, however. It is a matter of a common recognition on the part of otherwise quite divergent thinkers that time and soul are profoundly linked, in the depths, in the interiority of each. As part of this plummeting to the interior, the Saturnine preoccupation with keeping, measuring, and telling time needs to be seen through in its defensive denial of the fluidity of time and soul alike: in its attempt to dry out the moisture-loving soul and to channel the course of still waters running so deep as to be uncapturable in any chronometric units.[51]

As against Saturn and the adultified Senex consciousness, exhibited so flagrantly in that very time-calculation and time-reckoning in which we all take part as a matter of practical necessity, stands Time as "a child moving counters in a game" and who in so doing possesses the "royal power."[52] Such childish time—at once carefree and urgent, playful and particular—is the time of soul.[53] Or, rather, *a* time of soul, for the soul's time exists in many forms: as many possible forms as can be imagined for it, ranging from stolid to supple, mercurial to mired-down, retracted to robust. For where soul imagines, there it exists and has its time, however bizarre or irregular this time may appear to be by the standards of world-time.[54] "Image *is* psyche" is Jung's axiom of soul-making.[55] In imagining, we make soul; or, more adequately, we thereby make time *for* soul. In contrast with the marking of time, this making of time is a *taking of time for soul*— allowing time for attention to its afflictions and claims, whether this time be taken in psychotherapy, self-reflection, in the *agora*, or wherever. It is also a *creating of time in soul,* a psychical production of something sensuous and non-sensuous at once, a "time-space" (as Heidegger, parodying Einstein, calls it).[56] Being-in-soul (*esse in anima*) is then a being-in-time: in the soul's own good time.

Such a time makes possible, indeed encourages, the soul's erratic wanderings—as irregular, and yet also as regular, as those of the planets themselves. And as the movements of the latter constitute the "everlasting" basis for the periodicity of cosmic time, so the movements of the soul in imagining constitute the everlasting basis for the periodicity of psychical time. This latter periodicity is not necessarily numerable (to have thought so was precisely Fliess's failing in Freud's eyes) short of giving back to numbers the numinousness which the Pythagoreans first discerned in them and which Plato in his esoteric teachings extended still further. There may well be numbers of the Soul just as there are "numbers of Time";[57] but if so, they will somehow have to be equal to, and to express, the soul's wet wanderings in the tributaries of its own time.

These wanderings are possibilizings of the soul's existence and as such the creations of imagination. The expansive time brought into being by the soul's imaginings is a time of the possible: of what soul might, or would, or could do on a given occasion, and of where it could *be*. The result is a temporal indefiniteness reminiscent of Plato's indefinite dyad, with its mixture of odd and even, limited and unlimited. The temporality of the soul is a like combination of the same and the different. While occupying one and the same time, its unique and non-transferable time, soul also has a different time at its disposal in which it veers off oddly from the regular path. In its possibilizing power, imagining clears the time-space of sameness and difference, even and odd, limited and unlimited. In this making of time, soul is made as well as brought to movement, so that time and movement become in the soul, as in the world-about-us, inseparable even if not identical: as we see in souls that are manic or paralyzed, enlivened or reprobate, shiftless or energetic. By imagining fully and freely, soul expands, soaking up the moisture of its own streaming, flowing beyond or beneath the Saturnine boundaries of world-time. This extendedness, this self-stretching and overflowing, is time for and in soul:

> It seemed to me that time is nothing else than an extendedness; but of what sort of thing it is an extendedness, I do not know; and it would not be surprising if it were not *an extendedness of the soul itself.*[58]

IV

If what I have said strikes you as a bit fantastic, your response is quite appropriate. For time in the soul is brought forth and founded on just this: fantasy. Fantasy is full-fledged imagining, often assuming a narrative or quasi-narrative form.[59] When this form is assumed (as in a more or less coherent daydream), a temporal structure is superimposed on soul which acts as an internal analogue of the sheer succession that quantifies and typifies world-time. Such a structure is inherently orderly, e.g., in possessing the regularity of beginning-dénouement-end. The fact is that narratized fantasy, fully lived-through in soul, is more highly structured than many of the soul's other divagations; it is, to this extent, less possibilized: more intact and in place. Myths are narrative in structure too and thus possess a consecutiveness that fills up many a psychical *lacuna* in time. This is so even though we rarely live out in fantasy a complete myth from beginning to end; the myth of soul ends by narrating itself rather than repeating pre-established mythemes: "the myth [is] in the mess,"[60] and not floating freely above it in eternal Olympian serenity.

Despite the mess (indeed just because of it), in drawing to a close we need to do some drawing together: some battening down and tidying up, thereby giving to the Senex a last chance to reassert itself. This will be done in the form of one syllogism, three concrete instances, and two corollaries.

A. The syllogism, which sums up much of what has been discussed so far, runs as follows:

Major Premise: *Imagining is intrinsic to being in time:*

—to mundane time-consciousness, where it is responsible for projecting the near-term and the far-term future, as well as for possibilizing the past and the present;

—to the soul's temporality in the ways suggested above: primarily by expansion or outreach but also by opening onto the circuitous and irregular.

Minor Premise: *Imagining is intrinsic to soul:*

—to its very existence as well as to its pathologizing and prospering, both of which have multiple temporal modes; imagining is the moving agent of soul, its main motor and primary possibilizer.

Conclusion: *Being-in-time and being-in-soul are linked through imagining,* which puts time into soul (otherwise an abstract reflective power only) and soul into time (otherwise an exoskeleton of empty moments).

The fullness of time is reached in the fullness achieved by the imagining soul. For when the psyche is imagining, it is extending itself *through* time, filling itself with time, and time with soul, by means of the modalities of time—past, present, future, conditional, subjunctive, and all other forms of temporalizing.

B. The three concrete instances all concern the question of time in psychotherapy: "timing" in the richest sense of this word (a sense not restricted to the "correct timing" of an intervention).

Instance 1. If we focus on "incorporation" as this term was used by Freud and then extended by Melanie Klein, we notice that it runs a very unusual course. *Just when* does incorporation occur? *How long* does it take? When can we say that it *begins* or *ends*? These questions are as difficult to answer in relation to the early life of the infant (where Klein's claims are most controversial) as in relation to the situation in psychoanalytic therapy, where the actual duration of the analysis is no adequate measure of the exact progress of incorporation. Not only do we not know just when it is taking place in the process of analysis, but there is evidence that it pre-exists the clock-time of this process (e.g., by the previous incorporation of the *figures* of the analyst, though not yet his or her person) as well as post-exists it (i.e., by the continuing assimilation of, and identification with, the analyst). Now all such incorporation is manifestly psychical, and the time that it takes is psychical time, here in the special form of the anticipation, deferment, and subtle simultaneity of which only the soul in *its* time is capable.

Instance 2. Further attesting to the specialness of the psyche's time is the much-wondered-at but still little-understood phenomenon of the increasing length of analyses since Freud and Jung first began to practice this Hermetic art. The conventional explanation, that there is an increase in the incidence of character disorders (especially narcissistic ones) as over against classical neuroses, is hardly convincing, since character per se is no more impenetrable than ego. Nor is it plausible to say that patients are more knowledgeable or more wily today; they may well be, but by the same token so too are the very analysts with whom they enter into such long-term relations. A more promising approach is to be found in looking to the temporality of the soul. It is the soul, after all, that is taking all this extra time, and it must be doing so for reasons of its own. The reasons, one suspects, have primarily to do with expanding its own space of time: with taking more world-time so as to encourage the efflorescence of its own imaginal time. My point here is not that this is good or sound reasoning—there is certainly no guarantee that increased time of one kind will lead to an augmentation of time of the other kind—but that the strategy at least makes sense in temporal terms, the terms of the soul's own making. It is as if the soul were saying to itself: Expand or perish![61] Or as if it were respecting still another of Heraclitus's gnomic utterances: "You could not discover the limits of soul, even if you traveled every road to do so; such is the depth of its meaning."[62]

Instance 3. One cannot help but be struck by the idea, espoused by some Jungians, of doing a finite bit or stretch of analysis. Of course, all therapy is finite, and its termination (as Freud himself came to stress) more or less arbitrary. But a discontinuist model of therapy is importantly different from a continuist model of the sort that Freud proposed. Beneath the notion that one can—and perhaps even should—start and stop the process at irregular intervals, that one can break off and then pick up at distinctly different times, is, I suspect, an appreciation of the very soul-time to whose incongruous shapes I have been pointing. Unlike Bergson's *moi profond*, the time of soul is not to be presumed continuous—much less non-existent (as in Freud's claim concerning the id's timelessness). It is basically discontinuous, therein mocking the continuity of the time-line by which it is so often represented.[63] If so, though, it is discontinuous not simply as having breaks or gaps—to assert this is still to cling to the metaphor of the line, only now a dotted line—but as having many avatars, many kinds and modes. The polycentricity of the psyche[64] demands no less than this, namely, a polyform time with many turning centers and few strictly still points. The soul has many ways to be in time (only several of which I have been able to indicate), and this being so it is not at all surprising that its therapy is not monolinear but dispersed and diasporadic. Heidegger speaks of the "ecstatico-horizonal" character of Dasein's temporality.[65] So we might speak correspondingly of the expansive-disjunctive character of psychical time. This time deepens itself by fits and starts—by temporal fizzles and fissures—as much as by prolonged plumbings. Perhaps in the end both forms of exploration-and-expansion of the soul's limits are required: there is room for each in a psyche having only those limits it imagines itself to have.

C. This last observation leads to two concluding corollaries of our considerations. (1) The first is that the time of soul is infinite, not as an actual infinity (the positive infinite that applies strictly speaking to cosmic time alone), but as an "indefinite infinite" in Kant's conception.[66] An indefinite infinity of time is one that, rather than representing an actual totality of temporal moments, is at most *on the way* toward such a totality—taking steps to get there without, however, its being known just where it is along the way. The soul similarly cannot determine with assurance that it is exactly half-way, or a quarter of the way, to the entirety of its time. Its work in time—its working *of* time, its timing—yields to no such objective assessment, even though it often frets about just how much time is left in a given experience or in life itself (how many years do I have left? when is my 'date with death'?). Like the patient labor of the negative in Hegel's view, the work of the psyche is never simply over and done with, and is not to be measured in such discrete units as hours, days, or even years. The work itself is one of reflection, of condensation and rarefaction, of vaporization from the moist, and of moisturization from the vaporous. As in the alchemical search for transmutation, there is no end to this labor, nor should one expect a worldly success in these matters. None other than Sir Isaac Newton labored many of his adult years in an alchemical "elaboratory," filled over two thousand pages of manuscript with his observations of what he saw there (none of which were published in his lifetime),[67] and yet was quite undaunted by a lack of tangible, reportable results. So too is soul-making a movement without definite end, issue, or outcome. The time of transmutation, alchemical or psychical (where the "or" is inclusive and not exclusive), is infinite in the root sense of endless, without an exact end, un-ending. Of time in the soul thus regarded as perduring process of permutation and percolation, we have to say simply: *there is no end to it.* Not because the soul is puffing itself up pridefully, gaining or hoarding increasing amounts of time, getting ahead of time or staying on top of it—all of which the Greeks would have considered a state of excessive *megalopsychia*, "great-souledness." There is no such thing as gaining, getting ahead, or staying on top of time in the soul. There is just being in and of time—a time of turmoil which cannot be mastered or meted out in the manner of world-time. But we can be in and of such a turbulent time endlessly, with no precise 'before' and 'after' ("ridiculous the waste sad time stretching before and after"[68]), with no exact beginning-time or end-time: no closing time as such. Here we cannot say in the manner of the bartender in *The Waste Land:* "HURRY UP PLEASE ITS TIME." Nothing *is* time in the soul, so that nothing can close it off.

Consequently, a first way of being out of time—out of finite, worldly time—presents itself in this 'good infinite' of psychical time, and it takes the express form of being such time by persisting in it endlessly. One is out of one kind of time—has suspended its stranglehold on us—by staying in another kind of time: staying with it, following it (creating it!) whither the soul listeth, making *it* the turning center. This happens nightly, and often flamboyantly, in dreams; but what is episodic and sporadic in dreams may become diasporadic in waking life, where soul and its time belong too. The fullness of time, its true infinity, is attained only when soul-making is going on in both at once, ceaselessly.

(2) A quite different line of thought emerges when we turn to a second corollary of these reflections. This is that the soul's time is the very basis of our sense of time's transiency. In the term "transiency" is included an entire set of closely affiliated notions:

—the *irreversibility* of time: its one-wayness; our inability to live through it twice in exactly the same way (which is not to say, either, that we exhaust it the first time through);

—time's *passing,* particularly its passing away, its transitoriness, the way that it seems to go on, or move on, without our being able to do anything about it: as is felt with special acuteness when we say that time "passes us by" as if indifferent to our individual interests and fate;

—the sense of time *running out:* not only in relation to a given event but to the whole time of our life, mortal as it is; it is not accidental, then, that we designate dying by "passing away" (just as *vergehen* in German means both 'to perish' and 'to go by, to elapse');

—the conviction that there is always *too little time:* again not only for particular projects but for life itself, our own life, which almost always expires too soon, so that death can only rarely be considered a proper end, a fruition or fulfillment; as Heidegger reminds us, being-toward-death is not to be confused with being toward a predesignated end in the sense of a *telos* or final purpose of human life.[69]

Now all of this must be acknowledged: being in time as we are, being timelings, we are subject to time's transiency in all of these forms, including those that co-constitute us as deathlings. Time is experienced as transient and we are transient in it: we are beings-of-the-between, beings-in-transition. And it is by now evident that none of this is explicable on the model of world-time or of cosmic time. World-time tends to shrink into a series of vacant nows, while cosmic time tends to inflate into the actual infinite of eternity. Neither the actual now nor the eternal now (a now that stands still, a *nunc stans* as the Medieval theologians called it) offers any basis for transiency as it has just been characterized. No irreversibility, no directionality even, is inherent in a sheer succession of instants, much less in eternity. Nor will we ever discover any passingness, any running out or running short, in what is by definition inexhaustible and such as never to be run through in its entirety. Mortality, moreover, has no place at all in the schema of time as geared exclusively to the regularities of external physical motion, a time which is defined by Aristotle as "the number of motion in respect of 'before' and 'after.' "[70]

It is in the motion of soul, its e-motions and com-motions, that the genuine basis for transiency lies. Soul moves in many ways. This is part of its possibilizing power. Among these movements are those with direction (whether multilinear or not linear at all), but just as possible are movements without direction, the soul's vagaries. Insofar as a movement of some sort is taken, a course of some kind traversed, a sense of time's passing will arise. Further, the passing through will be a passing away of the earlier positions on the trajectory, and with this comes a conviction of irreversibility. Not that the soul cannot go back (pass back along) its course; nonetheless it will never again reach a perfectly pristine point of departure, when the whole course lies ahead and unknown. As Husserl said, "I can re-live [*nachleben*] the present, but it can never be given again,"[71] i.e., as it was first given. It perishes as new even if it can be relived as old. Passing away and perishing therefore bear as much on the *beginning* as on the end of a given set of movements; and it is just insofar as they do that the sense of time running out, of never being enough, is engendered. For having come *some* way on the course, I know that time has been taken; the time once available to me is no longer available to me in its totality. Even if more time, or time of a different kind, does come my way as I proceed (to assume that it cannot is just the Saturnine sense of the stinginess of time), the original totality will never again be that unique possibility which it once was. *Its* time is being consumed (Hegel speaks of time as "the abstraction of consumption"[72]), and there will never again be as much of it. When this "as much" is generalized to "enough" and is made to stand for my life's passing as a whole—as if this life were graspable as a single "basic project" in Sartre's term—then we have the anguishing feeling that time is *always*, 'chronically,' in short supply. Fortunately, this is not true; soul finds new time all the time. In soul, if not in cosmos, it is right to say with Aristotle that "time will not fail; for it is always at the beginning."[73] Authentic existence in particular always has enough time, as Heidegger avers:

. . . just as he who exists inauthentically is constantly losing time and never "has" any, the temporality of authentic existence remains distinctive in that such existence, in its resoluteness, never loses time and "always has time."[74]

Despite Aristotle's and Heidegger's optimism, in ending I must point to a darker side of the situation. Soul may well be capable of perpetual renewal, as theories of metempsychosis and the Myth of Er suggest, but it is also perpetually ending. Soul, like time itself, "is always at a beginning *and at an end.*"[75] Which is to say that it is also always dying. Death too is one of soul's possibilities: the "possible impossibility" of its existence in Heidegger's oxymoron.[76] It may expand endlessly in time, but it also finally contracts there. It contracts in a compact made much earlier in its life, since there is no soul without its dying, without its shading off into the realm of shades, the underworld. This underworld has its own temporality which is neither eternal time nor now-time nor non-time. We can only imagine what it is like, though just in doing so we enter it and partake in it as if we had known it all along. As perhaps we have: in the soul and of it, subtending it, and being at once its sameness and its difference.

To point thus to the soul's essential finitude is not a merely nugatory gesture. Nor does it contravene (even if it does seem to contest) what has been said of the in-finitude of psyche. There is no closing of time in the underworld, no ending of it there, no terminal time. Time, or at least time of soul, has no term, no fixed terminus. Death itself is not a form of non-time. But it is a way out of time now, out not only of world-time and cosmic time but even out of the soul's unlimited meanderings in this life, its life projects, its life as pro-ject—into a dying time, a time of dying, down and out.

So we move twice out of time, and each time soul is made: made by its expansive movements and made equally by the dying that it does at all times too. If soul is made, time is made, and in the two senses distinguished earlier: taken and created. These two senses merge, as time and soul themselves merge, in a dis-soluteness in which being in and out of time become one: in the kind of imagining which soul does and, doing, dies.

1. Charles Baudelaire, "L'Ennemi" in *Les Fleurs du Mal.*

2. C. G. Jung, *Modern Man in Search of Soul*, trans. W. S. Dell and C. F. Baynes (New York: Harcourt, Brace, 1933), p. 207. I have slightly modified the translation.

3. St. Augustine, *Confessions,* Book XI, chap. 14.

4. Cf. Edmund Husserl, *The Phenomenology of Internal Time-Consciousness,* trans. J. S. Churchill (Bloomington: Indiana University Press, 1964), p. 21; and Friedrich Waismann, "Analytic-Synthetic," reprinted in *The Philosophy of Time,* ed. R. M. Gale (New York: Doubleday, 1967), p. 55.

5. Heraclitus, Fragment 20 in the numbering and translation of Philip Wheelwright, *Heraclitus* (New York: Atheneum, 1968), p. 29. The full statement is "everything flows and nothing abides; everything gives way and nothing stays fixed."

6. Aristotle, *Physics* IV 218 b 12–13 in the translation of R. P. Hardie and R. K. Gaye (Oxford: Oxford University Press, 1930).

7. Ibid., 217 b 35–36.

8. I modify here T. S. Eliot's words in "Burnt Norton," in *The Four Quartets*: "the light is still/At the still point of the turning world."

9. "One part of it has been and is not, while the other is going to be and is not yet. Yet time—both infinite time and any time you like to take—is made up of these [parts, i.e., now's]. One would naturally suppose that what is made up of things which do not exist could have no share in reality" (Aristotle, *Physics* IV 217 b 36–218 a 3).

10. "Dasein knows fugitive time in terms of its 'fugitive' knowledge about its death" (Martin Heidegger, *Being and Time*, trans J. Macquarrie and E. Robinson [New York: Harper & Row, 1962], p. 478; in italics in original).

11. Jacques Derrida, "*Ousia* and *Grammē*," trans. E. S. Casey in F. J. Smith, ed., *Phenomenology in Perspective* (The Hague: Nijhoff, 1970), p. 66.

12. Or, alternatively, to be "in number": Aristotle, *Physics* IV 221 a 10–11.

13. Cf. Heidegger, *Being and Time*, p. 80.

14. Heidegger uses this phrase in *On Time and Being*, trans. J. Stambough (New York: Harper & Row, 1972), pp. 15–16. Cf. also his essay "The Thing," in *Poetry, Language, Thought*, trans. A. Hofstadter (New York: Harper & Row, 1971), pp. 177–78.

15. Robert Sokolowski, *Husserlian Meditations* (Evanston: Northwestern University Press, 1974), p. 139. Sokolowski is commenting on Husserl's notion of the "apodictic reduction" as this is conceived in *Erste Philosophie* (The Hague: Nijhoff, 1959), II, sec. 38.

16. This is Heidegger's term for time which is datable, shared, and public. See *Being and Time*, sec. 79–81.

17. Plato, *Timaeus* 40b: "those stars that having turnings and in that sense 'wander' came to be in the manner already described." F. M. Cornford, whose translation of the *Timaeus* I cite here below, comments on this passage: "but only in that sense. They are not really 'wanderers', but keep to their regular paths, though they 'turn' back at the limits of their spiral tracks" (*Plato's Cosmology* [New York: Liberal Arts Press, 1957], p. 118).

18. Cf. Husserl, *The Phenomenology of Internal Time-Consciousness*, sec. 24 and 26.

19. Alfred Schutz writes: "I have to visualize the state of affairs to be brought about by my future action before I can draft the single steps of my future acting from which that state of affairs will result. . . . In order to project my future action as it will roll on I have to place myself in phantasy at a future time when this action will already have been materialized" (*Collected Papers*, ed. M. Natanson [The Hague: Nijhoff, 1962], I, pp. 69 and 87).

20. T. S. Eliot, "Burnt Norton."

21. Ibid.

22. Martin Heidegger, *An Introduction to Metaphysics*, trans. R. Manheim (New Haven: Yale University Press, 1959), p. 92.

23. Ibid.

24. Plato, *Timaeus* 37e–38a.

25. "All these parts of Time, and 'was' and 'shall be', are forms of time that have come to be; we are wrong to transfer them unthinkingly to eternal being" (Plato, *Timaeus* 37e).

26. On the *modo futuri exacti*, see Schutz, *Collected Papers* I, p. 76.

27. See, inter alia, A. N. Prior, *Past, Present, and Future* (Oxford: Oxford University Press, 1967) and the same author's *Papers on Time and Tense* (Oxford: Oxford University Press, 1968).

28. Plato, *Timaeus* 37d; my emphasis. Cornford translates this as "moving likeness," reserving "image" for *agalma* as at *Timaeus* 37c.

29. See the entry under *kinesis* in F. E. Peters, *Greek Philosophical Terms: A Historical Lexicon* (New York: New York University Press, 1967), pp. 101–03.

30. On the role of "turnings" (*tropai*) in the *Timaeus*, see Cornford, *Plato's Cosmology*, pp. 116 ff.

31. Plato, *Timaeus* 38a; my italics.

32. Heraclitus, Fragment 21 in Wheelwright, *Heraclitus*.

33. Aristotle, *Physics* IV 219 a 1–2.

34. Thomas Hobbes, *Leviathan*, ed. C. B. MacPherson (London: Pelican, 1968), part I, chap. 8.

35. Cf. my *Imagining: A Phenomenological Study* (Bloomington: Indiana University Press, 1976), chap. 5, 9.

36. The image, says Plato, is "the ever moving semblance of something else" (*Timaeus* 52c).

37. C. G. Jung, *Collected Works* 16, ¶454. (Hereafter *CW*.)

38. The phrase "the thing that is self-moved" (Plato, *Timaeus* 37b) refers strictly speaking to the heaven; but this latter, as Cornford remarks, is "self-moved by its own self-moving soul," *Plato's Cosmology*, p. 95 n.

39. Proclus, cited by Cornford at *Plato's Cosmology*, p. 119. Cf. also Plato, *Phaedrus* 245c–246a and *Laws* X 894c.

40. Plato, *Timaeus* 37a. Cf. also 36e: the soul "revolves upon herself."

41. Cf. ibid., 36c–37c.

42. Heraclitus, Fragment 43.

43. Aristotle, *Physics* IV 223 a 22–26.

44. Ibid., 218 b 29–35; my italics.

45. "We perceive movement and time together: for even when it is dark and we are not being affected through the body, if any movement takes place in the world we at once suppose that some time also has elapsed" (Aristotle, *Physics IV* 219 a 3–6). I substitute "soul" for "mind" here.

46. Derrida, "*Ousia* and *Grammē*," p. 72.

47. Immanuel Kant, *Critique of Pure Reason*, trans. N. K. Smith (New York: Humanities, 1950), A 32 B 48, p. 77.

48. See especially *Critique of Pure Reason* A 139 B 178, pp. 181–82: "Thus an application of the category to appearances becomes possible by means of the concepts of understanding [and] mediates the subsumption of the appearances under the category. . . . The schema is in itself always a product of imagination."

49. G. W. F. Hegel, *Philosophy of Nature*, trans. A. V. Miller (Oxford: Oxford University Press, 1970), sec. 258 (Remark), p. 35.

50. Heidegger, *Being and Time*, p. 479; his italics.

51. "Saturn will shape order slowly through time" (James Hillman, *Re-Visioning Psychology* [New York: Harper & Row, 1975], p. 130).

52. Heraclitus, Fragment 24.

53. "The dynamic principle of fantasy is *play*, a characteristic also of the child . . . without this playing with fantasy no creative work has ever yet come to birth" (C. G. Jung, *CW* 6, ¶93; his italics).

54. One such standard is enunciated by John Locke: "duration is as it were the length of one straight line, extended *in infinitum*" (*An Essay Concerning Human Understanding*, Book II, chap. 15, sec. 11).

55. James Hillman comments on this statement from *CW* 16, ¶75, as follows: "Since psyche is primarily image and image always psyche, [psychological] faith manifests itself in the belief in images: it is 'idolatrous', heretical to the imageless monotheisms of metaphysics and theology. . . . Trust in the imaginal and trust in soul go hand in hand" (*Re-Visioning Psychology*, pp. 50–51).

56. Cf. Heidegger, *On Time and Being*, pp. 14 ff.

57. "In virtue, then, of this plan and intent of the god for the birth of Time, in order

that Time might be brought into being, Sun and Moon and five other stars—'wanderers' as they are called—were made to define and preserve the numbers of Time" (Plato, *Timaeus* 38c).

58. St. Augustine, *Confessions,* Book XI, chap. 26; my italics.

59. On the distinction between fantasy and imagination, see my essay "Imagination, Fantasy, Hallucination, and Memory," in this volume.

60. Hillman, *Re-Visioning Psychology,* p. 101.

61. To which we should compare Nietzsche's advice to psychologists: "Discern or perish!" (*The Dawn of Day,* sec. 460; cited by Hillman, *Re-Visioning Psychology,* p. 260).

62. Heraclitus, Fragment 42.

63. Cf. Kant's remark: "we represent the time-sequence by a line progressing to infinity, in which the manifold constitutes a series of one dimension only" (*Critique of Pure Reason,* A 33 B 50, p. 77).

64. On psychic polycentricity, see Hillman, *The Myth of Analysis* (New York: Harper & Row, 1978), p. 287.

65. Cf. Heidegger, *Being and Time,* sec. 78–81.

66. See Kant, *Critique of Pure Reason,* A 511 B 539, pp. 451 ff. "Indefinite" connotes "indeterminately great" and a continuing process of production (or division) in contrast with an actually achieved amount. It is first suggested in Anaximander's notion of the *apeiron* or "the unlimited."

67. An extensive study of Newton's alchemical works is found in Betty Jo Teeter Dobbs, *The Foundations of Newton's Alchemy, or 'The Hunting of the Green Lion'* (Cambridge: Cambridge University Press, 1977).

68. T. S. Eliot, "Burnt Norton." This line of Eliot's in effect rewrites Shelley's "Ozymandias": "Nothing beside remains. Round the decay/Of that colossal wreck, boundless and bare/The lone and level sands stretch far away."

69. On Being-toward-death as end, see Heidegger, *Being and Time,* sec. 48 and 52.

70. Aristotle, *Physics* IV 219 b 1–3.

71. Husserl, *The Phenomenology of Internal Time-Consciousness,* p. 66.

72. Hegel, *Philosophy of Nature,* sec. 258 (Zusatz). Miller translates *Verzehrung* as "destruction," but its literal meaning is consumption, as in the consumption of food or fuel.

73. Aristotle, *Physics* IV 222 b 7–8.

74. Heidegger, *Being and Time,* p. 463.

75. Aristotle, *Physics* IV 222 b 3–4; my italics.

76. Cf. Heidegger, *Being and Time,* sec. 53.

Getting Placed: Soul in Space

Where are we at all? and whenabouts in the name of space?

—James Joyce
Finnegans Wake

We could not conceive of empty space unless we could see the ground under our feet and the sky above. Space is a myth, a ghost, a fiction for geometers.

—J. J. Gibson
The Ecological Approach to Visual Perception

I

JUNG CLAIMS, more than once, that archetypes "can be found every-where."[1] This is hardly surprising in view of the Platonic, neo-Platonic, and Kantian origins of Jung's conception of archetypes as formal a priori structures—where "a priori" means necessary and universal in Kant's defini-tion of the term. Like Platonic Forms, or a Plotinian World Soul, or Kant's own forms of intuition and categories of the understanding, archetypes for Jung are "entirely universal"[2] in extension: everywhere in space, time, and causality. *No place is without archetypes*—without an archetypal basis or at least resonance. If the gods have become diseases, then archetypes (in which gods inhere) represent something of a worldwide epidemic.

And yet archetypes, so conceived, *have no place*, no proper or even prox-imate place. They are a common place—a place of places, a place for places—and in this abstracted role threaten to become commonplaces, taken for granted in their very universality. Keeping them in this Ur-Place (which is what we do whenever we think of them as belonging to the col-lective unconscious and as having existed "from time immemorial")[3] is precisely to deny them a place of their own. Such was already the fate of the Heaven (*ouranos*), the outermost sphere of the universe in ancient Greek cosmology and as such "the place of [and for] the whole world."[4] As Aristotle argued, any such ultimate place cannot possess its own place: it is not in place itself because it is not *in* anything else at all.[5] Essential to place is being in something that covers, contains, subtends, or shelters.

In fact, the matter is even more dire than this. Not only is to exist everywhere to exist nowhere—to be, therefore, u-topic, though not necessarily Utopian—it is, strictly speaking, *not to exist at all*. The argument is again Aristotle's:

> . . . what is somewhere is itself something. (*Physics* 212 b 15)

> . . . all suppose that things which exist are *somewhere* (the nonexistent is nowhere—where is the goat-stag or the sphinx?). (208 a 29–31; translators' italics)

What Aristotle asks of the goat-stag and the sphinx, those Greekmost personifications of archetypes, we must ask of archetypes themselves: *Where are they*, anyway? On this depends whether they *are* at all.

The problem, thus, is one of situating archetypes, finding out their local habitations, since any imputed universal location turns out to be locusless, a placeless place. What would such situating consist in? Heidegger says:

> To situate means . . . first of all to point out the proper place or site of something. Secondly, it means to heed that place or site. These two methods, placing and heeding, are both preliminaries to a topology. And yet it will require all our daring to take no more than these preliminary steps in what follows. The topology, as befits a path of thought, ends in a question. That question asks for the location of the site.[6]

What then is location to archetypes? To ask this question is to consider the nature, not of archetypology (that is, of the classification and cross-classification of archetypes), but of *archetopology*.[7] And "to consider," as Heidegger also reminds us, is *erörten* in German: literally, to determine the place, the *Ort*, of something.[8]

II

Before we can make any further headway, we need to ask a quite fundamental question: What kind of thing is place itself? This is a question which we do not ask enough, if we ask it at all anymore. The reasons for this conspicuous neglect of place in our era are two-fold in origin.

(i) First of all, place has become swept up into *space* conceived as a universal medium which is at once empty, homogeneous, and isotropic. After Descartes and Newton, space was considered as a three-dimensional co-ordinate system. Physical body and its place are seen as subsumable into space so regarded; according to Descartes:

> A space, or intrinsic place, does not differ in actuality from the body that occupies it; the difference lies simply in our ordinary ways of thinking. In reality the extension in length, breadth, and depth that constitutes the space is absolutely the same as that which constitutes the body.[9]

The phrase "intrinsic place" is especially ominous. Place is no longer (as it was for the Greeks) the place of a particular thing, and this is due to the dissolution of movable bodies (the proper occupants of place) into bits of three-dimensional extension. Descartes continues:

> The nature of matter, or of body considered in general, does not consist in its being a thing that has hardness or weight, or colour, or any other sensible property [here is the characteristic seventeenth-century disparagement of mere "secondary qualities"], but simply in its being a thing that has extension in length, breadth, and depth.[10]

In Newtonian nomenclature, space has become one of God's two infinite *sensoria* (the other is time), an infinite container of things having absolute, and not merely relative, positions within its unlimited embrace. "Intrinsic place" thus entails infinite space—which, as we know, means no place at all. Indeed, Locke, in the wake of Newton and Descartes, can deliver the coup de grâce to place by reducing it to sheer "relative position," a mere interval between pre-established points in "the indistinguishable inane of infinite space."[11] From here it is only a short step to Leibniz, who does not even pay lip service to place. By the Enlightenment, therefore, and quite symptomatic of what "enlightenment" means in the West, place has been dissipated in space defined as an infinite "order of co-existence," that is, the way in which things (insofar as there still can *be* things without place) find themselves merely side-by-side in space.

(ii) A second surpassing of place is by *time*, conceived by Leibniz as "the order of succession." This is hardly surprising, considering the austerely neutral and voidlike status to which space has been consigned. Beginning with Kant (and precisely in response to Leibniz, Locke, and Descartes), time was assigned priority over space. First, time is (in Kant's own conception) the form of *inner* sense and so more encompassing than the spatiality delivered by outer sense; then, time is the only adequate expression of Becoming (compared with which, for Bergson, space is only an artificial imposition); and, finally, time is the most authentic modality of all human existence (for Husserl and especially for Heidegger).

The point of this excursion in the history of ideas is that place has been doubly displaced since Descartes—first by "space" of a universal sort that has no place for local place, and then by time, which since Kant and the Romantics has overtaken space itself as having the privileged position. (One effect of this last step is to have precipitated theories of memory into a time-bound framework from which they have still not recovered. It is by no means accidental that William James juxtaposes "The Perception of Time" with "Memory" as the titles of two successive chapters in his *Principles of Psychology*, though he was anticipated in this, as in many other ways, by St. Augustine. Books 10 and 11 of Augustine's *Confessions* are entitled, respectively, "A Philosophy of Memory" and "Time and Eternity." Consider also that Husserl, decisively influenced by James and citing the *Confessions* in the very first section of his seminal 1905 lectures on "internal time-consciousness," conceived of such consciousness as mainly a matter of memory.)

Contrast with this virtual demise of place in post-Cartesian thinking the proclamation of Archytas, the second-generation Pythagorean (and friend of Plato), who was the first among the ancients to write a separate treatise on place (*topos*):

> Since what is moved is moved into a certain place and doing and suffering are motions, it is plain that place, in which what is done and suffered exists, is the first of things. Since everything which is moved is moved into a certain place, it is plain that the place where the thing moving or being moved shall be must exist first. Perhaps it is the first of all beings, since everything that exists is in a place and cannot exist without a place.[12]

Place—"the first of things"!? Even if the first shall have become last in the eventual course of Western thought, it behooves us to try to recapture and to understand what is meant by such a claim. In what, in other words, does the firstness of place consist?

Aristotle, who discusses place first before void, motion, and time, opens Book IV of his *Physics* with the demanding declaration that "the physicist must have a knowledge of place" (208 a 27). Place is first for Aristotle, as for Archytas, because existent beings must be somewhere and because the somewhere is best determined as a container of movable bodies. In the first capacity, place is essential to the very existence of movable bodies; in the second, it provides definition and limit, as well as enclosure and aegis, to these same bodies. Place has, further, the remarkable property of situating things while being separable from them, unlike the form and the matter of things which are *not* separable from them.[13]

But place is prior in Aristotelian cosmology for another quite crucial reason: *it exerts an active force* on the things it situates. Far from being a void (as the atomists, especially Democritus, held) and more even than being a homogeneous but non-isotropic medium (as Epicurus and Lucretius came to assert), place has a power of its own to change the course of events:

Further, the typical locomotions of the elementary natural bodies—namely, fire, earth, and the like—show not only that place is something, but also that it *exerts a certain influence* [*dynamis:* also "power," "potency"]. Each [natural body] is carried to its own place, if it is not hindered, the one up, the other down. Now these are regions or kinds of place—up and down and the rest of the six directions. (*Physics* 208 b 8–14; my italics)

Others before Aristotle had recognized such regions, which are abiding locations for the basic material elements. They had attributed the formation of these regions either to a natural process such as condensation and rarefaction (as in Anaximenes)[14] or to quasi-mythical powers invoked for this very purpose, as in Plato's account of the violent shaking motions of the "Recipient" or "Nurse of Becoming."[15] But Aristotle was the first to take the bold step of suggesting that the regionalization of things is due to the inherent power of place itself, that *place itself places*, engenders, effects, makes a difference by itself alone.

III

Let us pause for a moment before we consider just what difference place makes for Aristotle. What is it for place to have such influence as to be (in his panegyric) "a marvelous thing, and [to] take precedence of all other things" (208 b 34–35)? It is easy enough to grasp how time has this kind of influence: we need only notice the way in which things waste away in it (though whether time actually *causes* the wastage or is just the occasion for it remains more moot),[16] or the way in which we despair in and of time, come to joy or grief through it, get depressed by it, etc. But place? How can it ring such changes, especially if place is itself something unchanging—as Aristotle himself affirms by defining it as "the innermost *motionless* boundary of what contains" (212 a 20–21; my emphasis)? Yet it is clear that place, as it is experienced by human beings, is very much a moving force; it changes the character and direction of our lives.

The mere mention of one particular place—say, 'San Francisco'—suffices to bring this point home. San Francisco is a place that exerts a quite active influence on many who reside or visit there.[17] The city has an undeniable attractive power; it is the sort of place you can leave your heart in. And "heart" is the *mot juste* since the heart is the ultimate place of human attachments: "you have a place in my heart," we say, meaning that you and more particularly memories involving you belong to me, constitute me in the most intimate way. "Heart-mysteries there," said Yeats in "The Circus Animals' Desertion," where "there" always implies place. (Eliot adds that "I can only say, *there* we have been: but I cannot say [just] where./And I cannot say, how long, for that is to place it in time.")[18] Here is an extraordinary, a most moving, conjunction: city and heart, whose intimate interplay is echoed in phrases such as "city arteries" and "heart of the city." It is not just the inherent plasticity of place, it is this intrinsic memorability that contributes most powerfully to its psychical efficacy. 'San Francisco' is a place-marker as much for the memories we have of this city as for any more existential or pragmatic consequences it may have had in our lives. *Place–heart–memory:* here is a genuine *mysterium coniunctionis* which yields heart as the place of memory, memory as the place where heart is, place as the memory where heart is left, heart as what is left of remembered place.

IV

It is becoming increasingly evident *that* place can indeed exert an active influence on us (though this is nothing new to pilgrims), and we have begun to understand just *how* it can do so via its memorability and its tie to the human heart. But things other than place are memorable too, and heart-mysteries range very broadly in human experience. We need to scrutinize place more closely to discover what is uniquely efficacious in it. Once more we shall follow Aristotle's lead since he is, in my view, the first and still the most systematic phenomenologist of place. I will pursue here two themes which recur with insistence in Aristotle's discussion of place in the *Physics:* the "up" and "down" as determining the main directionality of place, and the "in" as its primary locus.

(i) *Up/Down.* "All place," said Aristotle, "admits of the distinction of up and down" (211 a 3). You will recall that "up" and "down" were already mentioned in one of the passages from the *Physics* cited above: indeed, not just mentioned, but singled out as paradigmatic precisely when the influence of place is being boldly asserted. Let me cite this passage in full:

> Further, the typical locomotions of the elementary natural bodies—
> namely, fire, earth, and the like—show not only that place is something,
> but also that it exerts a certain influence. Each is carried to its own place,
> if it is not hindered, the one up, the other down. Now these are regions
> or kinds of place—up and down and the rest of the six directions. Nor
> do such distinctions (up and down and right and left, etc.) hold only in
> relation to us. To *us* they are not always the same but change with the
> direction in which we are turned: that is why the same thing may be both
> right *and* left, up *and* down, before *and* behind. But *in nature* each is
> distinct, taken apart by itself. It is not every chance direction which is
> "up," but where fire and what is light are carried; similarly, too, "down"
> is not any chance direction but where what has weight and what is made
> of earth are carried—the implications being that these places do not dif
> fer merely in relative position, but also as possessing distinct potencies.

This is made plain also by [contrast with] the objects studied by mathematics. Though they have no real place, they nevertheless, in respect of their position relatively to us, have a right and left as attributes ascribed to them only in consequence of their relative position, not having by nature these various characteristics. (208 b 8–28; my emphasis)

Affirmed here are the following propositions: (1) The primary example of an element's being "carried to its own place" is movement up or down— as if to say that the most definitive places, the places of places, are those established by such directions. This will be confirmed by Aristotle's linking of "up" with heaven and "down" with the earth a few pages later.[19] (2) All of the six directions spontaneously distinguished by human beings (up and down, right and left, before and behind) seem to be relative to the position of our bodies—to be a mere matter of "relative position," just as Locke will say is true of place itself as a whole. But Aristotle claims that *in nature*, in the world, each direction is "distinct," i.e., independent of our position in relation to it.[20] (And yet once more the only sample he offers of such independence is the up and the down. Rightly so, too, for the other four directions are certainly much more dependent on our body's position in relation to them.) (3) The independence of the up and the down is then equated with the regionalization of elements by virtue of their "distinct potencies": fire and light are drawn up *by* the up, and earth and whatever has weight (i.e., water as well) are drawn down *by* the down. (4) In contrast with this, place in mathematics is entirely a matter of relative position only and, for this very reason, mathematical objects "have no real place." This is not only to lock out Locke's position in advance; it is to shed a sardonic light on the contemporary situation, in which topology, having vanished from physics and philosophy, now belongs almost wholly to mathematics.[21]

Notice precisely what Aristotle has accomplished in making these claims. He has, in effect, established inherent *vectors of place*. The distinct potencies of up and down are such as to mark off two cosmically crucial directions into which all the material elements will eventually drift or fall. Indeed, "it is not every *chance* direction which is 'up' . . . [or] 'down.' " There is a factor of cosmological necessity in the non-arbitrariness and non-relativity with which the up and the down polarize the known universe as its essential epicenters. The right and the left, the before and the behind, lack such necessity and scope, for they relate only to particular perceived things and do not apply to entire elements such as air, aether, or water. (And yet, in a modern perspective, *they* would be the more critical, restricted as we have become to a leveled-down cosmology in which the horizontal— where right / left, before / behind naturally belong—is more determinative than the vertical.)[22]

But more than cosmology is at issue here—indeed, more than physics too. Aristotle's *Physics*, like Plato's *Timaeus* on which it is so often commenting, is a veritable treatise in *psycho*physics. This is nowhere more evident than in the case of the up and the down. These vectors, and the movements which realize them, are as much directions of the psyche as of the material elements. Consider the following passage from the *Physics*:

> Hence since the light is what is naturally carried up, and the heavy what is carried down, the boundary which contains in the direction of the middle of the universe, and the middle itself, are down, and that which contains in the direction of the outermost part of the universe, and the outermost part itself, are up. (*Physics* 212 a 25–28)

Instead of construing this in strictly physicalistic terms, think of how the mind, and more particularly the imagination, makes just such movements: upward, when images and thoughts are aerial or fiery and naturally seek to soar; downward, when our ruminations are aqueous or tellurian and descend with their own psychical gravity.

It is Bachelard, of course, who has mapped in exquisite detail these contrary directions of the material imagination. Conspicuously missing from Bachelard's five books on this subject, however, is any sense of what Aristotle has just called "the middle," that is, "the boundary which contains in the direction of the middle of the universe." The middle, or centerpoint, of the universe is the earth, on which we stand, build, and gaze—on which, in short, we dwell. The middle point for human beings is a dwelling point, a place of inhabitation. Such a place is again as much psychical as physical, and its role in the present context is to mediate between the extremities of up and down, to be a *tertium quid* in relation to them, to be their buffer zone. For we would be torn apart psychically if we had as our only alternative directions upmost and downmost, heaven and hell, peaks and vales, high-flying imagination and morbidly remorseful memory. In the face of these exclusive and diremptive directionalities, we need to be able to take a stand somewhere in between—somewhere on earth, on the world's body, a body that is conterminous with the World Soul. Such a stand would occur in a dwelling place that enables us to experience our souls *in extremis* without reducing soul itself to the extremes.

Only in taking this stand can we begin to bear the tearing apart of which mania and depression are the psychopathological representatives in many particular variations (such as the "aethereal world"/"tomb world" juxtaposition we find in Ludwig Binswanger's case of Ellen West). Only in this way too can we begin to appreciate the cyclical character of such matters and, indeed, of the 'up' and the 'down' themselves: "the way up and the way down are one and the same," said Heraclitus, who did not mean that they are indifferently the same or the same only in relation to each other. Rather, they form part of the same cycle: "fire lives in the death of earth, air in the death of fire, water in the death of air, and earth in the death of water."[23] Such a cycle of transformations can best be discerned from a place in the middle—or, rather, *measured* from there in the richest sense of this term, as when we say "to take the measure of." Hear Heidegger on this:

> The upward glance passes aloft toward the sky, and yet it remains below on the earth. The upward glance spans the between of sky and earth. This between is measured out for the dwelling of man. We now call the span thus meted out the dimension. The dimension does not arise from the fact that the sky and earth are turned toward one another. Rather, their facing each other itself depends on the dimension. Nor is the dimension a stretch of space as primarily understood; for everything spatial, as something for which space is made, is already in need of the dimension, that is, that into which it is admitted. The nature of the dimension is the meting out—which is lightened and can be spanned—of the between, the upward to the sky as well as the downward to earth.[24]

The dimension of the between can be measured, however, only if taking this measure is itself based on taking a stand, which in turn depends on our finding a *place* in which to stand between heaven and earth, the up and down, and to determine its "distance." This place is called a "location" (*Ort*) by Heidegger, who conceives it as the gathering-place for mortals and gods as well as earth and sky. It is in such a place that we "dwell poetically on earth" in Hölderlin's phrase that serves as a leitmotif for Heidegger's reflections on "building, dwelling, thinking." A bridge, for example, is not only a spanning of a stream for the sake of convenience; it "gathers the fourfold [just mentioned], but in such a way that it allows a site for the fourfold."[25] As such, it is a location, a place. It is striking how close to Aristotle is Heidegger's description of the bridge-as-location:

> . . . only something that is itself a location can make space for a site. The location is not already there before the bridge is. Before the bridge stands, there are of course many spots along the stream that can be occupied by something. One of them proves to be a location, and does so *because of the bridge.*[26]

This is only to repeat Aristotle's point: there are not antecedently specifiable, independently existing places that come to be occupied by things. Such a conception of empty, to-be-occupied space holds only for "sites," determined by intervals between pre-established positions on a uniform grid or *spatium*, which, generalized to three dimensions, yields Cartesian *extensio.*[27] Sites are made possible by places—just as geography is by landscape[28]—but place itself is always the place of a particular thing, a given movable body whose place it is. The location or place of the bridge is a genuine *locus* (and not merely a *situs*) "because of the bridge," that is, because of the fact that this particular built thing has the surface and volume, as well as the structure and function, which it possesses uniquely. Place remains "the innermost motionless boundary of what contains," even if we must now add that it is also a "boundary which contains in the direction of the middle of the universe"—which is to say, a boundary from which we take the measure, span and mete out, the betweenness or dis-tance of the psychophysical extremities of the up and the down.

(ii) *In.* But beyond, or rather under, the "between" is the "in." If we were not standing *in* a place, we could not take measure *from* it of that which it is itself between. And if standing in a place is a dwelling there, it is (by) in-habiting it. This is not mere prepositional play, since place is, strictly speaking, *pre-positional.* Or we might say that the situation leads us to take prepositions with a new philosophical seriousness: Could it be that it is more in prepositions than in nouns and verbs, adjectives and adverbs that the syntax of place (and thus also of space and perhaps even of time as well) manifests itself most transparently?[29] Before we can begin to decide on this, however, we must consider something of the psycho-logic of the "in." Without this, we shall never get place itself in place.

Aristotle lists eight ways in which one thing can be said to be "in" another.[30] These include the manner in which a part is in a whole and vice versa, a species is in a genus and the converse, form is in matter, the existence of something lies in its end (*telos*), and the affairs of Greece center in the King. But, adds Aristotle, "the strictest sense of all [is] as a thing is 'in' a vessel, and generally 'in' place" (210 a 23–24). The analogy of the vessel is not brought in frivolously. It is introduced early in Book IV of the *Physics* by the remark that "place is supposed to be something like a vessel" (209 b 28) and is employed prominently on five or six subsequent occasions, including the late mention that "place is thought to be a kind of surface, and as it were a vessel, i.e., a container of the thing" (212 a 28–29).

But the value of the vessel for Aristotle's purposes goes beyond the mere fact that it is a container. First, it is the kind of container which is separable from what it contains—in contrast with form and matter, which (as mentioned earlier) are inseparable from what they are the form and matter of.[31] "The vessel," in brief, "is no part of what is in it" (210 b 28). Second, however, though strictly separable, the inner surface of the vessel is exactly coincident with the outer limit of what is contained in it, whether water or air.[32] This is not just a matter of a tight jeans-like fit but of a containment so complete that not the least gap can be left between container and contained. More like a plaster cast mold than anything merely hand-in-glove, it exhibits Aristotle's penchant for conceiving place as a plenum; thus what we would call "space" or the "universe" is for him a totality of filled-up places.

The positing of this plenum also makes manifest a horror of the vacuum—a defense against the idea of a void, which Aristotle defines revealingly as "place bereft of body" (208 b 26), wherein we can detect more than an echo of separation anxiety, of finding absence intolerable. He defends against absence and void by thinking of place as perpetual plenitude, whether at the level of proper place (the place of movable bodies) or at the vaster level of the common place, "the place of the whole world" that contains all particular places. Both kinds of place hold in, and keep, their contents without remainder through a containing action which is not unlike the continual anti-cathexis that Freud posited as the main motor of repression. This action is not only a gathering but an *in*-gathering, a retaining within, which is also a protecting of what is thereby kept inside.

This is not to say, of course, that the vessel is a perfect analogy of place (no analogy is perfect, not even one that repeats a structure tautologously).[33] Aristotle brings place and vessel to a point of near-coincidence, only to separate them at a critical concluding moment:

> Just, in fact, as the vessel is transportable place, so place is a non-portable vessel. So when what is within a thing which is moved, is moved and changes its place, as a boat on a river, what contains plays the part of a vessel *rather than that of place*. Place on the other hand is rather what is motionless: so it is rather the whole river that is place, because as a whole it is motionless. (212 a 13–19; my italics)

A vessel as a portable place both carries water within it and is itself carried; a river carries currents of water within it but is not itself carried. Even if Heraclitus was right that you cannot step twice into the same river (for "other waters are continually flowing on"),[34] still the river as a whole, as *one* river, is without motion. The riverscape becomes a landscape, and the marvelous immobility of the latter makes it a paradigm for any place-scape, including an urban one.

But portability aside, the common element of water is strikingly present in vessel and river. What does this signify? Here Heraclitus is again apposite:

> Souls take pleasure in becoming moist. (47)

> It is death to souls to become water, and it is death to water to become earth. Conversely, water comes into existence out of earth, and souls out of water. (49)

> Souls are vaporized from what is moist. (44)

> [Soul] is the vaporization out of which everything else is derived; moreover it is the least corporeal of things and is in ceaseless flux, for the moving world can only be known by what is in motion. (43)

Soul, in other words, gets drawn *downward* into water as if to its natural element (and drawn *in* it too: reflected there in aqueous relief), and yet it is essentially constituted by an *upward* movement of vaporization into the drily aerial. The paradox is that it is only as vaporized—Anaximenes had said: "just as our soul, being air, holds us together, so do breath and air encompass the whole world"[35]—that soul becomes structurally most like the water it is rarefied from: "in ceaseless flux," says Heraclitus in anticipating Husserl's idea of "absolute flux," the deepest level of time-consciousness. Still, a body of water as a whole, whatever the activity of its constituent parts, makes up one motionless place, as immobile as the Heideggerian bridge that spans it.

Soul, which is not only moving but *self*-moving (as Plato adds), comes to inhabit any such place as a river or a bridge over it, either by means of bodiless imagining or by embodied occupancy. Soul gets into place in these two ways as well as by remembering (a form of self-*re*-placing), and place in turn becomes ensouled—becomes genuinely inhabited by soul. Soul, despite its aerial proclivity, becomes situated in the still waters of place; and they become by this very action located: they become a local habitation. These waters pull soul in and down, drifting into death like Phlebas the Phoenician: "a fortnight dead, forgot . . . the profit and loss./A current under sea/Picked his bones in whispers. . . ."[36] Soul animates the waters, making them a psychical habitat as well as a natural phenomenon. In contrast with earth—which is crucial for soul mainly as a dwelling place situated midway between the extremities of up and down—water matters for soul as the element of its own interiority, as the basis for its being-*in*: in dreams and reveries as well as in the world it so uneasily inhabits.

Vessel–soul–river: all participate in place. The river in its ongoingness is a place par excellence, while the vessel is a para-place, part place only. Soul is situated in the 'in' of the between; it is carried by the body and yet self-moving in its imaginative and memorial flights—even to the manic point of ceaseless flux, rejoining the river's madly flowing torrents. The vessel, once more, carries water while being itself transportable; the river, unmoved as a whole, *is* swiftly moving water in any of its parts; the soul, self-instigating and to this extent uncontainable by any particular place, comes nonetheless to reside, to find and leave its heart, in various places, including rivers. And if the soul resides in places, these latter are in soul as well: ensouled there. From the soul's engaging perspective, nothing is out, much less outermost; everything is in . . . and in . . . and in. Not simply as water is in the vessel is in the hand; but as soul is in water is in world is in dream. The model of the Chinese box gives way to the interpenetrating multiplicity of the currents of the riverrun of the dream world.

The way out and the way in are one and the same, and it is in the inness of place, where inner boundary and outer limit coincide, that soul can be found. Or, rather, a place for soul, soul in place, gathered in upon itself and yet conterminous with all that would contain it, whether from above or from below. *Soul situated:* by no means the same as *soul sited*!

It is to the unsitedness of soul, its refusal to be contained within carto-graphic limits, that Heraclitus points when he says that "you could not discover the limits of soul, even if you traveled every road to do so; such is the depth of its meaning."[37] You may not be able to discover the limits of soul—especially if you follow roads staked out in geographic space—but you *can* find the place of soul in the proper landscape fully traversed; for here, in-placed, soul is discovered and discovers itself. And if soul is thus found in place, soul in turn puts place in its own proper place, giving to place itself a being and a depth which it lacks as site alone.

V

In coming toward a conclusion, let me try to draw things together under four headings: place versus site, place versus time, placing archetypes, and placing ourselves.

1. *Place versus Site.* In various ways we have been witnessing the truth of Archytas's claim that place is "the first of things." It is what things themselves require in order to exist; Aristotle's initial thesis that "every sensible body is in place" (208 b 28–29) has been expanded to include soul as well: souls, too, in order to exist, must be *somewhere* and not only in the human body as Aristotle presumed in his *De Anima* (where soul is held to be the form of the body).

Site is not similarly essential to the existence of things, whether bodies or souls. In fact, its own existence depends on place, of which it is a modification. What kind of modification? Where place is utterly particular and unique (think again of San Francisco, and think of how pointless are comparisons of it with, say, Paris or Rio), site is non-unique and replace-able. *On* a given site, *at* it, something else could exist—another McDonald's at this very address!—whereas *in* a given place nothing else could be without its becoming another place altogether. Sites modify places by level-ing them down, razing them, making them indifferently planar, so that horizontality comes to count for more than verticality; and the dimensions of up/down and in/out matter less than distinctions between right and left, before and behind. Notice that these latter are all determined by sheer confrontation with sensible bodies—by standing *in front of* them—while the four essential dimensions of place require concerted actions of look-ing up or down, in or out. On this earth, "in this realm," as Heidegger says, "man is allowed to look up, out of it, through it, toward the divinities."[38] Measuring place in this active sense is done not only with one's eye, but also with one's entire body; both ways contrast with measur-ing sites, which is always mediated by instruments and for the sake of pur-poses other than the measuring itself. Sites are less seen than overseen, supervised. They are, after all, sites *for* some more ultimate activity (thus we speak of "building sites"), while just taking the measure of a place suf-

fices in itself and calls for no further activity. Think of the difference between being in a cityscape or landscape and becoming sensuously attuned
to it, versus gazing at a map of some placescape. We typically use the map,
an isometric representation of ordered sites, to get somewhere *other* than
where we are standing; in the case of the landscape we do not need to
get anywhere else than where we *are;* we stand in it, dwell in it, and are
satisfied therewith. The intrinsically surpassable, and willfully established,
positions of sites ('site' is *thesis* in Greek; literally, a 'positing') give way
to spontaneously given, unsurpassable locations within the placescape. So,
too, the outgoing outlines of sites (out precisely onto other contiguous sites)
are replaced by the indwelling inlines of places, which provide their own
boundaries rather than borrowing these from surrounding space. And place
provides its own boundaries—"regionalizes," we might say—because it
possesses an immanent power that site lacks. This power, as I have suggested, is a considerable part of what makes place more inherently memorable, more an affair of the heart, than site; if we remember certain sites
(e.g., as addresses), this is characteristically only inasmuch as they serve
as indices of memorable places.

2. *Place versus Time.* I have been attempting in this final chapter to question some prominent post-Cartesian assumptions concerning spatiality. One
of these has been the primacy of site and space over place; another is the
priority of time over all of these. As there is not space enough to argue
adequately against this last assumption, I shall limit myself to noting some
distinctive differences between place and time. Place, as we certainly know
by now, is a matter of containment. The Greek word for container is *peri-
echon*, a having or holding around. To be in place is to be embraced within
a containing boundary; it is to be held there. This is why being in place
is a matter of enclosure or encapsulment, of in-gathering—and also why
images like the vessel and the river capture what is most crucial in the notion of place regarded as "the innermost motionless boundary of what contains."

Time, in vivid contrast, is dis-closing rather than en-closing, opening
up or out rather than closing down. Time, says Aristotle, "disperses subsistence" (*Physics* 221 b 2), and it does so by its characteristic activity of
"standing away" (*ekstatikon*): "we say 'beforehand and afterward' in relation to standing away from the now, where the now is the border of the
past and the future" (223 a 5–6).[39] There is something ecstatic, outgoing,
about time in contrast with the ingoing, in-standing character of place.
Place holds in while time breaks out. Place conserves where time destroys:
lays waste by always standing away from whatever has been accomplished
or experienced in the now, which exists only (like positions in space) to
be surpassed.[40] Toward what? Toward a past and a future which do not,
strictly speaking, exist now; or, rather, they exist only as horizons of the
now, *outer* limits of its corrosive activity. Hence Heidegger, very much indebted to Aristotle for his entire conception of human temporality, speaks

of its "ecstatico-horizonal" nature in *Being and Time*. Self-detonating from within (in the always-to-be-surpassed now), time is also detonated from without (since its horizons recede apace). As ec-static, time takes us out of ourselves—out of our mind and body, and out of our place as well.

It is significant that when Heidegger gives, many years later, a more positive account of horizon, it is only with reference to location and space, not to time:

> A boundary is not that at which something stops but, as the Greeks recognized, the boundary is that from which something *begins its presencing*. That is why the concept is that of *horismos*, that is, the horizon, the boundary.[41]

The horizon of landscape is not merely a vanishing point but a constitutive element of the scene and sometimes (as at dawn or sunset) the most energic element in it. In time's flow, however, the proximate horizons of beforehand and afterward (renamed "protentions" and "retentions" by Husserl)[42] continually "sink away," while the distal horizons of past and future vanish even more radically, as we know from the difficulties of prophecy and the vexations of amnesia. No wonder Heraclitus could say that "time is a child moving counters in a game; the royal power is a child's"[43]—for the child will push the counters right off the board, that is, the border of an organized and known place, undoing its enclosure.

But place is never entirely dispossessed by time, even if this latter does possess the royal power of laying places (and people) to waste. It is instructive to realize that the very idea of the beforehand and the afterward, which are so indispensable in the constitution of time as we know it, is derived ultimately from properties belonging to place:

> The beforehand and the afterward are first of all in place, therein, however, in respect to position, and since the beforehand and afterward hold in magnitude, they must also hold in motion too, it [motion] having analogy to them [position and magnitude]. But then in time too is the beforehand and afterward, through the ever-corresponding of [time and motion] to one another. (*Physics* 219 a 16–19)

Place proves primary to time in regard to the latter's own internal horizons of before and after. Here is revenge indeed upon the avenging tooth of time! Triumph or not, however, it should make us pause whenever we are tempted (and we always *are* tempted) to give dominion to Time's remorseless disarray. And in any case place, by its very nature, protects against this disarray, provides aegis before the ravage; which may be one reason why we act to protect places, to "conserve" these life-preservers themselves, from the decline and ruination wrought in (if not by) time's lethal advance.

3. *Placing Archetypes*. Here the task is not to counter or contrast but

to ground. It was with the groundlessness of archetypes that this chapter commenced; and that archetypes can be "found everywhere" is equivalent, I said, to their existing nowhere. Placelessness is groundlessness. For place gives ground, *is* ground in its most profound dimension: more than earth qua physical ground, as well as other than a logical (an explanatory or justifying) ground too. But the question remains: How do we give ground or place to anything so numinous, so omnitemporal and universal as an archetype? How, in other words, can archetypology become archetopology?

There are two essential steps in constructing an adequate archetopology: making particular and what I shall call, for lack of a better word, "placement."

(i) *Making Particular.* This is no other than the task of reconceiving archetypes as images rather than as symbols. The universalist pretensions of symbols put them into the same limbo—the same void—as that enjoined upon archetypes seen as all-encompassing contents of the collective unconscious. Such a void can be avoided only by refusing the lures of symbology and by turning instead to the particularities of imagery. Depth psychology began, after all, with Freud's rejection of an *oneirocritica* or lexicon of universal dream symbols. The history of such psychology has, however, testified to continual backsliding on this very point, beginning with Freud himself and continuing with Jung and Jungians. Only very recently, with Rafael López-Pedraza's insistence on "sticking to the image," has the situation begun to reverse itself once again, such that particularizing is beginning to get the attention previousiy reserved for universalizing (itself no doubt a reflection of the scientific aspirations of the new form of psychology, seeking as it did *laws* of the psyche).

Particularizing has its natural habitat in the image, which, as "a sudden salience on the surface of the psyche,"[44] comes to us in an intrinsically unique format. Symbols, like universals (indeed, *as* universals), are there to be exemplified and repeated. An image only exemplifies itself and cannot be repeated as such. Hillman has suggested an essential reason why this is so: images present themselves spontaneously as personified, as having a "face."[45] And this in turn implies their quasi-corporealization, their imaginal embodiment as sensible concreta of soul. "Imagination," as Shakespeare said unerringly, "*bodies forth* the forms of things unknown. . . . and gives to airy nothing a local habitation and a name."[46] Without body, albeit a subtle body, there is no fully particularized image.

(ii) *Placement.* But how do archetypes embodied and enfaced in images gain a "local habitation"? They gain it mainly in and through *myth*. Put succinctly: insofar as myth is im-plotted—finds itself caught up in the configurational 'topic' of a story—it is also im-placed. For the mythic story must have a place, a *topos*, in order to take place; it requires a *mise en scène,* a scene of action. Such a scene is itself a place and possesses all the particularity that belongs to place in contrast with site. And this is so not despite its imaginal status but very much because of it—just as a dream scene is highly specific to the dream for which it provides the place. The oneiric scene, like the mythic scene for which it is in so many ways the prototype, is non-transferable and non-generalizable. As with place in non-imaginal contexts, both types of scene play a containing and a protecting role; they shelter their content, gather it in within the perimeter they trace out. Anything beyond their limits is off-limits with regard to what shows itself in them. Freud borrowed from Fechner the phrase *"der andere Schauplatz"* for the dream scene. In myth, as in dream, it is a matter of determining that 'other show-place,' where the only action that counts is located. What takes place *takes place in such a place,* however deeply enciphered it may be.

Archetopology is the study of such specific places—such regions. It seeks for the *archetopoi* that particularize and ground archetypal presences in image-forms. We have already considered vectorial structures of basic places: up and down, in (and, by implication, out). These structures have been regarded as psycho-physical in status: physical, as incorporating or reflecting the material elements; psychical, as indicating areas or directions of inhabitation for the soul. The psychical side emerges, for instance, when we think of how many purely imaginary places are "up" or "out" there somewhere or when we take "down" depth-psychologically and find its proper place, its own domain, to be the underworld—which is, in Hillman's words, "a realm of only psyche, a purely psychical world. . . . Being in the underworld means psychic being, being psychological, where soul comes first."[47] To which I would only add the question: Is it soul, taken alone, that comes first or *soul-in-place*? There is certainly displaced soul (perhaps soul is always being displaced and displacing itself); but is there any such thing as *un*-placed soul?

4. *Placing Ourselves.* "Getting Placed" is my main title. Notice that I have not said "getting in place," which means assuming an assigned and serially ordered position, as when we get into line at a theater. Sartre compares all such queuing or "series" behavior with the "group in fusion" that is spontaneous and place-oriented (his leading example is the storming of the Bastille, whose constituent actions could not have taken place anywhere other than on the streets of a certain *arrondissement* in Paris).[48] Getting in, or into, place is thus a matter of site rather than place, of *thesis* rather than *topos*. Here the preposition controls too much, locking us into more than we need to bargain for in psychical topology.

In contrast, "getting placed" is a direct combination of active and passive verb forms, unmediated and unmodified by any preposition (it is of interest that in Latin and Greek prepositions were at first adverbs, hence appendages of verbs).[49] The "getting" is not the getting of "getting and spending," of acquiring and only then disbursing. This latter getting is equivalent to *having* and is thus allied with such expressions as "having a place of your own" with all that this entails of possession and possessiveness. It is sites, not places, that are owned in this fashion. And yet it is just because of a basic confusion between site and place, between having and creating space, that it has been assumed that *all* space is inimical to the soul's inhabitation and that time, by default, must be more amenable. Husserl is speaking not just for himself but for an entire tradition when he writes that "it has always been noted that psychic being in and for itself has no spatial extension and no location."[50] (It has "always been noted" only insofar as it has always been assumed that space is reducible to the kind of thing which you *have* and of which three-dimensional *extension* is a paradigm case.)

The *getting* of "getting placed" is equivalent to *being*—where "being" has an active sense of coming-to-be placed, not just accepting a place or fitting into one. We may be said to place ourselves, where such self-placing is fully psychophysical in status. Husserl himself posits kinesthesia as the most likely sensory modality by which such being-placed could occur bodily; and what is more psychophysically pivotal than kinesthetically sensed movements?[51] Soul, as we have already seen, is self-moving by its very nature; body becomes so by kinesthetic actions of various kinds.

Lest we be tempted to a new psychical activism, however, it is important to recall the other side of the formula: it is a matter of getting, or being, *placed*, where the passive construction reminds us that in questions of place something always precedes our own self-moving actions. Not a simply or sheerly unoccupied place (as in the "spots" along the stream at which Heidegger's bridge is *not* located) but a potentially occupied place, not definable with precision in advance but always to be specified by the movable thing that comes to be situated in it.[52] This "thing," which can be a soul as well as a body (and a soul *in* a body), lends to place its peculiar dimensions; and it is in this way that placing occurs: in animating a locale by a particular presence. Henry Corbin was thinking of the same dialectic between the situated and the situating when he wrote that "a human presence has the property of spatializing a world around it."[53] This signifies: finding and creating places in the world around it. And if creating places, giving them dimension, is the active element in getting placed, finding a place and getting oriented there ("getting one's bearings" as we say significantly) represent the passive moment. Every finding, as Freud asserted, is in fact a *re*finding; finding and refinding rejoin each other as intimately as do giving dimension and receiving orientation, placing and being placed. Soul inhabits space in getting placed.

1.   See C. G. Jung, *Two Essays on Analytical Psychology* (New York: Meridian, 1970), p. 76. Cf. also *CW* 9, i, ¶3.

2.   Jung, *Two Essays,* p. 76. He is speaking directly of the collective unconscious in this passage, but whatever holds true of it holds true of archetypes also.

3.   Ibid., p. 75.

4.   Aristotle, *Physics* 211 b 28–29 (Hardie & Gaye translation).

5. For this argument, see ibid., 212 b 12–22. Further references in the text will be to *Physics* IV.

6. Cited by Reiner Schürmann in his essay "Situating René Char: Hölderlin, Heidegger, Char and the 'There is,' " in *Heidegger and the Question of Literature*, ed. W. V. Spanos (Bloomington: Indiana University Press, 1979), p. 173.

7. This term condenses "archetypal topology," a term which is discussed further in my essay "Toward an Archetypal Imagination," in this volume.

8. See Martin Heidegger, *Unterwegs zur Sprache* (Pfullingen: Neske, 1959), p. 37.

9. René Descartes, *Principles of Philosophy*, trans. E. Anscombe and P. Geach and reprinted (in part) in J. J. C. Smart, *Problems of Space and Time* (New York: Macmillan, 1964), p. 75.

10. Ibid., p. 73. Gibson remarks: "Geometrical space is a pure abstraction. Outer space can be visualized but cannot be seen. . . . The visual third dimension is a misapplication of Descartes' notion of three axes for a co-ordinate system" (J. J. Gibson, *The Ecological Approach to Visual Perception* [Boston: Houghton Mifflin, 1979], p. 3).

11. John Locke, *An Essay Concerning Human Understanding*, Book II, chap. 13.

12. Archytas, as reported by Simplicius in his *Aristotelis categorias commentarium* and cited by Max Jammer, "The Concept of Space in Antiquity," in Smart, *Problems of Space and Time*, p. 28.

13. See Aristotle, *Physics* 209 b 5–30, where the argument is directed mainly against Plato's attempt in the *Timaeus* to identify place with matter.

14. Anaximenes recognizes air alone as the basic element; about it he says that "it differs in different substances in virtue of its rarefaction and condensation" (cited in J. Burnet, *Early Greek Philosophy* [New York: Meridian, 1957], p. 72).

15. "The four kinds [i.e., material elements] were shaken by the recipient, which was itself in motion like an instrument for shaking, and it separated the most unlike kinds farthest apart from one another, and thrust the most alike closest together; whereby the different kinds came to have different regions. . ." (Plato, *Timaeus* 52 d; Cornford's translation in *Plato's Cosmology* [New York: Liberal Arts Press, 1957], p. 198).

16. Aristotle reverses himself on this very point, first saying that time is "the cause of wasting away rather than of becoming" (*Physics* 222 b 20–21) and then adding that "still, time does not do this; even this change happens incidentally in time" (ibid., 222 b 25–26).

17. This essay was first delivered at the opening of the Second Archetypal Psychology Institute, July 1981, in San Francisco.

18. T. S. Eliot, "Burnt Norton," *Four Quartets;* his italics.

19. Cf. Aristotle, *Physics* 212 b 20–22: "The earth is in water, and this in the air, and the air in the aether, and the aether in heaven."

20. It is striking that "quark symmetries" (e.g., of the hadron) include equivalents of up/down and right/left. Aristotle would be delighted by such developments in recent physics! See Fritjof Capra, *The Tao of Physics* (New York: Bantam, 1975) and P. C. W. Davies, *The Forces of Nature* (Cambridge: Cambridge University Press, 1979).

21. I say "almost," for there are the exceptions of Heidegger (who speaks in his later writings of a "topology of Being") and of Gaston Bachelard (who talks of a "topo-analysis" in *The Poetics of Space*).

22. On the importance of "vertical being," see Maurice Merleau-Ponty, *The Visible and the Invisible*, trans. A. Lingus (Evanston: Northwestern University Press, 1968), pp. 221, 223–24, 234, 244, 253, 265, 268.

23. Fragment 34 in Wheelwright's numbering and translation: Philip Wheelwright, *Heraclitus* (Princeton: Princeton University Press, 1959). The fragment cited in the previous sentence is 108.

24. Martin Heidegger, *Poetry, Language, Thought,* trans. A. Hofstadter (New York: Harper & Row, 1975), p. 220.

25. Ibid., p. 154.

26. Ibid.; his italics.

27. For Heidegger's own reconstruction of this successive impoverishment of place see ibid., pp. 155–56.

28. On this distinction, see Erwin Straus, *The Primary World of Senses,* trans. J. Needleman (Glencoe, Il.: Free Press, 1963), pp. 318–23.

29. On the importance of prepositions, see Robert Sokolowski, *Presence and Absence* (Bloomington: Indiana University Press, 1978), pp. 122–28.

30. At Aristotle, *Physics* 210 a 15–25.

31. "The place of a thing is neither a part nor a state of it, but is separable from it. . . . [And] the vessel is no part of the thing" *(Physics* 209 b 27–29).

32. Cf. ibid., 212 a 30–31: "Boundaries are coincident with the bounded."

33. On this point, see Jacques Derrida, *The Archeology of the Frivolous,* trans. J. P. Leavey, Jr. (Pittsburgh: Dusquesne University Press, 1980), pp. 17, 43–44, 81–83.

34. Heraclitus, Fragment 21.

35. Cited by Burnet, *Early Greek Philosophy,* p. 73.

36. T. S. Eliot, "Death by Water," Section IV of *The Waste Land,* lines 312–16.

37. Heraclitus, Fragment 42.

38. Heidegger, *Poetry, Language, Thought,* p. 220.

39. I am indebted to Peter Manchester of the Department of Religious Studies, Stony Brook, for his masterful translation of the passages in the *Physics* which bear on time.

40. "Time is not a whole, for the simple reason that it is itself the instance which prevents the whole" (Gilles Deleuze, *Proust and Signs,* trans. R. Howard [New York: Braziller, 1972], p. 143).

41. Heidegger, *Poetry, Language, Thought,* p. 154; his italics.

42. See Edmund Husserl, *The Phenomenology of Internal Time-Consciousness,* trans. J. S. Churchill (Bloomington: Indiana University Press, 1964), esp. sec. 10, where retentions and protentions are explicitly labeled "horizons" in the time-diagram.

43. Heraclitus, Fragment 24.

44. Gaston Bachelard, *The Poetics of Space,* trans. Maria Jolas (New York: Orion Press, 1964), p. xi.

45. Indeed, for Hillman, strictly speaking "the given itself is shaped; everything comes with a face" ("Egalitarian Typologies *versus* the Perception of the Unique" [*Eranos Jahrbuch 24–1976*], p. 272; rept., Dallas: Spring Publications, Inc., 1984).

46. Shakespeare, *A Midsummer Night's Dream,* V, 1, 7; my italics.

47. James Hillman, *The Dream and the Underworld* (New York: Harper & Row, 1979), pp. 46–47.

48. Jean-Paul Sartre, *Critique of Dialectical Reason* (New York: Schocken, 1976).

49. On this point, see Sokolowski, *Presence and Absence,* pp. 122 ff. Sokolowski claims that the "first sense" of all prepositions is spatial. Only subsequently are temporal and causal interpretations of prepositions added on. Should we not say that the most important "first sense" is that of place, not space per se? Cf. also James Hillman, "Further Notes on Images," *Spring 1978:* 152–82.

50. Edmund Husserl, *The Crisis of European Sciences and Transcendental Phenomenology,* trans. D. Carr (Evanston: Northwestern University Press, 1970), p. 216.

51. See ibid., pp. 217 ff.

52. This line of thought is again anticipated by Aristotle: see *Physics* 221 b 12–29.

53. Henry Corbin, *The Man of Light in Iranian Sufism,* trans. B. Pearson (Boulder: Shambhala, 1978), p. 1.

Sources of Essays in This Volume

"Toward an Archetypal Imagination," *Spring 1974,* first given as a set of three lectures at the C. G. Jung Institute, Zürich, 1973; "Toward a Phenomenology of Imagination," *Journal of the British Society for Phenomenology* (1974), first delivered to the British Society for Phenomenology, Oxford University, 1973; "Imagination as Intermediate," English translation of "L'imagination comme intermédiaire," *Vers une esthétique sans entrave,* ed. G. Lascault (Paris, 1975), a contribution to a Festschrift for Mikel Dufrenne; "Imagination, Fantasy, Hallucination, and Memory," *Research in Phenomenology* (1976); "Image and Memory in Bachelard and Bergson," previously unpublished and first given at a conference on Gaston Bachelard sponsored by the Dallas Institute of Humanities and Culture, 1985; "How Important Are Images for Memory?"—composed as a guest address to the International Imagery Association, New York City, 1984; "Imagining and Remembering," *Review of Metaphysics* (1977), delivered as an invited paper to the annual meeting of the American Philosophical Association, Eastern Division, 1976; "Remembering and Perceiving," *Review of Metaphysics* (1979); "The Memorability of the Filmic Image," *Quarterly Review of Film Studies* (1981), first given at a symposium on film at Cornell University, 1980; "Time out of Mind," *Dimensions of Thought: Current Explorations in Time, Space, and Knowledge,* ed. R. H. Moon and S. Randall (Berkeley, 1980); "Time in the Soul," *Spring 1979,* delivered at the first Institute of Archetypal Psychology, Notre Dame, 1978; "Getting Placed: Soul in Space," *Spring 1982,* delivered at the second Archetypal Psychology Institute, San Francisco, 1981; "The Memorability of Inhabited Space," a contribution to a special issue of *Dragonflies* that never appeared; "Memory, Time, and Soul," given as an invited paper at the Jung Institute, New York, at the Jung Society of Western New York, the Jung Society of Connecticut, and at Syracuse University, in the period 1985–88.

PUER PAPERS—*James Hillman, ed.*

The archetypal young man and young lover, radiant, sensitive, charming, aloof, high-flying. *Puer Papers* gives back the wings to this archetype as he appears in diagnosis, symptoms, dream analysis, literary interpretations, and social movements. Nine basic papers, complete with a rich index of motifs, cover the wide range of that figure who is both spirit guide to the farthest reaches of imagination and seducer—cause of broken hearts and failed dreams. Includes Tom Moore on Artemis and the Puer, articles on Joyce and on Melville, and four papers by James Hillman, one his classic paper "Peaks and Vales" that lays out the differences between spiritual disciplines and depth psychology.

GOD IS A TRAUMA—*Greg Mogenson*

A book that presents a radical theology of *soul*, rather than of spirit, a theology that spells out why the conflict between monotheism and polytheism is really important. Because the monotheism of a no-name God pushes the psyche into a territory with no signposts, no subtle complexities and differences, the soul lacks a context to place its pain. Suddenly, we see that God is not distant, because the divine appears wherever we are overwhelmed. Any trauma of daily soul-making affords an experience that is both religious and psychological at once.

RETURN TO FATHER—*Gregory Max Vogt*

A manifesto for the new patriarch, whose metals are being forged in those craft guilds called men's groups and in the daily lives of individual men. The father has been blamed for all the wrongs in our culture; hence, the male psyche and body limp fatherless through the modern landscape, alien and confused, history-less and impoverished. Vogt challenges each man in his guts and spirit to revive in a new way the great patriarchal tradition of hunter and builder, lover and philosopher, protector of society and visionary. He opens the masculine imagination, showing that man can indeed live on earth with courage, reverence, purpose, and strength.

OEDIPUS VARIATIONS—*Karl Kerényi, James Hillman*

The spirit of the fathers weighs most heavily on psychology through the famous Oedipus complex. James Hillman takes on Father Freud, inverting the emphasis of the complex: why do fathers kill their sons? Looking at the anima landscape of Colonus where old Oedipus—helped by his daughters—dies, Hillman further shows that, in addition to the curse, murder, incest, and disease, the myth contained beauty, blessing, love, and loyalty. The famous mythographer Karl Kerényi gives details from classical sources for the Oedipus myth and incisively comments on its dramatic variations by Sophocles, Seneca, Corneille, Hofmannsthal, Gide, and others.

Spring Publications, Inc. • *P.O. Box 222069* • *Dallas, Texas 75222*

REMARKABLE TRANSLATIONS

GAIUS VALERIUS CATULLUS'S COMPLETE POETIC WORKS
Jacob Rabinowitz, tr.

William S. Burroughs says of this brilliant new work, "Beautifully translated
. . . trivial, frivolous, profound, obscene. Read the fossils of lust."
Rabinowitz grasps the elegance, passion, and nastiness not only of this
Roman rude boy, but also of first-century B.C. Rome. Fun to read, this
bold, yet literal translation supersedes the weary and stale bourgeois versions of these verses that have kept the lusty language of the poet from
the equally lusty minds of his readers. Translator's preface. (150 pp.)

OVID'S METAMORPHOSES
Charles Boer, tr.

All the classic tales of Western mythology come to life in a striking new
translation. Ovid's *Metamorphoses* has always been recognized as the
greatest single narration of what the myth world of antiquity looked,
thought, and felt like at its climax. Boer's rendering brings the reader a
fuller-bodied Ovid, one closer to the Ovid of Shakespeare or Ezra Pound.
Faithful to the poet's literal level, Boer parts company with the standard
American versions of the fifties. Glossary. (ix, 359 pp.)

THE HOMERIC HYMNS
Charles Boer, tr.

Nominated for the National Book Award and acclaimed by critics and
public, this stunning translation has established itself as a classroom text.
These thirty-five poems, the earliest extant depiction of the divinities as
individuals, evoke the Greek mythic imagination. Wm. Arrowsmith writes:
"[though] there were translations in plenty, there was nothing like this
remarkable work in which Greek gods appear not as abstract presences
but as moving and radiant irruptions of the sacred." (vi, 182 pp.)

THE BOOK OF LIFE
Marsilio Ficino—Charles Boer, tr.

In this fluent translation—the first in English—this underground classic
of the Italian Renaissance is a guide to food, drink, sleep, mood, sexuality,
song, and countless herbal and vegetable concoctions for maintaining the
right balance of soul, body, and spirit. Translator's introduction (with bib-
liography), index. (xx, 217 pp.)

Spring Publications, Inc. • *P.O. Box 222069* • *Dallas, Texas 75222*